The Making of Japanese Settler Colonialism

This innovative study demonstrates how Japanese empire builders invented and appropriated the discourse of overpopulation to justify Japanese settler colonialism across the Pacific. Lu defines this overpopulation discourse as "Malthusian expansionism." This was a set of ideas that demanded additional land abroad to accommodate the supposed surplus people in domestic society on the one hand and emphasized the necessity of national population growth on the other. Lu delineates ideological ties, human connections, and institutional continuities between Japanese colonial migration in Asia and Japanese migration to Hawai'i and North and South America from 1868 to 1961. He further places Malthusian expansionism at the center of the logic of modern settler colonialism, challenging the conceptual division between migration and settler colonialism in global history. This title is also available as Open Access.

SIDNEY XU LU is Assistant Professor of History at Michigan State University.

Studies of the Weatherhead East Asian Institute, Columbia University

The Studies of the Weatherhead East Asian Institute of Columbia University were inaugurated in 1962 to bring to a wider public the results of significant new research on modern and contemporary East Asia.

A list of titles in this series can be found at the back of the book.

The Making of Japanese Settler Colonialism

Malthusianism and Trans-Pacific Migration, 1868–1961

Sidney Xu Lu

Michigan State University

CAMBRIDGE
UNIVERSITY PRESS

CAMBRIDGE
UNIVERSITY PRESS

University Printing House, Cambridge CB2 8BS, United Kingdom

One Liberty Plaza, 20th Floor, New York, NY 10006, USA

477 Williamstown Road, Port Melbourne, VIC 3207, Australia

314–321, 3rd Floor, Plot 3, Splendor Forum, Jasola District Centre, New Delhi – 110025, India

79 Anson Road, #06–04/06, Singapore 079906

Cambridge University Press is part of the University of Cambridge.

It furthers the University's mission by disseminating knowledge in the pursuit of education, learning, and research at the highest international levels of excellence.

www.cambridge.org
Information on this title: www.cambridge.org/9781108482424
DOI: 10.1017/9781108687584

First published 2019

Printed in the United Kingdom by TJ International Ltd, Padstow Cornwall

A catalogue record for this publication is available from the British Library.

Library of Congress Cataloging-in-Publication Data
Names: Lu, Sidney Xu, 1981– author.
Title: The making of Japanese settler colonialism : Malthusianism and trans-Pacific migration, 1868–1961 / Sidney Xu Lu.
Description: Cambridge; New York, NY : Cambridge University Press, 2019. | Series: Studies of the Weatherhead East Asian Institute, Columbia University | Includes bibliographical references and index.
Identifiers: LCCN 2019012169 | ISBN 9781108482424 (alk. paper)
Subjects: LCSH: Japan – Colonies – History – 19th century. | Japan – Colonies – History – 20th century. | Japan – Emigration and immigration – History – 19th century. | Japan – Emigration and immigration – History – 20th century. | Malthusianism. | Demographic transition – Japan. | Japan – Foreign relations – 1868–
Classification: LCC JV5227 .L8 2019 | DDC 304.80952/09034–dc23
LC record available at https://lccn.loc.gov/2019012169

ISBN 978-1-108-48242-4 Hardback

To Eileen, teacher and best friend

Contents

Illustrations

Figures

Tables

Acknowledgments

To condense the fruits of a decade-long research project into a book is a challenging task, yet it is perhaps a more difficult one to express in only a few paragraphs even a fraction of my gratitude for the love, friendship, company, and support that I have received. Frederick Dickinson has been the most staunch and patient supporter of my research. As my mentor in the doctoral program at Penn, he transformed not only my knowledge of Japan and Asia but also my understanding of history as an academic discipline. He read every word I wrote at every stage of my graduate study and dissertation writing, and I have benefited tremendously from his encouragement and insights. Through his broad knowledge, passionate dedication, and indomitable spirit as a scholar, his kindness and generosity as a teacher, and his charming personality and great sense of humor as a friend, Fred has guided a wide-eyed student onto the career path of a historian.

At Penn, I was equally blessed with the opportunity to study under Eiichiro Azuma. It was Eiichiro's incisive research about the histories of Japanese Americans and modern Japan as well as his incredible insights into transnational history that had drawn me to the exciting field of migration history in the first place. He shared with me not only his own collections and academic networks but also his knowledge and wisdom. In more ways than one, this book would not have been possible without him. I also had the incredible fortune to have studied under Takashi Fujitani at Doshisha University in Japan when I conducted my dissertation research there in 2011. With his uncompromising commitment to social justice and critical thinking, Tak gave me a key to the boundless riches of postcolonial studies. He showed me what it means to be a socially responsible scholar.

Similarly, with great generosity and enthusiasm, Ayako Kano introduced me to exciting debates in Japanese feminism and pushed me to refine my arguments with her insightful critiques. Siyen Fei provided me with rigorous training in both teaching and research. I have always benefited from her knowledge and encouragement, both as a graduate student and as a professional academic. At Penn, I am also indebted to Peter Holquist, Kathy Peiss, Jennifer Amyx, the late Michael Katz, Lynn Lees, Rachel

Troop, Heather Sharkey, and Eve Powell. All of them have shaped the development of this book in their own ways. My approach to Asian history was also profoundly influenced by the stimulating discussions in Janet Chen's seminar on modern China at Princeton.

At MSU, I thank Charles Keith, Ethan Segal, Naoko Wake, Aminda Smith, Siddharth Chandra, and Catherine Ryu. As my fellow Asianists, they warmly welcomed me as their colleague and gave a junior scholar the most enormous amount of support one could possibly imagine. I also want to thank Walter Hawthorne, Pero Dagbovie, LaShawn D. Harris, Liam Brockey, Lewis Siegelbaum, Helen Veit, Leslie Moch, David Wheat, Edward Murphy, Peter Beattie, and Lisa Fine in the History Department for their kind support during the writing of this book. I am grateful for the insights of Jonathan Glade during our writing group discussions as well as the generous financial support from the MSU Asian Studies Center. A TOME award from the MSU College of Arts and Letters is allowing this book to be published in an open-access format.

The book workshop hosted by MSU's History Department on my behalf was a critical step in the development of this book. I want to thank Louise Young, Takashi Fujitani, Charles Keith, Naoko Wake, and Aminda Smith for their participation. Their comments and suggestions were enormously helpful as I sharpened my arguments. I also want to thank Jordan Sand, Jun Uchida, Ken Ruoff, Mariko Tamanoi, Katsuya Hirano, Laura Nancy, Noriko Horiguchi, Shellen Wu, Andrea Geiger, Hyung Gu Lynn, Pedro Iaccobelli Delpiano, Lori Watt, and John Swanson for offering their insights during various stages of my writing. I thank Michael Bourdaghs for generously sharing his sources with me.

In Japan, I would like to thank Ryō Yoshida for kindly sponsoring my one-year research stay at Doshisha University and adopting me as his advisee. I am extremely fortunate to have studied the history of Japanese American migration under his meticulous guidance. Jun'ichi Isomae at the International Research Center for Japanese Studies and Toyomi Asano at Waseda University inspired me to bring more depth and complexity to this project. I appreciate the kindness of Yukuji Okita and Makoto Hara at Doshisha, who brought me to their seminars. I would also like to thank Brian Hayashi for generously sharing his personal collections and offering valuable suggestions, and I thank Rumi Yasutake, Hironori Watari, and Ken'ichi Yasuoka for their helpful comments.

Conducting transnational research is quite impossible without the support of many librarians, archivists, and curators. It is not possible to list all of the individuals who have kindly helped me in each archive, library, and museum that I visited around the Pacific Rim, but I want to give special thanks to Naoki Tanaka at the Nippon Rikkō Kai, Masaki Fukui at Nagano Prefecture Museum of History, Eduardo Kobayashi at Museu Histórico da Imigração Japonesa no Brasil, Tokiko Y. Bazzell and Sachiko Iwabuchi at the University of Hawai'i, Kaoru "Kay" Ueda at Stanford, Tomoko Bialock at UCLA, Molly Des Jardin at

Penn, Keiko Yokota-Carter at the University of Michigan, as well as Mary Jo Zeter and Xian Wu at MSU.

It is my true fortune to have the brilliant copyediting assistance of Tian Huang. I can never thank her enough for the insights, passion, and perseverance that she has put into every page of this book. I am also very grateful for Ross Yelsey at Weatherhead East Asian Institute, Columbia University, and Lucy Rhymer and Lisa Carter at Cambridge University Press, who kindly guided me through the entire publication process with care and patience.

Since I began my pursuit of a PhD in Japanese history a decade ago, I have been fortunate enough to be surrounded and supported by wonderful friends. It is perhaps impossible to express the extent of my gratitude to Jiexi Zheng, Nagatomi Hirayama, Leander Seah, Rachel Epstein, Sheng Mao, Minlei Ye, Yuanfei Wang, Jamyung Choi, Robert Heywood, Victor Seow, Nathan Hopson, Kimura Mizuka, and many others for their enduring friendship. They have shared my joys and sorrows and given me the strength needed to complete this book.

I would like to thank my parents for always having faith in me. My love to Noella. Her arrival in this world has given me so much joy as a father. Finally, I dedicate this book to my dear wife Eileen, who has illuminated my life with her boundless love and support.

Note on Names, Terms, and Translations

Except for names of scholars and historical figures who have written and published their works in English, Japanese, Korean, and Chinese names in this book are in the original order, with family names first. The romanization of Japanese names and terms follows the revised Hepburn system. Exceptions are given to terms that already have standard English expressions, such as Tokyo, Hokkaido, Sapporo, Kobe, and Osaka. Chinese names and terms follow the Pinyin system. All translations in the book, unless otherwise noted, are my own.

Publication of this open monograph was the result of Michigan State University's participation in TOME (Toward an Open Monograph Ecosystem), a collaboration of the Association of American Universities, the Association of University Presses, and the Association of Research Libraries. TOME aims to expand the reach of long-form humanities and social science scholarship including digital scholarship. Additionally, the program looks to ensure the sustainability of university press monograph publishing by supporting the highest quality scholarship and promoting a new ecology of scholarly publishing in which authors' institutions bear the publication costs.

Funding from Michigan State University made it possible to open this publication to the world.

Introduction
Malthusian Expansion and Settler Colonialism

In 1924, the year when the United States shut its doors to all Japanese immigrants, Nagata Shigeshi embarked on a trip to Brazil to complete a land purchase. As the president of the Japanese Striving Society (Nippon Rikkō Kai), a leading Japanese migration agency of its day, Nagata planned to build Aliança, a new Japanese community, in the state of São Paulo to accommodate the supposed surplus population of rural Nagano. In addition to poverty relief, Nagata envisioned that the migration would turn the landless farmers of Nagano prefecture into successful owner-farmers in Brazil, who would not only serve as stable sources of remittance for their home villages but also lay a permanent foundation for the Japanese empire in South America. Rooted in social tensions in the archipelago, the anxiety of "overpopulation" in Japan was intensified by decades of anti-Japanese campaigns that raged in North America. White racism in the United States forced many Japanese migration promoters, including Nagata, to abandon their previous plans of occupying the "empty" American West with Japan's "surplus" population. Instead they turned their gaze southward to Brazil as an alternative, seeing it as not only an equally rich and spacious land but also free of racial discrimination. A direct response to Japanese exclusion from the United States, the community of Aliança was designed to showcase the superiority of Japanese settler colonialism over that of the Westerners.[1] Meaning "alliance" in Portuguese, Aliança was chosen as its name to demonstrate that unlike the hypocritical white colonizers who discriminated against and excluded people of color, the Japanese, owners of a genuinely civilized empire, were willing to cooperate with others and share the benefits.[2] This idea quickly grew into the principle of *kyōzon kyōei* – coexistence and coprosperity – a guideline of Japanese Brazilian migration in general.[3]

---

[1] In this book, I define some Japanese migration campaigns beyond the territorial boundaries and the spheres of influence of the Japanese empire as practices of settler colonialism because of the settler colonial logic and intentions behind these campaigns. This definition is explained in detail later in the introduction.

[2] Nagata Shigeshi, *Shinano Kaigai Ijūshi* (Nagano: Shinano Kaigai Kyōryokukai, 1952), 79–80, and Nagata Shigeshi, *Kaigai Hatten to Wa Ga Kuni no Kyōiku* (Tokyo: Dōbunkan, 1917), 19–21.

[3] A 1924 article in *Shokumin*, a leading Japanese journal promoting colonial migration, claimed that the ultimate goal of Japan's migration-centered expansion should be the coexistence and coprosperity of the entire human being. Responding to the US government's ban on Japanese

1

As the main direction of Japanese expansion shifted from South America to Northeast Asia in the 1930s, overpopulation anxiety was utilized by the imperial government to justify its policy of exporting a million households from the "overcrowded" archipelago to Manchuria, Japan's new "lifeline." Nagano prefecture continued to take on a leading role in overseas migration, sending out the greatest number of settlers among all Japanese prefectures to the Asian continent.[4] Nagata Shigeshi served as one of the core strategists assisting the imperial government's migration policymaking, and he often referred back to Aliança as a model for Japanese community building in Manchuria.[5] Coexistence and coprosperity, the guiding principle of Japanese migration to Brazil, also became the ideological foundation of Japan's Greater East Asia Co-Prosperity Sphere (Daitōa Kyōei Ken). After the empire's demise, Nagata continued to identify overpopulation as the root of all social programs in the war-torn archipelago and kept on promoting overseas migration as the ultimate cure. Under his leadership, the Striving Society worked closely with the postwar government and managed to restart exporting "surplus people" from Japan to South America by reviving migration networks established before 1945.[6]

The claimed necessity for Japan to export its surplus population has been dismissed by postwar historians as a flimsy excuse of the Japanese imperialists to justify their continental invasion in the 1930s and early 1940s. Likewise, according to conventional wisdom, the slogan of coexistence and coprosperity is nothing more than deceptive propaganda that attempts to cover up the brutality of Japanese militarism during World War II. Common examinations of Japanese expansion usually stop at 1945, when the Japanese empire met its end.

However, submerged in archives across the Pacific are stories of hundreds of Japanese men and women like Nagata Shigeshi, which the current nation-based, territory-bound, and time-limited narratives of the Japanese history fail to capture. They embraced the discourse of overpopulation and led and

---

immigration going into effect the same year, the author believed that this new goal should guide Japanese migration to South America as well as other parts of the world in the following years. Arai Nobuo, "Shokumin to Kyōiku," *Shokumin* 3, no. 3 (March 1924): 84. Moreover, Kurose Hiroshi, vice president of the Japanese-Brazilian Association (Nippaku Kyōkai), a major migration organization of the day, recognized in 1932 too "Kyōzon Kyōei" as the guideline for Japanese-Brazilian migration. Kurose Hiroshi, "Kyōzon Kyōei ni susume," *Burajiru: Ishokumin to Bōeki* 6, no. 5 (May 1932): 2.

[4] Louise Young, *Japan's Total Empire: Manchuria and the Culture of Wartime Imperialism* (Berkeley: University of California Press, 1998), 329–330.

[5] Nippon Rikkō Kai Sōritsu Hyaku Shūnen Kinen Jigyō Jikkō Iinkai Kinenshi Hensan Senmon Iinkai, *Nippon Rikkō Kai Hyakunen no Kōseki: Reiniku Kyūsai, Kaigai Hatten Undō, Kokusai Kōken* (Tokyo: Nippon Rikkō Kai, 1997), 213; Nagata Shigeshi, *Nōson Jinkō Mondai to Ishokumin* (Tokyo: Nihon Hyōronsha, 1933), 61–62.

[6] Nippon Rikkō Kai, *Nippon Rikkō Kai*, 332–343.

participated in Japanese migration-driven expansion that transcended the geographic and temporal boundaries of the Japanese empire. Their ideas and activities demonstrate that the association between the claim of overpopulation and Japan's expansion had a long and trans-Pacific history that began long before the late 1930s. The idea of coexistence and coprosperity, embodied by Japanese community building in South America, was both a direct response to Japanese exclusion in North America and a new justification for Japanese settler colonialism based on the argument of overpopulation. It emerged in the 1920s, long before the announced formation of the Greater East Asia Co-Prosperity Sphere during the total war.[7] Furthermore, not only did Japan's migration machine precede the war, it also survived it. The logic, networks, and institutions of migration established before 1945 continued to function in the 1950s and 1960s to spur Japanese migration to South America.

Why and how did the claim of overpopulation become a long-lasting justification for expansion? In what ways were the experiences of Japanese emigration within and outside of the empire intertwined? How should we understand the relationship between migration and settler colonialism in modern Japan and in the modern world? These are the questions that this book seeks to answer. This is a study of the relationship between the ideas of population, emigration, and expansion in the history of modern Japan. It examines how the discourse of overpopulation emerged in Japanese society and was appropriated to justify Japan's migration-driven expansion on both sides of the Pacific Ocean from the mid-nineteenth century to the 1960s. Through the history of the overpopulation discourse, this study redefines settler colonialism in modern Japan by demonstrating the institutional continuities and intellectual links between Japanese colonial migration in Asia and Japanese migration in Hawai'i and North and South America during and after the time of the Japanese empire. It further reveals the profound overlaps and connections between migration and settler colonialism in the modern world, two historical phenomena that have been conventionally understood in isolation from one another.

Malthusian Expansionism and Malthusian Expansionists

I define the discourse of overpopulation that legitimized Japan's migration-driven expansion on both sides of the Pacific as "Malthusian expansionism." This is a set of ideas that demanded extra land abroad to accommodate the claimed surplus people in the domestic society on the one hand and emphasized the necessity of the overall population growth of the nation on the other hand.

[7] Arai, "Shokumin to Kyōiku," 84. By the term "total war," this book refers to the Asia-Pacific War that began with the Marco Polo Bridge Incident on July 7, 1937, and ended with Japan's surrender on August 15, 1945.

As two sides of the same coin, these seemingly contradictory ideas worked together in the logic of Malthusian expansionism. It rationalizes migration-driven expansion, which I call "Malthusian expansion," as both a solution to domestic social tensions supposedly caused by overpopulation and a means to leave the much-needed room and resources in the homeland so that the total population of the nation could continue to increase. In other words, Malthusian expansionism is centered on the *claim* of overpopulation, not the actual *fear* of it, and by the desire for population growth, not the actual *anxiety* over it.

On the one hand, Malthusian expansionism echoed the logic of classic Malthusianism in believing that the production of a plot of earth was limited and could feed only a certain number of people. As early as 1869, three years before the newly formed Meiji government carried out the first nationwide population survey, it pointed to the condition of overpopulation (*jinkō kajō*) as the cause of regional poverty in the archipelago. As a remedy, the government concluded, surplus people in Japan proper should be relocated to the empire's underpopulated peripheries.[8] From that point forward, different generations of Japanese policymakers and opinion leaders continued to claim overpopulation as the ultimate reason for whatever social tensions of the day were plaguing the archipelago. They also embraced emigration, first to Hokkaido and then to different parts of the Pacific Rim, as not only the best way to alleviate the pressure of overpopulation but also an effective strategy to expand the power and territory of the empire.

On the other hand, unlike Malthus's original theory that held that population growth should be checked,[9] Malthusian expansionism celebrated the increase of population. The call for population growth emerged as Meiji Japan entered the world of modern nations in the nineteenth century, when the educated Japanese began to value manpower as an essential strength of the nation and a vital component of the capitalist economy. The size of population and the speed of a nation's demographic growth, as Japanese leaders observed, served as key indicators of a nation's position in the global hierarchy defined by modern imperialism. Accordingly, the emigration of the surplus people over-seas would free up space and resources in the crowed archipelago to allow the Japanese population to continue its growth.

This study examines overpopulation as a political claim, not as a reflection of reality. Japan did experience periods of rapid population growth once it began the process of modernization, and it has historically been known as a densely populated nation/empire.[10] However, the word "overpopulation" should never

---

[8] Yoshida Hideo, *Nihon Jinkō Ron no Shiteki Kenkyū* (Tokyo: Kawade Shobō, 1944), 250–252.

[9] Thomas Malthus, *An Essay on the Principle of Population* (London: J. Johnson, 1789), 6, 28.

[10] For example, world-renowned sociologist Warren Thompson in 1929 listed the Japanese empire, together with China, India, and Central Europe, as the world's "danger spots" due to their extremely high population densities. Thompson warned that if the population pressures in

be taken as given when discussing the contexts of emigration and expansion because the very definition of "overpopulation," as this study has shown, has always been subject to manipulation. Like elsewhere in the world, the claim of overpopulation was associated with a variety of arguments and social campaigns in modern Japan. As Japanese economist and demographer Nagai Tōru observed at the end of the 1920s, the issue of overpopulation served as an excuse for different interest groups to advance their own agendas. Those who called for birth control were in fact working toward the liberation of proletarians and women; those who focused on the issue of food shortage might have cared more about political security than overpopulation per se; and in the same vein, migration promoters' ultimate goal was the expansion of the Japanese empire itself.[11] By the concept of Malthusian expansionism, this book aims to explain how the claims of overpopulation were specifically invented and used to legitimize migration-driven expansion.

To this end, I focus on the ideas and activities of the Japanese migration promoters, men and women like Nagata Shigeshi, whom I call "Malthusian expansionists." In other words, this is a study of the migration promoters, not the individual migrants who left the archipelago and settled across seas. Malthusian expansionists were different generations of Japanese thinkers and doers, who viewed migration as an essential means of expansion. Their diverse backgrounds shaped their agendas for emigration in different ways—those inside the policymaking circles envisioned that emigration would expand the empire's territories and political sphere of influence, business elites saw emigration as a vital step to boost Japan's international trade, intellectuals believed that migration would propel the Japanese to rise through the global racial hierarchy, social activists and bureaucrats used emigration to realize their plans to reform the domestic society, owners and employees of migration organizations and companies hoped for the growth of their wealth and networks, and journalists aimed to expand readership and influences.

However, as advocates of Malthusian expansionism, they claimed in unison that the archipelago, in part or as a whole, was overcrowded even though it was essential that the Japanese population continue its growth. They thus agreed with each other that emigration was both an ideal solution to the problem of overpopulation at home and a critical means of expansion abroad. In different historical contexts and in their own ways, they took on the primary responsibility to plan, promote, and organize Japan's migration-driven expansion. Many not only extolled the merits of emigration through articles and speeches

these regions were not correctly dealt with, they might lead to international wars. Warren S. Thompson, *Danger Spots in World Population* (New York: Knopf, 1929), 18–48, 113–114.
[11] Nagai Tōru, *Nihon Jinkō Ron* (Tokyo: Ganshōdō, 1929), 3.

but also actively participated in migration campaigns by making policies and plans, investigating possibilities, or recruiting migrants.

To be sure, Malthusian expansionism was not the only design of empire in modern Japan. The ideas that the empire needed more population instead of less were constantly challenged by different forces from within and without. Kōtoku Shūsui, a pioneer of Japan's socialist movement, made one of the earliest and most powerful critiques of Malthusian expansionism at the turn of the twentieth century. The argument that overpopulation necessitated emigration, he pointed out, was merely rhetoric for imperial expansion because the true reason behind the rise of poverty was not population growth but the increasingly imbalanced distribution of wealth.[12] From the late 1910s to the early 1930s, leaders of socialist and feminist movements in Japan were vocal in their push for contraception and birth control. Their birth control and eugenics campaigns were both inspired and empowered by contemporary international Neo-Malthusian and eugenic movements.[13] Similarly, not every Japanese empire builder favored emigration as a practical solution to Japan's social problems and a productive means of expansion. As the tide of anti-Japanese sentiment began to rise in the United States, liberal thinkers like Ishibashi Tanzan argued that Japan should acquire wealth and power through trade instead of emigration. Ishibashi urged Tokyo to relocate all Japanese migrants in the United States back into the archipelago in order to avoid diplomatic conflicts.[14] As a whole, though Malthusian expansionists at times worked with other interest groups such as merchants, labor union leaders, and women's rights advocates, they were also constantly vying for leadership and influence.

Not all types of emigration fit into the ideal scenario of expansion imagined by Japanese Malthusian expansionists either. Few of them saw the Korean Peninsula and Taiwan, two major colonies of the empire, which had two of the largest Japanese overseas communities by the end of World War II, as vital parts in their maps of expansion. Due to the high population densities of the native residents and the low living standards of the local farmers, the Japanese agricultural migration, favored by the Malthusian expansionists, had seldom succeeded there. Due to similar reasons, Okinawa, a colony turned prefecture of the empire, was rarely mentioned in the discussions of the Japanese Malthusian expansionists. The rich histories of Japanese migration in the Korean Peninsula, Taiwan, and Okinawa, therefore, do not feature prominently in this book.

---

[12] Kōtoku Shūsui, *Teikoku Shugi* (Tokyo: Iwanami Bunko, 1901), 106–108, 112.

[13] Fujime Yuki, *Sei no Rekishigaku: Kōshō Seido, Dataizai Taisei kara Baishun Bōshihō, Yūsei Hogohō Taisei e* (Tokyo: Fuji Shuppan, 1997), 245–281.

[14] Oguma Eiji, *Nihonjin no Kyōkai: Okinawa Ainu Taiwan Chōsen Shokuminchi Shihai kara Fukki Undō made* (Tokyo: Shinyōsha, 1999), 232–235.

Instead, I focus on the histories of Japanese migration in Hokkaido, California, Texas, Brazil, and Manchuria, where Japanese settlement was crucial for the evolution of Japanese Malthusian expansionism. Similarly, in the visions of Japanese Malthusian expansionists, not every ethnic group in the empire was qualified for emigration. Though having substantial differences among themselves, colonial subjects in the Korean Peninsula and Taiwan as well as outcast groups were generally excluded from the pool of ideal subjects of emigration.[15] Although Okinawa had one of the greatest numbers of emigrants among all Japanese prefectures, Malthusian expansionists did not consider Okinawans as ideal migrants either.[16]

Malthusian Expansionism as a Logic of Settler Colonialism

By moving beyond geographical and sovereign boundaries, this study brings new ways to understand settler colonialism in the histories of modern Japan and the modern world. At a concrete level, it analyzes the links, flows, and intersections between Japanese migration within the imperial territory in Asia and that outside of the imperial territories in Hawai'i and North and South America and the continuities between Japanese overseas migration during and after the time of the empire. The connections between Japanese colonial migration in Asia and Japanese migration across the Pacific Ocean also present an intellectual necessity to conceptualize the overlaps between migration and colonial expansion. Thus, at a more theoretical level, by recognizing certain types of migration into the territories of other sovereign states as expansion, this study reconfigures the scope, logic, and significance of settler colonialism in world history.

---

[15] Although these marginalized groups are generally absent in the Japanese Malthusian expansionists' proposals, their stories as emigrants have been well documented. Noah McCormack, "Buraku Emigration in the Meiji Era – Other Ways to Become 'Japanese,'" *East Asian History*, no. 23 (June 2002): 87–108; Andrea Geiger, *Subverting Exclusion: Transpacific Encounters with Race, Caste, and Borders, 1885–1928* (New Haven, CT: Yale University Press, 2011), 36–71; Ronald Takaki, *Strangers from a Different Shore: A History of Asian Americans* (Berkeley: University of California Press, 1998), 270–286.

[16] Malthusian expansionists' discrimination against Okinawan migrants was exemplified by Tokyo's ban on Okinawan migration to Brazil from 1912 to 1917. The imperial government justified the decision by labeling the Okinawans as inferior to the Japanese and attributing the rise of anti-Japanese sentiment in South America to the Okinawan migrants' "inappropriate" behavior there. Yabiku Mōsei, *Burajiru Okinawa Iminshi* (São Paulo: Zaibu Okinawa Kenjinkai, 1987), 48–52. In 1942, Japanese colonial thinker Yanaihara Tadao, too, complained that the inferior Okinawan migrants had damaged the Japanese settlers' civilized image in the South Seas. Yanaihara Tadao, "Nanpō Rōdō Seisaku no Kichō," *Shakai Seisaku Jihō*, no. 260 (1942): 156–157, cited from Tomiyama Ichirō, "Colonialism and the Sciences of the Tropical Zone: The Academic Analysis of Difference in 'the Island Peoples,'" *Positions: Asia Critique* 3, no. 2 (1995): 385–386.

Until recently, the experience of Japanese overseas migration has been divided into two contrasting narratives: a story of settler colonialism inside of the empire's sphere of influence in Asia on the one hand and a story of Japanese migrants' bitter struggles against white racism and immigration exclusion in other areas across the Pacific on the other. Recognizing the divergence between emigration (*imin*) and colonial migration/expansion (*shokumin*) remains absolutely necessary for us to grasp the different dimensions in the experience of the Japanese overseas. However, recent scholarship has moved our understanding of Japanese colonialism and expansionism beyond geographical and temporal boundaries of the Japanese empire.[17] As a result, the concepts of emigration and colonial expansion, together with the two separated narratives they represent respectively, are no longer sufficient because they cannot explain the continuities and connections between various waves of Japanese emigration on both sides of the Pacific Ocean from the beginning of the empire to the decades after its fall.

By not taking the conceptual division between migration and colonial expansion as given, this study illustrates the ideological and institutional continuities centered around the overpopulation discourse that persisted through different periods of Japanese emigration. The history of Japan's Malthusian expansion transcended both the space and time of the Japanese colonial empire. I trace the origins of Japan's Malthusian expansion to the beginning of Meiji era. I demonstrate how the migration of declassed samurai (*shizoku*) to Hokkaido during early Meiji, an episode commonly omitted from the history of Japanese colonial expansion, was a precursor to the ideas and practices of Japanese migration to North America and other parts of the Pacific Rim in later years. Likewise, Japanese migration to the United States that began in the last two decades of the nineteenth century also provided crucial languages and resources for Japanese expansion in South America and Northeast Asia from the early twentieth century to the end of World War II. I also extend the analysis into the postwar era and consider Japanese migration to South America in the 1950s and 1960s as the final episode in the history of Japan's Malthusian expansion: though no longer performed by a militant and expanding empire, the postwar migration was still legitimized by the same discourse of overpopulation while driven by the same institutions and networks that were

---

[17] The representative studies in recent years include, but are not limited to, Young, *Japan's Total Empire*, 312–318; Sandra Wilson, "The New Paradise: Japanese Emigration to Manchuria in the 1930s and 1940s," *International History Review* 17, no. 2 (May 1995): 251–253; Eiichiro Azuma, "'Pioneers of Overseas Japanese Development': Japanese American History and the Making of Expansionist Orthodoxy in Imperial Japan," *Journal of Asian Studies* 64, no. 4 (November 2008): 1187–1226; Takashi Fujitani, *Race for Empire: Koreans as Japanese and Japanese as Americans* (Berkeley: University of California Press, 2011); Geiger, *Subverting Exclusion*; Jordan Sand, "Reconfiguring Pacific History: Reflections from the Pacific Empires Working Group," *Amerasia Journal* 42, no. 3 (2016): 1–5.

established during Japanese migration to South America and Manchuria before 1945.

That settler colonialism as a concept to describe the settler-centered colonial expansion and rule is different from military- or trade-centered colonialism has been widely accepted by scholars in recent decades. Yet researchers have utilized varied definitions of the term depending on the historical and political contexts of their subjects. The existing literature has offered at least three different definitions. First, in Anglophone colonial history, scholars use "settler colonialism" to describe the settling in colonies by colonizers and the establishment of states and societies of their own by usurping native land instead of exploiting native labor. The elimination of native peoples and their cultures and the perpetuation of settler states in the Anglophone history have led Patrick Wolfe to conclude that settler colonial invasion "is structure, not an event."[18] Second, careful examinations of twentieth-century colonialism around the globe have extended our understanding of settler colonialism beyond the Anglophone model. Unlike the expansion of the Anglo world in the previous centuries, settler colonialism in the twentieth century was marked by the instability of settler communities. Whether in the Korean Peninsula, Abyssinia, or Kenya, colonial settlers from Japan, Italy, and Britain alike had to constantly negotiate their political and social space with more numerous indigenous populations. Their stories often ended with repatriation, not permanent stay. Accordingly, Caroline Elkins and Susan Pedersen have defined twentieth-century settler colonialism as a structure of colonial privileges based on the negotiation between four political groups: the settlers, the imperial metropole, the colonial administration, and the indigenous people.[19] Third, recent studies have started to extend the definition of settler colonialism beyond formal colonial sovereignty and power relations by exploring the overlaps and similarities between the experience of colonial settlers and that of migrants. Looking from indigenous perspectives, colonial histories of Hawai'i, Southeast Asia, and Taiwan, in their own ways, have all offered plenty of evidence of how immigrants ended up fostering the existing settler colonial structures.[20]

---

[18] Lorenzo Veracini, "'Settler Colonialism': Career of a Concept," *Journal of Imperial and Commonwealth History* 41, no. 2 (2013): 313; Patrick Wolfe, *Settler Colonialism and the Transformation of Anthropology: The Politics and Poetics of an Ethnographic Event* (London: Cassell, 1999), 2.

[19] Caroline Elkins and Susan Pedersen, eds., *Settler Colonialism in the Twentieth Century: Projects, Practices, and Legacies* (London: Routledge, 2005), 3–4. Jun Uchida further defines the Japanese settlers in colonial Korea as "brokers of empire" based on ambivalent and constantly shifting relations they had with different forces in the Korean Peninsula and Tokyo. Jun Uchida, *Brokers of Empire: Japanese Settler Colonialism in Korea, 1876–1945* (Cambridge, MA: Harvard University Press, 2011), 5–8.

[20] Candace Fujikane, "Introduction: Asian Settler Colonialism in the U.S. Colony of Hawai'i," in *Asian Settler Colonialism: From Local Governance to the Habits of Everyday Life in Hawai'i*, ed. Candace Fujikane and Jonathan Y. Okamura (Honolulu: University of Hawai'i Press, 2008),

Recognizing the overlaps between the experiences of settlers and migrants is the starting point of this research. I use the term "settler colonialism" by its most extended meaning, close to the third definition. However, different from all the approaches above, this book sheds new light on settler colonialism through the lens of migration itself. The migration of settlers is an essential component of settler colonial experience but has often been neglected. The migration-centered approach requires us to examine settler colonialism from both the sending end and the receiving end of settler migration. Existing literature of settler colonialism has provided rich insights from the receiving end. Scholars have explained in depth how a settler state is established and how the power structure of a settler colonial society is maintained.[21]

This book examines the ideas and practices of settler colonialism at both ends of settler migration, highlighting the interactions between the social and political changes in the home country and those in the host societies. It seeks to explain how the emigration of setters was reasoned in the home country, why settlers demanded land more than anything else, and how settlers' appropriation of the land owned by others was justified in both settler communities and the home country. I argue that Malthusian expansionism, which celebrates population growth and, in the meantime, demands extra land abroad to alleviate population pressure at home, lies at the center of the logic of settler colonialism in the modern era.

The migration-centered approach also allows me to examine the ideas and practices of settler colonialism beyond conventional boundaries. Though existing indigenous critiques have successfully problematized the very definitions of "settlers" and "migrants," they are almost exclusively anchored in the host societies. I challenge the conceptual division between migration and settler colonialism from both ends of settler migration. Through the prism of Malthusian expansionism, this book shows that Japanese migration campaigns to the Americas and Hawai'i, territories of other sovereign states, were not only closely connected with the empire's expansion in Asia but also propelled by settler colonial ambitions in Japan's home archipelago.

3; Dean Itsuji Saranillio, "Why Asian Settler Colonialism Matters: A Thought Piece on Critiques, Debates, and Indigenous Difference," *Settler Colonial Studies* 3, nos. 3–4 (2013): 287; Shu-mei Shih, "Theory, Asia and the Sinophone," *Postcolonial Studies* 13, no. 4 (2010): 478; Katsuya Hirano, Lorenzo Veracini, and Toulouse-Antonin Roy, "Vanishing Natives and Taiwan's Settler-Colonial Unconsciousness," *Critical Asian Studies* 50, no. 2 (2018): 196–218.
[21] Patrick Wolfe, "Settler Colonialism and the Elimination of the Native," *Journal of Genocide Research* 8, no. 4 (December 2006): 387–409; Wolfe, *Settler Colonialism and the Transformation of Anthropology*; James Belich, *Replenishing the Earth: The Settler Revolution and the Rise of the Anglo-World, 1783–1939* (Oxford: Oxford University Press, 2009); Lorenzo Veracini, *Settler Colonialism: A Theoretical Overview* (Houndmills: Palgrave Macmillan, 2010); Lorenzo Veracini, *The Settler Colonial Present* (Houndmills: Palgrave Macmillan, 2015).

Malthusian Expansionism in Four Threads

Why did Malthusian expansionism possess such appeal and adaptability in modern Japanese history? How did it make sense to Japan's nation and empire builders from distinct socioeconomic backgrounds? How was this demographic discourse embraced in drastically different historical contexts to justify Japan's migration driven expansion? To explain the power, mechanism, and significance of Malthusian expansionism, one must look beyond the realm of thoughts and words of the elites. My analysis focuses on how ideas interacted with social realities, political actions, and historical changes. It pinpoints four different but overlapping threads within the big picture of Japanese Malthusian expansion: the intellectual, the social, the institutional, and the international.

First and foremost, the history of Malthusian expansionism is a unison of two schools of thoughts – overpopulation and expansion. I explain how the claim of overpopulation that justified emigration originated and how it continued as a dominant discourse in modern Japan's shifting intellectual debates of empire building, both among academics and in the public sphere. Second, this is also a study of social and cultural history that discusses how Malthusian expansionism took root in and was also transformed by the changing social and political contexts within the archipelago. It explores how a succession of social movements, each in response to specific sociopolitical tensions, turned to overpopulation for an easy diagnosis and portrayed emigration as the panacea. Beyond social movements, Malthusian expansionism also found expression in the form of specific laws and state apparatuses. Thus, the third thread reveals how it both influenced and was strengthened by government institutions, policies, and legislations, at both central and local levels, that aimed at managing reproduction and emigration. Finally, as a major player in the arena of modern imperialism, Japan's expansion was inevitably shaped by its uneasy relationship with other empires. The fourth thread examines how the Japanese empire's imitation of – as well as struggles against – Anglo-American expansion both molded and transformed the ideas and activities of Japanese Malthusian expansionists.[22]

The Intellectual: Population, Land, the Lockean Principle of Ownership

From the beginning of the Meiji era, educated Japanese both within and outside of the government started collecting massive amounts of information about

---

[22] This book uses the terms "Anglo-American expansion" and "Anglo-American settler colonialism" to describe both British settler colonial expansion around the world and US territorial expansion because these experiences, both driven by Malthusian expansionism, had jointly served as the central inspiration for Japan's own settler colonialism.

their nation, including its population, land, and produce.[23] Follow the example of their Western counterparts, Meiji leaders believed that the country could not be known and managed effectively without the collection of data. From 1872 onward, as a part of this "statistics fever" (*tōkei netsu*),[24] the Meiji government began conducting nationwide population surveys based on information provided by the newly reconstituted household registration system.[25]

Along with this faith in numbers, Meiji intellectuals also found new ways of understanding the meaning of ordinary life. The masses were no longer a sea of ignorant people (*gumin*) who were destined for political exclusion. Instead, educated Japanese began to see every individual in the archipelago as a valuable subject of the new nation, whose well-being was a critical indicator of the nation's strength and prosperity.[26] Beginning in early Meiji, as a result of the introduction of modern medicine and hygiene, the archipelago entered a phase of rapid population growth. Japanese intellectuals spared no efforts to celebrate the population boom as evidence for both the success of the new government and the superiority of the racial stock. In this spirit, they ranked the Japanese as one of the most demographically expanding races in the world, right alongside the Europeans.[27]

It was in this intellectual context that educated Japanese introduced Thomas Malthus to their domestic readers. From the late nineteenth century onward, while the call for birth control was constantly contested,[28] the Malthusian argument that land had a finite limit on the population it could sustain was widely accepted as common sense in the society. Thus overpopulation, a natural result of the rapidly growing population within the limited territory of the empire, became a critical issue that Japanese thinkers of different generations would all contend with.

The discovery of the existence of a "surplus population" in Japan came at a time when Meiji intellectuals began to reexamine the world's political geography by referring to past – and ongoing – Western colonial expansions. In particular, the history of Anglo-American settler colonialism became their

---

[23] Takashi Fujitani, "Kindai Nihon ni okeru Kenryoku no Tekunorojii: Guntai, Chihō, Shintai," trans. Umemori Naoyuki, *Shisō*, no. 845 (November 1994): 164–165.

[24] Hayami Akira, "Jinkō Tōkei no Kindaika Katei," in *Kokusei Chōsa Izen, Nihon Jinkō Tōkei Shūsei*, reprint ed., vol. 1, ed. Naimushō Naikaku Tōkeikyoku (Tokyo: Tōyō Shorin, 1992), 3, cited from Takashi, "Kindai Nihon ni okeru Kenryoku no Tekunorojii," 166.

[25] Hayami, "Jinkō Tōkei no Kindaika Katei," 4.

[26] One of the earliest demographers in Meiji Japan, Sugi Kōji, for example, argued in his speeches and writings that the life of a nation's ordinary subjects can reveal the nation's prosperity. Yoshida, *Nihon Jinkō Ron no Shiteki Kenkyū*, 127.

[27] Nishiuchi Yōsan, "Shokumin Jigyō to Kokka Keizai no Kankei," *Kōchi Shokumin Kyōkai Hōkoku*, no. 1 (October 1893): 3–4, cited from Yoshida, *Nihon Jinkō Ron no Shiteki Kenkyū*, 200–201.

[28] Fujime Yuki has documented the complicated and overall unsuccessful birth control movement in pre-1945 Japan. Fujime, *Sei no Rekishigaku*, 117–150, 245–282.

primary source of inspiration. Unlike the Iberian expansionists, whose central goals for colonization were securing tribute, labor, taxes, and the ostensible loyalty of indigenous inhabitants, the Anglo-American colonialists focused on the acquisition of land itself.[29] Armed with a new language drawn from the Enlightenment, they also sought to justify their taking of aboriginal lands in the name of reason and progress.[30]

This conceptual shift was spearheaded by the British Enlightenment thinker John Locke. Through his involvement in drafting and revising *The Fundamental Constitutions of Carolina* in the late seventeenth century, Locke had participated in the British Empire's expansion in North America.[31] In his widely acclaimed *Two Treatises of Government*, Locke defined agrarian labor, which included both the act of enclosure and the act of cultivation, as the only legitimate foundation of claiming land ownership. Any land without the presence of agrarian labor, no matter if occupied or not, was wasted and thus open to appropriation.[32] The Lockean principle of land ownership was cited by colonial thinkers on both sides of the Atlantic Ocean to justify British settlers' rejection of the indigenous land rights and legitimize the establishment of settler colonies in North America.[33] While the postindependence US government initially recognized some Native

[29] The divergence in their goals led to the intrinsic differences between the colonial model of the Iberian empires and that of the British Empire. Recent scholarship has shown that the territories that the Spanish acquired overseas were initially "kingdoms" instead of "colonies," in terms of both their titles and their relationship with Madrid. Mark Burkholder, "Spain's America: From Kingdoms to Colonies," *Colonial Latin American Review* 25, no. 2 (2016): 125–126. During the early years of Spanish rule in the Caribbean, African migrants functioned as surrogate colonists, not as plantation slaves, as they were expected to maintain and defend the Spanish order, as David Wheat has argued. Wheat, *Atlantic Africa & the Spanish Caribbean, 1570–1640* (Chapel Hill, NC: Omohundro Institute and University of North Carolina Press, 2016). Elites in Spanish colonies also enjoyed more power in controlling colonial administrative budgets than their counterparts in the British colonies did. Regina Grafe and Alejandra Irigoin, "A Stakeholder Empire: The Political Economy of Spanish Imperial Rule in America," *Economic History Review* 65, no. 2 (2012): 609–651.
[30] To be sure, initially the British colonists had acquired land in North America mostly through settlement and purchase; they also acknowledged, to a certain degree, the Native Americans' land rights. This was done both to differentiate themselves from the Spanish colonists, who were criticized by the British for their maltreatment of the Native Americans, and to minimize the attacks by Amerindian forces on British settlement communities. See Barbara Arneil, *John Locke and America: The Defense of English Colonialism* (Oxford: Oxford University Press, 1996), 70–71, 80–81.
[31] David Armitage, "John Locke, Carolina, and the *Two Treatises of Government*," *Political Theory* 32, no. 5 (October 2004): 602–627.
[32] Arneil, *John Locke and America*, 138–143. For a general discussion of John Locke's influence in the revolutionary-era United States, see ibid., 170–200.
[33] Locke's association of property ownership with agrarian labor enabled early eighteenth-century British settlers to comfortably ignore the Mohegans' ownership of their land in Connecticut. It also inspired Emer de Vattel to claim the establishment of colonies "extremely lawful" in his *Droit des gens* (*Law of Nations*), published in 1758. David Armitage, "John Locke: Theorist of Empire?," in *Empire and Modern Political Thought*, ed. Sankar Muthu (Cambridge: Cambridge University Press, 2012), 100–101.

American tribes' land ownership, by the late nineteenth century it had dispos-
sessed Native Americans of most of their lands through negotiation, purchase,
political maneuver, and military action. The Lockean principle, meanwhile,
continued to serve as a central justification for this process.[34] In the nineteenth
and twentieth centuries, it not only propelled British colonial expansion and land
acquisition in other parts of the world but also inspired other modern empires in
their own expansion projects.[35]

Informed by the experience of Anglo-American settler colonialism and this
new concept of land ownership, Japanese expansionists considered it the natural
right of the Japanese, members of a civilized and industrious race, to participate
in the imperial scramble for *vacuum domicilium* in the nineteenth and twentieth
centuries. As Japan's colonial empire continued to grow, different generations of
Malthusian expansionists saw a succession of locales – Hokkaido, Karafuto, the
Bonin Islands, Okinawa, the Korean Peninsula, Taiwan, and eventually
Manchuria – as empty and unworked, eagerly waiting for Japanese settlers to
claim. The inconvenient fact that many of these places were already densely
populated had no bearing on their narratives. Furthermore, in different historical
contexts but according to the same Lockean principle, Japanese expansionists
also saw potential targets of Malthusian expansion in the de facto territories of
Western colonial powers and independent nations, such as the United States,
Brazil, Peru, Hawai'i, Australia, New Zealand, and the Philippines. In their
imaginations, although already under the control of nation-states or colonial
empires, these territories remained partially empty and unworked due to the
low density of white population. As an equally civilized people from an overpopulated archipelago, the Japanese had the right to claim a share of ownership
by competing against or cooperating with white settlers in these lands.[36]

---

[34] As early as 1803, Thomas Jefferson argued that the Native Americans should concede some of
their "waste" lands to white settlers who were willing to "labor on them." This idea was later
carried out by President Andrew Jackson, who authorized the forced relocation of several
Native American tribes in the South to the western side of the Mississippi River. Through the
Homestead Act of 1862 and a series of related legislations following it, the US federal
government distributed millions of acres of Indian territory to non-Indian farming settlers.
See Arneil, *John Locke and America*, 192–193; Clyde A. Milner II, Carol A. O'Connor, Martha
A. Sandweiss, eds., *The Oxford History of the American West* (New York: Oxford University
Press, 1994), 162, 190.

[35] During the nineteenth century, British settlers embraced the Lockean principle while depriving
the Māori of their ancestral lands in New Zealand and Australia. Stuart Banner, *Possessing the
Pacific: Land, Settlers and Indigenous People from Australia to Alaska* (Cambridge, MA:
Harvard University Press, 2007), 62; Armitage, "John Locke: Theorist of Empire?," 101. It
was also picked up by imperial and later Nazi Germany in the nineteenth and twentieth centuries
to justify eastward expansion in Europe. Robert L. Nelson, "Colonialism in Europe? A Case
against Salt Water," in *Germans, Poland, and Colonial Expansion to the East: 1850 through the
Present*, ed. Robert Nelson (New York: Palgrave Macmillan, 2009), 5.

[36] The founder of modern Japanese demography, Sugi Kōji, argued in 1887 that overpopulation
within the archipelago made it justifiable for the Japanese to emulate the Europeans by

While Japanese Malthusian expansionists drew their world maps of expansion according to the Lockean principle, modern capitalism enabled them to view the emigration of surplus people as a process of economic growth and material accumulation. For them, the purpose of emigration was to enlarge the empire's population and increase its wealth. Since the very beginning of the empire, population increase was celebrated alongside economic development. The inseparability between demographic and economic growth in Meiji colonial thoughts was self-evident in the literal meaning of some Japanese terms used to describe colonialism and expansion. The word *shokumin* 殖民, a translation of "colonial migration," was an early Meiji invention that combined the character *shoku* 殖 (meaning "to increase") and the character *min* 民 (meaning "people").[37] This translation was a clear indicator of how colonial migration was understood in the early Meiji period – it was, at least partially, an action designed for population enlargement. The fact that the programs of *shokusan* 殖産 (to develop the economy) and *shokumin* 殖民 often appeared in tandem revealed the ideological connections between the increase of economic output and that of manpower throughout the history of the Japanese empire.[38] Another word, *takushoku* 拓殖, was also invented around the beginning of the Meiji period to combine *takuchi* 拓地 (to explore land) with *shokumin* 殖民.[39] It indicated that the acquisition of material wealth and the increase of population were consistently regarded as two sides of the same coin.

Such a connection was only natural because for Japan, as it was for other modern empires, the act of projecting power beyond its original territory went hand in hand with its embrace of modern capitalism. Ever since the beginning

migrating overseas to utilize unexplored foreign lands. Sugi specifically referred to the United States as an ideal destination because it had abundant unused land. Sugi Kōji, *Sugi Sensei Kōen Shū* (Tokyo: Chūaisha, 1902), 150–151. In 1924, in response to the US ban on Japanese immigration, Tazaki Masayoshi called for a globally scaled land redistribution plan. According to Tazaki, by redistributing lands based on the actual needs of each nation according to population sizes, white men's global monopoly on land resources would come to an end. Tazaki Masayoshi, "Yukizumareru wa ga Kuni no Jinkō Mondai," *Tōyō*, February 1924, 46, cited from Hasegawa Yūichi, "1920 Nendai Nihon no Imin Ron (3)," *Gaikō Jihō (Revue Diplomatique)*, no. 1279 (June 1991): 102.

[37] According to Nitobe Inazō, the expression of *shokumin* as the translation of colonial migration first appeared around 1871 or 1872. See Nitobe Inazō, *Nitobe Hakushi Shokumin Seisaku Kōgi Oyobi Ronbunshū*, ed. Yanaihara Tadao (Tokyo: Iwanami Shoten, 1943), 40–41. The earliest two books in Japan that used the word *shokumin* were both published in 1872: Shibue Tamotsu, *Beikokushi*, vol. 1 (Tokyo: Manganro, 1872) and Yoshida Kensuke and Sudō Tokiichirō, *Kinsei Shidan*, vol. 1 (Tokyo: Kyōritsusha, 1872).

[38] For example, a book calling for colonial exploration of the Kuril Islands (Chishima) includes chapters on both *shokusan* and *shokumin*. Noboru Momotari, *Waga Chishima* (Tokyo: Gojōrō, 1892). Similarly, annual reports of Tōyō Takushoku Kabushiki Gaisha (Oriental Development Company), one of the two flagship colonial companies in the history of the Japanese empire, listed the sections of *shokumin* and *shokusan* next to each other. Tōyō Takushoku Kabushiki Gaisha, *Eigyō Hōkokusho*, no. 15 (1923).

[39] Nitobe, *Nitobe Hakushi Shokumin Seisaku Kōgi Oyobi Ronbunshū*, 40–41.

of the modern era, the territorial expansion of nation-states had been inter-twined with their search for materials and markets. As Japan's migration-driven expansion evolved in response to the changes of domestic and global environments, places such as Hokkaido, California, Mexico, Hawai'i, the South Pacific Islands, Texas, Brazil, the Korean Peninsula, and Manchuria, one after another, came to be described as the empire's "sources of wealth" (*fugen*). These destinations were invariably portrayed as spacious, empty lands with abundant natural resources, ideal for not only accommodating the surplus Japanese people but also supplying materials to feed the hungry archipelago.[40] In the 1930s, as the empire's total war put unprecedented demands on resources, the trope of fugen took on a life-or-death significance and evolved into that of "lifeline" (*seimeisen*) during Japan's mass migration to Manchuria.[41] As Japan's overseas migration restarted at the beginning of the 1950s, South American countries that received most of the Japanese postwar emigrants were no longer portrayed as empty; nevertheless, they continued to be described as primitive but abundant in natural wealth, waiting for the civilized Japanese to explore and utilize.[42]

The Social: Class, Conflicts, and Overpopulation

The discourse of Malthusian expansionism in Japan was deeply rooted in the political contexts of the society and was constantly influenced and galvanized by a succession of social movements in the archipelago. For Malthusian expansionists, the core purpose of emigration was a two-pronged one: to export surplus people abroad in order to alleviate domestic tensions and, at the same

---

[40] As examples, the following are only a few books and articles authored by Japanese expansio-nists in different times of the empire that described different areas of the world similarly as the empire's sources of wealth. Perhaps the most representative works were part of the book series titled *Kaigai Fugen Sōsho*, which included specific volumes discussing the natural resources of the South Pacific and Hawai'i, Manchuria and Siberia, Southern China, and North America. Hirayama Katsukuma, ed., *Kaigai Fugen Sōsho* (Tokyo: Ryūbunkan, 1905). Some other examples include Shimizu Ichitarō, *Nihon Shin Fugen: Ichibei Hokkaido Jimu* (Tokyo: Kinkōdō, 1890) on Hokkaido; Yamashita Keitarō, *Kanata Fugen* (Tokyo: Maruzen Shōsha, 1893) on Canada; Yoshimura Daijirō, *Hokubei Tekisasushū no Beisaku: Nihonjin no Shin Fugen* (Osaka: Kaigai Kigyō Dōshikai, 1903) on Texas; Nanba Katsuji, *Nanbei Fugen Taikan* (Dairen: Ōsakaya-gō Shoten, 1923) on South America.

[41] In the words of Matsuoka Yōsuke, who headed Japan's South Manchuria Railway between 1935 and 1939, "Manchuria and Mongolia were the lifeline of the nation [Japan]." Mori Kiyondo, *Matsuoka Yōsuke o Kataru* (Tokyo: Tōhō Bunka Gakkai, 1936), 227.

[42] A representative book was Izumi Sei'ichi and Saitō Hiroshi, *Amazon: So no Fūdo to Nihonjin* (Tokyo: Kokin Shoin, 1954). The book encouraged Japanese migration to the Amazon River basin in Brazil by describing the region as an empty and unexplored land full of natural wealth. For example, see 244–259. Another book promoting Japanese farmer migration to South America in 1959 described certain areas in other countries in South America in a similar tone. Zenkoku Takushoku Nōgyō Kyōdō Kumiai Rengōkai, *Kaigai Nōgyō Ijū* (Tokyo: Zenkoku Takushoku Nōgyō Kyōdō Kumiai Rengōkai, 1959), 39–68.

time, to pursue wealth and power for the empire by turning these displaced people into useful subjects abroad. The coexistence of these two identities of the emigrants – troublemakers in the overcrowded archipelago and trailblazers of the empire overseas – closely tied Malthusian expansionism to different social movements in modern Japan.[43] Some of these social movements were initiated by the state, others were spearheaded by nongovernmental groups, but they all responded to specific social tensions and economic pressures of their times. As the following chapters explain in detail, the early Meiji movement to resettle shizoku was motivated by the perceived political threat posed by the newly declassed samurai. The socialist movement at the turn of the twentieth century was triggered by the rise of the working class and their call for political and economic rights. The agrarian movement that peaked in the 1930s was ushered in by prolonged economic depression and intensified land disputes in the countryside. The post–World War II land reform and land exploration programs were, in a way, responding to the urgent need for accommodating the millions of Japanese who lost their livelihood due to the war and the subsequent decolonization. Be they unwilling or unable to challenge the powerful status quo, leaders of different social movements often pointed to overpopulation as a root cause of the social crises of their times. Similarly, because it circumvented political confrontation, emigration constantly served as one of the most pragmatic prescriptions for Japan's social ills.

As Japan's nation-making and empire-building processes proceeded hand in hand, its Malthusian expansionists also incorporated the calls for domestic changes into their blueprints for the empire's expansion. Coming from different social backgrounds and active during different periods, they held divergent and at times contradictory views on what the Japanese nation-empire was and should be. Yet they uniformly imagined that large-scale emigration would not only free Japan from population pressure but also transform idle individuals into vanguards of the empire. For this reason, the questions of who exactly these surplus people were and how they should be called into service for the empire were as political as the definition of overpopulation itself.

In response to different social and political tensions, Malthusian expansionists had designated men and women of specific social strata as the ideal candidates for migration. The definition of strata also grew more diverse, moving from an inheritance-based caste to social and economic classes. This evolution itself testifies to the gradual horizontalization of the Japanese society, with the vertical feudal hierarchy yielding to the supposedly egalitarian social structure of the modern era. Those who were identified as "surplus" people

---

[43] Certainly not all troublemakers in the society were equally suitable for migration. As explained in the following two pages, the social groups that would make ideal emigrants were carefully chosen by Malthusian expansionists according to their specific political agendas and in response to the social tensions of their times.

shifted from the declassed samurai who posed immediate political dangers to the newly established Meiji regime to the commoner youth in late Meiji who had scant opportunities to realize their ambitions, from poor farmers suffering from continuous rural depression in the early twentieth century to almost everyone who failed to find a place in the war-torn archipelago after 1945.

For each of the successively targeted social groups, the Malthusian expansionists had designed specific missions for their migration according to their historical contexts. The declassed samurai in early Meiji were instructed to dedicate their talent and energy to defend the empire's northern territory and to civilize the barbarian land by tapping its natural wealth.[44] Ambitious youth from common families at the turn of the twentieth century were to establish themselves in the United States by acquiring education, managing businesses, or running farms; they were expected to secure a strong foothold for the Japanese race in the white men's world by the merit of their personal success.[45] Between the 1920s and 1945, the rural poor were urged to become owner-farmers in Brazil and Asia and put down permanent roots for the Japanese empire.[46] Finally, the postwar homeless and jobless were called upon to tame the wild lands in South America and represent the new Japan as a surrogate of the West during the Cold War, bringing the blessings of democracy and modernization to the underdeveloped countries.[47] Emigration, in sum, was expected to transform Japan's surplus people into productive subjects of the empire and nation.

The Institutional: The Control of Reproduction and the Making of the "Migration State"

Beyond the existence of an intellectual foundation and deep-reaching socio-political roots, Malthusian expansionism was also codified into laws and implemented by a number of governmental or quasi-governmental institutions. The history of Japanese Malthusian expansionism was thus also a history of state expansion in both biopolitics of controlling population reproduction and geopolitics of managing expansionist migration. This process of state expansion culminated in the formation of what I call the "migration state" in the late 1920s. By the end of World War II, the migration state had sponsored and

---

[44] "Yūshisha no Jimu," *Hokkaido Kaitaku Zasshi (HKZ)*, no. 27 (February 5, 1881): 50–51.

[45] Katayama Sen, *Tobei Annai* (Tokyo: Rōdō Shinbunsha, 1902), 2–6, reprinted in *Shoki zai Hokubei Nihonjin no Kiroku, Hokubeihen*, vol. 44, ed. Okuizumi Eizaburō (Tokyo: Bunsei Shoin, 2006).

[46] Katō Kanji, "Nōson Mondai no Kanken," in *Chihō Kairyō Kōenshū*, vol. 8, ed. Tokyo Chihō Kairyō Kyōkai (Tokyo: Tokyo Chihō Kairyō Kyōkai, 1927), 229–232; Nagata, *Nōson Jinkō Mondai to Ishokumin*, 81–153.

[47] Sugino Tadao, *Kaigai Takushoku Hishi: Aru Kaitaku Undōsha no Shuki* (Tokyo: Bunkyō Shoin, 1959), 4.

managed the migration of hundreds of thousands Japanese subjects to South America, Manchuria, and Southeast Asia. Except for a temporary interruption immediately after World War II, this migration state continued to function into the 1960s. The expression of Malthusian expansionism in the form of state policies and regulations was part and parcel of the modern Japanese state's social management, a process that involved constant negotiations with intellectuals and social groups.[48]

Like its Western counterparts, the modern Japanese state took shape hand in hand with its discovery of population as a political force that had to be not only monitored and controlled but also cultivated and guided.[49] Considering population to be an essential indicator of national strength, the Meiji state swiftly inserted itself into the sphere of reproduction. In 1868, the same year of its own formation, the government banned midwife-assisted abortion and infanticide. In 1874, the Ministry of Education (Monbushō) began to regulate the midwifery profession by requiring prospective midwives to receive professional training and gain state-issued licenses. In 1899, the government further promulgated a set of laws that recognized midwifery as a modern profession and put it under state monitoring. Modeled after its counterparts in modern Europe, the new and professionalized midwifery was quickly enshrined as a crucial occupation that safeguarded the life of infants, thereby laying the foundation for "enriching the nation and strengthening the army" (fukoku kyōhei).[50] In 1880, the government criminalized the act of abortion itself, and in 1907 it further clarified the definition of the crime and increased its punishment.[51] However, despite increasingly strict regulations on paper, their spotty enforcement was evidence that the government's stance toward reproductive crimes was not always consistent.[52]

In addition to ensuring population growth, Japan's policymakers also consciously drew a causal relationship between the existence of overpopulation

---

[48] Through the notion of "social management," Sheldon Garon has demonstrated the collaborations and negotiations between government bureaucrats and leaders of social interest groups in general. Sheldon Garon, *Molding the Japanese Minds: The State in Everyday Life* (Princeton: Princeton University, 1998).

[49] Joshua Cole has shown how the emergence of the modern nation-state in France ushered in the rise of the modern idea of population to meet the political needs of the state to understand "the social." Cole, *The Power of Large Numbers: Population, Politics, and Gender in Nineteenth Century France* (Ithaca, NY: Cornell University Press, 2000), 10–11.

[50] Fujime, *Sei no Rekishigaku*, 121.   [51] Ibid., 120, 123.

[52] Susan Burns suggests that there were contradictions in the Japanese government's attitudes toward reproductive crimes. On the one hand, it is true, as Fujime argued, that the Japanese government criminalized abortion and infanticide for the purposes of Japan's nation making and empire building. But on the other hand, the actual sentences for reproductive crimes became lighter and lighter in the first two decades of the twentieth century. Susan L. Burns, "Gender in the Arena of the Courts: The Prosecution of Abortion and Infanticide in Early Meiji Japan," in *Gender and Law in the Japanese Imperium*, ed. Susan L. Burns and Barbara J. Brooks (Honolulu: University of Hawai'i Press, 2014), 103.

and social issues (*shakai mondai*) such as poverty, economic inequality, and crimes. For the government, overseas emigration gradually became a primary solution to a host of domestic problems. Even before the first nationwide population survey was conducted, Meiji leaders had already concluded that the unequal distribution of population within Japan proper and Hokkaido was a cause of regional poverty and used this claim to rationalize their policies of sending the declassed samurai to the empire's northern frontier.[53]

Yet before the 1920s, the institutional links between emigration and domestic affairs remained inconsistent. The matter of overseas migration was classified under the umbrella of diplomacy and largely managed by the Ministry of Foreign Affairs. Even as the ministry strove to explore new destinations overseas for Japanese emigration, it also imposed increasingly stringent restrictions on emigration in order to maintain Japan's international image as a civilized empire. In 1894 it issued the Emigration Protection Ordinance, which went into effect two years later. Revised a few times through 1909, the ordinance gave the government the right to restrict and even suspend overseas travel for Japanese subjects.[54] The Japanese government's restriction on emigration reached its peak with the Gentlemen's Agreement of 1907, according to which it banned all Japanese subjects from migrating to the continental United States as laborers.

From the 1920s through the end of World War II, the imperial government redoubled its efforts to control reproduction and facilitate emigration. In 1920, the government started to conduct national censuses regularly.[55] Also beginning in the early 1920s, the majority of the births in the archipelago were assisted by professionally trained and state-certified midwives who had no tolerance for infanticide or abortion. The reproductive laws were also enforced more vigorously.[56] Although advocates for birth control and eugenics gained increasing popularity after World War I, the imperial government never legalized contraception. The state also managed to further expand its control over reproduction by collaborating with some prominent eugenicists under the common goal of strengthening the empire's racial stock. In 1941, during the total war, the government promulgated the National Eugenic Protection Law,

[53] To be sure, the government's involvement in emigration did not begin with the colonization of Hokkaido. In the first year of Meiji, for the purpose of poverty relief, the government managed to dispatch a group of Japanese subjects to the Kingdom of Hawai'i as contract laborers to work on its sugar plantations. But the shizoku migration to Hokkaido was the first time in which the discourse of overpopulation was used to justify migration-driven expansion.
[54] Alan Takeo Moriyama, *Imingaisha: Japanese Emigration Companies and Hawai'i, 1894–1908* (Honolulu: University of Hawai'i Press, 1985), 39, 46.
[55] Hayami, "Jinkō Tōkei no Kindaika Katei," 11.
[56] Fabian Drixler, *Mabiki: Infanticide and Population Growth in Eastern Japan, 1660–1950* (Berkeley: University of California Press, 2013), 222–223.

aiming to both permanently maintain a high birth rate and improve the physical quality of the Japanese population.[57]

In the early twentieth century, the Ministry of Home Affairs emerged as a key government branch in migration management. Two years after the Rice Riots of 1918, the ministry established the Bureau of Social Affairs in charge of unemployment issues and emigration promotion.[58] The formation of the bureau marked the beginning of the state's institutional integration of overseas emigration with domestic social issues. From then on, the imperial government – at both central and local levels – became involved in the processes of migration promotion and management on an unprecedented scale, eventually giving birth to what I define as the Japanese "migration state." The Ministry of Home Affairs began to subsidize emigrants to Brazil in 1923, and later also provided financial aids to emigrants heading to other destinations. In 1927, the Tanaka Gi'ichi Cabinet established the Commission for the Investigation of the Issues of Population and Food (Jinkō Shokuryō Mondai Chōsakai) and staffed it with prominent demographers, economists, and emigration advocates. As a cabinet think tank that continued to function into the 1930s, the commission was put in charge of designing government policies on both reproduction and emigration. Members of the commission saw overpopulation as a root cause of Japan's social ills, but they were also convinced of the absolute necessity of maintaining Japan's population growth.[59] For them, overseas migration was an ideal solution to many problems faced by the Japanese empire.

The promulgation of the Overseas Migration Cooperative Societies Law (Kaigai Ijū Kumiai Hō) in 1928 authorized each prefecture to launch its own overseas emigration projects and build communities abroad.[60] As a result, a few prefectural governments played important roles in the mobilization of Japanese migration to Brazil and later Manchuria between the late 1920s and 1945.[61] Beginning in the early 1930s, the Ministry of Agriculture and Forestry (Nōrinshō) also participated in emigration promotion and management.[62] Embracing the logic of Malthusian expansionism, its policymakers claimed

---

[57] Fujime, *Sei no Rekishigaku*, 351.
[58] Sakaguchi Mitsuhiko, "Dare ga Imin wo Okuridashita no ka: Kan Taiheyō ni okeru Nihonjin no Kokusai Idō Gaikan," *Ritsumeikan Gengo Bunka Kenkyū* 21, no. 4 (March 2010): 55.
[59] Hiroshima Kiyoshi, "Gendai Nihon Jinkō Seisaku Shi Shōron: Jinkō Shishitsu Gainen o Megutte, 1916–1930," *Jinkō Mondai Kenkyū*, no. 154 (April 1980): 51–54.
[60] Nobuya Tsuchida, "The Japanese in Brazil, 1908–1941" (PhD diss., University of California, Los Angeles, 1978), 250.
[61] For example, Nagano, Kumamoto, Toyoma, and Tottori prefectures managed to establish prefecture-centered settler communities in Brazil by taking advantage of the Overseas Migration Cooperative Societies Law. Tsuchida, "Japanese in Brazil," 267. Nagano and Kumamto also later became two major suppliers of Japanese emigrants to Manchuria in the 1930s and 1940s. Young, *Japan's Total Empire,* 329–330.
[62] Itō Atsushi, *Nihon Nōmin Seisaku Shiron: Kaitaku Imin Kyōiku Kunren* (Kyoto: Kyoto Daigaku Gakujutsu Shuppankai, 2013), 127.

that the vast land in Manchuria was the ultimate rescue for landless farmers in the overcrowded archipelago.[63]

The empire's collapse and the subsequent US occupation brought emigration-related apparatuses of the imperial government to a halt. However, significant institutional continuities between the imperial and postwar governments allowed Malthusian expansionism to reemerge in postwar Japan. The new government embraced the discourse of overpopulation to explain its inability to solve a number of urgent social problems right after the war. After the US occupation ended, the migration state quickly came back to life; with the institutional structures and networks built back in the 1920s and 1930s, it now redirected Japanese migrants to South America. The Ministry of Foreign Affairs and Ministry of Agriculture and Forestry, engines of the migration state before 1945, continued to drive the migration machine in the postwar era until the decline of Japanese emigration and Malthusian expansionism itself in the 1960s.[64]

The International: Anglo-American Expansion, White Racism, and Modern Settler Colonialism

In addition to the intellectual, social, and institutional contexts, the advent and evolution of Malthusian expansionism in Japan was also a byproduct of Anglo-American expansion around the world. At first glance, the parallels between imperial Japan's call for additional land to accommodate its surplus population, the Third Reich's thirst for Lebensraum, and the demand for Spazio vitale by Mussolini's Italy appear self-evident. As this book demonstrates, however, it was the British settler colonialism in North America and the US westward expansion that truly inspired and informed the Japanese Malthusian expansionists. Japan's uneasy interactions with the Anglo-American global hegemony had a significant impact on the trajectory of Japanese Malthusian expansionism.

From the beginning of the Meiji era, Japan's leaders were impressed by the history of Anglo-American expansion and followed it as a textbook example for Japan's own project of empire building. To rationalize this imitation, they spared no effort to claim similarities between the Japanese and the Anglo-Saxons. The influential Meiji economist and journalist Taguchi Ukichi, for example, argued that Japan's population growth proved that the Japanese were as superior as the Anglo-Saxons.[65] The colonization of Hokkaido, the first

---

[63] Namimatsu Nobuhisa, "Nōson Keizaikosei to Ishiguro Tadatsu Hōtoku Shisō to no Kanren o Megutte," *Kyōto Sangyō Daigaku Ronshū, Shakai Kagaku Keiretsu*, no. 22 (March 2005): 119–120.

[64] Nōgyō Takushoku Kyōkai, *Sengo Kaigai Nōgyō Ijū no Shokan to Kikō*, vol. 1 (Tokyo: Nōgyō Takushoku Kyōkai, 1966), 10–11, 13–14.

[65] Taguchi Ukichi, *Nihon Keizai Ron* (Tokyo: Keizai Zasshisha, 1878), 73–76.

target of the Meiji empire, was carefully modeled after Anglo-American settler colonialism in general and the US westward expansion in particular.[66] As the Japanese expansionists' gaze shifted overseas, the American West became one of the first ideal destinations for Japanese emigration: by going to the western frontier of American expansion, not only would the Japanese be able to learn firsthand from Anglo-American settlers, they would also participate in the colonial competition against them.[67]

To be sure, though bearing close connections and parallels, the histories of the British and the US empires followed divergent paths. Even in the region of North America, British settler colonialism and the US westward expansion stood apart from each other in both temporal and political contexts. What the Japanese empire builders described as the expansion of the "Anglo-Saxons" was usually based on their oversimplification and misunderstanding of these two highly complicated experiences.[68] Nevertheless, these misinterpretations did not prevent them from borrowing the core ideas of Malthusian expansionism from their British and American counterparts.[69]

The decades of the 1910s and 1920s marked a watershed in the history of Japanese Malthusian expansionism. Up until this point, the legitimacy of Japanese emigration rested upon the self-claimed similarities of the Japanese to the Anglo-Saxons, but now Japanese thinkers began to challenge Western settler colonialism and Anglo-American hegemony in order to promote Japan's own version of settler colonialism. This change was a response to the waves of anti-Japanese sentiment in the Anglo world that culminated in

[66] To this end, the Meiji government employed over forty American experts to advise and facilitate the empire's colonization of Hokkaido in the 1870s. Fumiko Fujita, *American Pioneers and the Japanese Frontier: American Experts in Nineteenth-Century Japan* (Westport, CT: Greenwood, 1994), 10. Meiji expansionists not only compared shizoku migrants in Hokkaido with Mayflower settlers in North America but also envisioned turning Hokkaido into Japan's California. "Kaitaku no Shisatsu," *HKZ*, no. 2 (February 14, 1880): 1–4; Tsuda Sen, "Nihon Teikoku no uchi ni Amerika Gasshūkoku wo Genshutsu Suru wa Atarasa ni Tōki ni Arazaru Beshi," *HKZ*, no. 3 (February 28, 1880): 51.
[67] Fukuzawa Yukichi, "Beikoku wa Shishi no Seisho Nari" and "Fuki Kōmyo wa Oya Yuzuri no Kuni ni Kagirazu," in *Fukuzawa Yukichi Zenshū*, vol. 9 (Tokyo: Iwanami Shoten, 1960), 442–444, 546.
[68] In the interest of historical authenticity, this book uses the term "Anglo-Saxons" in the same way the historical actors (the Japanese expansionists) had employed it, sometimes referring to either the British colonial settlers or the white Americans but often referring to both.
[69] By illustrating the impact of American westward expansion on Japan's own process of empire building, this study echoes US historian David M. Wrobel and others who have pointed out that, contrary to conventional wisdom, the experience of its westward expansion did not mark the United States as "exceptional." Instead, it was part and parcel of the age of New Imperialism in the modern world. Through the example of Japan, my study reveals the specific ways in which the history of the American West had inspired other modern empires to conduct their own projects of settler colonialism. See David M. Wrobel, *Global West, American Frontier: Travel, Empire and Exceptionalism from Manifest Destiny to the Great Depression* (Albuquerque: University of New Mexico Press, 2013), 21–28.

two international events: the Allies' rejection of Japan's proposal to write the clause of racial equality into the Treaty of Versailles in 1919 and the passage of the Immigration Act of 1924 in the United States.[70] Japanese Malthusian expansionists believed that as their empire was suffering from the crisis of overpopulation, Japan naturally deserved the right to export its surplus people overseas. However, this impeccably reasoned request, in their imaginations, was frequently denied, for the racist white men had reserved their vast and largely empty colonial territories around the Pacific Rim for their own people.[71]

As tensions between Japan and the United States continued to mount in the Asia-Pacific region, an increasing number of Japanese expansionists began to underscore and glorify the uniqueness of Japanese settler colonialism. Though Japan's Malthusian expansion continued to draw inspirations from the Anglo-American model in reality, it was increasingly portrayed as being guided by the unique principle of "coexisting and coprospering" with the native peoples. This principle, they argued, demonstrated the benevolent nature of Japanese expansion, which set them apart from the hypocritical white imperialists.

From the late 1930s to 1945, when Japan embarked upon a total war with the United States and the United Kingdom in the Asia-Pacific region, the idea of coexistence and coprosperity was enshrined as the ideology of its new world order known as the Greater East Asia Co-Prosperity Sphere. In their assuredly righteous struggle against white racism and the Anglo world, Japanese Malthusian expansionists considered a strong and growing population to be their best weapon: not

---

[70] Japan's influential political journal *Gaikō Jihō* periodically published articles in the 1920s and 1930s to commemorate the US Immigration Act of 1924 as Japan's national humiliation. See, for example, Inahara Katsuji, "Hainichi Dai Yon Shūnen o Mukau," *Gaikō Jihō* 46, no. 542 (1927): 1–18; "Hainichi Dai Nana Shūnen o Mukau," *Gaikō Jihō* 55, no. 614 (1930): 11–44; "Hainichi Imin Hō Dai Hachi Shūnen o Mukau," *Gaikō Jihō* 59, no. 638 (1931): 24–45; Ōyama Ujirō, "Hainichi Imin Hō Dai Kyū Shūnen," *Gaikō Jihō* 63 (1932): 1–13; "Hainichi Imin Hō Dai Jūni Shūnen," *Gaikō Jihō* 75 (1935): 44–56; "Hainichi Imin Hō Dai Jūsan Shūnen o Tomurau," *Gaikō Jihō* 79 (1936): 79–90; "Hainichi Imin Hō Dai Jūgo Shūnen o Tomurau," *Gaikō Jihō* 87 (1938): 75–83; "Hainichi Imin Hō Dai Jūroku Shūnen o Tomurau," *Gaikō Jihō* 91 (1939): 80–89.

   Except for a small number of studies, the impact of Japan's failure regarding the clause of racial equality in 1919 and the enactment of the Immigration Act of 1924 on the history of the Japanese empire has not been sufficiently recognized or examined in the extant literature. For a few salient works on these topics, see Naoko Shimazu, *Japan, Race and Equality: The Racial Equality of 1919* (London: Routeldge, 1998); Nancy Stalker, "Suicide, Boycotts and Embracing Tagore: The Japanese Popular Response to the 1924 US Immigration Exclusion Law, "*Japanese Studies* 26, no. 2 (2006): 153–170; Izumi Hirobe, *Japanese Pride and American Prejudice: Modifying the Exclusion Clause of the 1924 Immigration Act* (Stanford: Stanford University Press, 2002); Miwa Kimitada, ed., *Nichi-Bei kiki no Kigen to Hainichi Iminhō* (Tokyo: Ronsōsha, 1997); Minohara Toshihiro, *Hainichi Iminhō to Nichibei Kankei: Hanihara Shokan no Shinsō to Sono Jūdainaru Kekka* (Tokyo: Iwanami Shoten, 2002); Minohara Toshihiro, *Amerika no Hainichi Undō to Nichi-Bei Kankei: "Hainichi Imin Hō" wa Naze Seiritsushita Ka* (Tokyo: Asahi Shinbun Shoppan, 2016).

[71] Nasu Shiroshi, *Jinkō Shokuryō Mondai* (Tokyo: Nihon Hyōronsha, 1927), 86–87, 108–111, 162–163; Hasegawa, "1920 Nendai Nihon no Imin Ron (3)," 100–102.

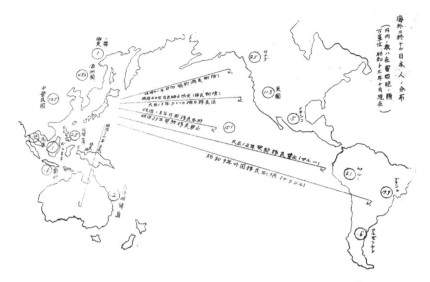

Figure I.1 This map, made in 1937 based on data from the Japan's Ministry of Foreign Affairs, illustrates the sizes of Japanese overseas communities around the Pacific Rim. It also presents a causal link between the exclusion of the Japanese migration in Australia and North and South America and the Japanese migration-driven expansion in East Asia. Kōseishō, Jinkō Minzokubu, *Yamato Minzoku o Chūkaku to Suru Sekai Seisaku no Kentō*, no. 6, in *Minzoku Jinkō Seisaku Kenkyū Shiryō: Senjika ni Okeru Kōseishō Kenkyūbu Jinkō Minzokubu Shiryō*, vol. 8 (repr., Tokyo: Bunsei Shoin, 1982), 2811.

only did it point to an increase of the overall strength of the empire, it also offered evidence of Japanese superiority over white men. In the minds of Japanese expansionists, racism was the indelible mark of Anglo-American hypocrisy that would lead white men to their downfall. A wartime survey published by the Japanese Ministry of Welfare gleefully noted that the population of Australia had already begun to decline due to a long history of excluding of Asian immigrants from the country.[72] In contrast, the overall population in the Co-Prosperity Sphere continued to grow at an impressive speed. More importantly, the Japanese, as the leading race (*shidō minzoku*), were willing to cooperate with the lesser races. Therefore, they were fully capable of using this formidable resource to empower

[72] Kōseishō, Jinkō Minzokubu, *Yamato Minzoku o Chūkaku to Suru Sekai Seisaku no Kentō*, no. 3, in *Minzoku Jinkō Seisaku Kenkyū Shiryō: Senjika ni Okeru Kōseishō Kenkyūbu Jinkō Minzokubu Shiryō*, vol. 5 (repr., Tokyo: Bunsei shoin, 1982), 1294–1295.

their empire; by doing so, they would succeed in their mission to build a new and liberated Asia.[73]

These imperial designs, however, would have to remain unrealized. Japan's defeat in World War II and the subsequent US occupation led to yet another turning point in the evolution of Japan's Malthusian expansionism. Postwar Japan's policymakers and migration promoters quickly embraced the American hegemony in the Western world by characterizing Japanese emigration as not only a solution to social crises in the war-torn archipelago but also a mission of exporting modernization. Emigration now became a way for the new Japan to solidify its position in the Western Bloc by enlightening Third World countries during the Cold War.

A Global History of Malthusian Expansionism

Examining the history of modern Japan from the perspective of Malthusian expansionism allows us to rethink the relationship between life and land, between migration and expansion in the global history of settler colonialism. As students of modern imperialism, Japanese leaders were quick to adapt to social Darwinism, and they saw the Western empires' territorial and demographic expansion as the guidebook for Japan's own project of empire making. Though this might strike today's readers as utterly counterintuitive, educated Japanese in different periods of the empire had imagined the snowy Hokkaido as Japan's very own California and hailed the northern Korean Peninsula as "Brazil in the frigid zone" (*Kantai Burajiru*).[74]

Similarly, Malthusian expansionism was not a Japanese invention. As a global discourse that served to justify modern settler colonialism, it had a long history that predated the rise of the Japanese empire. Its intellectual roots can be traced back to the formative years of modern nation-states in Europe, when Enlightenment thinkers began to discover the news meanings of population. Philosophers and political theorists such as Voltaire, Montesquieu, David Hume, Jean-Jacques Rousseau, and Thomas Paine all saw a large and growing population as evidence of social prosperity. The ability to sustain a rapid rate of population growth became a standard criterion by which a modern government's performance was judged.[75] The celebration of population increases also grew together with the emergence

---

[73] Kōseishō, Jinkō Minzokubu, *Yamato Minzoku o Chūkaku to Suru Sekai Seisaku no Kentō*, no. 1, in *Minzoku Jinkō Seisaku Kenkyū Shiryō: Senjika ni Okeru Kōseishō Kenkyūbu Jinkō Minzokubu Shiryō*, vol. 3 (repr., Tokyo: Bunsei Shoin, 1982), 507–508.

[74] Tsuda, "Nihon Teikoku no Uchi ni Amerika Gasshūkoku," 51; Kawamura Toyomi, "Naisen Yūwa no Zentei Toshite Hōyoku Naru Hokusen o Kaitaku Seyo," *Shokumin* 5, no. 2 (February 1926): 45.

[75] Karl Ittmann, Dennis D. Cordell, and Gregory H. Maddox, eds., *The Demographics of Empire: The Colonial Order and the Creation of Knowledge* (Athens: Ohio University Press, 2010), 4;

of demography as a modern discipline in Europe, allowing the nascent modern states to collect and use demographic data in order to control and manage their subjects.[76]

Due to the fear that people's fertility rate would drop once they settled overseas, population surveys were conducted in settler colonies earlier and more often than back in the metropoles.[77] The superior population growth rate in the North American colonies, however, convinced the British expansionists that settler colonialism was an ideal strategy to boost population size of the entire empire. In 1755, Benjamin Franklin, then still a loyalist to the British Crown, published a book in Boston to drum up support for the ongoing Seven Years' War. From a demographic perspective, he took pains to convince his readers that the war was worth fighting in order to secure and expand British colonies in North America. A swelling population, he argued, was crucial for the fate of every nation. However, if a land was fully occupied, those who did not have land would become mired in poverty because they would have to labor for others under low wages. Then due to poverty, landless people would have to stave off marriage in order to keep their living standards. This, in turn, would stop population growth.[78]

Contrasting to the overcrowded Europe, Franklin argued, the vast and empty North America was occupied by only a negligible number of Indian hunters. It had an abundance of cheap land that both European settlers and their offspring could easily obtain. For this reason, the average age of marriage among the British settlers in North America was younger than that in Britain. Franklin thus believed that the population in the British colonies in North America had been growing at full speed, with its size doubling every twenty-five years. Within a century, he predicted, the number of British settlers in America would exceed the population in the British Isles.[79]

With this vision, Franklin rejoiced in the population growth of the British settlers in North America and what it portended for the British Empire: "What an accession of Power to the British Empire by the Sea as well as Land! What increase of trade and navigation! What numbers of ships and seaman! We have been here but little more than one hundred years, and yet the force of our Privateers in the late war, united, was greater, both in men and guns, than that of the whole British Navy in Queen Elizabeth's time."[80] To emphasize the importance of North American colonialization, Franklin further explained

Mohan Rao, "An Imagined Reality: Malthusianism, Neo-Malthusianism and Population Myth," *Economic and Political Weekly* 29, no. 5 (January 29, 1994): 40, 42.

[76] Ittmann, Cordell, and Maddox, *Demographics of Empire*, 4.

[77] Alison Bashford and Joyce E. Chaplin, *The New Worlds of Thomas Robert Malthus: Rereading the Principle of Population* (Princeton: Princeton University Press, 2017), 27–28.

[78] Benjamin Franklin, *Observations concerning the Increase of Mankind and the Peopling of Countries* (Boston: S. Kneeland, 1755), 217.

[79] Ibid., 218.   [80] Ibid., 223.

how settler colonialism would foster both demographic and territorial expansion for the British Empire. A nation, he reasoned, was like a polyp: "Take away a limb, its place is soon supplied; cut it in two, and each deficient part shall speedily grow out of the part remaining." Referring to the land of North America, he continued, "if you have room and subsistence enough, as you may by dividing make ten polyps out of one, you may of one make ten nations, equally populous and powerful."[81] In his vision, the British colonies in North America offered the essential space for the British Empire to continue growing in both population and strength.

Franklin's theory about the rapid population increase in British North America was soon picked up by many publications in the British Isles as joyful common sense. In particular, Franklin's assumption that the size of British settlers' population in America would double every twenty or twenty-five years became a central inspiration for Thomas Malthus to compose his fundamental thesis on population.[82] In 1789, in *An Essay on the Principle of Population*, Malthus laid out his demographic theory that human population, if left unchecked, would grow in a geometrical ratio while subsistence for mankind could increase only in an arithmetical ratio.[83] To prove this theory, Malthus took the newly independent United States and Britain as two contrasting empirical cases. He picked up Franklin's hypothesis and defined American settler communities as an illustration for how fast human population could grow when given an abundance of land and subsistence. Britain, on the other hand, was a lesson on how overpopulation would take its toll by pushing millions into poverty.[84]

The publication of *An Essay on the Principle of Population* was indeed a milestone event in the global history of demographic thoughts. By proposing that food production could never keep up with population growth within a given amount of land, Malthus forcefully established a causal link between population growth, poverty, and social disorder and gave a scientific voice to the anxieties about overpopulation that had already been emerging in Britain and France at the time.[85] The flame of fear was further fanned by the explosion of urban population and revolutions throughout Europe during the first half of the nineteenth century.[86] During the following decades, as Malthusianism gained increasing prominence, it also became a point of contention among different social forces. Nevertheless, it would be difficult to overestimate Malthusianism's impact on social movements and state policies throughout the world to this day.

---

[81] Ibid., 224.
[82] Bashford and Chaplin, *New Worlds of Thomas Robert Malthus*, 51–52, 70–71; Rao, "Imagined Reality," 41.
[83] Malthus, *Essay on the Principle of Population*, 6.   [84] Ibid., 7.
[85] Ittmann, Cordell, and Maddox, *Demographics of Empire*, 4.
[86] Cole, *Power of Large Numbers*, 1.

However, the rise of Malthusianism by no means brought an end to the celebration of population growth in the imperial West. Throughout the nineteenth century, expansionists in the British Isles continued to hail population growth as an indicator of power and progress both in the metropole and in the colonies. In 1853, the *Manchester Guardian* happily claimed that the enormous increase of the Anglo-Saxons since the beginning of the century marked Great Britain's grand transition from a kingdom into an empire.[87]

In this context, visionaries of imperialism embraced the idea of the "Malthusian nightmare" as a central justification for settler colonial expansion. While educated Britons had advanced the idea that the coexistence of an overpopulated and industrious nation and the vacant foreign land necessitated the expansion of the former to the latter as early as the sixteenth century,[88] it was Malthus who, for the first time, vested this idea with scientific reasoning. None other than Malthus himself had praised the British colonies in North America as a successful example of how population growth could reach its full scale given sufficient land.[89] The ideas of Malthus became the intellectual foundation of Robert Wilmot-Horton's proposals to relocate the British poor to Upper Canada. Wilmot-Horton managed to implement some of his emigration plans and chaired the Select Committee on Emigration in the British government in the 1820s.[90] The Malthusian theory also inspired Wilmot-Horton's acquaintance, Robert Gouger, to establish the National Colonization Society in England in 1830: by promoting colonial migration to Australia, he would free the United Kingdom of its paupers. Gouger is known as one of the founders of South Australia and also served as its first colonial secretary.[91] In 1895 Cecil Rhodes promoted British settler colonialism in Africa in the same logic by declaring, "My dearest wish is to see the social problem solved: that is to say that in order to save the forty million inhabitants of the United Kingdom from bloody civil war, we colonial politicians must conquer new lands to take our excess population and to provide new outlets for the goods produced in our factories and mines. The empire, as I have always said, is a question of bread and butter. If you do not want civil war, you must become imperialists."[92]

---

[87] Kathrin Levitan, "'Sprung from Ourselves': British Interpretations of Mid-Nineteenth-Century Racial Demographics," in *Empire, Migration and Identity in the British World*, ed. Kent Fedorowich and Andrew S. Thompson (Manchester: Manchester University Press, 2013), 62.

[88] For example, Thomas More had drawn the link between the vacant land and the overflowing and industrious nation in *Utopia*, his famous work of fiction published in 1516. Arneil, *John Locke and America*, 80. This idea was also mentioned by John Locke and other British thinkers in his generation in the seventeenth century. See Arneil, *John Locke and America*, 110.

[89] Bashford and Chaplin, *New Worlds of Thomas Robert Malthus*, 4.   [90] Ibid., 211.

[91] Ibid., 226.

[92] V. I. Lenin, *Imperialism, the Highest Stage of Capitalism* (Chippendale, Resistance Books, 1999), 84.

Malthusian expansionism also undergirded the westward expansion of the United States. In 1803, Thomas Jefferson argued that the rapid increase of the white American population made it necessary for the Native Americans to abandon hunting in favor of agriculture in order to free up more land for white settlers.[93] To this end, he began to envision a relocation of the Native American tribes to the western side of the Mississippi in order to leave the entire eastern side of the river to white farmers.[94] Jefferson's idea was eventually materialized in the passage of the Indian Removal Act by the American Congress in 1830, which authorized US president Andrew Jackson to relocate Native Americans residing in the Southeast to the other side of the Mississippi. The promulgation of the Homestead Act of 1862, on the other hand, hastened US westward migration and agricultural expansion by granting eligible settlers public land in the American West after five years of farming.[95] In 1903, looking back to the history of US expansion in the nineteenth century, Frederick Jackson Turner celebrated the "free land" in the western frontier as the safety valve of American democracy and individualism. Whenever the civilized society in the East was troubled by population pressure and material restraints, he concluded, settlers could always pursue freedom by taking the empty land in the West.[96]

While the "closing of the frontier," observed by Turner at the turn of the twentieth century, led to a rising overpopulation anxiety among conservative American intellectuals, their liberal counterparts continued to celebrate population growth as the fountain of the nation's wealth and power.[97] Similarly, the falling birth rates in the United Kingdom and France and the rise of imperial Germany in the late nineteenth century further marginalized the cause of birth control advocacy in British and French societies. The educated Europeans were also worried that the declining birth rate of the upper classes and the rising birth rate of the lower classes would lead to an overall degeneration of their racial stocks. The eugenic movement gained momentum in Europe and North America at the turn of the twentieth century by encouraging the reproduction

---

[93] Arneil, *John Locke and America*, 192–193.

[94] Alison Bashford, "Malthus and Colonial History," *Journal of Australian Studies* 36, no. 1 (March 2012): 104.

[95] Allan Bogue, "An Agricultural Empire," in Milner, O'Connor, and Sandweiss, *Oxford History of the American West*, 288–289.

[96] Frederick Jackson Turner, "Contribution of the West to American Democracy," *Atlantic Monthly*, January 1903, cited from Frederick Jackson Turner, *The Frontier in American History* (New York: Henry Holt, 1920), 259–260. In his earlier and more famous essay, "The Significance of the Frontier in American History," Turner also echoed Thomas Jefferson by contending that population pressure necessitated the American westward expansion. See Turner, *Frontier in American History*, 7.

[97] Derek S. Hoff, *The State and the Stork: The Population Debate and Policy Making in US History* (Chicago: University of Chicago Press, 2012), 44–45.

of the "fit" and forbidding that of the "unfit."[98] Major international wars from the end of the nineteenth century to the mid-twentieth century, including the Second Boer War, the Russo-Japanese War, World War I, and World War II, turned both the quantity and quality of population into an issue of life and death for policymakers of all major powers.

The Japanese empire entered the global scene of imperial rivalry at a time when the majority of land territories around the world had already been seized either formally or informally by other colonial powers. The Japanese expansionists could no longer replicate the sweeping conquest of *terra nullius* like their Anglo-Saxon counterparts. Along with warfare, emigration to sovereign territories (either colonies of other empires or settler nations) became one of the few options the empire had to pursue wealth and power. The Japanese empire builders embraced Malthusian expansionism at this particular moment. They celebrated the demographic explosion in the archipelago as evidence of the racial superiority of the Japanese and demanded an outlet for the empire's surplus population. At the turn of the twentieth century, they believed that California, a sparsely populated frontier of American westward expansion, not only was a guide for Japan's own expansion in Hokkaido but also should be a frontier of the Japanese subjects themselves.[99] The "empty" and "wealthy" land of Brazil was likewise seen in the 1920s as an ideal destination for millions of Japanese landless farmers rather than a mere metaphor to encourage Japanese migration to Northeast Asia.[100]

The immigration of Asians to European colonies and settler nations soon triggered the first concerted efforts to regulate global migration. At the turn of the twentieth century, the United States, Australia, Canada, as well as European colonies in the Asia-Pacific region began to impose race-based immigration restrictions that aimed to exclude Asian immigrants. However, as Tokyo had justified Japanese emigration using the logic of Anglo-American expansion, the Anglophone scholars and politicians were forced to take the Japanese empire's demands seriously. In the 1920s and 1930s, overpopulation in Japan was widely recognized as scientific truth in the West.[101] Warren Thompson, a leading American sociologist and one of the most widely cited scholars in demographic studies in the West, argued in 1927 that due to the population pressure in Japan, "we should recognize that the urge towards expansion is just

[98] Richard A. Soloway, *Demography and Degeneration: Eugenics and the Declining Birthrate in Twentieth-Century Britain* (Chapel Hill: University of North Carolina Press, 1995), 57.

[99] Fukuzawa Yukichi, "Fuki Kōmyo wa Oya Yuzuri no Kuni ni Kagirazu," in *Fukuzawa Yukichi Zenshū*, vol. 9, 546.

[100] Nanba, *Nanbei Fugen Taikan*, 1–20.

[101] For example, see J. B. Condliffe, "The Pressure of Population in the Far East," *Economic Journal* 42, no. 166 (1932): 204; Thompson, *Danger Spots in World Population*, 114, 117–118; W. R. Crocker, *The Japanese Population Problem: The Coming Crisis* (London: George Allen & Unwin, 1931), 192, 202–203, 194–195, cited from Wilson, "New Paradise," 254.

as legitimate in the Japanese as in the Anglo-Saxons."[102] Thompson believed that in the interest of avoiding military conflicts, the Anglophone countries should cede some unused lands in the Pacific region to meet the needs of an expanding Japan.[103] Although Thompson's call for land share failed to convince the politicians inside the Anglosphere, it demonstrated that the logic of Malthusian expansionism was widely accepted even among the most educated minds in the West in the early twentieth century.

Germany and Italy also joined the global competition in colonial expansion in the second half of the nineteenth century, and the German and Italian empire builders shared their Japanese counterparts' predicament. They pointed to Malthusian expansionism as a justification for their efforts to carve out extra "living spaces" for their empires within a world of increasingly shrinking possibilities. Like it was for the Japanese empire, the emigration of "surplus" subjects into sovereign nations was a vital strategy for the German and Italian empires in their quest for wealth and power. Not surprisingly, the German and Italian emigration to other sovereign nations had profound ideological and institutional connections with the territorial expansion of these two colonial empires.[104] The convergence of the "battle for births" and "battle for land" of Germany and Italy culminated in the rise of fascist imperialism.[105] In the 1930s, like the Japanese demand for Manchuria as the empire's "lifeline," the push for Lebensraum and Spazio vitale eventually became the two fascist regimes' justification for wars.

Influential Western scholars like Walter Prescott Webb, who became the president of the American Historical Association in 1958, continued to embrace Malthusian expansionism after World War II in their grand narratives of modern world history. Webb saw the US westward expansion as part of the global

---

[102] Thompson, *Danger Spots in World Population*, 278, cited from Alison Bashford, "Nation, Empire, Globe: The Spaces of Population Debate in the Interwar Years," *Comparative Studies in Society and History* 49, no. 1 (2007): 192.

[103] Thompson, *Danger Spots in World Population*, 123–126.

[104] Mark Choate demonstrates the material and cultural ties between Italian settler colonialism in Africa and Italian migration to the two Americas by highlighting the role of the Italian government in promoting nationalism among the Italian overseas communities. Mark I. Choate, *Emigrant Nation: The Making of Italy Abroad* (Cambridge, MA: Harvard University Press, 2008). Stefan Manz, through a similar perspective, examines close connections between German imperial expansion and the rise of nationalism among German overseas communities in Russia and the United States. Manz, *Constructing a German Diaspora: The "Greater German Empire," 1871–1914* (New York: Routledge, 2014). German colonial thinkers such as Frederick List and Wilhelm Roscher in the late nineteenth century had already used the idea of overpopulation to legitimize both German expansion in the Americas and settler migration to Eastern Europe. Matthew P. Fitzpatrick, *Liberal Imperialism in Germany: Expansionism and Nationalism, 1848–1884* (New York: Berghahn Books, 2008), 58–61.

[105] Alison Bashford, "Population Politics since 1750," in *The Cambridge World History, Volume VII: Production, Destruction and Connection, 1750–Present*, Part I: *Structures, Spaces and Boundary Making*, ed. J. R. McNeill and Kenneth Pomeranz (Cambridge: Cambridge University Press, 2015), 222.

expansion of Western civilization since the sixteenth century. The lands and seas outside of Europe, which he termed in general as the Great Frontier, did not merely save a static Europe plagued by overpopulation and poverty. The multiple forms of wealth in the Great Frontier, Webb argued, also furnished the further growth of population and the development of capitalism, individualism, and democracy, which he saw as the essential components of Western civilization.[106]

Nevertheless, in the few decades following World War II, the discourse of Malthusian expansion itself had gradually fallen out of favor around the globe. As large-scale international migration and global land share schemes remained elusive in a world of nation-states, the biopolitics of fertility and mortality began to dominate intellectual debates on overpopulation and its solution.[107] Right after the war, US policy makers were convinced that overpopulation was a cause of Japanese militarism. The promulgation of the Eugenic Protection Law of 1948 in Japan, endorsed by the US occupation authorities, turned postwar Japan into one of the first countries in the world to legalize abortion.[108] What's more, groundbreaking technologies had divested land of its absolute primacy in food production.[109] The condition of overpopulation could no longer fully justify a nation's demand for additional land or emigration outlet, thus Malthusian expansionism disappeared from intellectual debates and political discourses around the world.

Chapter Overview: The Four Phases of Malthusian Expansionism

Malthusian expansionism in Japan evolved in four phases—emergence, transformation, culmination, and resurgence. In every stage, responding to specific social tensions within domestic Japan and the empire's interactions with its Western counterparts, Japanese Malthusian expansionists hailed men and women of distinct social strata in the archipelago as ideal subjects for emigration. Specific locations across the Pacific also emerged in each phase as ideal places for these migrants to put down the roots of the empire. Accordingly, this book examines each of these phases by following a chronological order.

Chapters 1 and 2 focus on the formative period of Malthusian expansionism, from the very beginning of the Meiji era to the eve of the Sino-Japanese War in the mid-1890s, and examine the international and domestic contexts in which

---

[106] Walter Prescott Webb, *The Great Frontier* (Boston: Houghton Mifflin, 1952), 8–10, 15–16, 30, 174–175, 292–294, 303–304.

[107] Alison Bashford, *Global Population: History, Geopolitics, and Life on Earth* (New York: Columbia University Press, 2016), 317.

[108] For the GHQ's influence on the legalization of abortion in Japan and the role of Warren Thompson in it, see Fujime, *Sei no Rekishigaku*, 358–361.

[109] Bashford, *Global Population*, 38.

Malthusian expansionism emerged in the archipelago. By defining the home archipelago as overpopulated while Hokkaido as conveniently empty, the Meiji government justified its policy of shizoku migration as a way to balance domestic demography and a strategy to turn these declassed samurai into the first frontiersmen of the empire. Japan's imitation of Anglo-American settler colonialism in Hokkaido also inspired the Japanese expansionists to turn their gaze to the American West as an ideal target of shizoku expansion in the 1880s. The blunt white racism that Japanese settlers and travelers encountered in California, however, forced the Japanese expansionists to shift their focus to the South Seas, Hawai'i, and Latin America. In their imaginations, these areas remained battlegrounds of racial competition in which the Japanese still had chances to claim a share, and the declassed samurai in the overpopulated archipelago were the ideal foot soldiers in this fight.

Unlike in Hokkaido and the American West, shizoku migration to the South Seas, Hawai'i, and Latin America failed to materialize on a significant scale. The decline of shizoku as a social class itself brought Japanese Malthusian expansionism to its second phase that lasted from the mid-1890s to the mid-1920s, examined in chapters 3, 4, and 5. These chapters detail how the focus of Japanese expansionists returned to North America when they replaced shizoku with the urban and rural commoners (*heimin*) as the backbone of the empire. These chapters also explain how the Japanese struggles against white racism in the US West Coast and Texas set the agendas for Japanese expansion in Northeast Asia, the South Seas, and South America and turned farmer migration into the most desirable model of Japanese settler colonialism in the following decades.

Following a series of domestic and international changes around the mid-1920s, Japan's migration-driven expansion entered its heyday phase that lasted through the end of World War II, examined in chapters 6 and 7. Two aspects distinguished Japanese Malthusian expansionism in this phase from the previous decades. First, the Japanese government involved itself in migration promotion and management on an unprecedented scale at both the central and prefectural levels, giving rise to "the migration state." Second, most Japanese expansionists who had been pursuing a seat for Japan in the club of Western empires were left severely disillusioned by the Immigration Act of 1924. They turned to an alternative model of settler colonialism to challenge Anglo-American global hegemony, marked by the principle of coexistence and coprosperity on the one hand and the emigration of grassroots farming families from rural Japan on the other. This new model was first carried out in Brazil and then applied to Japanese expansion in Manchuria and other parts of Asia during the 1930s and 1940s.

The collapse of the empire at the end of World War II brought an abrupt end to Japanese colonial expansion, but the institutions in charge of previous migration campaigns largely remained intact during the US occupation. Chapter 8, also the final part of this book, analyzes the unexpected resurgence of Japanese Malthusian expansionism during the 1950s and 1960s. This was also the final phase in its history. Policymakers and migration leaders, many of whom had led and participated in Japanese expansion before 1945, saw the returnees from the former colonies of the empire – as well as others who lost their livelihood due to the war – as the new nation's surplus people. Utilizing pre-1945 migration institutions and networks, they were able to restart Japanese migration to South America right after the enactment of the Treaty of San Francisco. In the 1960s, Japanese overseas emigration quickly declined as a rapid growing economy enabled its domestic society to accommodate most of the Japanese labor force. Malthusian expansionism eventually lost its material ground in the archipelago.

To grasp the complexity and dynamics in the relationship between demography and expansion and between emigration and settler colonialism in Japanese history, we must start our story from the very inception. It is with the Japanese colonial expansion in Hokkaido in early Meiji that our story shall begin.

Part I

Emergence, 1868–1894

1   From Hokkaido to California: The Birth of Malthusian Expansionism in Modern Japan

Malthusian expansionism emerged in the Japanese archipelago during the nascent empire's colonization of Hokkaido in early Meiji. Taking place when the nation-state itself was still in formation, the colonial expansion in Hokkaido constitutes the beginning chapter in the history of the Japanese empire. It not only offers a unique lens to look at the convergence between the process of nation making and that of empire building but also reveals the inseparability between migration and colonial expansion. To build a modern nation, the Meiji government abolished the Tokugawa era's status system and started turning the social structure into a horizontal one. By 1876, the samurai or *shizoku*, who were at the top of the Tokugawa social hierarchy, had lost almost all of their economic and political privileges. The government also implemented the policy of developing industry and trade (*shokusan kōgyō*) in order to boost the national economy, hiring American and European specialists to formulate concrete plans to modernize Japan's political and economic infrastructure. At the same time, the Meiji leaders were well aware that domestic changes alone were not sufficient to secure Japan's independence in the world of empires. To be admitted into the ranks of Western powers, Japan needed to have its own colonies. Hokkaido, the island in the northeast that had been a constant object of exploitation by forces in Honshu since the late Tokugawa period, was an easy target.

The Meiji empire's settler colonialism in Hokkaido was carefully modeled after the British settler colonialism in North America and the US westward expansion. Such imitation turned the specific social and political contexts in early Meiji into a cradle of Malthusian expansionists. Like their predecessors on both sides of the Atlantic Ocean who demanded colonial expansion in North America through the discourse of Malthusian expansionism, the Meiji expansionists rationalized colonial migration in Hokkaido by voicing the anxiety of overpopulation and calling for population growth at the same time. By a stroke of irony, this colonial imitation also inspired the Meiji expansionists to envision the American West as one of the first targets of Japanese expansion in the 1880s and 1890s.

The Shizoku Migration and the Anxiety on "Surplus People"

In 1869, the Meiji government established the Hokkaido Development Agency (Kaitakushi) to manage the colonization of Hokkaido. After Kuroda Kiyotaka took charge in 1871, the agency monopolized almost all political and financial policy-making powers in Hokkaido until its abolition in 1882. Kuroda was originally a samurai of lower rank in the Satsuma domain who held a profound interest in the West, and his empathy for shizoku and his passion for modernizing the nation according to the Western model came together in his blueprint for Hokkaido colonization. Kuroda regarded Hokkaido as a land of promises that would provide immediate help to the imperial government on two of its most urgent tasks: resettling the declassed samurai and developing its economy. He believed that the land of the island was large enough for the government to distribute to the declassed samurai settlers and that Hokkaido could provide enough natural resources to boost the entire nation's economic development. These two missions thus converged in the colonial migration of shizoku to Hokkaido under the direction of the Development Agency.

The two flagship migration programs launched by the Development Agency were the farmer-soldier program (*tondenhei*) and the program of land development (*tochi kaitaku*). The farmer-soldier program recruited domestic shizoku as volunteer soldiers and settled them in Hokkaido by providing free land, houses, as well as other living and farming facilities.[1] These settlers were expected to conduct both military training and working the land in assigned settlement locations. The program of land development, on the other hand, encouraged nonmilitary shizoku settlement in Hokkaido by providing free lease of land between about one and a half to three *chō* to each shizoku household up to five years. If their farming proved successful, the shizoku settlers could own the land for no charge.[2] These policies led to a wave of collective settlements of the declassed shizoku that were financially sponsored by their former lords. These collective projects were usually

---

[1] Kuroda Kiyotaka hoped to recruit farmer-soldiers exclusively among the newly declassed shizoku. This goal was also reflected in the regulations of recruitment. However, in reality, not all the farmer-soldiers were actual shizoku. Even in the early stage of the farmer-soldier program, men without shizoku status were admitted in order to ensure that enough soldiers were recruited. The Development Agency did not differentiate those who held shizoku status and those who were from shizoku families but did not inherit such status. In 1899, the Meiji government changed the recruitment policy of the tondenhei program, which officially opened the doors to men without shizoku status. Itō Hiroshi, *Tondenhei no Kenkyū* (Tokyo: Dōseisha, 1992), 276–279.

[2] One chō is equal to approximately 0.99 hectares. Kikkawa Hidezō, *Shizoku Jusan no Kenkyū* (Tokyo: Yūhikaku, 1935), 128.

launched and organized by private migration associations. Though different in format, both programs aimed to export the impoverished shizoku to Hokkaido and turn them into an engine for colonial development.

The programs of shizoku migration to Hokkaido considered both the migrants and the land of Hokkaido itself to be invaluable national resources. Through migration, the policymakers aimed to turn the declassed samurai into model subjects of the new nation and trailblazers in its frontier conquest. The land of Hokkaido was imagined as a source of great natural wealth, and the policymakers expected to convert this wealth into strategic economic resources through the boundless energy and massive manpower of the shizoku migrants.

Though Hokkaido was described as an empty, untouched land, justifying the proposal of migration was not an easy task for the early Meiji leaders. Government official Inoue Ishimi, for example, observed in 1868 that the size of the existing population in Japan proper was limited, and most of the residents shouldered the responsibility for providing food to the entire country. Unless its agricultural productivity increased, he believed, the nation could not afford to send people to Hokkaido.[3] The concern about population shortage in Japan proper was further voiced by Horace Capron, the American advisor hired by the Japanese government to guide this colonial project. Based on his investigation, Capron reported to the Meiji government in 1873 that even within Japan proper, only half of the land was occupied and explored.[4]

While both Inoue and Capron were supporters of Hokkaido migration, they considered the domestic population shortage a barrier and believed that it was necessary to have a surplus population in Japan proper first. They both mentioned that modernizing agricultural technology would free some labor from food production. However, such developments still could not provide the timely source of migration that the state immediately needed. A solution was found, instead, by reinterpreting demography. Based on the assumption that a certain size of land has a maximum number of people that it can accommodate, a document issued by the Meiji government in 1869, *Minbushōtatsu* (Paper of the Ministry of Popular Affairs), defined the existing population distribution in the nation as imbalanced, with an excess in Japan proper, where most areas were so densely populated that there was not even "a place to stick an awl" and a shortage in Hokkaido and other peripheries where the spacious land was in dire need of human labor.[5] This imbalance, the report claimed, led to surplus people and their poverty. To allow for existing resources to be used more evenly, these redundant people in overpopulated areas had to migrate to unpopulated areas to utilize unexplored land.[6] Therefore, the uneven distribution of the Japanese

---

[3] Yoshida, *Nihon Jinkō Ron no Shiteki Kenkyū*, 250.   [4] Ibid., 252.   [5] Ibid., 250–252.
[6] The interpretation of Japanese demographic distribution as imbalanced was used in the 1870s and 1880s to rationalize migration campaigns to other borderlands of the expanding empire, such as the Ogasawara (Bonin) Islands and the southwest corner of Kagoshima. Ibid., 214.

population, defined by this report, provided the logical ground for the government-sponsored shizoku migration programs to Hokkaido.

The Birth of Demography and the Celebration of Population Growth

The idea of seeing the empty land of Hokkaido as a cure for domestic poverty was by no means new. Tokugawa intellectuals like Namikawa Tenmin had used it to rationalize their proposals for northward expansion as early as the eighteenth century.[7] However, the discourse of overpopulation that emerged in early Meiji was a direct result of Japan's embrace of the modern nation-state system and New Imperialism in the nineteenth century. The government report of 1869 that investigated and interpreted the demographic figures in the archipelago was a result of the Meiji leaders' efforts to make information about people, society, and natural resources visible to the state through quantitative methods.

As it did in Europe and North America, demography as a modern discipline emerged in Japan as a critical means for the government to both monitor and manage the life and death of its subjects.[8] A central figure behind the push for state expansion in population management during the Meiji era was Sugi Kōji. Growing up in late Tokugawa Nagasaki and trained in Dutch Learning (Rangaku), Sugi first encountered the discipline of statistics while translating Western books into Japanese for the Tokugawa regime. He was particularly impressed by data books of social surveys conducted in Munich in the Kingdom of Bavaria.[9] Sugi started working for the Meiji government in 1871 as the head of the newly established Department of Statistics (Seihyō Ka), the forerunner to the Bureau of Statistics. In 1872, based on information collected by the national household registration system it had recently established, the Japanese state began to regularly conduct nationwide population surveys.

However, unsatisfied with this type of survey, Sugi conducted a pilot study in 1879 on demographic data in the Kai region in Yamanashi prefecture that was modeled on censuses conducted in Western Europe. This study was the first demographic survey in Japan that was based not on household registration but on individuals' age, marriage status, and occupation.[10] After spending two years calculating and analyzing the collected data, Sugi publicized the survey results in 1882. He urged the Meiji government to conduct a national demographic survey

---

[7] Kaiho Mineo, *Kinsei no Hokkaido* (Tokyo: Kyōikusha, 1979), 126.

[8] Demography as a field of academic study came into being in the eighteenth century together with the rise of nation-states in Europe. It fostered modern states using quantitative techniques to collect information on the masses. Ittmann, Cordell, and Maddox, *Demographics of Empire*, 4.

[9] A member of the German Confederation, the Kingdom of Bavaria joined the German Empire in 1871.

[10] Hayami Akira, *Rekishi Jinkōgaku de Mita Nihon* (Tokyo: Bungei Shunjū, 2001), 146.

modeled after this pilot study in order to produce high-quality census data like those in Europe and North America.[11] However, an enormous government budget cut by Minister of Finance Matsukata Masayoshi made Sugi's proposal impractical for the time being. In 1883, Sugi left his government post to cofound the School of Statistics (Kyōritsu Tōkei Gakkō), a private institution training students in quantitative methods using German textbooks.[12] Although the school was shut down amid the Matsukata Deflation, its pupils would go on to spearhead the Empire of Japan's first census, conducted in Taiwan in 1905.[13]

A central motive behind the quest for demographic knowledge in Meiji Japan was to provide scientific evidence to confirm the commonsense observation of rapid population growth in the archipelago at the time, a phenomenon brought on by the modernization of medicine and public hygiene. Japanese intellectuals, like their Western counterparts since the Age of Enlightenment, interpreted demographic expansion as a symbol of progress and prosperity. Since the size of population was considered a direct indicator of a nation's military strength and labor capacity, its increase was widely celebrated in the archipelago as Japan was finding its feet in the social Darwinist world order. More importantly, the celebration of population growth in Japan, as it was in the West, took place in the context of modern colonialism. Joining hands with the claim of overpopulation, it legitimized the Japanese empire's quest for wealth and power overseas. The necessity for population growth on the one hand and the anxiety over the existence of surplus people on the other hand formed the central logic of Malthusian expansionism that justified Japan's migration-driven expansion throughout the history of the Japanese empire.

This logic was well elaborated in the writings of the prominent Japanese enlightenment thinker Fukuzawa Yukichi at the end of the nineteenth century. According to the rule of biology, Fukuzawa argued, a species always had a quantitative limit to its propagation within a certain space. "There is a cap on how many golden fish can be bred in a pond. In order to raise more, [the breeder] either needs to enlarge the pond or to build a new one." The same was true, he argued, for human beings. While thrilled by the demographic explosion in the archipelago of the day, Fukuzawa warned that with such a speed of growth, the Japanese population would soon reach the quantitative limit set by Japan's current territory and stop reproducing. However, population growth, Fukuzawa also reminded his readers, was crucial for a nation's strength and prosperity. No nation, he argued, could achieve substantial success with an insufficient population. A nation had to maintain its demographic growth

---

[11] Hayami, "Jinkō Tōkei no Kindaika Katei," 10.
[12] Hayami, *Rekishi Jinkōgaku de Mita Nihon*, 147.
[13] Among the central statisticians during the census, five of seven had studied in Sugi's School of Statistics. Ibid., 150.

because demographic decline would lead only to the decline of the nation itself.[14]

Inspired by Anglo-American settler colonialism in the recent past, Fukuzawa concluded that the only solution to Japan's crisis of overpopulation was emigration. Although the domestic population of England was even smaller than that of Japan, he reasoned, the British Empire enjoyed the unmatched prestige and power around the world thanks to the vibrant productivity of the Anglo-Saxon race. The limited space in the British Isles pushed the Anglo-Saxons to leave their home country and conquer foreign lands. The Japanese, Fukuzawa believed, should follow the British example by building their own global empire.[15]

Malthusian Expansionism and Japanese Settler Colonialism in Hokkaido

As the thoughts of Fukuzawa Yukichi also revealed, Malthusian expansionism was originally an Anglo-American invention. It was first transplanted into the Japanese soil by Meiji leaders during Japan's colonial expansion in Hokkaido. The following paragraphs examine how Malthusian expansionism took root in the social and political contexts of late nineteenth-century Japan and was used to legitimize the colonization of Hokkaido, the first colonial project in the Japanese empire. This initial phase of Japanese Malthusian expansionism also provides a valuable lens to look at how Japanese empire builders modeled the colonial expansion in Hokkaido in early Meiji after Anglo-American settler colonialism. This imitation can be revealed in three aspects, including the settlement of shizoku, the acquisition of Ainu land, and the accumulation of material capital. Together these three aspects further explain how the call for population growth worked in tandem with the complaint of overpopulation to legitimize Japanese setter colonialism in Hokkaido.

Making Useful Subjects: Shizoku as Mayflower *Settlers*

While the Meiji government defined imbalanced demographic distribution as the cause of poverty and argued that relocating the surplus people to Hokkaido would lift them from destitution, the majority of the selected migrants were not those who lived in absolute poverty but the recently declassed samurai. The abolition of the status system deprived them of their previous affiliations and transferred the loci of their loyalty from individual lords to the Meiji nation-state

---

[14] Fukuzawa Yukichi, "Jinkō no Hanshoku," in *Fukuzawa Yukichi Zenshū*, vol. 15 (Tokyo: Iwanami Shoten, 1961), 347–350.
[15] Fukuzawa Yukichi, "Jinmin no Ishoku," in *Fukuzawa Yukichi Zenshū*, vol. 15, 350–352.

itself.[16] Losing almost all inherited privileges and lacking basic business skills, the shizoku were pushed to the edge of survival. These politically conscious shizoku, who struggled for both economic subsistence and political power in the new nation, posed a serious challenge to the safety of the early Meiji state from both within and without. The angry shizoku formed the backbone of a series of armed uprisings in the 1870s that culminated in the Satsuma Rebellion in 1877 and the Freedom and People's Rights Movement spanning from 1874 to the 1890s.

Instead of perceiving the struggling shizoku solely as a burden or threat, Meiji intellectuals and policymakers believed that they could be put to better use. The question of how to resettle these potentially valuable subjects – and to some extent restore their leadership in the new nation – remained a central concern of Meiji policymakers and a hot topic in public debate until the 1890s. The idea of personal success (*risshin shussei*), which would later grow into a dominant and persistent discourse of overseas expansion in Japanese history, emerged at this particular moment. Risshin shussei was invented initially to provide alternative value systems for the declassed samurai. In his popular book *Saikoku Risshi Hen* (an adapted translation of *Self-Help*, a best seller in Victorian Britain by Samuel Smiles), Nakamura Masanao (Keiu) told his shizoku readers that their accomplishments and advancements in society should come not from inherited privileges but from their own virtues such as diligence, perseverance, and frugality.[17] Whereas the road to success proposed by Nakamura remained abstract and spiritual, another route, promoted by Fukuzawa Yukichi, was specific and pragmatic. In his widely circulated book *Gakumon no Susume* (Encouragement of Learning), Fukuzawa argued that learning practical knowledge (*jitsugaku*) should be the way for shizoku to regain their power. Specifically, it was knowledge in Western learning, achieved through education, that would give them wealth and honor in the new Japan. The independence of shizoku would then lead to the independence of Japan in the world.

One of the most influential promoters of shizoku success was Tsuda Sen, whose career demonstrated the intrinsic ties between the discourse of shizoku independence and that of national prosperity. Born into the family of a middle-rank

[16] As Stephen Vlastos insightfully points out, the Meiji reformations of the old political structures deprived the samurai's ability to rebel. In Stephen Vlastos, "Opposition Movements in Early Meiji, 1868–1885," in *The Cambridge History of Japan, vol. 5: The Nineteenth Century*, ed. Marius Jansen (Cambridge: Cambridge University Press, 1989), 367–431.

[17] Such individual spirit is also crucial for national progress. Inspired by this call, a group of shizoku in Shikoku formed Risshi Sha (Self-Help Association) in 1874, which later established branches throughout the nation. Out of the premise of saving shizoku's vigor for the nation, it conducted various programs to help shizoku find new occupations such as farming and crafting. Earl H. Kinmonth, *The Self-Made Man in Meiji Japanese Thought: From Samurai to Salary Man* (Berkeley: University of California Press, 1981), 35–36.

samurai, Tsuda acquired English proficiency through education and visited the United States in 1867 as an interpreter on a diplomatic mission for the Tokugawa regime. Impressed by the critical role of agriculture in fostering American economic growth and westward expansion, he began a lifelong career in Westernizing Japan's agriculture. Shortly after the formation of the Meiji nation, he founded the *Agriculture Journal* (*Nōgyō Zasshi*), a widely circulated magazine that disseminated the knowledge of Western agricultural science and advocated the importance of agricultural production. A nation's independence, he argued in the opening article in the inaugural issue, could be achieved only when the production of the nation became sufficient so that exports exceeded imports.[18] He also established a school, the Society of Agriculture Study (Gakunō Sha), to train shizoku in practical farming skills. He sought to overcome shizoku's traditional contempt for farming and persuade them to "return to agriculture" (*kinō*) with Western technologies and become "new farmers" (*shinnō*) of the new nation.[19] He firmly believed that the modernization of agriculture would restore shizoku's honor and wealth as well as further enable Japan to find its footing on the social Darwinist world stage.

Tsuda's initiative matched well with the Meiji government's policy of shizoku relief (*shizoku jusan*) that aimed to help the declassed samurai to achieve financial independence while turning them into productive subjects of the nation.[20] Tsuda himself played a central role in promoting shizoku migration to Hokkaido. With the support of Kuroda Kiyotaka, Tsuda founded the *Hokkaido Kaitaku Zasshi* (*HKZ, Hokkaido Development Journal*) in 1880. This journal served as the mouthpiece of the Hokkaido Development Agency to the general public, promoting its migration programs by linking the individual careers of shizoku with the colonial development of Hokkaido. Though it was decidedly short-lived (it folded after two years due to the agency's demise),[21] this biweekly journal provides a valuable lens to look at how the idea of making useful subjects worked together with Malthusian expansionism to foster shizoku settlement in Hokkaido.

In an editorial, Tsuda reasoned that the peasant population in Japan already exceeded what the existing farmland in Japan proper could accommodate. At the same time, there were many newly declassed samurai who had to turn to farming for their livelihood. Relocating them to Hokkaido served as a perfect solution to the issue of farmland shortage.[22] The natural environment of

---

[18] Takasaki Sōji, *Tsuda Sen Hyōden: Mō Hitotsu no Kindaika o Mezashita Hito* (Urayasu: Sōfūkan, 2008), 66.

[19] Ibid., 39. Tsuda's activities also reflected the government's general goal of turning the declassed samurai into new farmers in the early Meiji era. David Howell, "Early Shizoku Colonization of Hokkaido," *Journal of Asian History* 17 (1983): 62.

[20] State support ranged from direct stipends to landownership after a period of cultivation.

[21] The journal lasted from January 1880 to October 1881. Takasaki, *Tsuda Sen Hyōden,* 96–97.

[22] "Kazoku Shokun Shikiri ni Hokkaido no Chi o Aganau," *HKZ,* no. 8 (May 8, 1880): 170–171.

Hokkaido, Tsuda also reminded his readers, was demanding. For Japanese pioneers in Hokkaido, it was extremely difficult to carve out a livelihood in the wilderness. They had to be resolute in the face of such enduring hardships if they were to achieve any measure of success.[23] The fact that Nakamura Masanao's essay appeared in the first issue of the journal demonstrated the importance of the ideology of shizoku self-help as a driving force behind the Hokkaido migration. Nakamura, who enthusiastically applauded Tsuda Sen's efforts, argued that Hokkaido was an ideal place for those who had no land or property to achieve success through their own hands.[24]

Though Tsuda used the opportunity for personal success to encourage shizoku individuals to migrate, it was the prosperity of the Japanese empire that gave the Hokkaido migration its ultimate meaning. Tsuda took pains to use the legend of the *Mayflower* Pilgrims to encourage shizoku migrants to connect their lives with the very destiny of the Meiji empire. Conflating the story of the Pilgrims and that of the Puritans during the British expansion in North America, Tsuda described how the *Mayflower* "Puritans" risked their lives to sail across the Atlantic Ocean to North America in order to pursue political and religious freedom due to persecution in their homeland. Not only was their maritime journey long and often deadly, the initial settlement in the new land was also challenging. In Tsuda's narrative, after enduring every kind of shortage imaginable (food, farming equipment, fishing and hunting tools), the "Puritan" settlers eventually survived. They overcame all these difficulties and turned the barren earth of America into an invaluable land of resources. It was the efforts of these earliest settlers, Tsuda argued, that established the foundation of the United States as one of the most prosperous nations in the world.

For Tsuda, the situation of shizoku was reminiscent of the persecuted *Mayflower* settlers in that they were deprived of inherited privileges. Like the "Puritans" who sailed to America for political rights and religious freedom, the shizoku were supposed to regain their honor and economic independence by migrating to Hokkaido. The success of the *Mayflower* settlers, therefore, served as a model for the shizoku migrants. Resolved to overcome extreme difficulties and carve out the path for the future empire builders in Hokkaido by sacrificing their own lives, the shizoku migrants could make their achievements as glorious as their British counterparts.[25]

The Loyal Hearts Society (Sekishin Sha), a migration association established in 1880 in Kobe, aimed to relocate declassed samurai to Hokkaido. Tsuda applauded it as a success in emulating the example of the *Mayflower* settlers. The prospectus of the society argued that it was more meaningful for shizoku to

---

[23] "Kaitaku no Shisatsu," 4.   [24] *HKZ*, no. 1 (January 31, 1880): 5–7.
[25] "Kaitaku no Shisatsu," 1–4.

Figure 1.1 This picture appeared on the second issue of *Hokkaido Kaitaku Zasshi*. The caption reads, "The picture of the Puritans, the American ancestors, who landed from the ship of Mayflower and began their path of settlement." *HKZ*, February 14, 1880, 1. This is a reprint of the artwork originally painted by Charles Lucy 1754 titled *The Landing of the Pilgrim Fathers, America, A.D. 1620*.

find ways to live a happy life than to simply waste their time complaining about their dire conditions. Among all the paths to success, it claimed, the "exploration of Hokkaido" was the most effective and realistic choice. More importantly, participating in the exploration would allow these poor shizoku to associate "their small and humble life with great and noble goals" since their personal careers would sway the fate of the empire.[26] The regulations of the society further required them to prepare for permanent settlement in Hokkaido, building it both for their descendants and for the empire. For Tsuda, the

[26] "Sekishin Shain no Funhatsu (2)," *HKZ*, no. 7 (April 24, 1880): 147.

members of the society further served as living examples of how common Japanese subjects should take on their own responsibilities for the nation.[27]

Acquiring the Ainu Land via the Mission Civilisatrice: Ainu as Native Americans

If overpopulation in Japan proper legitimized the relocation of declassed shizoku, the growth of Japanese population served as a justification for the Meiji empire to acquire and appropriate the land of Hokkaido, originally occupied by the Ainu. In the writings of demographers and economists in early Meiji, the Japanese were listed as one of the most demographically expanding races in the world. In particular, the rapid increase of the Japanese population was considered to be proof that the Japanese were a superior race, equal to the Anglo-Saxons.[28] The image of the Japanese as a growing and thus civilized race was further solidified by being juxtaposed against the image of the disappearing Ainu natives in Hokkaido.[29] The discourse of Japanese growth and Ainu decline in Hokkaido drew parallels with the growth of the white settlers and the decline of the Native Americans in North America.[30] Through this comparison, not only were the Japanese grouped with the Europeans as the civilized, but the decrease of the Ainu was also understood as natural and unavoidable in the social Darwinist world.

Such a comparison mirrors the British explanation for the expansion of the English settlers in North America in contrast to the quick decline of the Native American population in the seventeenth and eighteenth centuries. British expansionists attributed the divergence in the demographic trends of the British settlers and the Native Americans to the physical and cultural superiority of the former over the latter.[31] Ignoring the fact that the fall of the Native American population was mainly the result of European epidemics brought by the settlers to the new land, Thomas Malthus believed that the savageness of the Native Americans, too, functioned as a check to keep the growth of their population within the capacity of the food supply. On the other hand, the

---

[27] "Sekishin Shain no Funhatsu (1)," *HKZ*, no. 6 (April 10, 1880): 122–123.

[28] Influential Meiji economist and journalist Taguchi Ukichi, for example, believed that Japan's population growth proved that the Japanese were as superior as the Anglo-Saxons, owners of the most successful settler colonial empire in human history. see Taguchi, *Nihon Keizai Ron*, 73–76.

[29] Along with the deepening of the colonial penetration of Hokkaido, Japanese intellectuals in the following decades continued to develop the idea that the Ainu were a "disappearing race" (*horobiyuku minzoku*) that needed to be protected. See Katsuya Hirano, "The Politics of Colonial Translation: On the Narrative of the Ainu as a 'Vanishing Ethnicity,'" *Asia-Pacific Journal* 4, no. 3 (January 12, 2009), https://apjjf.org/-Katsuya-Hirano/3013/article.html. The concept of "disappearing race" was later used to understand other native residents in Japan's new frontiers of expansion, such as the South Pacific, Taiwan, and Mongolia.

[30] Taguchi, *Nihon Keizai Ron*, 73.

[31] Bashford and Chaplin, *New Worlds of Thomas Robert Malthus*, 69.

demographic growth of the British settlers was a result of their superior manners and the abundance of room in the New World.[32]

The ideas of Thomas Malthus later inspired Charles Darwin to establish his theory of evolution, which explained the different fates of species as a result of natural selection.[33] The application of Darwinism in the understanding of human history and societies gave rise to modern racism that undergirded the existing discourse of racial hierarchy in the European colonial expansion through scientific reasoning. Faithful subscribers to social Darwinism, Meiji leaders, too, believed that only the superior races could enjoy a high speed of population increase while the inferior peoples were heading down a path of inexorable decline and eventual extinction. The destiny of the inferior races was sad but unavoidable because, due to their backwardness, they were not capable either to achieve social stability and community growth from within or to compete with the superior people from outside who came to colonize their lands.[34]

The demography-based racial hierarchy between the Japanese and Ainu further justified the Meiji leaders' appropriation of the Ainu land through the Lockean logic of land ownership. Like their European counterparts, the Meiji expansionists believed that the superior and the civilized had the natural right to take over the land originally owned by the inferior and the uncivilized so that the land could be better used. Therefore, it is not surprising that Kuroda Kiyotaka appointed Horace Capron, then the commissioner of agriculture in the US government, as the chief advisor of the Hokkaido Development Agency. Before working in the US Department of Agriculture, Capron was assigned by US president Millard Fillmore to relocate several tribes of Native Americans after the Mexican-American War.[35] Capron himself, while investigating the land of Hokkaido, found close similarities between the primitive Ainu and the savage Native Americans.[36]

For this reason, the migration from Japan proper to Hokkaido, the land of Ainu, was not only a solution to the issue of overpopulation in Japan but also an act of spreading civilization and making better use of the land itself. In the very first editorial of the *Development Journal*, Tsuda tried to convince his readers that Hokkaido of the day was no longer the land of Ezo. The existing understanding of Hokkaido, Tsuda argued, was based on the book *The Study of Ezo* (*Ezoshi*), which was authored by Confucian scholar Arai Hakuseki one and a half centuries earlier. It described the island as a sterile land with only a few

---

[32] Ibid., 70.   [33] Ibid., 268.

[34] A Japanese book that explicitly applied the logic of social Darwinism to the demographic dynamics in European expansion is Shiga Shigetaka, *Nan'yō Jiji* (Tokyo: Maruzen Shōsha Shoten, 1891), 13.

[35] Horace M. Capron, *Memoirs of Horace Capron – Vols. 1 and 2: Autobiography* (Special Collections, National Agricultural Library, 1884), 1:79.

[36] Ibid., 2:92–93, 98.

Figure 1.2 The caption of this picture in *Hokkaido Kaitaku Zasshi* reads "the picture of the native people (*dojin*) of Karafuto who were relocated to Tsuishikari." *HKZ*, September 11, 1880, 1.

crooked roads. However, Tsuda continued, times had changed. The time had come for the Japanese to reunderstand Hokkaido as a land of formidable wealth, where settlers from Japan proper could farm, hunt, and engage in commerce. Such a transition would be a result of the Japanese government's transplantation of civilization to the island.[37] The native Ainu saw their ancestral lands taken away from them due to their supposed "lack of civilization," and the land of Hokkaido was redefined by the Development Agency as unclaimed land (*mushu no chi*) based on the Hokkaido Land Regulation of 1872, thereafter distributed to the shizoku settlers.[38]

The logic that the civilized had the right to take over the land of the uncivilized so that it could be better used was more explicitly articulated in an article in the

[37] "Kaitaku Zasshi Hakkō no Shushi," *HKZ*, no. 1 (January 31, 1880): 2–3.
[38] Katsuya Hirano, "Thanatopolitics in the Making of Japan's Hokkaido: Settler Colonialism and Primitive Accumulation," *Critical Historical Studies* 2, no. 2 (Fall 2015): 207. Also see Ann B. Irish, *Hokkaido: A History of Ethnic Transition and Development on Japan's Northern Island* (Jefferson, NC: McFarland, 2009), 195.

Development Journal discussing a coercive Ainu relocation. In order to secure the control of Hokkaido, the Meiji government signed the Treaty of Saint Petersburg with the Russian Empire in 1875, recognizing Russian sovereignty over Sakhalin Island in exchange for full ownership of the Kuril Islands. Ainu residents in Sakhalin were, of course, excluded from the negotiation process. About 840 of them were forced to migrate from the Sakhalin Islands to Tsuishikari, a place close to Sapporo.[39] Though Tsuda recognized the unwillingness of these Ainu to give up their homeland and admitted that the forced relocation had caused them grief, he contended that such pain was necessary: Since the Ainu lacked both motivation and ability to develop their Sakhalin homeland into a profitable place, it would be a waste to let them stay there in hunger. The Japanese, on the other hand, not only put Sakhalin to better use by exchanging it for the Kuril Islands with Russia, but also had been civilizing these relocated Ainu. Tsuda happily noted that the Ainu in Tsuishikari, in addition of receiving new educational opportunities, were learning the modern ways of hunting, handcrafting, and trading. He posited that these Ainu were now satisfied with their new life and felt grateful for the protection offered by the Development Agency.[40] By this logic, the Meiji government's takeover of Ainu lands was portrayed as an altruist project that had the native residents' best interests at heart.

In reality, however, the relocation soon trapped these Ainu in misery. Unfamiliar with the new environment and incapable of adapting to the new ways of production introduced by the Meiji authority, they could not sustain their own livelihood. The community was further decimated by epidemics. Especially in 1886, the spread of smallpox claimed over three hundred lives. Many survivors later returned to Sakhalin.[41] The tragedy of this group of Ainu was only an example of the rapid decline of Ainu communities in general due to a series of Meiji policies that deprived them of their land, materials, and cultures in the name of spreading civilization.[42]

Accumulating Material Capital: Hokkaido as California

Meiji expansionists' acclamation of population growth was also a product of the development of Japan's nascent capitalist economy. Their desires to acquire more human resources as well as natural resources were driven by the impulse of

---

[39] Initially due to the strong protest of these Ainu, instead of Tsuishikari, the Development Agency temporarily settled them in the Sōya area at the north end of Hokkaido Island, next to Sakhalin, across the La Pérouse Strait (Sōya Strait), based on their own desire. However, to prevent these Ainu from interacting with the Ainu who remained in Sakhalin, the Development Agency forced them to move farther south to Tsuishikari shortly after they arrived in Sōya. Emori Susumu, *Ainu Minzoku no Rekishi* (Urayasu: Sōfūkan, 2007), 408.
[40] "Hokkaido wa Kosan no Chi Naru Setsu," *HKZ*, no. 17 (September 11, 1880): 387.
[41] Emori, *Ainu Minzoku no Rekishi*, 412.
[42] Hirano, "Thanatopolitics in the Making of Japan's Hokkaido," 197.

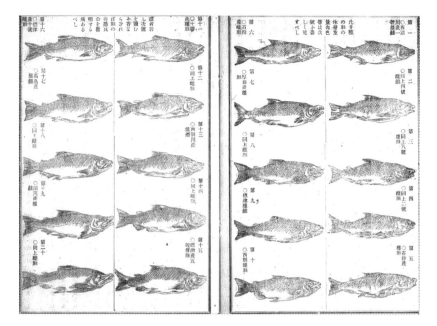

Figure 1.3 Two pages in *Hokkaido Kaitaku Zasshi* introduce different types of salmon in Hokkaido. The same issue also discusses tips in salmon hunting and canning as well as incubating salmon eggs. *HKZ*, June 5, 1881, 242–243.

capitalist accumulation. The migration of people from Japan proper to Hokkaido to explore and exploit the natural resources was to meet these demands. In their imaginations, the worthless land of yesterday's Ezo suddenly became a precious source of ever-growing wealth (*fugen*), because its earth, rivers, mineral deposits, plants, and wild animals all became potential resources for Japan's nascent capitalist economy.

In the eyes of Tsuda Sen, the enormous amount of natural wealth in Hokkaido was vital to finance industrialization, road building, and trade expansion of the Japanese empire.[43] To help readers in Tokyo understand the richness of Hokkaido through the vocabularies of capitalism, almost every issue of the *Development Journal* included articles that illustrated how various natural resources in Hokkaido could be either extracted for direct profit or used for material production. These included, to name but a few examples, tips for hemp processing, benefits of planting potato, knowledge of running winery, and methods of salmon hunting.[44]

---

[43] "Yūshisha no Jimu," 50–51.
[44] "Asano," *HKZ*, no. 2 (February 14, 1880): 9; "Jyagatara imo no rieki," *HKZ*, no. 3 (February 28, 1880): 56; "Budō saibai no rieki," *HKZ*, no. 5 (March 27, 1880): 97; "Sake no setsu," *HKZ*, no. 10 (June 5, 1880): 241.

For the Meiji empire's capitalist exploitation of Hokkaido through migration, the American westward expansion served as a key guide. The director of
the Development Agency, Kuroda Kiyotaka, appointed Horace Capron, the
commissioner of agriculture in the US government, as the main advisor to the
Development Agency. The agency also hired more than forty other American
experts who specialized in agriculture, geology, mining, railway building, and
mechanical engineering to guide its project of transforming natural deposits in
Hokkaido into profitable resources.[45]

To draw the parallel between Japanese colonial migration in Hokkaido and
American westward expansion, Tsuda Sen declared that soon an "America"
would emerge from the Japanese archipelago. While Japan currently could not
compete with America in terms of wealth, power, and progress in democracy
and education, he maintained, the soil of Hokkaido was as rich as that of the
United States, and their climates were equally suitable for farming. Tsuda
assured his readers that as the colonial project continued to develop, material
production from Hokkaido would match that in the United States.[46] In particular, he compared the position of Hokkaido in Japan to that of California in the
United States. Located on the West Coast of North America, Tsuda argued,
California had been no more than an empty land until it became a part of
America. Within two decades of American settlement, with the discovery of
gold and improvements to agricultural technology, its population and material
products grew exponentially. Hokkaido, Tsuda claimed, had not only similar
latitudes to California but also equal amounts of natural resources. With the
influx of settlers from Japan proper making progress in land exploration, the
Ezo of yesterday would surely become the California of tomorrow. It would
serve as a permanent land of treasure for Japan, the output of which would
sustain Japan's economic growth at home and bring in wealth from abroad
through exportation.[47]

At the center of Japan's imitation of American westward expansion was the
transplantation of American agricultural technology to Hokkaido. Tsuda believed
that in addition to the Puritan spirit of the early settlers, the Americans owed much
of their triumph to the fertility of its land and a high agricultural productivity.
Assuming Hokkaido's land would prove to be equally fertile, Tsuda concluded that
the key to the success of Hokkaido exploration was to increase the existing
agricultural productivity by transplanting American technology.[48] He not only
translated several books on new American farming practices from English to
Japanese, but also included many articles in the *Development Journal* calling on
farmers to adopt American farming tools and techniques in areas such as crop

---

[45] Fujita, *American Pioneers and the Japanese Frontier*, 10.
[46] Tsuda, "Nihon Teikoku no Uchi ni Amerika Gasshūkoku," 50.   [47] Ibid., 51.
[48] "Nōgu Kairyō Ron," *HKZ*, no. 3 (February 28, 1880): 59.

Figure 1.4 A picture of a new wheat-cutting tool in the United States in
Hokkaido Kaitaku Zasshi. HKZ, June 19, 1880, 1.

cultivation, animal husbandry, and pest control. Under the direction of the
Development Agency, a variety of American crops, livestock, and machines
were introduced and used in Hokkaido. In 1876, the agency established the
Sapporo Agricultural College (SAC, Sapporo Nōgakkō) to offer future generations
of empire builders advanced agricultural knowledge. It appointed William Clark,
the third president of the Massachusetts Agricultural College (now the University
of Massachusetts Amherst) in the United States and a specialist in agriculture and
chemistry, as the head of SAC for a year. Clark passionately promoted the model of
American agriculture in Hokkaido when serving in this position.[49]

The Transformation of Colonial Policies in Hokkaido

The colonial project led by the Development Agency was expensive. From
1872 to 1882, it cost more than 4.5 percent of the national budget each year on
average. In 1880, as much as 7.2 percent of total government spending went to
Hokkaido.[50] The extent of the financial support indicated a consensus among

---

[49] For example, the extended summary of a report by William Clark appeared in *HKZ*,
February 28, 1880, 53–55.
[50] The numbers are calculated based on the data provided by Nagai Hideo, *Nihon no Kindaika to
Hokkaido* (Sapporo: Hokkaidō Daigaku Shuppankai, 2007), 51.

the Meiji leaders on the overall strategic direction of the Hokkaido venture: the colonial project should be conducted through state planning and under the government's political and financial control.

Though the intellectuals were nearly unanimous in envisaging Hokkaido as an enormously profitable colony as well as a land for declassed samurai to find their own feet and prove their value in the new nation, they were divided on how the colonial project should be carried out. Some, like Wakayama Norikazu, a Meiji political strategist and high-ranking official in the Ministry of Agriculture and Commerce, believed that the colonial exploration of Hokkaido should be controlled and protected by the state, which should subsidize the migration of poor shizoku and help them settle down in Hokkaido as landowning farmers.[51] Others, however, were highly critical of the government's huge spending in Hokkaido. The liberalist thinker Taguchi Ukichi, the editor of *Tokyo Economic News* (*Tokyo Keizai Zasshi*) – one of the most influential newspapers in the Meiji era – was firmly in the latter camp. Attributing the success of British colonial expansion to the principle of free trade, Taguchi urged the Japanese government to cease its intervention in the colonization of Hokkaido. *Tokyo Economic News* acted as a platform for liberal thinkers to criticize almost every single Development Agency policy. Taguchi believed that Hokkaido exploration of the day was monopolized by the plutocrats in the government. The exclusion of common people from participation in the colonial project and the lack of fair competition, he warned, would eventually lead to the failure of the overall project.

The agency's sponsorship of the migration programs was a special target for Taguchi. People, he argued, were driven by profits. The temporary subsidy and governmental intervention would lead only to fake achievement, with settlers staying in Hokkaido only to profit from governmental aid. Once the support disappeared, so would the settlers. The successful settlement in Hokkaido, Taguchi argued, should be accomplished by independent individuals who would build a career on their own. He believed that instead of agriculture-based migration, the wealth of Hokkaido's natural resources should be first tapped by merchant settlers. Taguchi considered the monopoly of natural resources by Kuroda's plutocrat allies and the high tax rates in Hokkaido as fundamental obstacles for common shizoku to pursue success in Hokkaido by starting businesses of their own.[52]

The criticisms that the Hokkaido Development Agency faced as well as the government budget cuts amid the Matsukata Deflation propelled a liberalist turn for governmental policies in Hokkaido after the agency's abolishment in

---

[51] Wakayama Norikazu, "Shizoku Jusan no Shigi," in *Wakayama Norikazu Zenshū*, vol. 1 (Tokyo: Keizai Shinpōsha, 1940), 209–215. Also see Kuroda Ken'ichi, *Nihon Shokumin Shisōshi* (Tokyo: Kōbundō Shobō, 1942), 228.

[52] Taguchi Ukichi, "Hokkaido Kaitaku Ron," *Tokyo Keizai Zasshi*, no. 77 (1881): 669.

1882. The prefectural government of Hokkaido, established in 1886, placed capital importation at the center of colonial exploration, thereby reversing the agency's migration-centered approach.[53] The new policies stimulated inflows of private capital to Hokkaido, leading to the rapid concentration of land ownership in Hokkaido in the hands of private wealthy investors and the formation of a big farm economy similar to the agricultural model in the United States. The implementation of this big-farm model of colonial development was described by colonial thinker Satō Shōsuke as turning Hokkaido into "Japan's America."[54] As a result of the influx of private capital, most of the explored lands in Hokkaido were soon claimed by a small number of wealthy landlords, many of whom lived in Tokyo, while the majority of the local population were turned into agricultural laborers.[55]

The withdrawal of the state intervention opened the doors of Hokkaido to more migrants from Japan proper. Yet the majority of the newcomers since the mid-1880s were poor and landless farmers whose lives were devastated by the Matsukata Deflation.[56] For colonial thinkers who considered expansion a way to transform shizoku from seeds of instability to model subjects of the nation, Hokkaido was no longer an ideal land because agricultural labor without landownership was not sufficient for these shizoku to gain wealth and honor. New frontiers of expansion beyond the Japanese archipelago were thus needed.[57] Malthusian expansionism was embraced again to legitimize the proposals of migration overseas, which aimed to export the "surplus people" and in the meantime allow them to connect their personal ambitions with that of the nation. Tsuda Sen investigated the Bonin Islands (Ogasawara Guntō) as a possible place for shizoku migration in 1880.[58] One year earlier, an article in *Tokyo Keizai Zasshi* even proposed expansion to Africa.[59] Yet the agendas of expansion beyond Hokkaido materialized first in Japanese migration to the United States.

---

[53] "Hokkaido Nōgyō no Keisei," in *Nihon Nōgyō Hattatsushi: Meiji Ikō ni Okeru*, vol. 4, *Nihon Shihon Shugi Kakuritsuki no Nōgyō*, ed. Tōhata Sei'ichi and Norinaga Toshitarō (Tokyo: Chūō Kōronsha, 1978), 559–560.

[54] Inoue Katsuo, "Sapporo Nōgakkō to Shokumingaku no Tanjō," in *Teikoku Nihon no Gakuchi*, vol. 1, ed. Yamamoto Taketoshi et al. (Tokyo: Iwanami Shoten, 2006), 21.

[55] "Hokkaido Nōgyō no Keisei," 590–593.   [56] Ibid., 572.

[57] As a solution to the swelling rural poverty resulting from the Matsukata Deflation, in 1885 Tokyo answered the request of King Kalākaua by approving and sponsoring the migration of Japanese rural poor to the Hawai'ian Kingdom as contract laborers. Between 1885 and 1894, over twenty-nine thousand Japanese migrants reached the shores of the Hawai'ian Islands. Martin Dusinberre, "Writing the On-Board: Meiji Japan in Transit and Transition," *Journal of Global History* 11, no. 2 (2016): 282; Moriyama, *Imingaisha*, xviii.

This decade-long program – known as "government-sponsored emigration" (Kanyaku imin) – was successful in terms of migrants' numbers. But because most of these emigrants ended up as cheap laborers on sugar plantations, few Meiji expansionists found this program satisfactory.

[58] Takasaki, *Tsuda Sen Hyōden*, 103.

[59] "Afurika kaitaku no hakarigote," *Tokyo Keizai Zasshi*, November 15, 1897, 482–483.

From "America in Japan" to "Japan in America": The Rise of Japanese Trans-Pacific Expansion

I call the campaign of Japanese migration to the United States from mid-1880s to 1889, spearheaded by Fukuzawa Yukichi and his students, the first wave of Japanese migration to the United States. In terms of ideology, this movement was a direct offspring of the shizoku-based colonial expansion in Hokkaido of the previous years. Japan's imitation of Anglo-American settler colonialism in Hokkaido directly inspired the shizoku expansionists to consider the American West as an alternative to Hokkaido. The imagined similarities between Hokkaido and California also allowed the expansionists to replicate their visions on Hokkaido to Japan's expansion to the other side of the Pacific.

Though not as vocal as Tsuda Sen, Fukuzawa Yukichi was also a firm supporter of colonial expansion in Hokkaido. He believed Hokkaido's enormous wealth should be utilized, and he connected shizoku's personal success with the act of colonial expansion. Some of his students at Keiō School (Keiō Gijuku) participated in the Hokkaido Development Agency's shizoku-migration program. Among them, Sawa Mokichi served as president of the Loyal Heart Society and Yoda Benzō founded the Late Blooming Society (Bansei Sha), both of which were leading companies in Hokkaido migration of the day.

Fukuzawa shifted his gaze from Hokkaido to the United States for Japanese migration in 1884. In a public speech in that year, he used the example of British setter colonialism in New England to criticize the lack of expansionist spirit among the educated youth in Japan:

Let us suppose that Hokkaido is a British territory. . . . Its soil is rich, and it has great natural resources. If such a source of wealth were located 500 miles from London, I doubt that the British would ignore it. Certainly, they would compete with each other to settle Hokkaido and to develop the entire island; and then come up with another New England within a few years. . . . I am very embarrassed. The Europeans crossed five thousand miles of ocean to develop America, while the Japanese refuse to go to Hokkaido because they say that five hundred miles is too great a distance.[60]

In the second half of the speech, after acknowledging the difficulties of the natural and economic conditions in Hokkaido, Fukuzawa proposed, "If Hokkaido is really bad, why don't our young men change their direction and go to foreign countries?" In particular, he pointed out, "America is the most suitable country for anyone to emigrate to."[61] For Fukuzawa, the United States, just like Hokkaido, was a land of abundant wealth awaiting Japanese

---

[60] Wayne Oxford, *The Speeches of Fukuzawa: A Translation and Critical Study* (Tokyo: Hokuseido, 1973), 217–218.
[61] Ibid., 217–218.

exploration. As he described in *The Review of Nations in the World* (*Sekai Kuni Zukushi*),

[The United States] is equal to Great Britain in every kind of manufacturing and business, and it excels France in literature, arts, and education. Their land produces grains, animals, cotton, tobacco, grapes, fruit, sweet potatoes, gold, silver, copper, lead, iron, coal; indeed, nothing necessary in daily life is wanting. People who want to get clothes and food naturally come to the place where it is easy to make a living, so people gather from all over the world every day and every month.[62]

Not everyone in Japan was qualified to go to the United States, however. Only shizoku, with their education background, talent, and ambition, deserved the right of emigration.[63] Different from the rural poor who went to Hawai'i as contract laborers to survive, the emigrants to the US mainland were given the task of improving Japan's national image.[64] As an immigrant nation that had a vibrant spirit of progress and stood at the center of modern civilization, Fukuzawa argued, America was the place where shizoku could study and grow as Japanese subjects.[65]

Moreover, the United States was also an expanding nation that kept on opening up new lands through frontier conquest and migration. Fukuzawa encouraged the Japanese to follow the examples of European settlers and participate in American frontier expansion. A loyal follower of Benjamin Franklin, Fukuzawa also replicated Franklin's metaphor of polyps for settler colonialism in his own promotion of Japanese trans-Pacific expansion. One day, Fukuzawa expected, the Japanese offspring in the United States would gain political rights and sway American politics. In this way, the overseas migrants would establish ten or even twenty "new Japans" around the world.[66]

If the opportunities of serving the nation, acquiring wealth, and contributing to the progress of civilization were used to encourage shizoku to emigrate to the United States, the logic of Malthusian expansionism turned the migration into an absolute necessity. Although the land of the United States had already been enclosed by its national sovereignty, this fact by no means prevented the Japanese expansionists from having colonial ambitions over the American land. In their imaginations, the Lockean definition of land ownership that justified

---

[62] Fujita, *American Pioneers and the Japanese Frontier*, 6.
[63] Fukuzawa called the ideal emigrants *shishi*, meaning men with noble goals. Fukuzawa Yukichi, "Danji Kokorozashi o Tatete, Kyōkan o Izu Beshi," in *Fukuzawa Yukichi Zenshū*, vol. 9 (Tokyo: Iwanami Shoten, 1960), 457. To be sure, *shishi*, an abstract term, was not entirely the same as *shizoku*, that had a clearer implication of one's sociopolitical status. But undeniably, in the social context of the day, the majority of the men who had "noble goals" were those who grew up in shizoku families and were able to receive more education than others.
[64] Tachikawa Kenji, "Meiji Zenhanki no Tobeinetsu (1)," *Tomiyama Daigaku Kyōyōbu Kiyō* 23, no. 2 (1990): 3.
[65] Fukuzawa, "Beikoku wa Shishi no Seisho Nari," 442–444.
[66] Fukuzawa, "Fuki Kōmyo wa Oya Yuzuri," 546.

Anglo-American settler colonialism continued to be applicable to the Japanese settlement in the American West. In a revised Lockean logic, they believed that the territory of the United States was still open to appropriation by others because it was still largely empty and unutilized due to its low occupancy by white settlers. Thus, it was the natural right for the Japanese, civilized people from the overcrowded archipelago to settle in, then claim and make use of the land.

It is no wonder why one of the central promoters of Japanese migration to the United States at this time was the founder of demography in modern Japan, Sugi Kōji, himself. Sugi was also an intellectual friend of Fukuzawa who studied at Tekijuku, a school of Dutch Learning where Fukuzawa previously attended.[67] While the idea of population imbalance in Japanese archipelago was used to rationalize the migration from Japan proper to Hokkaido, Sugi applied this view in his description of the demography in the world at large. Backed up by demographic data about Japan and other countries in the world he collected, Sugi argued in a speech in 1887 that the overall distribution of people over land in the world was uneven. Therefore, to avoid regional poverty at the global level, migration across national borders was unavoidable.

He believed that the rapid speed of population growth in the archipelago gave Japan the natural right to overseas migration. Japan, he argued, was just like overcrowded Europe, where people were competing with each other unhealthily for limited space and opportunities and many had to struggle against poverty. Thus, the same as European countries, Japan had to export its surplus people overseas in order to maintain the domestic prosperity. In Sugi's mind, the United States was the ideal destination for Japanese emigration because it not only was an advanced nation that would lift the Meiji migrants up in the progress of civilization but also had vast unoccupied land with abundant space, wealth, and opportunities.[68]

Malthusian expansionism was also embraced by guidebooks for Japanese American emigration in the 1880s. Penned by shizoku travelers and settlers in the United States, these guidebooks described the American West as the heaven for the Japanese, with abundant natural resources and enormous opportunities for both education and work. They encouraged their domestic readers to leave the overcrowded archipelago and follow the example of the Europeans by pursuing their new lives across the ocean. Like the migration to Hokkaido, this route of self-help was also guided by the teleology of Japan's rise as a civilized empire, with the expectation of transforming emigrants into pioneers of overseas expansion.[69] Japanese settlers' colonial encounters with the

---

[67] Hayami, *Rekishi Jinkōgaku de Mita Nihon*, 145.   [68] Sugi, *Sugi Sensei Kōen Shū*, 150–151.
[69] Akamine Se'ichirō, *Beikoku Ima Fushigi* (Tokyo: Jitsugakkai Eigakkō, 1886); Mutō Sanji, *Beikoku Ijū Ron* (Tokyo: Maruzen, 1887); Ishida Kumataro and Shūyū Sanjin, *Kitare Nihonjin: Ichimei Sōkō Tabi Annai* (Tokyo: Kaishindō, 1886); Fukuoka Teru, *Kigyō Risshi no Kinmon: Ichimei Beikōsha Hikkei* (Tokyo: Nisshindō, 1887).

Ainu in Hokkaido also helped Japanese emigrants to fit themselves into the racial hierarchy in the American West as a dominant race on the same footing as the white settlers. In these guidebooks, Native Americans were called *dojin* (literally meaning "native people"), the same term used for the Ainu in Japan. A guidebook, *Beikoku Ima Fushigi* (*The United States Is Wonderful Now*), drew a further parallel between the Ainu in Hokkaido and the Native Americans in the United States by calling the latter the "Red Ainu" (aka Ezo).[70] The book described at length the backwardness of the Native Americans, such as their lack of a written language, the primitiveness of their religion, as well as the inequality in gender relations. As Japanese officials and scholars had written of the Ainu, *Beikoku Ima Fushigi* observed that the Native Americans were quickly vanishing. Amid the wave of civilization, the book observed, they were as vulnerable as "leaves in the autumn wind."[71]

From 1884 to 1888, quite a few graduates of Fukuzawa's Keiō School landed in California. In May 1888, the Alumni Association of Keiō School was established in San Francisco with thirty-five members.[72] In 1885, Fukuzawa initiated a project of collective migration to the United States with the financial support of Hokkaido entrepreneur Yanagida Tōkichi and Keiō graduate Kai Orie, who had opened his own business in California.[73] Fukuzawa's promotion of Japanese migration to the United States reached its peak in 1887. In an editorial in the first issue of *Jiji Shinpō* (*Jiji News*), an influential newspaper founded by himself, Fukuzawa proposed to establish a "Japanese nation in America" (*Nihon koku Amerika no chihō ni sōritsu*).[74] Thanks to the recent opening of the sea route between Tokyo and Vancouver, he rejoiced, people and goods could now easily move across the ocean. As tens of thousands of Japanese subjects began to populate the American West Coast, a Japanese nation (*nihon koku*) would soon emerge on the other side of the Pacific. He further expected that this newly established Japanese settler nation would become a permanent resource of wealth for the home archipelago.[75] To realize this goal, he collaborated with Inoue Kakugorō, his student who had migrated to the United States a year earlier. They planned on purchasing land in California in order to build an agricultural colony for Japanese settlers.[76] *Jiji*

---

[70] See Akamine, *Beikoku Ima Fushigi*, 141. *Ezo* was a common term for the native residents in Hokkaido in early Meiji. The term *Aka Ezo* was first used by Tokugawa intellectuals as a name for Russians. See Kudō Heisuke, *Akaezo Fūsetsukō: Hokkaido Kaitaku Hishi*, trans. Inoue Takaaki (Tokyo: Kyōikusha, 1979). But here it referred to Native Americans.

[71] Akamine, *Beikoku Ima Fushigi*, 144.

[72] Tachikawa, "Meiji Zenhanki no Tobeinetsu (1)," 17.

[73] Suzue Ei'ichi, "Yanagita Tokichi to Kariforunia Imin," *Fukuzawa Techō* 40 (March 1980): 1–5. While it was unclear why this plan failed, the plan itself demonstrated Fukuzawa's passion in promoting Japanese migration to the United States and his close connection with the early Japanese American communities in California.

[74] Tachikawa, "Meiji Zenhanki no Tobeinetsu (1)," 20.   [75] Ibid., 20–21.   [76] Ibid., 21–25.

Indian   War– Dance.

米國土人の戰舞踊

Figure 1.5 This picture appears in a guidebook for Japanese migration to the
United States published in Japan in 1886. The Native Americans were not
only described as savage but also termed *dojin*, the same label used for Ainu in
Japan. Akamine Se'ichirō, *Beikoku Ima Fushigi* (Tokyo: Jitsugakkai Eigakkō,
1886), 135.

Shinpō also published several articles throughout the year reporting Inoue's
activities in preparation for this plan.[77] This colonial project was terminated,
however, due to the sudden arrest of Inoue during his stay in Japan.[78]

---

[77] Ibid., 23–24.
[78] Inoue returned to Japan from California to discuss further details in establishing the colony with
     Fukuzawa. Right before he embarked on his return trip to the United States in January 1888, he
     was arrested by the Japanese police in Yokohama for his criticism of the Japanese government's

The failure of Inoue's colonial project brought Fukuzawa's promotion of American migration to an end. The early shizoku migrants who made their way to the United States experienced blunt white racism by observing the anti-Chinese campaigns. As Eiichiro Azuma has pointed out, these early Japanese American settlers were well connected with political debates of Japanese elites within and outside of policymaking circles in Tokyo. They read the anti-Chinese campaigns as a strong statement that the American West was reserved for the white European settlers and warned their domestic cohorts that the Japanese would soon be excluded like the Chinese.[79] Fukuzawa accordingly suspended his promotion for Japanese migration to the United States in 1888.[80]

Women in Malthusian Expansion

The history of shizoku expansion in Hokkaido and North America was not only a story of men but also that of women. If shizoku men were expected to regain their wealth and honor through colonial migration, women of samurai families, on the other hand, were hailed to become mothers of future empire builders. The Meiji government's attention toward women's education was initially drawn by the necessity of cultivating settlers of the next generation for Japan's first colony. One of the earliest governmental initiatives on women's education in modern Japan was Hokkaido Development Agency's sponsorship of a group of young women of shizoku families to study in the United States.

When Kuroda Kiyotaka conducted his investigation trip in the United States right before taking the chair of the Hokkaido Development Agency, he was particularly impressed by the influence women wielded in the American society. In a proposal submitted to the imperial government, he reminded Tokyo of the importance of women for the nascent empire. The success of Japan's colonization of Hokkaido, Kuroda argued, ultimately depended on whether the empire had capable people for this mission. Training of the empire builders should start with little children. It was thus necessary to establish women's schools to first train the mothers of these empire builders.[81]

Korean policy. Inoue Kakugorō Sensei Denki Hensankai, *Inoue Kakugorō Sensei Den* (Tokyo: Inoue Kakugorō Sensei Denki Hensankai, 1943), 128–131.

[79] Eiichiro Azuma, "A Transpacific Origin of Japanese Settler Colonialism: US Migrant Expansionists and Their Roles in Japan's Imperial Formation, 1892–1908" (Paper, Global Japan Forum, University of California, Los Angeles, May 9, 2014). Azuma's forthcoming book further demonstrates the critical roles of the Japanese American elites in advancing different ideas and practices of Japanese colonial expansion across the Pacific throughout the history of the Japanese empire. Eiichiro Azuma, *In Search of Our Frontier: Japanese America and Settler Colonialism in the Construction of Japan's Borderless Empire* (Berkeley: University of California Press, 2019).

[80] Tachikawa, "Meiji Zenhanki no Tobeinetsu (1)," 29–30.

[81] Takahashi Yūko, *Tsuda Umeko no Shakaishi* (Tokyo: Tamakawa Daigaku Shuppanbu, 2002), 23–24. Koyama Shizuko and Katayama Sei'ichi have pointed out that the imperial discourse of

In the proposal, Kuroda suggested two specific plans in order to prepare young Japanese women to become mothers in the empire's first colony.[82] One was for the Development Agency to establish a women's school. The other was to sponsor a selected group of young women to study in the West. As a result of Kuroda's proposal, five girls from shizoku families were chosen to study in the United States along with the Iwakura Mission.[83] Among these five girls was six-year-old Tsuda Umeko, the second daughter of Tsuda Sen himself. Tsuda Umeko arrived in San Francisco in 1871 and stayed in the United States until her return in 1882. Unsatisfied with the opportunities she had in Japan, she embarked on another study trip in the United States between 1889 and 1892 to receive a college education at Bryn Mawr College in Philadelphia. Through her successful efforts in fund-raising, Tsuda Umeko managed to establish a scholarship in 1893 to support other Japanese women to study in the United States.[84] Seven years later, she funded the Women's Institute for English Studies (Joshi Eigaku Juku), later known as Tsuda College, in Tokyo.[85]

Nakamura Masanao, a central advocate of shizoku resettlement and supporter of Hokkaido expansion, was also among the earliest Japanese modern thinkers to emphasize the importance of women's education. In an 1875 article, titled "On Creating Good Mothers," he argued that producing and cultivating qualified children were crucial for Japan to become a civilized nation and empire like the Western powers. All women in Japan thus should receive education in order to become competent mothers who could take on the mission to nurture the next generation of nation and empire builders.[86]

Fukuzawa Yukichi, another supporter of Hokkaido and American migration, was a passionate speaker for women's freedom and rights. Motherhood was the core in his reasoning. In response to the challenge of the West, Fukuzawa believed that the Japanese racial stock should be physically improved according to that of the Westerners. The first step, he argued, was to change the social condition of women. Under the backward custom of Tokugawa society, women lacked responsibility and joy in their daily life. For this reason, they were physically weak, as were the children they gave birth to. As a result of the social suppression of women over the past few hundred years, the physical body of average Japanese was weak and small. The nation would not have strong and

motherhood in modern Japan originated in Kuroda Kiyotaka's proposal. Koyama Shizuko, *Ryōsai Kenbō Toiu Kihan* (Tokyo: Keisō shobō, 1991), 25–41; Katayama Sei'ichi, *Kindai Nihon no Joshi Kyōiku* (Tokyo: Kenpakusha, 1984), 4–5.
[82] Nitobe Inazō, *The Imperial Agricultural College of Sapporo* (Sapporo: Imperial Agricultural College, 1893), 3.
[83] Iino Masako, Kameda Kinuko, and Takahashi Yūko, eds., *Tsuda Umeko o Sasaeta Hitobito* (Tokyo: Yūhikaku, 2000), 6–7.
[84] Ibid., 178–179.   [85] Ibid., 162.
[86] Takeda Hiroko, *The Political Economy of Reproduction in Japan: Between Nation-State and Everyday Life* (London: Routledge, 2005), 36.

healthy offspring unless Japanese women's mental and physical conditions were improved.[87]

Fukuzawa also observed that the freedom and rights of women should be understood in the context of Western imperial expansion and the global hierarchy it created. Women's position in a society, as he saw it, symbolized the degree of progress in civilization achieved by the nation. Fukuzawa called for more opportunities for women in education and employment and equal social rights like men in marriage and property ownership.[88] For him, women's position not only offered a barometer to gauge Japan's achievement in Westernization but also enabled Japan to establish its own imperial hierarchy with its Asian neighbors. Although Japan fell behind Western powers in the improvement of women's condition, Fukuzawa contended, Japanese women enjoyed much more freedom and joy than their counterparts in Joseon Korea and Qing China.[89] His famous essay "On De-Asianization," written in 1885, the same year when he celebrated the social condition of Japanese women as better than that of Chinese and Korean women, used the same logic to urge the nascent empire to embrace Western civilization on the one hand and to launch its own colonial expansion in East Asia on the other hand.[90]

In addition to the good women who would serve the empire as mothers, Fukuzawa also recognized that bad women were equally valuable. He argued that prostitution contributed to the society by providing an indispensable outlet for the energy of men who failed to marry due to poverty. Otherwise, these men might threaten social stability.[91] Ever the pragmatist, he found reasons to celebrate the emigration of a growing number of Japanese prostitutes around the Pacific Rim that began in the late nineteenth century.[92] While the shizoku men should take leadership in overseas Japanese communities,[93] the Japanese prostitutes abroad were a "necessary evil" (*hitsuyō aku*) for the empire in two ways: they would facilitate migration-driven expansion by satisfying the sexual needs of Japanese male emigrants,[94] and their remittances back to the

---

[87] Fukuzawa Yukichi, "Nihon Fujin Ron," in *Fukuzawa Yukichi Zenshū*, vol. 15 (Tokyo: Iwanami Shoten, 1961), 448, 466.
[88] Ibid., 470.   [89] Ibid., 471–472.
[90] Fukuzawa Yukichi, "Datsua Ron," in *Fukuzawa Yukichi Chosakushū*, vol. 8 (Tokyo: Keiō Gijuku Daigaku Shuppankai, 2003), 261–265.
[91] Fukuzawa Yukichi, "Hinkō Ron," in *Fukuzawa Yukichi Zenshū*, vol. 5 (Tokyo: Iwanami Shoten, 1970), 545–578.
[92] Sidney X. Lu, "The Shame of Empire: Japanese Overseas Prostitutes and Prostitution Abolition in Modern Japan, 1880s–1927," *Positions: Asia Critique* 24, no. 4 (November 2016): 839.
[93] Fukuzawa, "Beikoku wa Shishi no Seisho nari," 442–443; Fukuzawa, "Danji Kokorozashi o Tatete," 457.
[94] Men (students, laborers, businessmen, and colonial bureaucrats) constituted the absolute majority of the Japanese overseas population until the second decade of the twentieth century.

archipelago would be a boon to Japan's nascent capitalist economy, which was still at the stage of primitive accumulation.[95]

Conclusion

Malthusian expansionism, stressing the need to find extra land to accommodate the rapidly growing domestic population, was initially invented during British colonial expansion in North America in the seventeenth and eighteenth centuries. It legitimized the British transatlantic expansion by simultaneously warning against the dangers of overpopulation and celebrating the overall demographic growth of the British Empire. This chapter has demonstrated how Malthusian expansionism was transplanted to Japan in early Meiji. It was the Meiji empire's imitation of Anglo-American settler colonialism in its own colonial migration in Hokkaido that allowed Malthusian expansionism to take root in Japanese soil.

Such imitation, as demonstrated by the first wave of Japanese migration to the United States, spearheaded by Fukuzawa Yukichi, allowed Japanese expansionists to turn to North America as an ideal destination for Japanese migration in the mid-1880s. Shizoku expansionists later also cast their gaze on other parts of the Pacific Rim with the same mind-set.[96] After Japan acquired Taiwan as a colony from the Qing, Fukuzawa immediately called for mass migration from the overcrowded archipelago to Taiwan in order to explore the latter's natural wealth (*fugen wo kaihatsu suru*). To live out the true meaning of civilization (*bunmei no hon'i*), he suggested, the Japanese should follow the model of Anglo-American expansion by monopolizing the entire island and all its products as well as banishing the benighted aborigines from their own land.[97]

Tsuda Sen and his extended family also provide a telling example. After serving as the editor of the *Hokkaido Kaitaku Zasshi*, Tsuda Sen turned his colonial gaze toward Korea and later Northern China, while his son Tsuda Jirō migrated to California to foster Japanese American agricultural settlements.[98] Tsuda Umeko, one of the first women of modern Japan to receive an education in the West, remained single and childless her entire life. In this sense, she failed to fulfill her obligation to the empire as a mother of Hokkaido colonists, the original expectation of Kuroda Kiyotaka to support her first study trip in the United States. However, as one of the earliest promoters of women's education

---

[95] Fukuzawa Yukichi, "Jinmin no Ishoku to Shōfu no Dekasegi," in *Fukuzawa Yukichi Zenshū*, vol. 15 (Tokyo: Iwanami Shoten, 1961), 362–363.

[96] Sidney X. Lu, "Colonizing Hokkaido and the Origin of Japanese Trans-Pacific Expansion, 1869–1894," *Japanese Studies* 36, no. 2 (2016): 265–270.

[97] Fukuzawa Yukichi, "Taiwan Eien no Hōshin," in *Fukuzawa Yukichi Zenshū*, vol. 15 (Tokyo: Iwanami Shoten, 1961), 265–266.

[98] Takasaki, *Tsuda Sen Hyōden*, 138–155, 171–172.

in modern Japan, her lifelong career demonstrated the close connections between women's education and Japan's migration-based expansion from the very beginning. Among the awardees of the scholarship she established for Japanese women to study in the United States was Kawai Michi.[99] Kawai became an influential leader of the Japanese Young Women Christian Association and a central figure in the women's education movement who spearheaded the campaign to educate Japanese female migrants on the American West Coast. Tsuda Umeko's elder sister, Tsuda Yunako (later Abiko Yunako), was a direct beneficiary of the Women's Institute for English Studies. Growing up in Hakodate, Hokkaido, Tsuda Yunako both studied and then taught at the institute. She later migrated to San Francisco after marrying a Japanese American, Abiko Kyūtarō. Abiko Yunako founded the Japanese Young Women Christian Association in San Francisco in 1912 and served as its director until 1923. The primary goal of the association was to familiarize Japanese female migrants with American customs and child-rearing skills in order to facilitate Japanese community building in the United States.[100] Abiko Kyūtarō, husband of Abiko Yunako, was the editor of *Nichibei Shinbun* (Japanese American News), a leading San Francisco–based Japanese American newspaper. He was not only a community leader for Japanese Americans in California but also a trailblazer in Japanese land acquisition in Mexico.[101]

In a more general sense, Japan's colonization of Hokkaido in early Meiji established the intellectual foundation for Japanese colonial expansion and overseas migration in the following decades. Numerous late nineteenth-century participants in the Hokkaido colonial project as well as people who were directly influenced by them later became the arms and brains of Japanese expansion abroad. Satō Shōsuke and Nitobe Inazō, students at Sapporo Agricultural College (the predecessor of Hokkaido Imperial University), later taught classes on history and the policies of colonialism at the same college. They trained a group of scholars who would later sway public opinion and state policies on overseas expansion.[102] Shiga Shigetaka, Fukumoto Nichinan, and Kuga Katsunan, participants in the colonization of Hokkaido in early Meiji,

[99] Iino, Kameda, and Takahashi, *Tsuda Umeko o Sasaeta Hitobito*, 160.
[100] Ibid., 231, 237–238; Abiko Yonako, "Zaibei Nihonjin Kirisutokyō Joshi Seinen Kai Sōritsu no Shidai," *Joshi Seinen Kai* 9, no. 9 (October 1912): 17–18.
[101] Eiichiro Azuma, "Japanese Immigrant Settler Colonialism in the U.S.-Mexican Borderlands and the U.S. Racial-Imperialist Politics of the Hemispheric 'Yellow Peril,'" *Pacific Historical Review* 83, no. 2 (May 2014): 255–276.
[102] To name a couple of these graduates in Sapporo Agricultural School, Tōgō Minoru served the Japanese colonial government in Taiwan and promoted Japanese colonial migration to the Korean Peninsula and Manchuria in 1905, and Takaoka Kumao was an expert in Hokkaido colonial history who later became an advocate for Japanese migration to Brazil, Manchuria, and Northern China.

grew into key members of the Association of Politics and Education (Seikyō Sha).[103] The association became the cradle of Japanism (*kokusuishugi*) and other ideologies in favor of Japanese expansion into Hawai'i, the South Pacific, and Latin America. Other influential advocates for the Hokkaido expansion, such as Taguchi Ukichi and Wakayama Norikazu, held different ideas from Seikyō Sha members and also disagreed with each other. However, they also quickly looked to the South Pacific and Latin America as migration destinations. Sakiyama Hisae, a colonial settler in Hokkaido in the 1890s, established the School of Overseas Colonial Migration (Kaigai Shokumin Gakkō) in 1916, training Japanese youth and facilitating their migration to South America.[104] The next chapter elaborates on how the gaze of Meiji Malthusian expansionists shifted quickly from the North to the South and how the experience of colonial expansion in Hokkaido and Japanese migration to the United States in the 1880s paved the way for this transition.

[103] Shiga Shigetaka studied at Sapporo Agricultural College. Fukumoto Nichinan himself headed a shizoku migration campaign to Hokkaido. Kuga Katsunan served the state-owned sugar factory in Hokkaido.
[104] Yoshimura Shigeyoshi, *Sakiyama Hisae Den: Ishokumin Kyōiku to Amazon Kaitaku no Senkakusha* (Tokyo: Kaigai Shokumin Gakkō Kōyūkai Shuppanbu, 1955), 13–29, 91–181.

2 Population and Racial Struggle: The South Seas, Hawai'i, and Latin America

Fukuzawa Yukichi urged his fellow countrymen who migrated to the United States to follow the model of Anglo-American expansion – they needed to commit themselves to long-term settlement in order to have permanent achievement abroad.[1] The majority of the migrants during the last two decades of the nineteenth century, however, did not subscribe to this notion. With strong ambitions back home, the majority of Fukuzawa's students who made their way across the Pacific at that time had no intention to live out the rest of their lives in California. Some began to return to Asia in the late 1880s.[2]

The ease of migrant movement between Japan and California at the time was strengthened by another wave of Japanese migration to the United States, triggered by the Meiji government's suppression of the Freedom and People's Rights Movement. Initiated by the Tosa clan under the leadership of Itagaki Taisuke, this sociopolitical movement attracted many shizoku and rural elites from all over the country. It demanded the freedom of speech, the freedom of association, and the creation of a parliament in order to increase political representation for the common people. The Meiji government responded to this movement negatively. It promulgated the Public Peace Preservation Law in 1887, allowing itself to expel from the capital individuals considered detrimental to political stability and to imprison those who did not comply with this verdict of exile.[3] Thus chased out from the political center of the empire, some members of the movement chose to migrate to the United States, the nation they thought of as the true embodiment of freedom, to continue their political campaign. Using San Francisco as their base, these exiles formed the Federation of Patriots (Aikoku Yūshi Dōmei) in January 1888. They continued to criticize the political establishment in Japan by publishing periodicals in Japanese and sending copies of each issue back to Tokyo. To circumvent state censorship, they had to constantly change the

---

[1] Fukuzawa Yukichi, "Ijū Ron no Ben," in *Fukuzawa Yukichi Zenshū*, vol. 9 (Tokyo: Iwanami Shoten, 1960), 458–460.
[2] Tachikawa, "Meiji Zenhanki no Tobeinetsu (1)," 30.
[3] Ebihara Hachirō, *Kaigai Hōji Shinbun Zasshishi: Tsuketari Kaigai Hōjin Gaiji Shinbun Zasshishi* (Tokyo: Meicho Fukyūkai, 1980), 109.

names of their publications. In 1888 alone, the Meiji government banned the sale of more than twenty-one different newspapers shipped from San Francisco – a testament to the overlapping intellectual spheres in Tokyo and San Francisco.[4]

A boom in the publication of trans-Pacific migration guides and writings of Japanese travelers in the United States beginning in the late 1880s further connected the minds of Japanese expansionists on both sides of the Pacific Ocean. Most of these migration guides were authored by migrants themselves, aimed at encouraging Japanese audiences to prove themselves by earning wealth and honor in the Golden State. Travelers such as Nagasawa Betten and Ozaki Yukio also provided their domestic readers with a significant amount of information about the United States in general and its Japanese immigrant communities in particular. Their writings included messages they collected from Japanese Americans as well as their own observations. In summary, before the 1980s rise of migration companies that would play a critical role in the mass migration of laborers from the archipelago to the West Coast of the United States, Japanese communities in mainland America tended to be small in size, mainly composed of self-financed students and political exiles. Even though they were now physically located in San Francisco instead of Tokyo, these settlers were well connected with thinkers and politicians back in Japan.[5]

Meanwhile, the experience of the Chinese migrants who had reached the shores of North America decades before the Japanese had also shaped the minds of Japanese expansionists in Tokyo and San Francisco. On one hand, the Japanese intellectuals and policymakers saw American exclusion of Chinese immigrants as an ominous warning to get ready for the destined battle between the white and yellow races; on the other hand, they looked at the existence of numerous Chinese diasporic communities all around the Pacific Rim as both a potential threat and a possible model.[6]

It was within this context of trans-Pacific dialogue between the shizoku expansionists and political dissidents that the discourse of southward expansion (*nanshin*), a major school of expansionist thought throughout the history

---

[4] For a list of the banned newspapers, see ibid., 293–295.

[5] I heed the insights of historians Yūji Ichioka and Eiichiro Azuma, who have already pointed out the close connections between Japanese American communities and Japan in Meiji era. My discussion contributes to the existing literature by highlighting how the shizoku identity owned by the majority of Japanese American migrants of the day tied them with the political struggles in domestic Japan. For reference, see Yuji Ichioka, *The Issei: The World of the First Generation Japanese Immigrants, 1885–1924* (New York: Free Press, 1990), 16–28; Eiichiro Azuma, *Between Two Empires: Race, History, and Transnationalism in Japanese America* (London: Oxford University Press, 2005), 35–36.

[6] I echo the pioneering scholarship of Akira Iriye, who has pointed out that the experiences of Chinese overseas migration provided some initial inspirations for Japanese leaders to conduct the expansion of the Japanese empire. Akira Iriye, *Pacific Estrangement: Japanese and American Expansion, 1897–1911* (Cambridge, MA: Harvard University Press, 1972), 22–23.

of the Japanese empire, first emerged.[7] As the following pages demonstrate, if white racism forced Japanese expansionists to explore alternative migration destinations, Malthusian expansionism continued to legitimize Japanese migration-driven expansion. Both factors contributed to the construction of the nanshin discourse. The campaigns of shizoku expansion to Hokkaido and the United States together laid the ground for the initial phase of Japan's expansion to the South Seas and Latin America.

As it was with all schools of expansion within the Japanese empire, southward expansion – both as an ideology and as a movement – was a complicated construct from its very inception. Starting in the late 1880s, different interest groups proposed a variety of agendas for expansion, their primary aims ranging from commercial to naval and agricultural. The ideal candidates for migration in these blueprints also ranged from merchants, laborers, and farmers to outcasts known as the *burakumin*.[8] However, the domestic struggles of shizoku settlement continued to serve as the dominant political context in which the nanshin discourse was originally proposed and debated. Like it was for the preceding Hokkaido and American migration campaigns, shizoku were initially regarded as the most desirable candidates for southward expansion.

Existing literature tends to define nanshin, literally meaning "moving into the South," as a school of thought that promoted Japanese maritime expansion southward in the Pacific including the South Pacific and Southeast Asia.[9] This geography-bound understanding is mainly derived from the definition of *Nan'yō* as a geographical term in Japanese history. Literally translated as "the South Seas," Nan'yō had different meanings in different contexts. But it has been generally considered that in its widest scope, Nan'yō covers the land and sea in the South Pacific and Southeast Asia, the two geographical regions that the works on Japanese southward expansion by Mark Peattie and Yano

---

[7] Eiichiro Azuma has insightfully pointed out the role of Japanese American intellectuals in the construction of different routes of expansion that laid the foundation for Japanese expansionism throughout the modern era. See Azuma, *Between Two Empires*, 91–92.

[8] Seikyō Sha thinker Sugiura Jūgō, for example, proposed to relocate burakumin to the South Pacific to help them escape domestic discrimination on the one hand and to expand the influence of the Japanese empire in the world on the other hand. See Jun Uchida, "From Island Nation to Oceanic Empire: A Vision of Japanese Expansion from the Periphery," *Journal of Japanese Studies* 42, no. 1 (2016): 81–89. Shiga Shigetaka, on the other hand, advocated migrating lower-class Japanese subjects to Hawai'i as a way of training. See Shiga, *Nan'yō Jiji*, 200. Taguchi Ukichi was a supporter of mercantile expansion. Taguchi Ukichi, "Nan'yō Keiryaku Ron," *Tokyo Keizai Zasshi*, no. 513 (1890): 352. An important architect of nanshin, Tokutomi Sohō, was a promoter of the overseas migration of heimin, the commoners, in contrast to the shizoku. See chapter 3.

[9] Mark Peattie's discussion of Japanese southward expansion focuses on the South Pacific in general and Micronesia in particular. Yano Tōru's take of the nanshin history, on the other hand, focuses on Japanese expansion in Southeast Asia. See Yano Tōru, *"Nanshin" no Keifu* (Tokyo: Chūō Kōronsha, 1975) and Mark Peattie, *Nan'yō: The Rise and Fall of the Japanese in Micronesia, 1885–1945* (Honolulu: University of Hawai'i Press, 1988).

Tōru have focused on respectively.[10] However, as this chapter explains, for Japanese expansionists in the late nineteenth century the South Seas also included Hawai'i.[11] In addition to Hawai'i, other nanshin advocates in history did not confine their sights within the South Seas. Some also included Latin America in their blueprints of southward expansion.[12]

Currently the history of Japan's southward expansion is being studied as a subject within the nation-/region-based narrative of the Japanese empire, one that excludes the experience of Japanese migration to Latin America and Hawai'i.[13] However, as this chapter illustrates, the calls for expansion into Latin America and Hawai'i were proposed in conjunction with calls for expansion into the South Seas. The nanshin advocates envisioned that Japanese expansion to areas located geographically south to the Japanese archipelago and Japanese communities in the United States would be able to circumvent Anglo-American colonial hegemony. Following the experiences of shizoku expansion to Hokkaido in the 1870s and 1880s and to North America in the 1880s and 1890s, the campaigns for expansion to the South Seas and Latin America belonged to the same wave of shizoku expansion that was firmly buttressed by Malthusian expansionism.

Reunderstanding the World in Racial Terms

Experiences in the United States promoted shizoku migrants and visitors to adopt a race-centric worldview. Replicating the racial thinking of many expansionists in the West,[14] the Japanese expansionists' definition of race was directly derived from Charles Darwin's theory of natural selection. They were convinced that the world of mankind, like that of nature, not only was

[10] Mark Peattie's definition of *Nan'yō* in its widest scope does not include Hawai'i. See Peattie, "The Nan'yō: Japan in the South Pacific, 1885–1945," in *The Japanese Colonial Empire, 1895–1945*, ed. Ramon Myers and Mark Peattie (Princeton: Princeton University Press, 1987), 172. For consistency, in this book I use the term "South Seas" in its widest sense, which includes the land and sea in the South Pacific, Hawai'i, and Southeast Asia unless specifically defined.

[11] In the book published in 1891 titled *Nan'yō Jiji*, Shiga Shigetaka saw Hawai'i as the most important target of Japanese expansion in the region he called *Nan'yō*.

[12] For example, in the two special issues of the *Taiyō* magazine designated to the heated debate on the ways and directions of Japanese expansion in 1910 and 1913, expansion to the South Seas and Latin America was categorized as southward expansion. See "Nihon Minzoku no Bōchō," *Taiyō* 16, no. 15 (November 1910), and "Nanshin ya? Hokushin ya?," *Taiyō* 19, no. 15 (November 1913).

[13] The two most important works on the history of Japanese southward expansion are Yano, "*Nanshin*" no Keifu, and Peattie, *Nan'yō*. None of them included the history of Japanese expansion in Hawai'i or Latin America.

[14] Profoundly influenced by social Darwinism, European expansionists in the nineteenth century saw the nation in racial terms and considered wars and conflicts among nations as biological struggles for racial superiority in which both the size and the quality of the nation were decisive factors. Ittmann, Cordell, and Maddox, *Demographics of Empire*, 62.

composed of biologically different human races but also followed the principle of survival of the fittest. The contemporary competition among nations, they believed, was a reflection of the biological struggle for the limited space and resources among the races. Their perception of the world as an arena for racial competition converged with the intellectuals in domestic Japan on whether the nation should endorse mixed residence in inland Japan (*naichi zakkyo*) in order to revise the unequal treaties. This would allow Westerners (as well as Chinese and Koreans) to travel, settle in, and conduct business throughout the Japanese archipelago without restriction. A group of hard-liners, later known as promoters of national essence (*kokusuishugisha*), warned that the white races were taking over the world by not only excluding the yellow races from the West but also invading their homelands in the East. They formed the Association of Politics and Education (Seikyō Sha) in 1888, organizing public lectures as well as publishing journals and newspapers, urging their countrymen to assume a position of leadership in the inevitable worldwide racial competition. To avoid racial extinction, they argued, the Japanese needed to compete with the white races as the leader of the yellow races; in order to emerge victorious from this competition, they must reaffirm their cultural roots and launch their own colonial expansion.

The Japanese American experience's influence on the growing discourse of racial competition in Tokyo was particularly evident in the writings of Seikyō Sha thinker Nagasawa Betten. Nagasawa went to the United States to study at Stanford University in 1891, and there he joined the Expedition Society (Ensei Sha),[15] a political organization formed by exiled Freedom and People's Rights Movement activists in San Francisco, and participated in their debates about the future of Japanese expansion.

Drawing from his own experience in the American West, Nagasawa wrote to his intellectual friend and fellow Seikyō Sha member Shiga Shigetaka about the importance of adopting a race-centric worldview:

While the competition between nations is evident, the competition between races remains invisible. People take the visible competition seriously and prepare themselves for it, but only experts can sense the invisible competition and thus few efforts are made for its preparation. The crucial point lies not in the former but the latter. . . . Living among people of other races, my sense of urgency about the need for making preparations for racial competition grows each day. The urgent task now, as you have proposed, is to promote our national essence and to inspire our countrymen's spirit of overseas expansion.[16]

---

[15] Eiichiro Azuma's salient study has shown the central role of the Expedition Society in the land acquisition of issei Japanese American settlers in Mexico. Azuma, "Japanese Immigrant Settler Colonialism in the U.S.-Mexican Borderlands," 260–261.

[16] *Ajia*, no. 36 (February 28, 1894): 679–680.

Nagasawa thus shifted the primary subjects of global competition in expansion from nation to race, the power of which was not bound by national territory. This view allowed him to place overseas migration at the center of Japanese expansion. He concluded, "Overseas expansion is the most effective way to prepare for racial competition. . . . Once our fellow Japanese find their footing in every corner of the world, it will doubtlessly lead to our triumph in the racial competition."[17] In his book *The Yankees* (*Yankii*), published in Tokyo in 1893, Nagasawa Betten embraced American frontier expansionism and described the national history of the United States as a living example of it.[18] The *Mayflower* ancestors of the American people, he wrote, overcame many hardships to establish the first thirteen colonies as the foundation of their nation, and their expansion had not ceased ever since. The American borders had extended beyond the Mississippi River and the Rocky Mountains, reaching the coast of the Pacific Ocean. If the railway bridging the two Americas were completed, the United States would become a natural leader of the entire Western Hemisphere due to the wisdom and wealth of its people.[19] While Nagasawa did not believe that Japanese overseas expansion was triggered by religious and political persecutions, he argued that the Japanese should nevertheless emulate the *Mayflower* settlers' frontier expansionism in order to establish a new, large, prosperous, and mighty nation much like the United States.[20]

However, in this trans-Pacific reconstruction of Japanese expansionism, Anglo-American settler colonialism was not the only reference for the Japanese intellectuals. The omnipresent influence of Chinese Americans on their lives in San Francisco led the Japanese expansionists to include the Chinese expansion model as another point of reference. The existing literature on Japanese American history has well documented the fact that the Japanese immigrants replicated white racism toward their Chinese neighbors in the American West. To combat white racism, they strove to prove their own whiteness and spared no efforts to separate themselves from the "uncivilized" Chinese laborers.[21]

This attitude, however, constituted only one aspect of the Japanese migrants' complicated feelings about their Chinese counterparts in the late nineteenth century. Arriving in the American West decades earlier than the Japanese, the Chinese immigrants founded the earliest Asian communities that the first Japanese immigrants readily resided in.[22] While shizoku setters felt insulted

---

[17] Nagasawa Betten, "Raisei no Nihon to Sanbei Kantsū Daitetsudō," *Nihonjin*, no. 2 (October 20, 1893): 113–114.
[18] Azuma, "Japanese Immigrant Settler Colonialism in the U.S.-Mexican Borderlands," 258.
[19] Nagasawa Setsu (Betten), *Yankii* (Tokyo: Keigyōsha, 1893), 4–6.   [20] Ibid., 6.
[21] Azuma, *Between Two Empires*, 36.
[22] Tamura Norio and Shiramizu Shigehiko, eds., *Beikoku Shoki no Nihongo Shinbu* (Tokyo: Keisō Shobō, 1986), 109–110.

when they were mistaken for Chinese, they also admired Chinese achievements in the land of white men. Mutō Sanji, a Japanese business tycoon who sojourned in the United States during the Meiji era, published a guide for Japanese migration to the United States in 1888. In this book, he argued that in the destined global competition between the white and the yellow races, the Chinese had offered a good example for the Japanese on how to compete with the white races.[23]

Mutō's book went into detail illustrating the contributions that Chinese immigrants had made to American society in the fields of agriculture, mining, railway building, manufacturing, and domestic service.[24] He also commented on the strong presence of Chinese communities on the West Coast of North America: no matter where he traveled, be it California, Oregon, Washington, or British Columbia, he could always find Chinese communities there. Admiring "the courage of the Chinese in competing with the white people,"[25] Mutō believed that the Japanese should borrow a page from the successful Chinese experience.[26]

Compared to Mutō, Nagasawa was more critical of the Chinese American immigrants. He wrote extensively about what he saw as "uncivilized" behaviors of the Chinese in the United States that his fellow countrymen should take care to avoid. Even so, he still acknowledged the wide-reaching presence of Chinese migrants around the world and saw the Chinese as another rival for the Japanese in the competition of expansion.[27]

In summary, although Meiji settlers and travelers shared a discriminatory attitude toward the Chinese immigrants in the United States, at the same time there was also a sense of both admiration and fear. This mixed attitude reflected the general perception of the Qing Empire among Japanese intellectuals prior to the Sino-Japanese War, when it was considered to be a mighty geopolitical power in Asia, declining but still maintaining a strong potential for revival. Some Meiji Japanese intellectuals, Seikyō Sha thinkers in particular among them, espoused a type of proto Pan-Asianism and recognized the Qing Empire as the current dominating power in Asia; it was only in escaping from the Qing's clutches that Japan could win for itself the mantle of leadership in Asia.[28]

---

[23] After returning to Asia, Mutō Sanji called for economic cooperation between Japan and China and was involved in Japanese economic expansion in China in the Taishō era.
[24] Mutō, *Beikoku Ijū Ron*, 41–101.   [25] Ibid., 7.   [26] Ibid., 123–144.
[27] Nagasawa, *Yankii*, 11–22.
[28] Nakanome Tōru, *Seikyōsha no Kenkyū* (Kyoto: Shibunkaku Shuppan, 1993), 214. Fearing that the Japanese might be defeated in direct competition with the Chinese, Seikyō Sha thinkers opposed the idea of opening Japan's border to Chinese migrants during the nationwide debate on mix residence. Mizuno Mamoru, "Ekkyō to Meiji Nashonarizumu 1889 Nen Jōyaku Kaisei Mondai ni Okeru Seikyō Sha no Shisō," *Nihon Gakuhō*, no. 22 (March 2003): 47.

Figure 2.1 This picture appears in the front matter of the book *Beikoku Ijū Ron* authored by Mutō Sanji in 1887. Based on his observation in the American West, Mutō described the global competition of the world in this picture as the "conflict of races" among the Caucasians, the Chinese, and the Japanese.

For Japanese expansionists on both sides of the Pacific, the Qing Empire was a mighty rival in the age of colonial competition. At the same time, however, Qing was also seen as a possible ally whose model of expansion Japan could learn from. Such an understanding of the Qing Empire and Chinese overseas expansion substantially affected the ways in which the racial exclusion of Chinese immigrants in the United States transformed the ideology of Japanese expansionism in the last two decades of the nineteenth century.

Chinese Exclusion in the United States and the Rise of Nanshin

The first Chinese Exclusion Act was enacted by the US government in 1882, before most of the Japanese migrants had arrived in California. Anti-Chinese campaigns made it possible for the act to be renewed for another ten years in 1892 with the Geary Act, then becoming permanent in 1902.[29] The complexity of the Japanese racial identity, especially when considered in relation to that of the Chinese and white Americans, resulted in different responses to the Chinese Exclusion Act among the Meiji expansionists on both sides of the Pacific. Some of them unconditionally accepted the act's racist logic and believed that the uncivilized Chinese deserved to be excluded, at the same time emphasizing that the Japanese belonged to the civilized races and therefore would not suffer the same fate as the Chinese.[30] The "uncivilized Chinese" also served as a metaphor that the shizoku settlers used to disparage the unprivileged Japanese laborers who began to arrive in California en masse at the beginning of the 1890s. Asserting that these laborers' behaviors were almost as uncivilized as those of the Chinese, the Japanese intellectuals believed that their lower-class countrymen in the United States had dishonored the empire, leading to the argument that their migration should be restricted if not outright banned.[31]

Some other expansionists, however, contemplated the fate of the Chinese in the United States with a measure of empathy. An 1888 editorial in the *Nineteenth Century* (*Jūkyūseiki*), a mouthpiece of the Federation of Patriots, identified the Qing Empire and the Empire of Japan as the two leaders of East Asia, both of whom had to face the invasion of white people who were armed with civilization and gunpowder. The article warned its readers that even the Qing Empire, with its vast territory, great wealth, and over three hundred million subjects, could not avoid falling prey to white imperialism. Since these same Western powers would not spare Japan from its imperialistic

---

[29] It was in effect until being repealed in 1943.
[30] Ishida and Shūyū, *Kitare Nihonjin: Ichimei Sōkō Tabi Annai*, 2.
[31] He even extended his criticisms to the work-study students from Japan. He considered them lazy and uncivilized. Ozaki Yukio, "Beikoku Zakkan," in *Ozaki Gakudō Zenshū*, vol. 3 (Tokyo: Kōronsha, 1955–1956), 343–354.

clutches, it went on to argue, Japan should develop its material strength in order to survive through self-defense instead of worshipping Western nations.[32]

Some were further convinced by a series of anti-Japanese incidents in California at the end of the 1880s that the Japanese would eventually meet the same fate of racial exclusion as the Chinese immigrants had. Japanese diplomats in the United States began to send Tokyo copies of articles in local newspapers that called for excluding the Japanese from immigration because they were no different from the uncivilized Chinese who stole jobs from white workers.[33] In 1891, the US government established the Immigration Bureau and imposed strict immigration rules in order to exclude "undesirable" individuals from coming to the United States.[34] This wave of anti-Japanese sentiment reached its peak in 1892, marked by a sharp increase in the number of articles attacking Japanese immigrants in major San Francisco newspapers.[35] Exclusionists also began to give public speeches and hold gatherings all around the city. With the rise of Japan's colonial empire in Asia, the flow of Japanese laborers into California was considered an even greater threat than the Chinese had posed.[36]

In the same year, an editorial in *Patriotism* (*Aikoku*), another official newspaper of the Federation of Patriots, responded to the anti-Japanese sentiment in the United States with a blistering attack on white racism: "Extremely wretched! Extremely cruel! On the coast of Africa, when a ship steered by white people ran out of coal, they captured the natives and threw them into the fire as fuel. . . . The white people also captured native African children and used them as baits to hunt crocodiles. Once a crocodile took the bait, the child would die in its stomach. This is the way that the white races treat colored races. How cruel! How wretched!" The article then argued that white Americans treated the Chinese immigrants in a similar manner. The Americans had excluded the Chinese from their territory while invading the latter's home country with gunpowder, costing the Chinese countless lives and untold amounts of wealth. While the Europeans' massacres of Africans were cruel, the article claimed, "they are still forgivable when compared with what the Americans are doing today: they are bragging about their civilization to the entire world, but how can they do so when they are full of cruelty and prejudice?!" It then moved on to argue that the Japanese in the United States suffered from white racism as well and that the Japanese government should send the Imperial Navy to defeat the white Americans in retaliation against such humiliations.[37]

[32] Tamura and Shiramizu, *Beikoku Shoki no Nihongo Shinbu*, 150.   [33] Ibid., 124–125.
[34] For the impact of this change on the migration policy of the Japanese government, see Sakada Yasuo, "The Enactment of the 1891 Immigration Law of the United States and Conflicting American and Japanese Perceptions: 'The Undesirable' and the 'Undesired,'" *Kokusaigaku Ronshū* 9, no. 1 (June 1998): 21–69.
[35] Tamura and Shiramizu, *Beikoku Shoki no Nihongo Shinbu*, 74–75.   [36] Ibid., 79.
[37] Ibid., 81–82.

The expansionists in Tokyo, however, had little interest in waging an actual war against the United States. The Chinese Exclusion Act and their fear that the Japanese would eventually meet the same fate pushed them to try to make sense of the exclusionists' logic. Some took the Chinese exclusion as an announcement that the white races had secured their ownership of the North American land and thus had the right to exclude others. As a result, the United States was no longer a suitable destination for Japanese migration. Instead, the Japanese should make haste to occupy hitherto unmarked and unowned territories in the world; once they staked their claims of ownership, they could exclude other races just like the white Americans were now doing. Of course, in the minds of these Meiji expansionists, only the "civilized" races qualified as competitors for land ownership. Aboriginal peoples, such as Native Americans and Pacific Islanders like the Ainu in Hokkaido, were classified as uncivilized races who had no right to their ancestral homes.

An 1890 article vividly captured this moment of transformation in the discourse of Japanese expansionism. Authored by political journalist Tokutomi Sōhō, it was titled "The New Homes of the Japanese Race" ("Nihon Jinshu no Shin Kokyō"). Tokutomi began by reaffirming the importance of race in global politics: nations no longer struggled through military aggression but through race-centered colonial expansion. The Chinese were an example of a race that had spread to every corner of the world. While the Chinese migrants' status in local societies was usually low, they nevertheless added to the overall strength of their race. As a result, even though the Qing Empire was declining, the power of the Chinese race was in fact increasing because they continued to migrate overseas and increase in numbers there.

Tokutomi's call to emulate the Chinese in the quest for Japanese expansion was grounded in Malthusian expansionism. He believed that the Japanese, like the civilized Western nations, were an expanding race marked by a rapidly growing population. The Japanese empire urgently needed to join the global racial competition by exporting its surplus population overseas and turning them into trailblazers of racial expansion. Where, then, could the Japanese expand to? He named the Philippines, the Mariana Islands, the Carolina Islands, and many other islands dotted across the Pacific Ocean as the ideal targets. Tokutomi was not bothered by the facts that the majority of these areas were already colonized by European powers. Appropriating the Lockean logic used to justify Japanese settlement in the American West, Tokutomi believed that the white Europeans failed to claim their ownership over many of these areas because the land was left empty and unused. Aside from tropical flora and fauna, these islands were inhabited only by primitive barbarians. Once the Japanese actually claimed these "empty houses," Tokutomi argued, they could "shut the doors on everybody else."[38]

---

[38] Tokutomi Sōhō, "Nihon Jinshu no Shin Kokyō," *Kokumin no Tomo* 6, no. 85 (June 13, 1890): 829–838.

As a direct result of Chinese exclusion in the United States, the call for southward expansion also garnered supporters in the Japanese government. A particularly noteworthy supporter was Enomoto Takeaki, whose many roles in the government included a stint as minister of foreign affairs between 1891 and 1892, a time when the flood of consular reports about anti-Japanese political campaigns in California began to reach Tokyo. Responding to white racism on the other side of the Pacific, Enomoto established the Bureau of Emigration as a part of his ministry in 1891 to explore *vacuum domicilium* around the Pacific as alternative targets for Japanese expansion.[39] In the 1880s and 1890s, he played a crucial role in founding two schools of thought that together constituted the overall nanshin discourse – the expansion to the South Seas (*Nan'yō*) and the expansion to Latin America.

While the existing academic literature has clinically isolated the history of Japanese maritime expansion to the South Seas from the history of Japanese migration to Latin America, as the following pages will demonstrate, they were closely associated with each other in terms of both ideology and practice. A sense of urgency in searching for "unclaimed" territories, triggered by both white racism in North America and trans-Pacific migration of the Chinese, pushed the Japanese expansionists to cast their gaze southward on both the land and sea in the tropic zone and Southern Hemisphere. This wave of expansion also traced its ideological and political lineage back to the shizoku expansion into Hokkaido in the earlier decades.

Hawai'i and Calls for Expansion in the South Seas

Tokutomi's proposal was a part of a larger intellectual trend that pointed to the South Seas as the future of Japanese expansion. Throughout the history of the empire, Japanese thinkers had offered a variety of rationales for southward expansion into the Pacific, ranging from defending the archipelago against foreign invasion to protecting Japanese subjects abroad through naval power, from stretching the trans-Pacific trade network to fulfilling Japan's own Manifest Destiny as a maritime empire.[40] Originally, however, the call for southward expansion was promoted by Seikyō Sha thinkers in the latter half of the 1880s as a direct response to the Chinese Exclusion Act in the United States.

---

[39] Sasaki Toshiji, "Enomoto Takeaki no Imin Shoreisaku to Sore o Sasaeta Jinmi," *Kirisutokyō Shakai Mondai Kenkyū*, no. 37 (March 1989): 536.

[40] Sugiura Jūkō, *Hankai Yume Monogatari: Ichimei Shinheimin Kaitendan* (Tokyo: Sawaya, 1886); Shiga, *Nan'yō Jiji*; Tadakaze Suganuma, *Shin Nihon Tonan no Yume* (Tokyo: Iwanami Shoten, 1888); Taguchi, "Nan'yō Keiryaku Ron," 352–353; Hattori Tōru, *Nan'yō Saku* (Tokyo: Sanshōdō Shoten, 1891); and Tsuneya Seifuku, *Kaigai Shokumin Ron* (Tokyo: Hakubunsha, 1891).

Though relatively obscure, the earliest nanshin promoter was a Seikyō Sha thinker named Sugiura Jūkō.[41] In a book published in 1886, he argued that Japan was facing serious threat from the West and it could only survive through conducting its own colonial expansion. Sugiura saw that the Chinese migrants in North America were humiliated and excluded by the Anglo-Saxons. Worried that the Japanese migrants would eventually receive the same mistreatment in the world of the white settlers, he believed that the Japanese should look elsewhere to expand. According to him, the Qing Empire and Korea were to be Japan's allies, Southeast Asia was already claimed by the British and French, thus the only places where the Japanese could build colonies were the numerous islands located to the South of the Japanese archipelago in the Pacific.[42]

The book *Nan'yō Jiji,* authored by Sugiura's fellow Seikyō Sha member Shiga Shigetaka one year later, infused further political meaning into the word *Nan'yō,* which was previously only a loosely defined geographical concept. For Shiga, Nan'yō indicated the cultural space lying to the South of the Japanese archipelago independent from both the West (*Seiyō*), the white men's domain, and the East (*Tōyō*), home of the yellow races.[43] While a substantial part of Nan'yō was still unclaimed, Shiga warned that the white colonists had already begun their territorial scramble there; it was vital for the Japanese to enter the fray as soon as possible.

In particular, Shiga singled out Hawai'i, a wealthy kingdom that already had thousands of Japanese migrants, as a target worthy of Tokyo's attention. Though Hawai'i was officially independent, the land and politics of the kingdom were monopolized by the white settlers while its small business and farming sectors were controlled by the Chinese. Shiga argued that Japan should also claim a share of the prize by sending more migrants to Hawai'i and enhancing Japan's commercial power there.[44]

In the same year when *Nan'yō Jiji* became a bestseller in Japan, American settlers in Hawai'i forced the Hawai'ian King Kalākaua to sign a new constitution that deprived the all nonwhite migrants – as well as two-thirds of the native Hawai'ians – of their voting rights. *Hawai'i,* a book pushed in 1892 in Japan, argued that this constitution sent a clear message that the white people had already gained the upper hand in the racial competition in the Hawai'ian Islands. After the Americans took full control of Hawai'i, the book warned,

---

[41] Only recently have scholars begun to pay attention to the importance of Sugiura and Seikyō Sha thinkers in general in constructing the discourse of southward expansion. See Jun Uchida's pioneering article-length study, "From Island Nation to Oceanic Empire," 57–90.

[42] Sugiura, *Hankai Yume Monogatari,* 16–21.

[43] Miwa Kimitada, "Shiga Shigetaka (1863–1927): A Meiji Japanist's View of and Actions in International Relations" (Research Papers, Series A-3, Institute of International Relations, Sophia University, 1970), 14–16, cited from Peattie, *Nan'yō,* 8.

[44] Shiga, *Nan'yō Jiji,* 169, 174–175, 195–203.

they would shut its doors to the Chinese and the Japanese.[45] It reminded its readers that the Japanese empire could not afford losing its influence in Hawai'i: though small in size, Hawai'i was the center of communication and trade between the two sides of the Pacific Ocean and thus the center of the racial competition in the Pacific region.[46]

A year later, the American settlers overthrew the Hawai'ian monarchy and replaced it with a republic. Fearing that Hawai'i might soon entirely fall into the white men's hands, the Japanese Federation of Patriots in San Francisco dispatched four of its members to Hawai'i to make an attempt at retaining the Japanese residents' voting rights and dismantling the white men's monopoly of power in Hawai'ian politics.[47] They published a book titled *Japan and Hawai'i* (*Nihon to Hawai*) in Tokyo that recorded their observations and thoughts while in Hawai'i. The book urged the Japanese government to seize the "golden chance" of the political upheaval on the islands and use forceful diplomacy, backed up with naval power, to win political rights for Japanese settlers in Hawai'i. Given the geopolitical significance of the islands, Japan had to secure its interest there in order to fight the race war with the West. In addition to arguing for Tokyo to exert political pressure, *Japan and Hawai'i* also suggested that the Japanese government should follow the model of the Chinese immigrant companies in San Francisco by purchasing land on the islands and cultivating Japanese enterprises there.[48]

In the same year, Nagasawa Betten echoed the opinion of the Federation of Patriots members in Seikyō Sha's mouthpiece *Ajia*, emphasizing the importance of Hawai'i in the racial battle that loomed over the Pacific Ocean.[49] In his book *The Yankees*, also published in 1893, Nagasawa pointed out another advantage that would come from controlling Hawai'i: it would serve as a station for the Japanese empire in the mid-Pacific region and allow it to further expand into Latin America.[50]

Calling for Expansion in Latin America

The Yankees also served as a telling example of how the discourse of Japanese colonial expansion into the South Seas was closely tied to another expansionist discourse emerging around the end of the 1880s, one that called for Japanese migration to Latin America. Much like the case of the South Seas, the promotion of expansion into Mexico and further south in the Western Hemisphere was

---

[45] Seya Shōji, *Hawai* (Tokyo: Chūaisha Shoten, 1892), 8.   [46] Ibid., 1–4, 31–33.
[47] Toyama Yoshifumi, *Nihon to Hawai: Kakumei Zengo no Hawai* (Tokyo: Hakubunkan, 1893), 1–2.
[48] Ibid., 17–25.
[49] Nagasawa Setsu, "Hawai'i Iyoiyo Isogi Nari," *Ajia* 2, no. 11 (1893): 291–295.
[50] Nagasawa, *Yankii*, 130–131; Iriye, *Pacific Estrangement*, 42–43.

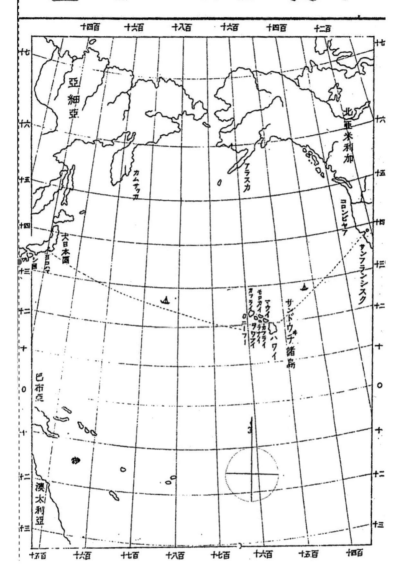

Figure 2.2 This map appears in *Hawai Koku Fūdo Ryakuki* (A Short Description of the Society and Culture of the Kingdom of Hawai'i), one of the earliest books published in Meiji Japan introducing the Kingdom of Hawai'i to the general public. The map describes the importance of Hawai'i by highlighting its location at the center of the sea route connecting Japan and the American West Coast. It demonstrates that Japanese colonial ambition in Hawai'i was developed hand in hand with Japanese migration to the American West. Konishi Naojirō, ed., *Hawai Koku Fūdo Ryakuki: Fu Ijūmin no Kokoroe* (Tokyo: Eishōdō, 1884), 1.

a collective response made by Japanese expansionists in Tokyo and San Francisco to the Chinese Exclusion Act in the United States, which they viewed as an episode in the colonial contest between different races.

Substantial efforts in promoting migration to Latin America began when Enomoto Takeaki became minister of foreign affairs in 1891. The same year, Enomoto established the Japanese consulate in Mexico City, collecting local information in order to facilitate migration planning. He assigned Fujita Toshirō, a previous Japanese consul in San Francisco whose reports had flooded Enomoto's office in Kasumigaseki, warning about the possibility of Japanese exclusion in California, to head the consulate in Mexico. Later that year, Enomoto sponsored Fujita to conduct a trip with a few other government employees to investigate locations in Mexico suitable for Japanese migration.[51] These activities illustrated the direct connection between the Chinese Exclusion Act in the United States and Enomoto's initiative in exploring Mexico as a possible destination for Japanese migration. Such a connection was further asserted by Andō Tarō, the first director of the Emigration Bureau appointed by Enomoto himself. In 1892, Andō published a series of articles aiming to steer the general public's attention toward migration to Mexico. Given the fact that the Asian immigrants in the United States were mistreated due to white racism, Andō told readers, Mexico was a more desirable destination for migrants from the overpopulated Japan because there "the natives welcomed us thanks to our racial affinity."[52]

Enomoto's initiative mirrored the rise of discussions about expansion into Latin America among the Japanese settlers in the United States. Disillusioned by white racism, some of them gave up on the dream of pursuing a Japanese colonial future in the American West. As an 1891 *Ensei* article lamented, white sellers not only prohibited the Japanese from establishing colonies in the United States, but also refused to treat Asian immigrants equally. The real Promised Land for the Japanese, it argued, lay to the south of the US border. Latin America had vast amounts of fertile land, and its natives were nothing like the white Americans – they were welcoming and obedient, easy for the Japanese to manipulate.[53] That year, *Ensei* began to publish reports of self-organized Japanese American expeditions to Mexico and South America. These reports offered Japanese American readers detailed information about Latin America's geography, culture, and social conditions, encouraging them to remigrate southward across the US border.[54]

---

[51] Fujita's report was published by the Ministry of Foreign Affairs as Gaimu Daijin Kanbō Iminka, *Mekishikokoku Taiheiyo Engan Shoshūn Jūnkai Hōkoku* (Tokyo: Gaimu Daijin Kanbō Iminka, 1891).

[52] Tsunoyama Yukihiro, *Enomoto Takeaki to Mekishiko Ijū* (Tokyo: Dōbunkan Shuppan, 1986), 68.

[53] "Shokuminchi ni Taisuru Honkai no Iken," *Ensei*, no. 5 (September 1891): 1–3.

[54] Eiichiro Azuma's pathbreaking article offers details on how issei Japanese American expansionists conducted land acquisition in Mexico in response to white racism in the United States. Azuma, "Japanese Immigrant Settler Colonialism in the U.S.-Mexican Borderlands," 255–276.

Figure 2.3 This map of Mexican territory appears in the report *Mekishikokoku Taiheiyō Engan Shoshū Junkai Hōkoku*, authored by Fujita Toshirō based on his investigation in Mexico.

In this trans-Pacific chorus clamoring for Latin American migration, the Chinese migrants, who were the actual objects of racial exclusion in the United States, also played a role. As they had done in the case of Japanese migration to the American West, Japanese expansionists used the Chinese experience in Mexico as a reference point to make their own proposals. In fact, it was the Chinese presence in Mexico that encouraged Japanese expansionists to view Mexico as a potential target in the first place. To promote expansion to Mexico and farther south, Nagasawa Betten argued in 1893 that the Chinese, being excluded from North America, Hawaiʻi, and Australia, were now moving into Mexico and South America. In order to avoid ceding these lands to Chinese control, the Japanese should occupy them first.[55]

Andō Tarō urged his fellow countrymen to learn from the Chinese example and pursue their future in Mexico. He argued that while the Japanese shied away from setting their feet on welcoming foreign lands, their fellow Asians were building "small Chinese nations" all over the world under adverse circumstances.[56] An article in *Ensei* further predicted that while the Qing Empire might collapse in the near future, the Chinese would remain as a powerful race in the world because of their omnipresent diasporic communities in Latin America and Southeast Asia; they would be a very important force for the Japanese to collaborate with in order to win the race war against the white people.[57]

In sum, the Chinese trans-Pacific migration and its exclusion from the white men's world served as both a reference and a stimulation for the rise of Japanese expansion in the South Seas and Latin America. But as the remaining pages in this chapter illustrate, the shizoku expansion in Hokkaido during earlier decades also provided intellectual and political foundations for southward expansion.

From North to South: Hokkaido and *Nanshin*

If the discourse of racial competition had shaped the practical direction of the expansion, it was the ideology of Malthusian expansionism that provided the logical foundation for the project. Malthusian expansionism emerged with the colonial project in Hokkaido and early Japanese migration to the United States. It argued for both the existence of surplus population and the necessity of further population growth, the apparent paradox of which was to be solved by migration-based expansion. At the end of the 1880s, the South Seas and

---

[55] Nagasawa, *Yankii*, 22.   [56] Tsunoyama, *Enomoto Takeaki to Mekishiko Ijū*, 69.

[57] "Raisei no shinajin narabini sono riyō (1)," *Ensei*, no. 14 (July 1892): 1–4; "Raisei no shinajin narabini sono riyō (2)," *Ensei*, no. 16 (August 1892): 192–193.

Latin America became new destinations where Japan's surplus population could be exported to.

In 1890, economist Torii Akita announced that Japan had seen a population increase numbering six million in the preceding fifteen-year period. He warned that with such a rapid rate of population growth and a small territory, the Japanese would soon become plagued by hunger and homelessness. Directly spending government money to relieve poverty would lead to a financial deficit, but reducing the birth rate by moral persuasion (as Thomas Malthus had suggested) might lead to a permanent decline of the racial stock. Instead, the nation should make long-term plans by moving the surplus people elsewhere to explore empty and fertile lands. Through two lists that outlined population density figures in different prefectures in Japan and different areas in the world, Torii identified the ideal destinations for migration as Hokkaido within Japan and the South Seas as well as the two Americas abroad.[58]

However, outside of Torii's thesis, the arguments for migration to Hokkaido and overseas did not always complement each other. The racism that Japanese migrants and travelers encountered in the United States since the late 1880s and the white plantation owners' poor treatment of Japanese laborers in Hawai'i triggered renewed calls for migration to Hokkaido *in place of* going overseas.[59] Such arguments played down the value of overseas migration in general by emphasizing that Hokkaido had the capacity to host all of Japan's surplus population. In a public lecture in 1891, Hamada Kenjirō argued that overseas migration would run the risk of harming Japan's national image and might result in material losses as well as diplomatic issues for the nation. Reminding his audience that the population density in Hokkaido was still extremely low, he argued that it would be beneficial to the nation if the surplus people would be used to explore Hokkaido instead of being exported abroad.[60] In the same year, Katsuyama Kōzō also opposed overseas migration by claiming that the Japanese people, due to their long history of isolation, were not yet used to living abroad. Hokkaido, he believed, was the ideal migration destination because it was a part of Japan's domestic territory and its vast lands, rich and fertile, were fully capable of accommodating all the surplus population to be found in the archipelago.[61]

Responding to these arguments, advocates for overseas migration disputed the assertion that Hokkaido could fully accommodate the archipelago's ever-

[58] Torii Akita, "Ijū Ron," *Tokyo Keizai Zasshi*, no. 514 (1890): 397–400.
[59] The call for stopping overseas migration and sending migration to Hokkaido instead also appeared in debates at the Imperial Diet in 1893. Yoshida, *Nihon Jinkō Ron no Shiteki Kenkyū*, 284. Another agenda of Hokkaido migration was counter to overseas migration in the Diet. Also see ibid., 278–279.
[60] Hamata Kenjirō, "Shokumin Ron," *Tokyo Keizai Zassh*, no. 600 (1891): 793–794.
[61] Katsuyama Kōzō, *Nihon Kaifu: Hokkaido Shokumin Saku* (Tokyo: Dainihon shokuminkai, 1891), 11–12.

growing surplus population. In his book *Strategies for the South* (*Nan'yō Saku*), southward expansionist Hattori Tōru argued that the advocates for domestic migration were wrong to believe that Hokkaido was sufficient to host all surplus people within Japan proper. He reasoned, "The Japanese population is growing at an astonishing rate. ... In 50 years, there will be 25,000,000 newborns in the archipelago. Since Hokkaido can only accommodate 9,150,000 more people, it means that Hokkaido's capacity will be filled to full within 20 years."[62] Hattori reminded his readers that based on his calculations, in order to make long-term plans for the country, they needed to think beyond Hokkaido and look overseas for migrant destinations. Ironically, the idea of looking for extra space to export the surplus population, originally drawn from the Hokkaido expansion, was now used against the same enterprise.

As it was with the colonial project in Hokkaido, however, the urgent necessity of exporting surplus population overseas was proposed in conjunction with the goal of promoting further population growth and wealth accumulation. Hattori pointed out that since nations competed with each other via racial productivity and the ability of expansion,[63] to gain the upper hand in this competition Japan should export its subjects from the overcrowded archipelago to the islands in the South Seas and build colonies there. The migration would not only stimulate further increases in Japan's manpower but also facilitate a transfer of natural resources from the colonies to the metropolis, expanding the nation's trading networks.[64] Mexico was also incorporated into the map of expansion by the same logic.[65] Similar to shizoku expansion in Hokkaido and the United States, it was the *need* for surplus population not the *fear* of it and the *celebration* of population growth not the *anxiety* over it that buttressed the discourses of expansion to the South Seas and Latin America. The three dimensions of Japanese colonial expansion shaped by the empire's imitation of Anglo-American settler colonialism, including making useful subjects, uplifting the Japanese in the global racial hierarchy, and increasing capitalist accumulation for the empire, continued to shape ideas and practices during this new wave of expansion.

---

[62] Hattori, *Nan'yō Saku*, 106–108.
[63] Ibid., 77. In this context, the Japanese word in the original text, *Shinshuryoku*, means the ability to be enterprising in expansion.
[64] Ibid., 77–79, 135–136.
[65] For similar arguments of Japanese Malthusian expansionism over Mexico, see Tōkai Etsurō, *Mekishikokoku Kinkyō Ippan: Fu Nihon Fukoku Saku* (1889), 35–36. Also see Itagaki Taisuke, "Shokumin Ron," *Jiyūtō Hō*, no. 10 (April 28, 1892), in *Itagaki Taisuke Zenshū*, ed. Itagaki Morimasa (Tokyo: Hara Shobō, 1980), 77–79; Tsuneya, *Kaigai Shokumin Ron*, 89–123.

Making Useful Subjects

The idea of using migration to produce more valuable subjects was embraced and further developed under the discourse of racial competition. Seikyō Sha thinkers saw Japan's own colonial migration as a necessary step to prepare the empire builders for their destined war with the white races. Shiga Shigetaka, for example, saw the Chinese Exclusion Act as evidence that the yellow races, including the Japanese, were not yet mentally and physically ready to compete with the white people head-on.[66] In order to avoid defeat, Japan should not only prohibit inter-racial residence in the archipelago but also export its subjects. Such a move, he further argued, would enable these subjects to acquire both knowledge of the outside world and an expansionist spirit.[67] Connecting nationalism with overseas expansionism, "the true patriots," he asserted, were those "who left the country for country's good."[68] For Nagasawa Betten, Hawai'i would be the first stage to test the Japanese race's ability to compete with the Caucasians. Gaining political rights in Hawai'i would allow Japanese immigrants to compete with the white settlers equally. This was the first test for the Japanese, the result of which could determine whether interracial residence should be allowed in Japan.[69] Even Taguchi Ukichi, who directly opposed the Seikyō Sha thinkers on the issue of interracial residence and was confident that Japanese were already fully capable to compete with Westerners, agreed that migration to the South Seas would better prepare the Japanese for the upcoming race war. Though previously lacking expansionist experience, he pointed out the Japanese could acquire a hands-on education on the subject in the South Seas.[70]

The expansionists had a well-defined profile of the ideal migration candidate. While some of them were open to the idea of merchants, peasants, and even burakumin going overseas, shizoku were the most ideal candidates for this project. Throughout the 1880s and into the early 1890s, shizoku relief remained the overarching political context for Japan's overseas expansion. Similar to the case of Hokkaido in the 1870s, the expansionist thinkers believed, the South Seas and Latin America would turn the declassed samurai into self-made men and model subjects of the empire. Taguchi Ukichi, for example, began his promotion of southward expansion by accepting a special shizoku relief fund from the governor of Tokyo. In 1890, this fund allowed him to establish and manage the Southern Islands Company (Nantō Shōsha) in the Bonin Islands that provided employment for shizoku from the Tokyo prefecture.[71] Taguchi also used a part of this fund to embark upon a six-month trip to Micronesia in the same year, investigating

[66] Shiga, *Nan'yō Jiji*, appendix, 51. [67] Ibid., 200–202. [68] Ibid., 202.
[69] Nagasawa, *Yankii*, 131–132.
[70] Kojima Reiitsu, *Nihon Teikoku Shugi to Higashi Ajia* (Tokyo: Ajia Keizai Kenkyūjo, Hatsubaijo Ajia Keizai Shuppankai, 1979), 21.
[71] Kojima, *Nihon Teikoku Shugi to Higashi Ajia*, 21.

possible opportunities for shizoku there.[72] Relocating "ambitious Tokyo shizoku to the South Seas," he believed, would enable them to achieve self-independence and expand Japan's power abroad at the same time.[73]

While Taguchi's activity in the South Seas did not last long, his passionate writings in *Tokyo Keizai Zasshi* brought the topic of South Seas expansion into the public discourse of the day.[74] He argued that southward expansion, like its Hokkaido counterpart, should be commerce based and free from governmental intervention. He believed that early Meiji migration to Hawai'i failed to benefit the empire because the impoverished farmer-migrants, lacking a spirit of independence, eventually became enslaved by Westerners.[75] With this historical lesson in mind, Japan's southward expansion should be conducted by independent merchants. Such a mercantile expansion would not only bring tremendous profit to Japan but also allow the empire to acquire unclaimed territories in the Pacific in a nonmilitary manner.[76]

While Taguchi redirected shizoku expansion from Hokkaido to the South Seas, his intellectual opponent on Hokkaido migration policies, bureaucrat and scholar Wakayama Norikazu, was a central figure in the campaign that brought Latin America to the map of shizoku expansion. Maintaining his migration agenda in Hokkaido, Wakayama believed that Japan's expansion into Latin America should be conducted not through commerce but rather through government-led agricultural settlement. In a letter to Ōkuma Shigenobu, minister of foreign affairs, Wakayama urged the government to mobilize a million shizoku to explore Latin America and establish colonies there. These colonization projects, he contended, would strengthen shizoku in both body and spirit. With appropriate education that would ensure their continued loyalty to Japan, these settlers would become permanent assets of the Japanese empire.[77]

Racial Uplifting

As it was in the case of Hokkaido expansion, the nanshin proposals cited Japanese population growth as a fact that proved the superiority of the Japanese race. The

[72] Taguchi Ukichi, "Wakare ni Nozomi Ichū o Arawasu," *Tōkyō Keizai Zasshi*, no. 521 (1890): 631–632.
[73] Inoue Hikosaburō, *Suzuki Keikun and Taguchi Ukichi, Nantō Junkōki* (Tokyo: Keizai Zasshisha, 1893), 353.
[74] As Mark Peattie shows, more than sixty articles regarding his trip were published in *Tokyo Keizai Zasshi*. Peattie, *Nan'yō*, 20.
[75] Between 1885 and 1894, the Japanese government managed to migrate twenty-nine thousand people from rural Japan to Hawai'i as laborers on sugar plantations. See Yaguchi Yūjin, *Hawai'i no Rekishi to Bunka* (Tokyo: Chūō Kōron Shinsha, 2002), 11–60.
[76] Taguchi, "Nan'yō Keiryaku Ron," 352–353, and Taguchi, "Wakare ni Nozomi Ichū o Arawasu," 633–634.
[77] Wakayama Norikazu, "Ōkuma Gaishō e Ataete Nanbei Takushoku o Ronzuru no Sho," in *Wakayama Norikazu Zenshū*, vol. 1 (Tokyo: Keizai Shinpōsha, 1940), 344.

Figure 2.4 This picture appears in the front matter of a book that recorded the observations of a group of Japanese expansionists during their expedition to Mexico. It describes the primitivity of Mexican farmers. Takezawa Taichi, Fukuda Kenshirō, and Nakamura Masamichi, *Mekishiko Tanken Jikki* (Tokyo: Hakubunkan, 1893).

South Seas expansionists contrasted Japanese population growth with a rapidly declining native population, painting an image of an empty space waiting for the expanding Japanese to rightfully occupy.

Japan's colonial experience in Hokkaido also enabled the South Seas expansionists to place the Japanese in the existing racial hierarchy between the white colonists and native islanders as another civilized race. Shiga Shigetaka, for example, found similarities between the native islanders of the South Seas and the Ainu of Hokkaido, categorizing both as inferior in relation to the Japanese and Westerners. He attributed the decline of the native population to their own racial inferiority – they lacked the ability to withstand epidemics and were incapable of competing with white settlers.[78] As an adherent of social Darwinism, he saw such racial decimation as cruel but unavoidable and believed that the Japanese, as a superior race, should claim their share in the South Seas like the Westerners.[79] On the other hand, unlike the Ainu and the Pacific Islanders who were doomed to

[78] Shiga, *Nan'yō jiji*, 6–9.   [79] Ibid., 13–15.

disappear, the local peoples in Latin America were not categorized as primitive races. However, they were still considered to be inferior to the Japanese; thus the latter could easily settle on their lands and bring the light of civilization to them.[80]

Increasing Capitalist Accumulation

Also similar to the case of Hokkaido, in the minds of Japanese expansionists, the declining and/or inferior natives in the South Seas and Latin America were juxtaposed with the abundant wealth these lands could provide for the empire. Sugiura Jūgō, for example, was amazed by the South Seas' low population density in contrast with the enormous amount of raw materials it provided for England.[81] In an article titled "Economic Strategies in the South Seas" ("Nan'yō Keiryaku Ron"), Taguchi Ukichi's most representative thesis on South Seas expansion, he similarly perceived the islands "below the equator" as "not only full of precious plants, animals, and rare minerals, but also rich in marine products."[82]

Advocates for migration to Latin America viewed their proposed destination in much the same way. Listing a series of data that compared the populations, territory sizes, and natural resources between Japan and Mexico, Tōkai Etsurō contrasted a small, resourceless, and overcrowded Japan with a spacious, wealthy, and empty Mexico. As the title of his book indicated, expansionist migration to Mexico was a "strategy to enrich the Japanese nation" (*nihon fukoku saku*). By the book's end, Tōkai had drawn a similar portrait of several other Latin American countries such as Columbia, Honduras, Brazil, and Chile, all of which were listed as possible future migration destinations for his countrymen.[83]

As the empire's first colonial acquisition, Hokkaido was constantly mentioned as a point of reference in the expansionists' descriptions of the South Seas and Latin America. Japanese Malthusian expansionists perceived native islanders as the equally primitive brethren of the Ainu. They identified the northern island of New Zealand, in particular, as similar to Hokkaido in terms of both ecology and economic potential.[84] They considered Latin American countries even more desirable than Hokkaido due to their larger and more fertile territories, more abundant mineral deposits, and better climate in general.[85] Through these comparisons, Japanese expansionists portrayed the South Seas and Latin America as new sources of wealth (*shin fugen*) that were

---

[80] Wakayama Norikazu, "Ōkuma Gaishō e Ataete Nanbei Takushoku o Ronzuru no Sho," 343; "Shokuminchi ni Taisuru Honkai no Iken," 1–3.
[81] Sugiura, *Hankai Yume Monogatari,* 21–22.   [82] Taguchi, "Nan'yō Keiryaku Ron," 352.
[83] Tōkai, *Mekishikokoku Kinkyō Ippan,* 48–54.   [84] Shiga, *Nan'yō Jiji,* 101.
[85] Tōkai, *Mekishikokoku Kinkyō Ippan,* 40–41, and "Imin no Kyūmu Tankenka no Ketsubō," *Ensei,* no. 32 (October 1893): 2–6.

similar to or even richer than Hokkaido. Their empty lands offered a perfect solution to the issue of overpopulation in the archipelago, and their limitless resources would help to sustain the ever-expanding empire.[86]

Human Connections

Aside from ideological consistency, the innate continuity shared by the Hokkaido and nanshin campaigns was also demonstrated by extensive human connections between the two. Both Taguchi Ukichi and Wakayama Norikazu, architects of the Hokkaido expansion project in the 1870s, became proponents of southward expansion in the late 1880s. They did so with different destinations in mind – Taguchi in favor of the South Seas and Wakayama arguing for Mexico – but it was Enomoto Takeaki who lent his political influence and personal efforts to both southward projects.

After serving as a high-ranking officer in the Hokkaido Development Agency, Enomoto rose to a series of key cabinet positions. He was successively in charge of the Ministries of Communications (1885–1889), Education (1889–1890), Foreign Affairs (1891–1892), and finally Agriculture and Commerce (1894–1897).[87] Believing that national strength could be acquired only through frontier conquest and colonial expansion, Enomoto made a few unsuccessful attempts to expand the empire into the South Seas by purchasing the Mariana Islands, the Palau Islands, and Borneo as early as the mid-1870s.[88] To promote studies on the Pacific Rim region with colonial ambitions in mind, he helped to establish in 1879 the Tokyo Geography Society (Tokyo Chigaku Kyōkai), modeled after the Royal Geographic Society in London.[89] The society's members included leading intellectuals and politicians of the day such as Shiga Shigetaka, Fukuzawa Yukichi, and Ōkuma Shigenobu. With his influence in the Imperial Navy, Enomoto also encouraged the Japanese intellectuals' interest in the South Seas by sponsoring trips via naval cruises. A number of Seikyō Sha expansionists took this opportunity to tour the South Seas, among them Miyake Setsurei and Shiga Shigetaka, the latter of whom wrote the book Nan'yō Jiji from his trip observations.[90]

After taking the charge of the Ministry of Foreign Affairs, Enomoto appointed his loyal follower Andō Tarō as the head of the Emigration Bureau.[91] Andō's Emigration Bureau only managed affairs of migration abroad

---

[86] Takezawa Taichi, Fukuda Kenshirō, and Nakamura Masayuki, *Mekishiko Tanken Jikki* (Tokyo: Hakubunkan, 1893), afterword, 1–3.

[87] Peattie, *Nan'yō*, 5–6.   [88] Ibid., 6.

[89] Ibid., 7; Usui Ryūichirō, *Enomoto Takeaki kara Sekaishi Ga Mieru* (Tokyo: PHP Kenkyūjo, 2005), 221–222.

[90] Peattie, *Nan'yō*, 6–8; Uchida, "From Island Nation to Oceanic Empire," 67.

[91] Andō faithfully followed Enomoto during the Boshin War on the side of the Bakufu.

and facilitated overseas expeditions to investigate migration destinations.[92] Though Enomoto and Andō managed to send a group of Japanese peasants to Mexico, this particular campaign soon failed due to poor planning and serious financial issues.[93] Nevertheless, it marked the beginning of Japanese migration to Latin America. In 1897, Mexico and Brazil were included in the Japanese Emigration Protection Law as migration destinations. This piece of legislation required Japanese subjects to name a guarantor when they submitted a passport application for the purpose of migration. Previously only the United States, Canada, Hawai'i, and Siam were deemed migration destinations.[94]

Enomoto's initiative also encouraged Japanese expansionists to carry out colonial projects of their own in the following years. *Ensei*'s July 1892 issue included a Japanese intellectual's public letter to Enomoto Takeaki. Writing from San Francisco, the author praised Enomoto's plan for Japanese expansion into Mexico as a glorious project that would bring permanent benefits to both the individuals involved and Japan itself for generations to come. He saluted Enomoto as the founding father of Japanese settler expansionism who jump-started the mission by founding the Republic of Ezo (Ezo Kyōwakoku).[95] While the Republic of Ezo was short-lived, the writer argued that if Enomoto transplanted his colonial project to Mexico, it would surely succeed.[96] Stimulated by both Enomoto's initiative and widespread racism in the United States, the Japanese expansionists residing in the American West began to consider Latin America as a possible migration destination. Such ambitions led to their land acquisition campaigns in Baja California in the first two decades of the twentieth century.[97]

The Peak of Shizoku Expansionism

In 1891, Tsuneya Seifuku, a government employee who had conducted an investigative trip to Mexico under Enomoto's auspices, published a book titled

[92] Tsunoyama, *Enomoto Takeaki to Mekishiko Ijū*, 59–61.   [93] Ibid., 185–198.
[94] Ibid., 76–77.
[95] During the Boshin War, under the leadership of Enomoto Takeaki, navy commander in chief of the Tokugawa Bakushu, diehard followers of Tokugawa regime fled to Hokkaido after losing Honshū to the supporters of the Meiji emperor. In December 15, 1868, they announced the formation of the Republic of Ezo in Hakodate. Enomoto Takeaki was elected president of this republic. Leaders of the republic continued resisting the pro–Meiji emperor forces by seeking diplomatic recognition and support from the Western powers. The republic quickly collapsed in June 1869 after its forces lost the Battle of Hakodate to the Meiji forces. Enomoto surrendered to the Meiji government.
[96] "Harukani Gaimudaijin Enomoto Takeaki ni Agaru no Sho,"*Ensei*, no. 13 (July 1892): 14.
[97] Azuma, "Japanese Immigrant Settler Colonialism in the U.S.-Mexican Borderlands," 255–276. Eiichiro Azuma has demonstrated how white racism triggered the Japanese American expansion in Baja California. This letter further tells us that the initiate of Enomoto Takeaki in Tokyo also played a role in shaping issei elites' colonial expansion.

On Overseas Colonial Migration (*Kaigai Shokumin Ron*). It gathered together the ideologies and proposals of shizoku expansion since Hokkaido migration in the 1870s.

In the first half of his book, Tsuneya urged the shizoku who were uncertain about their future in Japan to look beyond the archipelago.[98] He incorporated the ideas of racial competition, population growth, as well as economic development in his argument for shizoku expansion. Tsuneya described the world as one in which only the fittest races would survive; he emphasized the necessity for Japan to expand overseas and participate in the colonial competition against the Westerners. The Japanese, he further pointed out, were competent competitors: they had their own successful colonial conquests during the past few centuries, therefore they were the Westerners' equal.[99] He followed this theme of racial competition with demographic comparisons between different countries, highlighting the fact that Japan had the highest population density among them all. To propel the nation forward, Tsuneya concluded, Japan should relocate a great number of people to both Hokkaido and other parts of the world.[100] Migration-based expansion, he further pointed out, was also necessary for Japan to keep its currently rapid rate of population growth and increase its national wealth.[101] He also reconciled the contemporary debates about the different migration models and the role that the government ought to play in them. Since expansionist migration was a crucial issue for the empire, Tsuneya argued, it should be conducted through collaboration between the government and the people. He was open to all manners of migration but believed that for the migrants – be they merchants, peasants, or temporary laborers – to remain valuable for the nation, they must all be protected by Japan's naval power.[102] In the second half of the book, which examined the possible destinations of Japan's expansionist migration, Tsuneya included both the South Seas and Latin America in his map.

If *On Overseas Colonial Migration* served as a theoretical summary of the previous agendas on shizoku expansion, the Colonial Association (Shokumin Kyōkai), established by Enomoto Takeaki in 1893, put the theory into practice.[103] The establishment of the Colonial Association as the first nationwide organization of overseas expansion marked the culmination of shizoku-centered expansionism in Meiji Japan. The association sponsored investigation trips and expeditions around the Pacific Rim. It also held public lectures and published an official journal named *Reports of the Colonial Association*

---

[98] Tsuneya, *Kaigai Shokumin Ron*, 3.   [99] Ibid., 11–22.   [100] Ibid., 36.   [101] Ibid., 46–47.
[102] Ibid., 78.
[103] The association was initially established by Enomoto to carry out his plan of Mexico migration after he had to resign from his government position due to internal conflict in the Matsukata Masayoshi cabinet. Kodama Masaaki, "Kaisetsu," in *Shokumin Kyōkai Hōkoku Kaisetsu, Sōmokuji, Sakuin* (Tokyo: Fuji Shuppan, 1987), 9.

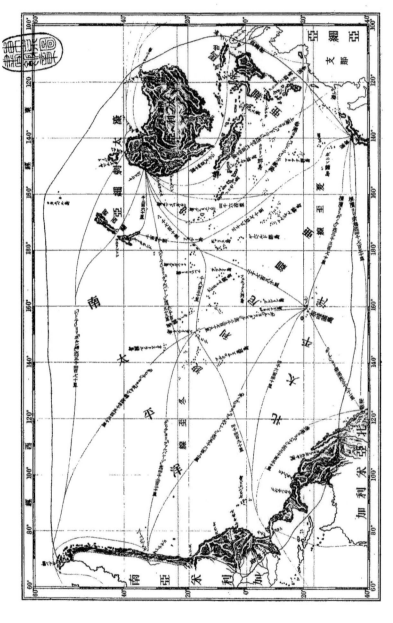

Figure 2.5 The map of Japanese expansion proposed by Tsuneya Seifuku that included both the South Seas and Latin America. Tsuneya Seifuku, *Kaigai Shokumin Ron* (Tokyo: Hakubunsha, 1891).

(*Shokumin Kyōkai Hōkokusho*) to disseminate information about and ideas for overseas expansion. The association's prospectus appeared in the journal's inaugural issue, and it reiterated all the major ideas for overseas expansion in the previous years as summarized by Tsuneya.[104]

The association's choice of advising council and membership composition revealed partnerships between government officials and public intellectuals, between the promoters of Hokkaido migration and those in favor of overseas expansion.[105] The fact that leading figures from separate migration campaigns – Inoue Kakugorō, Shiga Shigetaka, Taguchi Ukichi, and Tsuneya Seifuku to name but a few – were all involved in the association illustrated the common foundation that these different schools of expansion shared. As direct ideological descendants of early Meiji colonial expansion in Hokkaido, they were all motivated by the desire to both reduce population pressure at home and increase Japan's national power abroad. Shizoku, the group that posed the biggest threat to the new nation's stability, was singled out as the ideal candidate for these projects. The processes of migration and settlement were expected to transform them into exemplary subjects of the empire.

Conclusion

This chapter has explained how shizoku migration to the American West paved the way for the genesis of Japanese expansion in the South Seas and Latin America in the last two decades of the nineteenth century. Shizoku expansionists' encounter of white racism through Chinese exclusion in the United States allowed them to reinterpret the imperial competitions in the world as struggles between races. The exclusion of Chinese immigrants from the United States forced Japanese expansionists to temporarily move their gaze from North America to the South Seas and Latin America. In their imaginations, exporting the declassed samurai there to claim these still contested territories would allow the Japanese empire to claim its own colonial possessions amid the increasingly intensified global competition of race.

If white racism redirected Japanese expansion toward the Southern Hemisphere from outside, Malthusian expansionism continued to connect shizoku-centered political tension at home with colonial expansion abroad from the inside. Thinkers and participants in southward expansion had profound connections with shizoku migration in the recent past in Hokkaido, where the marriage between the discourse of overpopulation and migration-driven expansion originated. The formation of the Colonial Association and the

---

[104] "Shokumin Kyōkai Setsuritsu Shoisho," *Shokumin Kyōkai Hōkokusho*, no. 1 (April 1893): 105–107.
[105] *Shokumin Kyōkai Hōkokusho*, no. 1 (April 1893): 110–118.

campaigns of expansion it launched demonstrated the profound connections between the shizoku migration in Hokkaido, migration to the United States, and the ideas and activities of Japanese expansion in the South Seas and Latin America.

The Colonial Association continued to function and publish its journal until the beginning of the twentieth century. Yet the shizoku-based expansionist discourse, along with the generation of shizoku whose lives were fundamentally transformed by the turmoil of regime and policy changes, had faded from public consciousness by the mid-1890s. When the Japanese empire was on the cusp of a war with the Qing Empire that would redefine the geopolitics in East Asia, a new social discourse had already begun to emerge. It was rooted in the rise of urban decay and rural poverty, results of Japan's rapid industrialization and urbanization. Ideologues of expansion, joined by social reformers, began to propose migration abroad, particular to the United States, as a solution to rescue the common poor from their misery at home. The shizoku generation was giving way to the rise of unprivileged commoners in Japanese society; Japan's migration-driven expansion thus entered a new stage. The following chapter examines the commoner-centered Japanese migration to the United States that took place from the mid-1890s to 1907.

Part II

Transformation, 1894–1924

3   Commoners of Empire: Labor Migration to the United States

In December 1894, during the middle of the First Sino-Japanese War, Tokutomi Sōhō published a collection of his political essays under the title *On the Expansion of the Great Japan* (*Dai Nihon Bōchō Ron*), predicting that Japan's defeat of the Qing would become a starting point of the empire's destined global expansion in the decades to come.[1] The Japanese population, he asserted, had grown rapidly and soon would exceed the amount that its existing territory could accommodate. Meanwhile, since population size was a crucial indicator of national strength, as demonstrated by the success of the British global expansion in the recent past, Japan had to maintain its overall population growth. Like "surging water would flow over the riverbank," he concluded, Japan had to take on the mission of expansion by exporting its subjects overseas.[2]

Tokutomi urged the entire nation to unite and fight to hand the Qing Empire a total defeat rather than accepting a quick armistice that would grant Japan the control of Korean politics or an attractive amount of reparation. The Qing Empire was not simply a political threat to Japan's territorial ambitions in Asia, but as the Japanese were destined to expand overseas and "establish new homes around the world," the Chinese presented a key barrier to this global expansion because they were competing with Japanese emigrants in different parts of the world such as Hawai'i, San Francisco, Australia, and Vladivostok.[3] Tokutomi wanted his readers to understand the war as not only a clash of two geopolitical powers but also part of the inevitable rivalry of global expansion between the Chinese and the Japanese.[4] What to gain from winning the war, accordingly, was the opening of new routes and the removal of barriers to Japan's global expansion. Defeating the Qing, Tokutomi argued, would win Japan recognition in the world as an expansionist nation and allow it to join the competition of colonial expansion on equal footing with the Western powers.[5]

---

[1] Tokutomi Iichirō, *Dai Nihon Bōchō Ron* (Tokyo: Min'yūsha, 1894), 4.   [2] Ibid., 7–12.
[3] Ibid., 16–17.   [4] Ibid., 17–18.
[5] Ibid., 23. Tokutomi's view represented the mainstream opinion of the Japanese expansionists at the time. Even Kayahara Kazan, who would soon emerge as Tokutomi's rival in Japanese

On the Expansion of the Great Japan demonstrates that the discourse of Malthusian expansionism, which celebrated rapid population growth on the one hand and lamented the land's limited ability to accommodate it on the other, continued to serve as a central justification for overseas expansionism in the 1890s. However, the First Sino-Japanese War marked a turning point in the history of Japan's migration-driven expansion. The generation of shizoku who experienced the vicissitudes of the Tokugawa-Meiji transition was disappearing from public view, and shizoku-based expansionism was phased out along with it. In its stead rose a new discourse of expansion, one that was based on the pursuit of success for the common youth. Generally called "commoners" (*heimin*), they were born after the Tokugawa-Meiji transition with no inherited privileges, and theirs was a generation that was fundamentally different from the generation of shizoku before them.

Compared to the shizoku, the heimin class was much larger and more diverse in social backgrounds. Its ranks included both the well-off and the poor, both urban dwellers and rural farmers. Some came from the families of either shizoku or wealthy merchants and thus enjoyed certain types of upward mobility. Others were born to impoverished homes and become members of the first generation of the working class in Japan's fledgling capitalist economy. Despite such differences, they were collectively the first products of Japan's modern education system. They shared the painful struggles of reconciling the ideal of egalitarianism with the reality of social inequality, the exalted principle of rugged individualism with unaffordable cost of education and fierce competition for very limited professional opportunities, the conscious pursuit of personal freedom with Japanese society's numerous economic, cultural, and political barriers. How to make sense of these commoners as a rising sociopolitical force and what role they should play in the course of Japan's nation/empire building became two central questions for Japan's intellectuals, politicians, and social leaders at the time.

During the decade in between the First Sino-Japanese War and the Russo-Japanese War, the heimin class's emergent political consciousness – and the debates about it – was accompanied by the ascent of a new expansionist discourse. The newly proposed heimin overseas migration was aimed at providing the commoners with an opportunity to simultaneously achieve personal success and serve the expanding empire. The promoters of heimin expansion came from a variety of personal backgrounds and ideological persuasions, but the vanguards of this movement were Japan's earliest socialists who were introduced to the ideals of socialism together with Protestant Christianity. They attributed Japan's growing social gap to class-based exploitation, but

journalism, saw the Sino-Japanese War as a precious opportunity for Japan to become a global power and expand into the Pacific. Iriye, *Pacific Estrangement*, 45.

they looked for a solution to poverty not through violent revolution but through religious philanthropy and peaceful mediation between the classes. Adherents to social Darwinism and historical progress, they associated the economic and political rights of the working-class youth with the Japanese empire's rights to colonial expansion. Among possible migration destinations, the United States was singled out as the most ideal location because it was imagined as a land of abundant job opportunities and a beacon of civilization to the rest of the world. From the Christian Socialists' point of view, migration to the United States would allow the common Japanese youth to escape bourgeois exploitation and other forms of oppression at home; moreover, it would mold them into truly free subjects at the very center of civilization, where freedom, equality, and the value of labor were fully respected. Thus, materially enriched and mentally transformed, these youth would then lead the Japanese empire in its destined march toward global expansion.

This chapter examines the changes and continuities of Japan's migration-driven expansionism between the eve of the First Sino-Japanese War and the first decade of the twentieth century. While the discourse of population growth and the idea of making model subjects through migration continued to legitimize overseas expansion, the ideal candidates for migration were no longer a countable number of shizoku but hundreds of thousands of ordinary youth. Migration was still an essential component of national expansion, but on an individual level it was no longer framed as restoring the honor of declassed men. Instead, it now aimed to provide lower class people with access to economic success and political power. The US mainland once again became the main destination of migration.

The chapter begins with an analysis of the rise of heimin as a major socio-political force in the last two decades of the nineteenth century and discusses its convergence with the early labor movement after the First Sino-Japanese War. It then examines the new discourse of migration-driven expansion that emerged from this context and explains why migration to America returned to the forefront of Japanese overseas expansionism. This analysis is centered on the ideas and practices of the Japanese Christian Socialists in their promotion of migration to the United States until the Gentlemen's Agreement in 1908. The chapter concludes with a look at the decline of the heimin-centered discourse of America-bound migration after the Gentlemen's Agreement went into effect.

The Rise of Heimin

Starting in the late 1880s, domestic political tensions surrounding the shizoku issue became diluted by the fever of overseas expansion and the materialization of promised political reforms such as the formation of the Imperial Diet and the enact of the Meiji Constitution. The decline of the former samurai class as a political force was accompanied by the rise of the commoners (heimin) as a voice in the political debate. The term heimin, as a political concept, carries different meanings and connotations in different contexts, but here it is used to specifically indicate the class of common youth who belonged to the genera-tions born after the Tokugawa-Meiji transition. Most members of the heimin class had no inherited power or honor like the shizoku and possessed a distinct political consciousness.

The shift from shizoku to heimin as the center of Japanese political discourse mirrored the transition of Japanese social identity from one based on inheri-tance into one shaped by social and economic status. These changes reflected the horizontalization of Japanese society pushed by the forces of modernity. Although shizoku identity continued to be memorized as a symbol of honor and many continued to use their shizoku backgrounds for self-promotion, the title of shizoku no longer possessed the same political power as before. Some central heimin activists, though holding shizoku backgrounds themselves, embraced the idea of heimin as the idealized democratic subject position.[6]

The early heimin activists believed that Japan's existing political and social structures, still monopolized by inherited privilege and traditional value, had betrayed the spirits of egalitarianism and progress promised by the modern society. They argued that the nation should move forward by giving political and economic opportunities to individuals born without privilege. Tokutomi Sōhō, a prominent spokesperson for heimin, had grown up in a family of *gōshi*, wealthy peasants who obtained certain shizoku privileges by serving the Tokugawa Bakufu. Tokutomi strongly resented the full-fledged samurai who had looked down upon him since childhood because of his inferior social background.[7]

In 1886, Tokutomi published his heimin-centered blueprint for Japan's nation-building, *The Future Japan* (*Shōrai no Nihon*). He observed that the nineteenth-century world was an arena of international competition where only the fittest could survive.[8] Hidden behind the wars and arms race was the true rivalry of national wealth. In other words, nations ultimately competed with each other in terms of economic productivity and trade.[9] In the past the samurai had enjoyed political and economic privileges due to their status as military aristocrats without engaging in any form of economic production. But, argued Tokutomi, the samurai could no longer lead such a parasitic life in the new society now. The heimin, as the main body of economic production, were now

---

[6] Irwin Scheiner has demonstrated that many initial converts to Protestant Christianity in modern Japan were shizoku. See Scheiner, *Christian Converts and Social Protest in Meiji Japan* (Berkeley: University of California Press, 1970). As this chapter shows, Protestant Christianity also became a driving force behind the rise of heimin activism in Japanese society.

[7] Kinmonth, *Self-Made Man in Meiji Japanese Thought*, 105.

[8] Tokutomi Iichirō, *Shōrai no Nihon* (Tokyo: Keizai Zasshisha, 1886), 22–23.   [9] Ibid., 80–81.

replacing aristocracy and emerging at the center of national and global politics –
a trend that was proven by both the French Revolution and the American
Revolution.[10] In order to survive and gain the upper hand in international
competition, Japan had to follow this global trend by allowing its common
people to take up the mantle of leadership.[11]

In the next year, Tokutomi established the Association of the People's Friend
(Minyū Sha) to disseminate ideas of commonerism (*heiminshugi*), calling to
form a nation and empire led by commoners. The association's official journal,
Friend of the Nation (*Kokumin no Tomo*), began its circulation the same year.
Tokutomi's promotion of heimin-centered nationalism and the increasing
popularity of his works among the general reading public revealed the society's
lack of upward mobility. This predicament of common youth was well captured
by two contemporary works of fiction. Mori Ōgai's *The Dancing Girl*
(*Maihime*), first serialized on *Friend of the Nation* upon Tokutomi's request,
described a tragic romance between an ambitious but unprivileged Japanese
man and a German dancing girl. Under a plethora of social pressures, the
protagonist eventually had to discard his true love in order to gain his dream
job—an elite position within the government bureaucracy. Futabatei Shimei's
The Drifting Cloud (*Ukigumo*), on the other hand, told the story of a well-
educated and hardworking young man from an aristocratic family in the
Tokugawa era who failed in both his career and love because he refused to be
a sycophantic social climber in Meiji society.[12] The protagonists in both stories
were young men of promise who either graduated from a hyperselective university or were born into an established family. Most common Japanese youth
had no access to the privileges enjoyed by either of them. Nevertheless, the
protagonists' struggles against the social barriers that belied the premise of
modernization were shared by all the commoners in Meiji Japan. Even those
who were wealthy enough to study at the bourgeoning private colleges faced
serious discriminations compared with their counterparts from imperial universities on an already oversaturated job market. A journal, *The Youth of Japan*
(*Nihon no Shōnen*), claimed in 1891 that private college graduates in the fields
of politics and economics had only a 50 percent employment rate.[13] These
jobless graduates were joined by a much larger number of rural and urban youth
who could not afford higher education but still held high expectations for their
own future inspired by the spirit of egalitarianism.

Tokutomi blamed this lack of opportunities for the commoners on the
aristocrats who would not let go of their stranglehold on the country's politics
and economy. In his essay "Youth of the New Japan" ("Shin Nihon no Seinen"),
Tokutomi called those with inherited privileges "old men of Tenpō" who clung

---

[10] Ibid., 108–109, 112–113.   [11] Ibid., 213–216.
[12] Kinmonth, *Self-Made Man in Meiji Japanese Thought*, 143–145.   [13] Ibid., 133.

to traditional values and made no contribution to the nation's advancement.[14] In his view, these aristocrats should yield to the flow of history and make way for the commoners, who were the young and progressive harbingers of the future.

How, then, did Tokutomi envisage a society of commoners? It was not only an egalitarian society that gave political rights to the common people through electoral democracy, but also one that provided a fair platform where ordinary men could achieve economic success by their own efforts. In order to realize this goal, he argued, society needed to operate according to the principles of self-independence and self-responsibility. Unlike the old shizoku and kazoku aristocracies who lived as social parasites, everyone in the nation of heimin should earn their own living. "Their brows are wet with honest sweat . . . and they do not owe to any man."[15] Tokutomi deemed the desire for a career (*shokugyō no kannen*) so important in the formation of independent subjects of the nation that he went as far as calling it the "new religion of Japan."[16]

The ideal image of the heimin, therefore, was the working class that emerged from Japan's fledgling capitalist society in the late nineteenth century. *Friend of the Nation* described them as "workers" (*rōdōsha*). Accordingly, the publication was sensitive to class-based exploitation and sympathetic to the working class's poverty. An 1891 article, for example, argued that the working class was of a noble character and should receive fair payments for their labor. In order to transform itself into a nation of heimin, Japan should emulate the model of the Western countries where, according to the article, the workers were treated well and allowed to have a share of the profits.[17]

Tokutomi's promotion of the rights of the commoners was closely associated with his vision for Japan's empire building. The economic independence of the commoners and their rise to power as a sociopolitical force in domestic Japan mirrored the Japanese empire's claim of its own rights of expansion on a global stage that was previously dominated by the Western imperial powers. The development of a heimin nation, Tokutomi argued, would better prepare Japan to survive and prosper in a social Darwinist world. In the book *On the Expansion of the Great Japan*, he reasoned that the expansion of an empire was dependent upon the expansion of its individual subjects. He encouraged Japan's commoners to follow the examples of the British, the Chinese, and the Russians to migrate to every corner of the world as the pioneers of Japanese expansion.

---

[14] By "old men of Tenpō," Tokutomi meant those who were born between 1830 and 1844. Tokutomi Sōhō, "Shin Nihon no Seinen," in *Tokutomo Sohō Shū*, ed. Uete Michiari (Tokyo: Chikuma Shobō, 1974), 118. According to Kinmonth, it covered the majority of the oligarchs, government officials, and leading intellectuals of the day. See Kinmonth, *Self-Made Man in Meiji Japanese Thought*, 107.

[15] Tokutomi, "Shin Nihon no Seinen," 119.

[16] "Nihon Kokumin no Shinshūkyō," *Kokumin no Tomo*, no. 201 (September 13, 1893): 1.

[17] "Rōdōsha no Koe," *Kokumin no Tomo*, no. 95 (September 23, 1890): 9.

The First Sino-Japanese War and the Heimin Expansion

Prior to the First Sino-Japanese War, support for the heimin discourse was limited to Minyū Sha members and their intellectual followers who had few interactions with the working class. After Japan's victory over Qing China, however, the heimin discourse became closely associated with Japan's burgeoning labor movement. This movement arose amid the boom of Japanese industrial development triggered by the Sino-Japanese War. Tokutomi Sōhō's proto-socialist ideas of nation building were picked up, though in revised forms, by the socialist thinkers and activists in their campaigns calling for political and economic rights of the workers. The heimin-centered discourse of Japanese expansion was eventually materialized in the Christian Socialists' campaigns for moving working-class youth to the United States.

A year after the end of the First Sino-Japanese War, Tokutomi lamented the loss of Japan's "national energy": the Japanese policymakers ended the war without capturing the Qing Empire's capital of Peking (now Beijing), a decision that destroyed the Japanese populace's wartime passion for expansion and progress. Deluded by the illusion of peace, he observed, young people gave up their noble goals of studying politics, religion, science, and philosophy and turned to moneymaking.[18] In fact, Japanese nationalism and expansionism did not come to an end after the conclusion of the First Sino-Japanese War – it simply manifested itself in a different form. However, Tokutomi was correct to notice that the heimin discourse had taken a decidedly materialistic turn.

The common Japanese economic optimism and thirst for monetary gains, stimulated by war's end, was demonstrated by the sudden popularity of business schools. While they had a hard time filling their seats before the war, these business schools began to enjoy full registration, and some were even able to admit students selectively right after the war.[19] The decade following the war also witnessed a boom in writings on personal economic success in print media. *Business Japan* (*Jitsugyō no Nihon*), a journal aimed at selling business courses to students without a formal education, was founded in 1897.[20] Magazines of different ideological stances and backgrounds, such as the *Sun* (*Taiyō*) and the *Central Review* (*Chūō Kōron*), introduced special columns that published rags-to-riches stories and tips on moneymaking ventures. The most widely circulated journal representative of this era was *Seikō* (*Success*), founded by Murakami Shūnzō in 1902. Its circulation reached fifteen thousand within three years.[21]

---

[18] "Seinen Gakumon no Keikō," *Kokumin no Tomo*, no. 304 (August 21, 1896): 1–2, cited from Kinmonth, *Self-Made Man in Meiji Japanese Thought,* 157.
[19] Kinmonth, *Self-Made Man in Meiji Japanese Thought*, 157–158.   [20] Ibid., 158–159.
[21] Ibid., 166.

The discourse of success embodied by *Seikō* and other magazines of the day was directly derived from the idea of commonerism promoted by Tokutomi Sōhō. Like Tokutomi, Murakami characterized the heimin as a young and progressive group that should replace the "conservative" old men and lead the nation to a better future.[22] Like the Hokkaido expansionists decades ago, Murakami was promoting a story of personal achievement. However, this time the protagonist was no longer the declassed shizoku who would regain their previous honor and dignity: now the common youth, who were born without any privileges, would lift themselves up through hard work.

The flood of literature on material success was in direct contrast to the stark economic reality. The First Sino-Japanese War did stimulate military and civil industry expansions, marked by a rapid increase in the numbers of factories and wage laborers. Yet it was soon followed by a severe depression that resulted in a far-reaching wave of bankruptcy and unemployment. Income declines and deteriorating working conditions led to the rise of the labor movement. The backbone of this movement, the young working class, was also the main audience of the discourse of materialistic success. As its celebration of money-making spoke to the wage laborers' hope for financial advancement, its call for more employment opportunities for the common youth also matched the working class's resentment of class exploitation and economic inequality.

While Tokutomi expressed sympathy toward the laborers, this materialistic version of commonerism was associated more closely with the working class and converged with Japanese socialist thoughts at the turn of the twentieth century. Unlike the later wave of socialist movements that directly challenged the existing political structure after the Russo-Japanese War, this early version of socialism, while critical about the political status quo, did not seek to upend it. Influenced by Protestant Christianity,[23] Japanese Socialists of the day considered self-help as the ultimate solution to working-class poverty. They sought to bridge the social gap through interclass reconciliation as well as religious and moral suasion on the poor. Leading socialists such as Katayama Sen and Sakai Toshihiko were key supporters of the idea of self-help and published articles in *Seikō* to promote materialistic success. *Rōdō Sekai* (*Labor World*) – the mouthpiece of the labor movement of the day – and *Seikō* also carried advertisements for each other.[24]

In the heimin thinkers' agenda of nation building at the turn of the twentieth century, the ideal subjects of the empire were no longer the shizoku but the common working-class youth epitomized by work-study students (*kugakusei*), poor boys who worked their own way through school.[25] Like the shizoku

---

[22] Ibid., 171.
[23] John Crump, *The Origins of Socialist Thought in Japan* (London: St. Martin's Press, 1983), 91–93.
[24] Ibid., 172.   [25] Ibid., 181.

expansionists in earlier decades, some heimin ideologues also embraced overseas migration as the foundation of Japan's nation making and empire building.
The idea of Malthusian expansionism, lamenting the overcrowdedness of the
archipelago on the one hand and emphasizing the importance of migration in
producing desirable subjects on the other, continued to guide their various
agendas for expansion. Attributing the lack of opportunities for common youth
to the nation's growing size of surplus population, heimin expansionists
believed that overseas migration would allow ambitious young men to achieve
economic independence. Convinced that the future of the Japanese empire lay
in frontier conquest and territorial expansion, they expected that these common
youths would rise to positions of leadership in the empire by building settler
colonies abroad.

Resurgence of Japanese Migration to the United States

Japan's victory over Qing China in the First Sino-Japanese War relieved
Japan's racial anxiety caused by the Chinese Exclusion Act in the United
States, which previously had led the shizoku expansionists to explore alternative migration destinations. The war, as Tokutomi observed, cemented the
Japanese hierarchical superiority over the Chinese in the racial imaginations of
Japanese expansionism.[26] Tokutomi emphasized that the war opened the doors
for Japan's further expansion not only in Asia but also globally.[27] In other
words, the war was fought for Japan's global expansion and for its confidence
to do so.[28]

Tokutomi's intellectual friend Takekoshi Yosaburō penned an article in
Friend of the Nation at the end of the war, inviting his countrymen to consider,
without regional and racial bias, Japan's position in the world.[29] A graduate
from the Keiō School,[30] Takekoshi inherited the school founder Fukuzawa
Yukichi's faith in de-Asianization. He believed that the Japanese should abandon the labels of Asia and the yellow race and "stand at the top of the world" by
absorbing the essence of both East and West.[31] In 1896, a year after the war's
end, Takekoshi founded the journal *Japan of the World* (*Sekai no Nihon*),
repositioning Japan in the hierarchy of world politics as a force on equal footing
with the Western powers. For this venture he received financial support from
two politicians who were involved in Japan's diplomatic mission to revise its
unequal treaties with the Western powers, Saionji Kinmochi and Mutsu
Munemitsu.[32]

---

[26] Tokutomi, *Dai Nihon Bōchō Ron*, 35–46, 124–133.   [27] Ibid., 23.   [28] Ibid., 46.
[29] "Sekai no Nihon Ya, Ajia no Nihon Ya," *Kokumin no Tomo*, no. 250 (April 13, 1895): 1–4.
[30] Yano, *"Nanshin" no Keifu*, 65.   [31] "Sekai no Nihon Ya, Ajia no Nihon Ya," 2.
[32] Fukui Jūnko, "Kaidai," *Sekai no Nihon* 1 (repr., Tokyo: Kashiwa Shobō, 1992), 2.

This reembrace of the West was accompanied by a fundamental challenge to the Seikyō Sha thinkers' discourse of racial conflict. While Seikyō Sha intellectuals believed in a destined rivalry between the yellow races and the white races, between East (Asia) and West. Takekoshi, on the other hand, criticized the definition of Asia as a culturally or biologically homogenous racial entity:

The races in Asia are different from each other, just like the Japanese race is different from the European races. There are different races such as the Caucasians, the Mongolians, the Malays, the Dravidians, the Negritos, and the Hyperboreans. . . . These are only general terms. After conducting a closer analysis of the Chinese, who share the same language and racial origin with us, we can see that not all the Chinese share the customs and traditions of the Mongolian races. . . .

If we only collaborate with those of our own race and exclude all others, we would end up not only excluding the Europeans but also the Asians as foreign races. . . . Asia is not a unified racial, cultural, or political entity. It is simply a geographical term, without any real meaning. [33]

Takekoshi's deconstruction of Asia's racial homogeneity went hand in hand with his emphasis of the uniqueness of the Japanese race in relation to the rest of Asia. "Japan," he explained, "is geographically separated from the Asian continent and is close to the heart of the Pacific Ocean. Its civilization is not that of the Mongolians but an independent one synthesizing the essence of different cultures in the world."

This revision of Japan's racial identity, made possible by victory over Qing China, served to conceptually delink Japan from Asia in general and China in particular. It allowed Japanese expansionists to draw a distinction between Japanese migration to the United States and the tragedy of Chinese exclusion therefrom. They believed that the Japanese were people of a master race like Westerners; as such, they would be welcomed by the white Americans in the United States, just as Japan would be accepted as an equal member in the club of civilized empires.[34] Fukuzawa Yukichi, for example, resumed his promotion of overseas migration in 1896. In an article urging his countrymen to build "new homes overseas," he confirmed that the war had altered Japan's racial identity: "The single fact that Japan has defeated the ancient and great country of China has changed the minds of the conservative, diffident Japanese people." Fukuzawa further proudly announced that "in capability and in vigor, [the Japanese] are not inferior to any race in the world."[35]

---

[33] "Sekai no Nihon Ya, Ajia no Nihon Ya," 1–2.

[34] Abe Isoo, for example, was confident that the Japanese race had much better assimilability to the white American society than the Chinese. Abe Isoo, *Hokubei no Shin Nihon* (Tokyo: Hakubunkan, 1905), 102–104.

[35] "Kaigai no Shin Kokyō," *Jiji Shinpō*, February 3, 1896, cited from Wakatsuki Yasuo, "Japanese Emigration to the United States, 1866–1924: A Monograph," *Perspectives in American History* 12 (1979): 443.

Figure 3.1 This is the cover of an issue of a popular magazine, *Shōnen Sekai* (*The World of the Youth*), published in 1895. The cover celebrates Japan's victory in the Sino-Japanese War. With the world map at the center, this picture also illustrates how this victory ushered in passion among Japanese intellectuals for the empire's global expansion.

Thus, the rise of heimin as a sociopolitical force and the reimagining of the Japanese racial identity after the First Sino-Japanese War made the United States once more a favorable migration destination. Japan's imperial-minded socialists connected their domestic sociopolitical campaigns to the mission of empire building. They believed that relocating the common youth to the United States would bridge the domestic social gap while contributing to their agenda of building Japan as a heimin-led egalitarian empire. The rest of this chapter analyzes three most representative and influential migration promoters of the day: Katayama Sen, Abe Isoo, and Shimanuki Hyōdayū. By examining the convergence and divergence of their migration-related ideas and activities, the following pages shed light on the different ways in which this wave of American migration was connected with the process of Japanese nation building and imperial expansion in Asia.

Divergence and Convergence in the Discourses of Heimin Expansion to the United States

The mid-1890s witnessed a proliferation of private migration companies in Japan. The increase in the number of trans-Pacific sea routes after the Sino-Japanese War allowed many of these companies to include the United States on their commercial maps.[36] These for-profit companies targeted the rural masses, individuals who usually had to take a huge risk by selling their properties in order to pay for their passage. Equally profit-minded, these rural migrants simply hoped to find temporary work as laborers abroad in order to lift themselves – as well as their families back in Japan – out of destitution.[37]

In response to a series of anti-Japanese campaigns on the American West Coast targeting the migrant laborers since the early 1890s, the Japanese government enacted the Emigrant Protection Law in 1896. It was aimed at preventing "undesirable" migrants from entering the United States so that they would not bring "shame" upon the empire. It imposed financial requirements on both migration companies and the migrants themselves, hoping this would remove the uneducated and purely money-seeking laborers from the migrant pool. Within a few years, however, the imperial government realized that this law was all too easily circumvented, thus in 1900 it began to limit the number of passports issued for those who wished to travel to the United States.[38]

The discourse of commoner migration to the United States emerged at this moment. The heimin expansionists were critical of the government's restriction on overseas migration, considering it to be a shortsighted policy that dampened

---

[36] Kodama Masaaki, *Nihon Iminshi Kenkyū Josetsu* (Tokyo: Keisuisha, 1992), 521.
[37] Mitziko Sawada, *Tokyo Life, New York Dreams: Urban Japanese Visions of America, 1890–1924* (Berkeley: University of California Press, 1996), 45.
[38] Ibid., 47.

the common youth's expansionist spirit or, worse, a malicious strategy of the bourgeois state designed to confine the working class to perpetual domestic exploitation. However, they shared the government's view that the most desirable migrants were not the rural masses living in absolute poverty. While encouraging the migrants to accept laborer jobs, they believed that migration to the United States should not be solely for economic survival. These migrants should have long-term goals of self-improvement such as seeking higher education or business success; furthermore, they needed to connect their lives with the well-being of Japan. They also agreed with the government in that the for-profit migration companies should be blamed for indiscriminately sending "undesirable" subjects abroad, thereby stirring up anti-Japanese sentiments on the other side of the Pacific. Their own heimin migration campaigns, in contrast, would help the truly promising youth in Japan to circumvent government restriction and rescue them from the exploitative migration companies.

The thinkers and promoters of heimin migration were nearly unanimous in their Malthusian interpretation of Japan's demographic trends. Like the shizoku expansionists in the previous decades, they appreciated Japan's rapid population growth as a sign of swelling national strength. At the same time, the archipelago's incapacity to accommodate this growing population made overseas migration both necessary and unavoidable. The heimin expansionists also integrated the logic of Malthusian expansionism into specific criticisms against Japan's existing political and social order. Either sympathizers of the labor movement or outright socialists, they were also influenced by Protestant Christianity. They did not seek to fundamentally alter the structural foundations of the nation but strove for reconciliation and reformation, avoiding serious conflict rather than promoting it. Migration to the United States became a key component in their respective blueprints for transforming Japan into a commoner-centered nation and empire.

Different agendas of nation/empire building and different practical approaches shaped the heimin promoters' interpretation of Japanese demography and the meaning of migration to America in divergent ways. The following paragraphs offer an analysis of the thoughts of three leading promoters – Katayama Sen, Abe Isoo, and Shimanuki Hyōdayū. During this wave of migration movement, each of them championed a specific vision about how migration would transform Japan into a heimin nation and empire.

Katayama Sen, a renowned leader of Japan's socialist movement in the early twentieth century, followed the classic path of a struggling student in his own youth. He migrated to the United States in 1884 and worked to pay for his education. Having joined the socialist cause while in America, he returned to Japan right after the First Sino-Japanese War. He was a vanguard of the fledgling labor movement, working to organize labor unions and demanding improved working conditions and better pay for workers. From 1901 to 1907, he published a number of books and numerous articles in the mouthpiece of labor movement in Japan, *Labor World* (*Rōdō Sekai*), and beyond. In these writings he urged the common youth to migrate to the United States, offering them guidance through every step of the migration process, from how to circumvent governmental restriction to exploring job options and educational opportunities in America. To put his ideas into practice, he also established the Association for Migration to the United States (*Tobei Kyōkai*) and provided firsthand assistance to the migrants.

The existing scholarship has generally treated Katayama Sen's promotion of migration and his socialist career as separate from each other, but his initiative in American migration was crucial to understanding his approach to the socialist movement in Japan at the turn of the twentieth century. Katayama believed that overpopulation within the archipelago had partially enabled class-based exploitation. The rapid growth of population caused domestic inflation, an increase in landless peasants, and rising unemployment.[39] The shortage of food and jobs forced the struggling working class to accept jobs with extremely low payment. Katayama argued that the government's restriction on migration served only the interests of the rich: it was aimed to confine the working-class young men within the country, where opportunities for education and employment were scarce, so that the rich could better take advantage of this condition to exploit them.[40]

Katayama had little trust in the state, and his eventual goal for the labor movement was not to build a socialist society centered around the governmental power.[41] However, he did share his contemporary Japanese socialists' conservative stance, seeking to bridge the social gap not through revolution but by promoting ways for the working class to help themselves. While the formation of labor unions would strengthen the working class in general and put laborers in a better position vis-à-vis their employers, migrating to the United States, Katayama believed, would help them to escape capitalist exploitation in Japan altogether.

For Katayama and other migration promoters of the day, everything in the United States stood in glaring contrast to the miserable sociopolitical conditions in Japan. What's more, with what he described as the vast, empty, and unexplored land on its West Coast, the United States could easily accommodate hundreds of thousands of immigrants from Japan.[42] Katayama further idealized the United States as the model of a socialist nation, a place where the role of labor was highly respected and the laborers were well paid. American labor

---

[39] "Tobe no Kōjiki," *Shakai Shugi* 7, no. 12 (May 18, 1903): 23–24.
[40] "Kokumin no Katsuro," *Rōdō Sekai* 6, no. 16 (September 23, 1902): 16.
[41] Sumiya Kimio, *Katayama Sen, Kindai Nihon no Shisōka*, vol. 3 (Tokyo: Tokyo Daigaku Shuppankai, 1967), 84.
[42] "Tobe no Kōjiki," 24.

unions were strong and their interests were protected by politicians and intellectuals. As a result, the United States was a nation where common people could make their own way by honest labor and succeed with a spirit of self-help. Japanese mass media of the day also portrayed rich American businessmen as sympathetic figures – unlike the selfish and bloodsucking entrepreneurs in Japan, American businessmen treated their employees well. They celebrated rags-to-riches success stories of Andrew Carnegie and Cornelius Vanderbilt as examples of not only self-made men but also those of kind philanthropists.[43]

While Katayama saw assisting heimin youth to migrate to the United States as a way to fight the state's oppression of the working class, the prominent social reformer and politician Abe Isoo, on the other hand, believed that the Japanese government should take the lead in guiding migration to the United States. In contrast to Katayama, who distrusted the government, Abe believed that the welfare state was key to the formation of a socialist nation. Abe agreed with Katayama that overpopulation worsened class exploitation and exacerbated Japan's social problems; however, he argued that the condition of overpopulation meant there was a pressing need for state-centered socialist reforms.[44] He urged the government to take up the responsibility to improve the livelihood of common people. Migration was an effective way to provide employment and educational opportunities to members in a society plagued by overpopulation and inflation, thus the government should lift its restriction on migration and encourage the commoners to migrate overseas by providing both guidance and subsidization.[45]

While Katayama and Abe represented two divergent perspectives on the role of the Japanese government in their socialist visions of nation building, Shimanuki Hyōdayū emphasized the importance of Christianity in his blueprint for Japan's future. A Protestant priest and an enthusiast supporter of the Salvation Army's socialist approach to evangelicalism, Shimanuki saw social philanthropy and Christianity-based moral reform as two sides of the same coin.[46] While sharing other socialists' concerns about social inequality and poverty in Japan, he sought to combine materialistic solution with spiritual salvation. He established the Tokyo Labor Society (Tokyo Rōdō Kai) in 1897, later renamed as the Japanese Striving Society (Nippon Rikkō Kai). This organization was aimed at providing both financial aid and moral suasion to struggling students, whom he saw as the future of the nation.[47]

---

[43] Azuma, *Between Two Empires*, 24–25; Kinmonth, *Self-Made Man in Meiji Japanese Thought*, 264–265.
[44] Abe Isoo, "Byō Teki Shakai," *Shakai Shugi* 7, no. 8 (March 18, 1903): 4.
[45] Abe Isoo, "Seinen no Tameni Kaigai Tokō no To o Hiraku Beshi," *Shakai Shugi* 8, no. 4 (February 18, 1904): 4–7.
[46] "Kyūseigun o Ronzu," *Kyūsei* 1, no. 5 (July 1895): 1–11.
[47] Shimanuki Hyōdayū, *Rikkō Kai to wa Nan Zo Ya* (Tokyo: Keiseisha, 1911), 121.

Figure 3.2 This is a symbol of the Striving Society that appeared in 1905. It connected the words of American migration (tobei), work-study (kugaku), success (seikō), and aspiration (risshi) together around the concept of striving (rikkō) at the center. *Rikkō* (*Striving*) 3, no. 1 (January 1, 1905): 1.

Returning from a trip to the United States in 1901, Shimanuki was convinced that migration abroad, especially to the United States, was an effective way to realize his goal of national salvation.[48] Describing Korea as a hopeless and dying country, he warned that Japan was on the verge of a similar crisis. Overpopulation in Japan not only had enlarged the social gap and caused poverty but also would lead to a decline of the national spirit. Japan would follow the way of Korea if its young men refused to seek solutions abroad.[49] The United States was a country with vast, empty lands as well as many job opportunities. What's more, it was the center of both Western civilization and Christianity. A move to the United States would both lift the Japanese youth out

[48] Ibid., 71–72.   [49] "Rikkō Hyōron," *Kyūsei* 6, no. 87 (January 1, 1907): 1.

of poverty and save their soul by converting them to Christianity. Shimanuki referred to this process as "spiritual and physical salvation" (*reiniku kyūsai*), a phrase that became the Striving Society's enduring motto. This dual salvation of the common youth, he believed, would lead to the eventual salvation of the nation.[50]

Differing understanding of the predicament of the heimin class shaped the agendas of these three migration promoters in divergent ways. However, as all three were converts to Protestant Christianity and at times spoke together at public events in support of labor movement in Japan, their ideas had definite points of convergence. On their global map of Japanese expansion, the United States was no doubt the most desirable destination. In their minds, Taiwan, the Korean Peninsula, and Manchuria, areas controlled by or under the influence of Japan's expanding empire, were already densely occupied by their native peoples. The local labor costs were generally low; thus it only made sense for entrepreneurs to move to these territories. The United States, on the other hand, was the ideal destination for the common youth because its labor market was favorable to the Japanese.

Yet like their shizoku counterparts in earlier decades, these heimin migration advocates did not see migration merely as a form of poverty relief. They believed that their project would mold migrants into model imperial subjects and trail-blazers of expansion.[51] It only made sense, then, that migration should be a selective process. Though these advocates professed to be speaking for the working class, they nevertheless opposed temporary labor migration (*dekasegi*). Japanese temporary laborers usually made their way to the United States through migration companies or labor contractors; as most of them came from an impoverished rural background, they aimed only to make some quick money within a short period before returning to Japan. In the eyes of heimin expansionists, these temporary laborers had a dangerous resemblance to the "uncivilized" Chinese immigrants because they lacked in everything from education and social manners to long-term commitment.[52] They blamed these temporary laborers for sabotaging Japan's national image aboard and causing anti-Japanese sentiment in the United States, leading the Japanese race down an ignominious path that might end in racial exclusion as the Chinese had suffered.

Those who *did* qualify for the migration project were the common youth, endowed with a certain amount of financial resources and education and who had a strong will for personal success and ambition for national expansion. The expansionists urged working, as laboring would be only their first step to starting their life in the United States, one that would allow them to achieve

---

[50] Shimanuki, *Rikkō Kai to wa Nan Zo Ya*, 65–66.   [51] Azuma, *Between Two Empires*, 25.
[52] This was in response to the Chinese exclusion in 1882 as well as the passage of the US Immigration Act of 1891 that excluded temporary labor migrants in general, mainly targeting Asians and Southern Europeans.

financial independence. Their personal growth, moreover, would not end there: Katayama expected these youth to replicate his own experience by pursuing higher education,[53] Shimanuki wanted their materialistic achievement to lead them to Christianity,[54] and Abe believed that life in the United States would positively influence these Japanese subjects due to their physical proximity to Western civilization.[55]

While temporary laborers were considered undesirable and were likened to the excluded Chinese immigrants, the desirable candidates were expected to be colonial migrants (*shokumin*) with a commitment to long-term settlement. Heimin expansionists wanted them to build permanent communities in the United States as a part of Japan's global expansion in the mode of British settler colonialism. They hoped that Japanese immigrants would be able to establish themselves as equal members of American society, thereby gaining political rights and economic benefits.

In the heimin expansionists' blueprint for Japanese community building in the United States, the role of women was as important as that of men. Since the end of the 1880s, Japanese prostitutes had begun to arrive on the American West Coast, driven by their own poverty at home and the demand for commercial sex by the predominately male Japanese immigrant population across the Pacific. The expansionists condemned these prostitutes for bringing shame to the Japanese empire just like the low-class temporary Japanese laborers.[56] Katayama believed that prostitution was a result of the lack of education. To represent the civilized image of the empire abroad, Katayama urged that instead of prostitutes, more well-educated Japanese women should migrate to the United States. For Katayama, the arrival of educated women was also crucial for Japanese American community building, because he believed that the immoral behaviors committed by Japanese men in the United States, such as gambling and frequenting brothels, were due to the lack of women. These women of good nature and culture would thus improve the ethics of Japanese American communities in general by regulating the mind and behavior of Japanese men.[57] From a similar perspective, Abe Isoo called for a governmental ban on the migration of prostitutes to the United States and the formation of special organizations to facilitate Japanese women's trans-Pacific migration and their adjustment to the new life in the United States.[58]

[53] Katayama Sen, *Tsuzuki Tobei Annai* (Tokyo: Tobei Kyōkai, 1902), 1–4, in *Shoki Zai Hokubei Nihonjin no Kiroku, Hokubeihen*, vol. 44, ed. Okuizumi Eizaburō (Tokyo: Bunsei Shoin, 2006).
[54] Shimanuki Hyōdayū, "Shokan Nisoku," *Kyūsei* 6, no. 92 (1910): 6.
[55] Abe, *Hokubei no Shin Nihon*, 120–124.
[56] Katō Tokijirō, "Kokumin no Hatten," *Shakai Shugi* 8, no. 9 (July 3, 1904): 248–249.
[57] Katayama Sen, "Seinen Joshi no Tobei," *Shakai Shugi* 8, no. 1 (January 3, 1904): 17–19.
[58] Abe, *Hokubei no Shin Nihon*, 68.

The migrants' success in the United States, in the minds of the expansionists, would both increase Japan's political influence and stimulate the Japanese economy by enhancing bilateral trade. In addition to bringing economic benefits to Japan, heimin migration to the United States also provided ideological justification for the empire's expansion in Asia. Abe Isoo, for example, described Japan as "the broker of civilization," buying it from the United States and then selling it to China and Korea; it was thus natural for the Japanese to hold a base at the Western end of the North American continent.[59] While the United States had a mission of bringing the blessing of civilization to Japan, Abe argued, Japan had a similar obligation to spread the same blessing to the Asian continent.[60] Shimanuki Hyōdayū also believed that the migrants would be made into better Japanese subjects once they moved to the United States and converted to Christianity; thus migration was the first step in the empire's mission to transplant progress to East Asia.[61] To Shimanuki, who began his religious career as a missionary in Korea, the philanthropic assistance he provided to the struggling students was a way to achieve his ultimate goal of evangelizing Asia.[62] The prosperity of the Japanese communities in the United States, in terms of both economic success and spiritual salvation, was crucial in justifying Japan's acceptance of the global hierarchy arranged according to the degree of Westernization and legitimizing the empire's colonial expansion in Asia.

The Decline of Japanese Labor Migration to the United States

The heimin migration discourse peaked around the time of the Russo-Japanese War. In the minds of the Japanese expansionists, a victory over the Russians would give Japan yet another bargaining chip during its negotiation with the Western powers for global expansion. Foreseeing Japan's victory, an article on *Striving* (*Rikkō*), one of the official journals of the Japanese Striving Society, predicted that the war would bring a great opportunity to boost Japanese migration to the United States. The author argued that Japan's victory would end anti-Japanese discrimination in the United States because the Americans would finally recognize Japan as a strong power and treat the Japanese immigrants with respect.[63] A few days after the war ended, Abe published his most important work for the promotion of America-bound migration, urging Japan's

---

[59] Ibid., 124.   [60] Ibid., 121.
[61] "Tōyō Dendō Kaishi no Issaku," *Kyūsei*, no. 1 (March 1895): 2.
[62] Shimanuki, *Rikkō Kai to wa Nan Zo Ya*, 67. His ambition of evangelizing East Asia also led him to complete a thesis at the Tohoku Gakuin University, Department of Theology, titled "Christian Missions in East Asia and Poverty Relief," before embarking on his migration campaigns. Shimanuki, *Rikkō Kai to wa Nan Zo Ya*, 49.
[63] "Shin Kichōsha no Danwa," *Rikkō* 2, no. 6 (May 25, 1904): 2.

government and social leaders to work together in order to build a "new Japan in North America" (*hokubei no shin nihon*). He assured his readers that the US government, fearful of a powerful Japan's reprisal, would not dare to exclude Japanese immigrants. Moreover, as Japan had now achieved effective hegemony in East Asia, the empire could claim its own version of the Monroe Doctrine and exclude the interests of the United States from Manchuria and the Korean Peninsula.[64] Such optimism led to a sharp increase in the number of Japanese migrants to the United States after the Russo-Japanese War: the numbers of Japanese who migrated to the US mainland from Japan and Hawai'i in 1906 and 1907 more than doubled from their prewar levels.[65]

The eventual fate of Japanese migration to the United States, however, did not bear out such optimism. Contrary to Japanese expectations, the Russo-Japanese War triggered an unprecedented wave of Japanese exclusion campaigns in the United States. Japan's defeat of Russia ironically served as fresh ammo for the racial exclusionists who called for keeping the uncivilized and aggressive Japanese out of the white men's world. The decision by the municipal government of San Francisco in 1906 to exclude Japanese children from public schools demonstrated that anti-Japanese sentiment had gained support from the policymakers in the Golden State. In September 1907, a long article appeared in the *New York Times* titled "Japan's Invasion of the White Man's World," describing the Japanese as inassimilable intruders into American society. The Malthusian interpretation of Japanese demography, cited by the Japanese expansionists to justify their migration agendas, was used by the article as a reason to exclude the Japanese. It argued that having failed to export migrants to Hokkaido, Taiwan, Korea, and Manchuria, Japan was now sending its surplus population to America, the white men's domain. The Russo-Japanese War, the article warned, showed that Japan was a dangerous threat. If given the opportunity, it might invade America by force. The Japanese immigrants who refused to assimilate into US society would serve as Japan's vanguards in such an invasion.[66]

This lengthy report showed that anti-Japanese sentiment had spread beyond the American West Coast and gained a nationwide audience. Its political influence resulted in the Gentlemen's Agreement between Japan and the United States that came into effect in 1908, in accordance with which the Japanese government voluntarily stopped issuing new passports to those who planned to migrate to the United States as laborers. In exchange, the Roosevelt

[64] Abe, *Hokubei no Shin Nihon*, 93.
[65] This claim is based on data collected in Tachikawa Kenji, "Meiji Kōhanki no Tobei Netsu: Amerika no Ryūkō," *Shirin* 69, no. 3 (May 1, 1986): 74.
[66] "Japan's Invasion of the White Man's World," *New York Times*, September 22, 1907, 4, cited from Kumei Teruko, *Gaikokujin o Meguru Shakaishi: Kindai Amerika to Nihonjin Imin* (Tokyo: Yūsankaku, 1995), 112.

administration promised to not impose official restrictions on Japanese immigration and also managed to remove the ban on Japanese immigrant children from attending public schools in San Francisco through a negotiation with local officials.

Based on the Gentlemen's Agreement, the Japanese government enacted a near-complete ban on migration from Japan to the US mainland.[67] There were only a few exceptions to this ban, including remigrants, family members of migrants already in the United States, as well as government-approved agricultural settlers. As a result, the main body of trans-Pacific migration became the so-called picture brides, young women who entered the United States as the wives of Japanese immigrants already in the United States. They were urged to project a civilized image of the empire and foster Japanese community building in American society. The male-centered commonerist discourse of previous years, however, had died out due to this drastic policy change.

The Gentlemen's Agreement thus brought the decade-long wave of heimin migration to the United States to a sudden end. Hoping this unexpected roadblock would be quickly removed via diplomatic renegotiations, migration promoters continued to mobilize their countrymen with rosy images of the United States. However, the demises of *Amerika* (the successor of *Tobei Zasshi*) and *Tobei Shinpō* in 1909, respectively the mouthpieces of Katayama and Shimanuki's migration campaigns,[68] marked the total collapse of such an illusion.

The end of labor migration to the United States mirrored the decline of heimin expansionism in the late 1900s. The Gentlemen's Agreement forced Katayama and Abe to give up their plans of turning Japan into a heimin-centered nation and empire through migration. The powerful Hibiya Park rallies and riots between 1905 and 1908 also convinced them that making structural changes in domestic Japan was actually possible, though they disagreed completely as to how to bring these changes about – or indeed what these changes were.

Katayama began to follow a path similar to his radical comrade Kōtoku Shūsui. In 1909 he began to criticize the Christian churches in Japan for being

---

[67] A number of studies have provided insightful discussions of the Gentlemen's Agreement. Akira Iriye has examined the historical contexts of the enact of the Gentlemen's Agreement from the perspective of the imperial rivalry between the United States and the Japanese empire around the Pacific Rim. Iriye, *Pacific Estrangement*. Mitziko Sawada provides a history of Japan's emigration policy leading up to the Gentlemen's Agreement. Sawada, *Tokyo Life, New York Dreams*, 41–56. Jordan Sand has innovatively presented the flows and connections of ideas and people between Japan and the United States, the two Pacific empires, centered around the enactment of the Gentlemen's Agreement through a fragmented narrative. Jordan Sand, "Gentlemen's Agreement, 1908: Fragments for a Pacific History," *Representations* 107, no. 1 (Summer 2009): 91–127.
[68] Tachikawa, "Meiji Kōhanki no Tobei Netsu," 77.

dominated by the rich and thus lacking the initiative to solve the country's social and economic issues.[69] He abandoned his Christian faith and turned to materialist Marxism as the ultimate solution, seeking a more radical method to achieve his goals. He was arrested for leading a labor strike in Tokyo in 1911, the same year that Kōtoku Shūsui was executed for a failed plot to assassinate the Meiji Emperor. After being released, Katayama went to the United States again and took part in the labor movement in Japanese American communities. Inspired by the Bolshevik Revolution of 1917, he became a Leninist. He participated in the international communist movement and was eventually buried in the Kremlin.

Abe Isoo, on the other hand, continued to regard overpopulation as the central issue that blocked Japan's path to a better future. With the doors to the United States now shut, he turned to promoting contraception and played a key role in Japan's birth control and eugenic movement during the 1920s and 1930s. While the exclusionists in the United States taught the Japanese expansionists that migration to the white men's domain was impossible, it was another American, Margaret Sanger, who provided the Japanese with the "correct" solution to their "problem" of overpopulation. While the idea of birth control was introduced to the Japanese much earlier, it never gained nationwide support until Sanger visited Japan in 1922. Celebrated as the "Black Ship of Taishō,"[70] Sanger's speaking tour in Japan vested the advocates of birth control and eugenics in Japan with a degree of much-wanted legitimacy: progress and science.[71] In the year of Sanger's visit, Abe published the book *On Birth Control* (*Sanji Seigen Ron*) in which he turned away from his earlier criticism of capitalism and class-based exploitation. He now argued that overpopulation was the fundamental cause of social issues such as labor disputes, rural poverty, and gender inequality in Japan as well as the world at large. Contraception, accordingly, was the ultimate solution.[72]

However, Abe's agenda of population control was not simply aimed at reducing the birth rate. Abe, who subscribed to Sanger's idea of "more children from the fit, less from the unfit,"[73] had a clear eugenic teleology. He believed that the American exclusion of Japanese immigrants was caused by the migrants' undesirability,[74] and he called for improving the quality of the Japanese race by preventing the reproduction of the "unfit" who either had genetic flaws or did not possess enough resources. It was not uncontrolled

[69] Sumiya, *Katayama Sen, Kindai Nihon no Shisōka*, 186–187.
[70] Sabine Frühstück, *Colonizing Sex: Sexology and Social Control in Modern Japan* (Berkeley: University of California Press, 2003), 131.
[71] Abe Isoo saw Sanger as "the most well received woman in the world by Japanese men (foreign or native)." Frühstück, *Colonizing Sex*, 133.
[72] Abe Isoo, *Sanji Seigen Ron* (Tokyo: Jitsugyō no Nihon Sha, 1922), 110–170.
[73] Takeda, *Political Economy of Reproduction in Japan*, 65.
[74] Abe Isoo, "Imin to Kyōiku," *Yūben* 3, no. 8 (1912): 37–47.

population growth but the selective reproduction, coupled with quality control, that would lead Japan to success on the world stage.[75]

In the same year, Abe put his ideas into practice as the director of the Japanese Birth Control Study Society (Nihon Sanji Chōsetsu Kenkyūkai). Labor union leader Suzuki Bunji, whose moderate stance represented that of the labor movement in the 1920s and 1930s in general, became Abe's loyal supporter. Under what was insightfully defined by Andrew Gordon as "imperial democracy," Japan's labor unions at the time did not wish to pose radical challenges to the status quo. The labor movement sought to strengthen its political power by forming alliances with bourgeois parties; it celebrated imperial wars and expansion.[76] These moderate socialists and labor activists were soon joined by leading feminists and prominent physicians. Though they disagreed with each other on a multitude of issues, all of them considered eugenic-oriented contraception as an effective way to realize their social agendas. Together they constituted the main force of the birth control movement in Japan between the 1920s and 1930s.[77]

Conclusion

"Fighting with the Qing was fighting with the world."[78] Tokutomi's contemporary observation insightfully captured the fundamental changes the First Sino-Japanese War brought to Japanese expansionism: it ushered in the resurgence of Japanese migration to the United States and the rise of heimin expansionist discourse. This chapter has argued that the emergence of heimin as a sociopolitical force in Japan, stimulated by the First Sino-Japanese War, shifted the focus of migration-driven expansion from the declassed shizoku to working-class youth. The outcome of this war also convinced the Japanese of their racial superiority over the Chinese, creating an illusion among the expansionists that the Japanese, members of a civilized empire and a master race in their own right, could be treated by the Westerners as their equals. Buoyed by such optimism, they once again turned their gaze to the United States as the ideal destination for Japanese migration.

In 1907, Kōtoku Shūsui, a leader of Japan's socialist and anarchist movement, published the book *Commonerism* (*Heiminshugi*), outlining his political agenda for turning Japan into a nation of commoners. A pioneering critic of imperialism and a strong opponent of war and expansion, Kōtoku was on the very opposite end of the ideological spectrum from his contemporary Tokutomi Sōhō. Nevertheless, Kōtoku's vision of a heimin nation resembled Tokutomi's

---

[75] Abe, *Sanji Seigen Ron*, 81–82.
[76] Andrew Gordon, *Labor and Imperial Democracy in Prewar Japan* (Berkeley: University of California Press, 1991), 1–10.
[77] Frühstück, *Colonizing Sex*, 116–151.   [78] Tokutomi, *Dai Nihon Bōchō Ron*, 148.

own in terms of calling for the heimin to have political rights, adopting a sympathetic approach to the issue of working-class poverty, and celebrating historical progress.

As this chapter has shown, the leaders of Japan's socialist movement at the turn of the twentieth century became the loyal heirs of Tokutomi's heimin-centered nationalism and expansionism. They connected the pursuit of political rights for commoners with improving the economic conditions of the working class. The majority of the socialist leaders of the day did not adopt Kōtoku's revolutionary stance; they sought moderate ways to achieve their goals, ready to work with the political establishment and lending their support to imperial expansion.

In the first decade of the twentieth century, migration to the United States served as a way for socialists of different viewpoints to realize their particular blueprints of Japanese nation/empire building. As adherents of Malthusian expansionism, Katayama Sen, Abe Isoo, and Shimanuki Hyōdayū all blamed overpopulation for widening the social gap and causing poverty in Japan. Seeing the United States as a land of boundless wealth, a heaven of laborers, and the center of world civilization, they hoped migration to the United States would save Japan's working class from exploitation and poverty. Moreover, they envisioned that these migrants would be turned into model subjects who could fulfill the Japanese empire's own Manifest Destiny.

Racism on the other side of the Pacific led to the decline of Japanese labor migration to the United States at the end of the 1900s. While they subsequently followed divergent paths due to their different approaches to socialism, both Katayama Sen and Abe Isoo ceased their promotion of migration to the United States.[79] Shimanuki, however, continued to help young men to move to the United States via smuggling. Starting in the mid-1900s, reports on the Japanese Striving Society's members' expeditions to Korea, China, and Latin America began to appear in the society's official journals such as *Rikkō* and *Kyūsei*. While maintaining that the United States was the most ideal destination, Shimanuki began to encourage his followers to explore other parts of the world for migration purposes.[80]

The first decade of the twentieth century also witnessed a short-lived campaign of Japanese farmer migration in Texas. Like the labor migration to the US West Coast, the farmer migration was another campaign in the wave of heimin expansion. But different from the labor migration that was centered on the urban working class, the backbone of this campaign of migration was Japanese farmers, the nonprivileged but politically conscious rural commoners. This

---

[79] Though Abe did not completely stop supporting migration until 1924, he became much less vocal on migration promotion since the Gentlemen's Agreement went into effect.
[80] Shimanuki, *Rikkō Kai to wa Nan Zo Ya*, 173.

Figure 3.3 This is a symbol of the Striving Society that appeared in 1909.
Compared to the one from 1905, "colonial migration" (*shokumin*) has
replaced "American migration" (*tobei*). This demonstrates that after the
enactment of the Gentlemen's Agreement the Striving Society no longer
considered the United States as the only ideal destination for migration and
began to explore the possibility of migration to other parts of the world.
Kyūsei 5, no. 81 (November 1909): 1.

campaign was also a joint product of the anti-Japanese sentiment in the
American West and the rise of the Japanese agrarianism at the turn of the
twentieth century. Chapter 4 examines the Texas migration campaign and
explains the significance of this short-lived campaign in the history of
Japanese migration-driven expansion.

4   Farming Rice in Texas: The Paradigm Shift

In 1906, naturalist author Shimazaki Tōson published his first novel, *The Broken Commandment* (*Hakai*). The story explored the predicament of Segawa Ushimatsu, a schoolteacher in Japan coming from an outcast (*burakumin*) background. Segawa was struggling between the necessity to hide his burakumin identity in order to live a normal life and his desire to challenge the social prejudices faced by the outcast community. He eventually announced his burakumin identity in public, only to realize that there was no end in sight for his struggles against discrimination. By pure chance, an exhausted Segawa learned about an opportunity for him to migrate to Texas to embark upon a career in agriculture. The novel ended with Segawa departing for Texas in an attempt to escape from his hopeless struggles in Japan once and for all.

Segawa's decision to migrate across the Pacific testified to the image of the United States as the proverbial land of opportunity in the discourse of overseas migration in Japan at the time.[1] The United States as a country was indeed seen as a land of egalitarianism that provided boundless opportunities by ambitious but underprivileged Japanese men. However, it was telling that Shimazaki, the author of the novel, specifically chose Texas to be the protagonist's promised land of racial equality. This setup revealed that contemporary Japanese writers and observers were well aware of the existence of anti-Japanese racism on the American West Coast.[2] Thus it was Texas, not the states on the West Coast, that was portrayed as a utopia with no prejudice.

Equally significant was the fact that Segawa ultimately decided to pursue a career in farming. This move away from industrial labor toward agriculture mirrored the beginning of a significant transformation of Japan's migration-

---

[1] In her salient study of the trans-Pacific encounters of *burakumin* migrants in North America, Andrea Geiger has pointed out that Segawa's story demonstrates that immigration to the North American West was considered by Japanese outcaste communities as a way to escape caste-based discrimination in their homeland. Geiger, *Subverting Exclusion*, 15.

[2] Joseph Hankins's anthropological analysis of Burakumin identity points out that that Texas, a major state in animal farming in the United States, had historically been considered a place that valued, not discriminated against, human involvement in meat production. Joseph D. Hankins, *Working Skin: Making Leather, Making a Multicultural Japan* (Berkeley: University of California Press, 2014), xi.

based expansionist discourse. While the United States remained the most attractive migration destination in the minds of the heimin expansionists, they were losing interest in labor migration. They believed that because Japanese migrant laborers had no intention to stay for long or to contribute to the local society, their migration could only incite anti-Japanese sentiment in the United States. Instead, they assumed, common but ambitious Japanese men could find their footing in America through farming, and such a long-term career would demonstrate to white men that these Meiji subjects were indeed the salt of the earth.

The promotion of agricultural migration to Texas was not only a response to anti-Japanese campaigns on the American West Coast but also a result of the growing tension between the agricultural sector and the industry-centered model of development of the Meiji empire at the turn of the twentieth century. Alarmed by Japan's loss of self-sufficiency in rice supply and increasing concentration of farmland, agrarian thinkers argued that it was important to protect agriculture as the foundation of the Japanese economy and the owner-farmers as the backbone of the nation. Identifying the issue of overpopulation as the main cause for the crises in the Japanese countryside, agrarian expansionists proposed for common farmers to migrate overseas; they believed such a move would both stimulate Japanese agricultural productivity at home and plant the root of expansion for the empire abroad.

This chapter examines the origin, development, and demise of the short-lived campaign of Japanese farmer migration to Texas in the 1900s. Similar to the movement of labor migration to the United States that took place around the same time, the call for agricultural migration to Texas was also grounded in the discourse of personal success, inviting the common Japanese to become self-made men through migration. Though it was a part of the heimin migration wave, the Texas campaign marked the beginning of a paradigm shift in Japanese migration-driven expansion from labor to agriculture. Subsequently, the failure of this project prompted Japanese expansionists to cast their gaze farther south, paving the way for Japanese farmer migration into South America in the decades to come.

The Debate on the Role of Agriculture

Both laborers and farmers were key components of heimin, the class of commoners with no inherited privilege in Meiji Japan. The growth of their presence in the public discourse heralded the decline of shizoku's political influence. In the eyes of heimin activists, there was a substantial overlap between the categories of farmers and laborers, as migrants from the country-side constituted the main body of the burgeoning working class in the cities. The majority of migrants who made their way overseas by following the teaching of heimin expansionists like Tokutomi Sōhō, Katayama Sen, and Shimanuki Hyōdayū were young men who had grown up in the countryside.

However, the respective rise of laborers and farmers as political forces revealed different social changes within the Japanese society. The calls for labor migration reflected the growth of the Japanese urban working class at the end of the nineteenth century. The emergence of farmers in the discourse of Japanese expansionism, on the other hand, was a result of agriculture's shrinking importance in an increasingly industrialized empire.

In the minds of Meiji empire builders, the agriculture sector was an essential contributor to Japan's quest of modernization but not a direct beneficiary. The passage of the Land Tax Reform Law of 1873 legalized land ownership, allowing lands to be freely bought and sold. The government's land survey that came with the law registered a substantial amount of new land to be taxed, and the government's land tax income increased by 48 percent.[3] For most of the Meiji period, the agricultural sector remained the biggest source of the state's income, which in turn was used to finance industrial development. The privatization and marketization of land resulted in a concentration of landownership. The Matsukata Deflation in 1881 accelerated this process by causing a sharp drop in the prices of rice and silk. As a result, between 1884 and 1886, 70 to 80 percent of farming households in the Japanese countryside were in debt.[4] Many owner-farmers had no choice but to sell their land in order to pay off debts. After losing their land, they either stayed in the countryside as tenant farmers or migrated to urban areas to seek employment as wage laborers. Japan in the last two decades of the nineteenth century thus experienced both a rapid shrinkage of the owner-farmer population and an increase in landlord-tenant disputes.

The outbreak of the Sino-Japanese War dealt yet another blow to Japanese agriculture. The war boosted industrial development and lured even more people away from the countryside. The growing urban population and the rising standard of living turned Japan from a rice exporter into a rice importer. From the late 1890s, rice from Taiwan and later the Korean Peninsula began to flow into the Japanese market.[5] Shrinkage of the owner-farmer population and growing insufficiency in rice production received immediate attention from Japanese thinkers. Figures from both inside and outside of the policymaking circle warned the nation about the importance of farming and sought to improve the position of agriculture in the national economy.

---

[3] Thomas R. H. Havens, *Farm and Nation in Modern Japan: Agrarian Nationalism, 1870–1940* (Princeton: Princeton University Press, 1974), 34.
[4] Steve Ericson, "'Matsukata Deflation' Reconsidered: Financial Stabilization and Japanese Exports in a Global Depression, 1881–85," *Journal of Japanese Studies* 40, no. 1 (2014): 12–16.
[5] Havens, *Farm and Nation*, 90.

Two schools of thought emerged at this moment. Both of them emphasized the centrality of agriculture, but each had a different blueprint for Japan's national destiny in relation to the West. One school of thought was represented by Yokoi Tokiyoshi, a professor of agronomy at Tokyo Imperial University. In an 1897 essay titled "Agricultural Centralism" ("Nōhonshugi"), Yokoi launched a radical attack on the early Meiji principle of national development centering on industrialization and Westernization. The Western model of development was destined to fail, he argued, because its one-sided industrial development would inevitably widen the social gap. With increasingly flagrant disparity between the different segments of society, Western societies would eventually head down a path of revolution and chaos. Due to its blind imitation of the Western model, Yokoi believed, Japan's industrialization was also being built on the sacrifice of the agricultural population. Attached to the soil, farmers were naturally the most patriotic subjects and most qualified soldiers of the empire. Yet as urbanization drained both human and material resources from the countryside, these farmers were losing their land and becoming mired in poverty. To avert potential chaos, Yokoi argued, the government should make the development of agriculture – instead of industry – its top priority.[6]

The other school of thought was represented by Nitobe Inazō, the founder of the School of Japanese Colonial Policy Studies. In 1898, a year after Yokoi published his essay, Nitobe authored *On the Foundation of Agriculture* (*Nōgyō Honron*).[7] This book-length study was not as widely known as some of his other works, but it profoundly influenced the evolutionary course of Japanese colonialism and expansionism in the following decades. The book, like Yokoi's essay, emphasized agriculture's role as the very foundation of the empire. While sharing some of Yokoi's criticisms about the government's neglect of domestic agriculture, Nitobe firmly believed that Japan was destined to follow the path of the West and become an industrialized empire. Unlike Yokoi, Nitobe drew the conclusion that agriculture was not to replace industry as the top policy priority. Instead, Nitobe called for more attention to the development of agriculture in order to secure Japan's progress in industrialization.

Nitobe criticized the Western European powers such as the United Kingdom and France for achieving rapid industrialization at the price of sacrificing their agricultural sectors. As a result, he argued, the European empires eventually lost their agricultural self-sufficiency; they had no choice but to meet their domestic need for agricultural products through importation from their overseas colonies.

---

[6] For a more detailed analysis of Yokoi's essay, refer to Stephen Vlastos, "Agrarianism without Tradition: The Radical Critique of Prewar Japanese Modernity," in *Mirror of Modernity: Invented Traditions of Modern Japan*, ed. Stephen Vlastos (Berkeley: University of California Press, 1998), 82–83. Also see Havens, *Farm and Nation*, 98–110.

[7] Nitobe Inazō, *Nōgyō Honron*, 6th ed. (Tokyo: Shōkabō, 1905). The first edition of the book was published in 1898.

Nitobe urged Japan to avoid falling into the same trap, as agriculture was the empire's very foundation on which all other achievements – such as cultural progress, urbanization, and the improvement of public health – could be built. It was thus imperative for the Empire of Japan to maintain its agricultural self-sufficiency.

Nitobe's interest in agriculture, stemming from his study at Sapporo Agricultural College in Hokkaido and his personal connection with Tsuda Sen's Association of Studying Agriculture (Gakunō Sha), was infused with both Malthusian expansionism and colonial ambition. He believed that rapid population growth was essential for Japan's development as a civilized and expanding empire, and a flourishing agricultural sector was the key to keeping the population growing because it guaranteed sufficient food supply.[8] The protagonists in Nitobe's blueprint for Japanese empire building were no longer the shizoku of yesterday or the bourgeoning urban working class, but the owner-farmers (*jisakunō*) from the countryside. Working in the field on a daily basis, Nitobe argued, the owner-farmers were healthier and physically stronger than the urban dwellers and would make better soldiers for the empire. Moreover, they also enjoyed a higher fertility rate and longer life expectancy than the urban residents.[9] As both the primary food supplier for the nation and the biggest source of manpower for the imperial army, they should be protected from falling into poverty and performing excessive labor.[10]

Nitobe's agenda was better received than Yokoi's because most national leaders both within and outside of the government still saw Western-style industrial imperialism as the example to emulate for Japan. Within ten years after its original publication, *On the Foundation of Agriculture* was reprinted five times. Nitobe's idea of emphasizing the fundamental role of agriculture in Japan's development into an industrial empire also won him many supporters and converts among the thinkers and doers of Japanese expansion. *On Japanese Agricultural Centralism* (*Nihon Nōhon Ron*), authored by agronomist Hiraoka Hikotarō four years after the publication of Nitobe's book, for example, wholeheartedly accepted Nitobe's notion of agriculture as the foundation of Japan's national progress. It further offered several ways to reverse the agricultural sector's decline, including lowering the land tax, imposing protective tariff on imported agricultural products, as well as modernizing farming management techniques and equipment.[11] More importantly, Hiraoka also proposed the migration of Japanese farmers overseas. The migration and resettlement of a certain amount of rural population overseas, he argued, would speed up Japan's agricultural mechanization process and increase agricultural productivity. The growth of overseas Japanese communities would

[8] Ibid., 186–187.   [9] Ibid., 148.   [10] Ibid., 178.
[11] Hiraoka Hikotarō, *Nihon Nōhon Ron* (Tokyo: Yasui Ukichi, 1902), 36–53.

also increase the export of Japanese agricultural products abroad.[12] As a leading thinker and professor of colonial studies, Nitobe also trained and influenced a group of colonial thinkers. Among his protégés were Tōgō Minoru and Ōkawadaira Takamitsu, whose works demonstrated the impacts of both the Russo-Japanese War and the rise of anti-Japanese sentiment in the United States. As the following pages demonstrate, their writings marked the beginning of farmer-centered Japanese expansionism.

Japanese Exclusion in the United States and the Emergence of Farmer Migration

At the turn of the twentieth century, while Japanese intellectuals were trying to grapple with the empire's agricultural issues, anti-Japanese sentiment in the United States also began to swell. Japanese laborers, who constituted the majority of the overall Japanese immigrant population of the day, became the primary targets of anti-Japanese campaigns in America. These laborers were seen in the same light as the Chinese immigrants who were already excluded; they were labeled as lacking in social manners and education, and they were accused of being reluctant to contribute to the local community due to a lack of commitment to the new life.

Anti-Japanese sentiment on the American West Coast grew even stronger after Japan's victory in the Russo-Japanese War, when the exclusionists began to link the threat of the racially inferior Japanese immigrants to the American labor market with the threat that the Empire of Japan potentially posed to American national security. Japanese mass media paid close attention to the anti-Japanese campaigns on the American West Coast and expressed indignation toward the United States after the agreement was sealed. In June 1907, a popular journal of satire cartoons named *Tokyo Puck* published a special issue titled "The Issue of Anger toward the United States" ("Taibei Haffun Gō"), criticizing Americans' hypocrisy by juxtaposing their self-professed principles of humanism, justice, and freedom with the reality of American immigration restrictions, racism, and corrupted politics. Novels imagining a war between Japan and the United States, ending with total victory for Japan, also began to appear in 1907,[13] allowing the Japanese public to take a measure of fictional revenge against the hypocritical Americans.

While anger and vengefulness were the mass media's general response to American anti-Japanese sentiment, Japanese intellectuals, particularly those who were trained in Western colonial theories, sought to reconcile Japanese

---

[12] Ibid., 56–57.

[13] Okabayashi Nobuo, "Jinkō Mondai to Imin Ron: Meiji Nihon no Fuan to Yokubō," *Dōshisha Hōgaku* 64, no. 8 (March 2013): 153–154.

exclusion in the United States with the image of the United States as a righteous leader of the West that Japan sought to follow. They faithfully accepted the logic of the white exclusionists and saw temporary labor migration as an undesirable model of Japanese expansion in the United States. The rise of agricultural centralism and growing landlord-tenant disputes in Japan naturally drew their attention to agricultural migration as an alternative.

Malthusian expansionism provided an easy solution to Japanese thinkers who lamented the agricultural sector's decline while maintaining the necessity for industrial and commercial primacy. They attributed the fundamental cause of rural depression to overpopulation in the Japanese countryside, which in turn had led to an overall decline in agricultural productivity. The fact that Japan lost its main staple food self-sufficiency was seen as damning evidence of this overpopulation crisis.[14] Based on this assumption, they argued that the Japanese agricultural sector could be revived by relocating the surplus rural population overseas with no major changes to the existing economic structure of the country.

Two studies on colonialism that appeared right after the Russo-Japanese War marked the beginning of this shift in intellectual thought.[15] Both *Nihon Imin Ron* (*On Japanese Emigration*) and *Nihon Shokumin Ron* (*On Japanese Colonial Migration*) were written under the auspices of Nitobe Inazō. Authored respectively by Ōkawadaira Takamitsu in 1905 and Tōgō Minoru in 1906, these works were among the earliest original studies of colonialism by Japanese scholars, who previously had relied heavily on the existing colonial studies done by Western scholars. Produced during the formative years of the colonial policy studies in Japan (*Shokumin Seisaku Kenkyū*), these two works laid the foundation for the discourse of expansionism both in and beyond Japanese academic circles in the decades to come.

For both Ōkawadaira and Tōgō, the anti-Japanese campaigns in the United States served as lessons for Japan's further expansion. They believed that in order to avoid being excluded again in the future, Japanese emigrants should do away with their sojourning mentality (*dekasegi konsei*) and aim to settle abroad permanently. Under the sojourning mentality, the previous Japanese migrants

[14] Yoshimura, *Hokubei Tekisasushū no Beisaku*, 10–11. The official English title of the book is *The Cultivation of Rice and Other Crops in Texas*.
[15] Ōkawadaira Takamitsu, *Nihon Imin Ron* (Tokyo: Jōbudō, 1905) and Tōgō Minoru, *Nihon Shokumin Ron* (Tokyo: Bunbudō, 1906). These two books were not the first to propose agricultural migration as a remedy to the decline of Japanese agriculture. *On Japanese Agricultural Centralism* (*Nihon Nōhon Ron*), authored by agronomist Hiraoka Hikotarō in 1902, already suggested migration to Hokkaido and Taiwan as a way to revive agriculture in Japan. Calls for agricultural migration to Korea appeared in the public media in the same year. See Kimura Kenji, "Nichiro Sengo Kaigai Nōgyō Imin no Rekishiteki Chii," in *Nihon Jinushi Sei to Kindai Sonraku*, ed. Abiko Rin (Tokyo: Sōfūsha, 1994), 155. But the works of Tōgō and Ōkawadaira were the first book-length studies, authored by members of a think tank on Japanese colonialism, to place agricultural migration at the center of Japan's expansion.

to the United States planned to stay overseas only temporarily; after they saved a certain amount of wealth, they would return home. As a result, the authors asserted, they were unwilling to assimilate into American culture or make any contribution to their host country. Their self-isolation from the mainstream society became a major cause of anti-Japanese sentiment. The solution to this problem, Ōkawadaira and Tōgō argued, was for Japanese emigrants to prepare to resettle their lives abroad permanently; they should consider the host country their home and actively contribute to its development. Only in this way could they be accepted as equal members in the host country and secure new citizenship, thereby gaining voting rights and the ability to forestall any anti-Japanese policy in the future. Taking it a step further, they would also be able to make long-term contributions to Japan by swaying the politics of the host country and facilitating bilateral trade relations between the two states.[16]

Aside from dictating the appropriate mind-set for migrant overseas settlement, Ōkawadaira and Tōgō also contended that the model of Japan's migration-based expansion should be agrarian. Unlike other types of expansion that could achieve only temporary results, agriculture-centered expansion, they believed, would bring permanent benefits to the empire. Tōgō quoted the words of German historian Theodor Momsen in the beginning of his book: "That which is gained by war may be wrested from the grasp by war again, but it is not so with conquests made by the plough."[17]

The ideal candidates for migration were farmers in the countryside who were victims of continuous rural depression.[18] The deterioration of the farmers' quality of life was accompanied by Japan's loss of self-sufficiency in rice supply beginning at the end of the nineteenth century, leading to increasing concerns among Japanese policymakers and intellectuals about food shortages. It was in this context that Malthusian expansionism, an ideology that had already for decades served as the logical foundation for Japanese expansion, was offered up as the easiest explanation: rural depression and food shortage were the natural result of overpopulation in the Japanese countryside, and the only remedy was for the empire to expand further by relocating the surplus farmers abroad. Useless in Japan, they would acquire more land outside of the archipelago and work them to the empire's benefit.[19]

Tōgō shared classic Malthusianism's belief that a given size of earth had a certain limit on the food it could produce. If the population size exceeded what the earth could support, the earth would begin to lose its fertility, leading

[16] Ōkawadaira, *Nihon Imin Ron*, 212–217; Tōgō, *Nihon Shokumin Ron*, 286, 326–328.
[17] Tōgō, *Nihon Shokumin Ron*, 2.
[18] Kimura, "Nichiro Sengo Kaigai Nōgyō Imin no Rekishiteki Chii," 155–156.
[19] For example, calls for agriculture-based migration to Korea based on population pressure appeared in *Chūō nōji ho* (Central Agricultural News) in 1902 and 1904. See Kimura, "Nichiro Sengo Kaigai Nōgyō Imin no Rekishiteki Chii," 155.

to economic crisis and subsequently moral crisis. At the same time, like most intellectuals of his day, Tōgō maintained that population growth was absolutely necessary because it was a critical indicator of national strength. Japan's high fertility rate proved the nation's racial superiority, making them comparable to the Caucasians.[20] He believed that there was an intrinsic relationship between the increase of food production and that of population.[21] In order to sustain the current speed of demographic increase, Tōgō argued, Japan had to increase its agricultural productivity. At the same time, the current low productivity in agriculture was due to its excessive farming population: there were too many farmers and not enough arable land. Relocating these surplus peasants overseas to acquire and farm new lands would not only increase the efficiency of agriculture at home but also provide more food supplies from abroad.[22]

Tōgō further categorized expansion into two types: nonproductive and productive. Unlike nonproductive expansions such as military conquest, agricultural migration was a type of productive expansion because it aimed for long-term benefits and permanent settlement. While it could not provide a quick payoff due to the very nature of agriculture, it could steadily develop and consistently yield profits for a long time. Spanish expansion into South America had failed because their nearsighted colonists were satisfied with temporary profits, paying attention only to mining precious minerals; in contrast, the British had successfully expanded into North America due to their long-term investment into land settlement: having voyaged cross the Atlantic Ocean with plows and pruning hooks, they started their new lives by cultivating the land first.[23] Since agriculture was the foundation for population growth and the development of both industry and commerce, promotion of agricultural migration should be a top priority for the Japanese government in terms of its overseas expansion policies.[24]

Like Tōgō, Ōkawadaira also believed that Japan's rural depression was a result of overpopulation in the countryside. As there were too many farmers and not enough arable land in Japan, he argued, the rural economy suffered from unhealthy competition among the farmers and an overall decline in agricultural productivity.[25] The already oversaturated labor market in rural Japan took another blow when more than half a million veterans returned from the battlefields of the Russo-Japanese War. Ōkawadaira agreed with Tōgō in that relocating the "extra" farmers overseas was the best solution to Japan's rural depression.[26]

Both Tōgō and Ōkawadaira imposed certain standards for prospective migrants, stipulating that the candidates should be carefully selected and trained.

[20] Tōgō, *Nihon Shokumin Ron*, 110–111.   [21] Ibid., 202–205.   [22] Ibid., 238–241.
[23] Ibid., 46–47.   [24] Ibid., 68–69.   [25] Ōkawadaira, *Nihon Imin Ron*, 182–183.
[26] Ibid., 282–283.

For example, tenant farmers who had little land or money were not qualified because the trip itself and land acquisition abroad required a certain amount of capital. Only owner-farmers could meet the financial requirement. Land ownership also correlated with a certain degree of education, therefore the owner-farmers were more politically conscious as imperial subjects; they were more likely to be prepared to present Japan as a civilized empire to the foreigners.

As adherents of Malthusian expansionism, Tōgō and Ōkawadaira maintained that in order for agriculture-based migration to be successful, the migrants' destinations must have vast amounts of fertile land. Tōgō believed that Hokkaido and Taiwan, the two existing destinations, were no longer fertile enough to house Japan's rapidly growing peasant population. Though they were not opposed to migration to the United States, Tōgō and Ōkawadaira believed that the empire had to find alternative destinations beyond the reach of the Anglo-Saxons. Tōgō considered the Korean Peninsula and Manchuria, two territories that came under Japan's sphere of influence after the Russo-Japanese War, as the ideal targets for agricultural expansion.[27] Ōkawadaira, on the other hand, believed that Asia was already too densely populated, therefore South America was a better choice.[28]

As Tōgō and Ōkawadaira's plans demonstrated, the Japanese expansionists were operating on a global scale in their searches for settlement locations. Eventually, the state of Texas in the United States became the first test site for the idea of Japanese farmer migration, an experiment that was carried out with cooperation between the imperial government and a number of social groups. The campaign for Texas migration attracted nationwide attention in Japan and paved the way for Japanese agricultural migration to Asia and South America from 1908 onward.

From Laborers to Farmers

Japanese Texas migration constituted the initial step in the transformation of Japanese migration-driven expansion. Not only did it put the idea of farmer migration into practice, it also paved the way for Japanese farmer migration to Latin America. Texas came under the radar of Japanese expansionists due to the efforts of Japanese diplomats. In response to the anti-Japanese sentiment on the American West Coast, the Japanese Ministry of Foreign Affairs began to tighten its control on emigration in order to avoid further provoking anti-Japanese sentiment in the United States.[29] At the same time, however, Japanese diplomats were also looking for ways to continue Japanese migration

---

[27] Tōgō, *Nihon Shokumin Ron*, 363–380.   [28] Ōkawadaira, *Nihon Imin Ron*, 266–278.

[29] Before the enactment of the Gentlemen's Agreement in 1908, the Japanese government had already begun to restrict the migration of Japanese temporary laborers to the United States in 1902. Sawada, *Tokyo Life, New York Dreams*, 46–47.

to the United States. In 1902, Uchida Sadatsuchi, the Japanese consul in New York, made a pitch to Tokyo about relocating Japanese farmers to Texas for rice cultivation. Reprinted in mass media, Uchida's report triggered a boom in Texas migration from Japan that lasted from 1902 to 1908.[30]

As a result of Uchida's report, the Ministry of Foreign Affairs showed a strong interest in the prospect of Japanese migration to Texas and began to publish relevant reports in its official journals.[31] The imperial government's interest in the idea was echoed by public enthusiasm in mass media. By 1908, countless reports and stories of Japanese rice farming (*beisaku*) in Texas had appeared in different types of journals and newspapers at both national and local levels. Among these media outlets were leading migration journals such as *Amerika, Tobei Zasshi*, and *Shokumin Sekai*, mainstream media such as *Chūō Kōron* and *Tōyō Keizai Shinpō*, as well as those targeting specific or professional audiences such as *Kyōiku Jiron* (*Education Times*) and *Nōgyō Sekai* (*Agricultural World*).[32] Influenced by passionate rhetoric from both the government and mass media, hundreds of Japanese sailed across the Pacific and landed in southern Texas to pursue a career in rice farming.[33] Among these trans-Pacific rice farmers were some prolific writers who broadcasted their success, in rather exaggerated styles, to their countrymen back in Japan, further fueling the fever for Texas.

One of the most vocal proponents for agricultural migration was Yoshimura Daijirō, a Malthusian expansionist who had been enthusiastically encouraging Japanese youth to achieve personal success by leaving overpopulated Japan for United States to seek work-study opportunities.[34] He formed the Society of Friends of Overseas Enterprises (Kaigai Kigyō Dōshi Kai) in Osaka in 1903, aiming to assist Japanese farmers for migration to Texas.[35] Together with other society members, Yoshimura purchased 160 acres of land in League City, Texas, and established a rice farm there in 1904.[36] Though the farm was bankrupted the same year, this experience allowed Yoshimura to pen three guidebooks on American migration for Japanese readers between 1903 and

---

[30] Mamiya Kunio, *Saibara Seitō Kenkyū* (Kōchi-shi: Kōchi Shimin Toshokan, 1994), 313–314.

[31] Twelve reports appeared in official journals of the Japanese Foreign Ministries, including *Imin Chōsa Hōkoku* and *Tsūshō Isan*. This number is calculated based on the index of journals in Mamiya, *Saibara Seitō Kenkyū*, 314.

[32] Mamiya, *Saibara Seitō Kenkyū*, 315–319.

[33] According to calculations in a report made by the Japanese Ministry of Foreign Affairs in 1910, in 1908, when the Japanese agricultural migration to Texas reached its peak, there were 212 Japanese rice farmers in Texas.

[34] To this end, Yoshimura authored a few books, such as *Seinen no Tobei* (Tokyo: Chūyōdō, 1902), *Tobei Seigyō no Tebiki* (Tokyo: Okashima Shoten, 1903), and *Hokubei Yūgaku Annai* (Tokyo: Okashima Shoten, 1903).

[35] Yoshimura, *Hokubei Tekisasushū no Beisaku*, 203–205.

[36] Shimizu Seisaburō, "Hokubei Tekisasushu Iminchi Torishirabe Hōkoku," in *Gaimushō Tsūshōkyoku, Imin Chōsa Hōkoku*, vol. 1 (1908; repr., Tokyo: Yūshōdō Shuppan, 1986).

1905 that highlighted the promising future for rice farming in Texas. These guidebooks provide a valuable prism for us to analyze this phase of transition for the Japanese expansion discourse in the mid-1900s, when the empire moved away from labor migration and promoted agricultural migration in its stead. They also reveal that Malthusian expansionism continued to serve as the fundamental driving force in this new stage of Japan's migration-based expansion in the decades to come, with the agricultural sector at its front and center.

Texas as Japanese Frontier: Rice, Race, and History

How did Texas become an ideal target for Japanese agricultural expansion? There are a number of reasons for this phenomenon, all of them embedded in the historical contexts of both countries. First, the Lone Star State was an alternative to the American West Coast, which up to this point had been the most attractive destination for Japanese labor migrants. In response to the rise of anti-Japanese sentiment on the West Coast, migration promoters in Japan began to cast their eyes eastward to inland America. Yoshimura, for example, saw American exclusionism as a natural result of the arrival of a huge number of immigrants "who raided the coastal areas like locusts." He believed that Japanese immigrants would be welcomed if they moved to inland states such as Colorado, Texas, and Louisiana, places that had not yet received many Asian immigrants. In addition, these inland states' vast and rich lands were currently occupied by only very few residents.[37]

The attention shift of Japanese expansionists from the West Coast to inland America also matched the rise of the discourse of farmer migration in Japan that began to replace the discourse of labor migration. In his report to Tokyo, Uchida Sadatsuchi described the migration of Japanese farmers to Texas as a better alternative to labor migration to the West Coast. Unlike the unenlightened and low-class laborers who would only provoke the white residents' wrath, Uchida emphasized, the key to Japanese success in the United States was to export owner-farmers who had both a fair amount of wealth to purchase land and the resolution to settle in the United States permanently.[38] Texas, situated far away from the centers of anti-Japanese sentiment in the West Coast, looked particularly promising to Japanese expansionists. According to Yoshimura, the state of Texas was roughly twice as big as Japan but was occupied by only a small number of settlers.[39] Blessed with a pleasant climate, it was a cornucopia waiting for Japanese farmers to explore and develop.[40]

---

[37] Yoshimura, *Tobei Seigyō no Tebiki*, 56–57.
[38] Kikugawa Sadami, "Tekisasu Beisaku no Senkusha: Saibara Seito to Ōnishi Rihei," *Keizai Keiei Ronsō* 32, no. 4 (March 1998): 45.
[39] Yoshimura, *Hokubei Tekisasushū no Beisaku*, 140–141.   [40] Ibid., 139.

Figure 4.1 This map of Texas was included in Yoshimura's book *Hokubei Tekisasushū no Beisaku: Nihonjin no Shin Fugen*. It highlights the ideal areas for rice farming in Texas as well as railway routes that connected the areas with other parts of the United

Second, Texas was singled out as the most promising destination for Japanese migrants because it was beginning to take part in American agricultural capitalism's trans-continental expansion. Even though livestock husbandry remained Texas's economic engine when it became the twenty-sixth state in 1845, Texas quickly became a primary cotton supplier in the country by the turn of the twentieth century, and it had begun to supply cotton to the fledgling Japanese textile industry by the end of Sino-Japanese War.[41] After its neighbor Louisiana became the top producer of rice in the United States in 1889 by attracting rice farmers to work the coastal lands along the Gulf of Mexico, the Texan government sought to do the same in the southern part of the state, an area that shared the coastline with Louisiana. The completion of the Southern Pacific Railroad, connecting New Orleans with Los Angeles and running straight through Texas, also expedited agricultural settlement and the transportation of farm products. The Southern Pacific Railroad Company had obtained a large amount of Texan land along the railway lines. Motivated by profit, it spared no effort to attract agricultural settlers to the Lone Star State who would purchase its land for rice farming.[42] Originally tasked with investigating the conditions for cotton cultivation in the American South, Uchida was approached by leaders of agriculture in Texas. These Americans expressed an interest in attracting Japanese farmers to the state in order to jumpstart its own rice cultivation industry.

The opportunity of rice farming in Texas coincided with the rising calls for "rescuing" agriculture in Japan. For Japanese expansionists, relocating farmers from the overcrowded archipelago to Texas to grow rice was a masterful move that would kill two birds with one stone. The emigration of surplus population would help to balance Japan's domestic farmer-land ratio and improve its agricultural productivity. Moreover, Japanese success in rice farming in Texas would reaffirm the centrality of agriculture to the Japanese national identity, something that was endangered by Japan's loss of self-sufficiency in rice.

Yoshimura Daijirō argued that in the preceding decades, the demand for food had grown rapidly in the United States as the country's population skyrocketed. Out of many types of staple foods, rice was a particularly popular choice in the United States because its advantages had been amply demonstrated by Japanese robustness and productivity. "The courage of Japanese soldiers, the vigor of Japanese rickshaws, and the physical strength of Japanese women," Yoshimura proudly claimed, were all results of rice eating (*beishoku*).[43] He also believed that rice farming in Texas would further prove that the Japanese were the world champion in agriculture. While the demand for rice kept growing, Yoshimura pointed out, the white settlers preferred commerce and industry to

---

[41] Kikugawa, "Tekisasu Beisaku no Senkusha," 41.   [42] Ibid., 42–44.
[43] Yoshimura, *Hokubei Tekisasushū no Beisaku*, 93–94.

agriculture. For this reason, the Japanese would be welcomed in Texas because they were the nature-anointed kings of rice farming.[44]

Third, Texas was seen as the new frontier of Japanese expansion because of its own colonial history. In Yoshimura's imagination, the past and present of Texas were not only relevant but also closely connected to Japanese expansion at its moment of paradigm change. The history of Texas, he argued, was a tale of colonial competition and racial struggle. The land of Texas had changed hands from the Native Indians to Latin Europe colonists, the Mexicans, and eventually the Anglo-Saxons. The American expansion experience in Texas was particularly instructive to the Japanese because it was a testament to the merits of long-term settler expansion. The old colonial expansion, exemplified by the Spanish Empire, was conducted through military conquest and invasion.[45] Yet the era of military invasion had ended, announced Yoshimura, and the civilized powers now wrestled through peaceful means as migration became the primary method of expansion in this new era. For Japanese expansionists, Texas's recent history demonstrated the power of migration and settlement: The American migrants first arrived in this part of Mexico without any support from their national government. Through diligence and perseverance, they were able to entrench themselves in this foreign land and make it their own. Operating under the natural principle of survival of the fittest, they were eventually enthroned as the owners of Texas.[46] The colonization of Texas, Yoshimura contended, represented the overall model of American settler expansion that the Japanese should emulate. The key to such a successful venture was replacing temporary laborers with farmers who were prepared for long-term settlement in foreign lands.

If the colonial history of Texas offered a lesson for Japanese expansionists, the campaign for Japanese farmer migration to Texas was an indispensable part in their blueprints of the empire's expansion. It was expected that success in rice farming in Texas would allow the Japanese to claim a primary role in rice production, a field that would be of vital importance to the US economy in the future.[47] The victory of the Japanese farmers over white settlers in Texas would

---

[44] Yoshimura Daijirō, *Tekisasushū Beisaku no Jikken* (Tokyo: Kaigai Kigyō Dōshi Kai, 1905), 87.

[45] To clarify, Yoshimura's understanding of the history of the Spanish Empire was by no means accurate. As recent scholarship has demonstrated, the means of Spanish expansion in the Americas were far more complicated. In addition to military conquest, the Spanish usually utilized conflicts among Native American states by forming alliances with one side in order to defeat the other. Moreover, Spanish settlers also managed to access Native Americans' kin and political networks through intermarriage with indigenous elites. See Laura Matthew and Michel Oudijk, *Indian Conquistadors: Indigenous Allies in the Conquest of Mesoamerica* (Norman: University of Oklahoma Press, 2007) and Peter Villella, *Indigenous Elites and Creole Identity in Colonial Mexico, 1500–1800* (Cambridge: Cambridge University Press, 2016).

[46] Yoshimura, *Tekisasushū Beisaku no Jikken*, 144–145.

[47] Mamiya, *Saibara Seitō Kenkyū*, 322.

herald the success of Japanese expansion in the following decades in East Asia, Southeast Asia, and South America, new arenas of global colonial competition in the dawning century.[48]

Based in Osaka, the Society of Friends of Overseas Enterprises was established by Yoshimura and his peers to ensure the success of this new model of Japanese expansion in Texas. Yoshimura believed that like the American settlers who colonized Mexican Texas, the new Japanese migrants should have to resolve to make American Texas into a permanent home of the Japanese. The society's goal was to provide guidance to these empire builders to make long-term plans of settlement and help them to overcome temporary hardships while abroad.[49] Not only did the society have plans to build several branches in the United States, it also aimed to branch into Asia.[50] Even though this organization quickly collapsed, its vision for Japanese empire building demonstrated that under this new direction of agricultural expansion, Japanese migration to the United States was still intrinsically tied to Japanese expansion into the other parts of the Pacific Rim.

The involvement of Katayama Sen, a central leader of Japanese labor migration to the United States, in the movement of rice planting in Texas testified that Japanese migration-based expansion had become irreversibly centered on agriculture. In 1904, after investigating the existing Japanese farms in Texas, Katayama penned four consecutive articles in the *Oriental Economist* (*Tōyō Keizai Shinpō*) that passionately promoted agricultural migration to Texas.[51] At the same time, with the rise of anti-Japanese sentiment on the American West Coast in mind, Katayama offered his readers some words of caution. He pointed out that while Texas was a superior alternative to the West Coast because the Japanese were welcomed there and the procedure for them to purchase land was simple, not every Japanese could succeed. Temporary laborers were not qualified for rice farming in Texas because they did not have the specialized knowledge needed to choose the land, prepare farm facilities, and manage a farm. Farmers with limited means were also unsuitable, as they did not have enough money to purchase lands in Texas. The most desirable migrants for this project were thus those who owned sizeable land themselves in Japan with both the expertise in crops cultivation and the means to secure sufficient startup capital.[52]

Katayama soon put his rhetoric into practice. Between 1905 and 1907, he made several attempts at establishing rice farms in Texas and recruiting farmers from Japan, none of which succeeded. Ironically, his failure stemmed from his

[48] Yoshimura, *Tekisasushū Beisaku no Jikken*, 142.
[49] Yoshimura, *Hokubei Tekisasushū no Beisaku*, 203–204.   [50] Ibid., 205.
[51] Katayama Sen, "Tekisasu Beisaku to Nihonjin" (1)–(4), *Tōyō Keizai Shinpō*, nos. 305–308 (1904).
[52] Katayama Sen, "Tekisasu Beisaku to Nihonjin" (1), *Tōyō Keizai Shinpō*, no. 305 (May 1904): 25.

own inability to meet the two preconditions that he had laid out in his analysis: he had neither agricultural expertise nor stable financial support. When his long-term donor Iwasaki Kiyoshichi withdrew his money, Katayama had no choice but to end his Texas campaign once and for all.[53]

Subverting Racism through Farming

In order to raise money for their projects, Katayama Sen relied on big donors while Yoshimura Daijirō used collective funding. In contrast, many other Japanese farm owners in Texas were wealthy enough to establish their businesses in Texas with their own money. The most successful and influential Japanese farm in Texas was established and managed by Saibara Seitō and his family.

Saibara Seitō's life path illustrated the multidimensional connections between Japanese trans-Pacific migration and Japan's colonial expansion in Asia. An activist in the Freedom and People's Rights Movement, he was elected as a member of the Imperial Diet in 1898 and became the president of Doshisha University in the next year. A Malthusian expansionist, he began his career as a colonist in 1896 by funding a migrant farm in Hokkaido named the Society of Northern Light (*Hokkō Sha*).[54] Disappointed by the domestic political climate and stimulated by the fever of migration to America, Saibara resigned his positions in Japan and moved to the United States for a new start in 1902. Inspired by Uchida's report on Japanese rice farming in Texas and established his own farm on three hundred acres of land in Webster, Texas, at the end of 1903.

Saibara was well educated in specialized knowledge and in possession of substantial wealth. Though born to a shizoku family, he was an ideal candidate for success in this wave of heimin-centered agricultural migration and indeed became one of the most eminent Japanese settlers in Texas. From 1904 to 1907, his farm almost tripled in size and its output quadrupled. Due to Saibara's effort in seed refinement and the exploration of alternative crops, his farm was able to enhance its rice productivity and survive several natural disasters as well as unexpected drops in the price of rice, even while some other Japanese farms went bankrupt.[55]

Self-styled as a torchbearer of the Japanese agricultural expansion in the United States, Saibara became a spokesperson for Texas rice farming in Japan. Traveling back and forth between Texas and Japan, he persuaded his family members to join his cause and recruited farmers (mainly from Kōchi, his native

[53] Kazuhiko Orii and Hilary Conroy, "Japanese Socialists in Texas: Sen Katayama," *Amerasia Journal* 8, no. 2 (1981): 168–169.
[54] Mamiya, *Saibara Seitō Kenkyū*, 209.   [55] Ibid., 341–344.

prefecture) to work on his farm. He further participated in Texas migration promotion in Japan by advertising his success to the Japanese public: he made public speeches and wrote articles for various domestic journals to share tips with his countrymen who planned to follow his footsteps. Widely reported on and celebrated in migration circles, Saibara became the symbol of Japanese agricultural migration to Texas. His farm became an exhibition site of Japanese nationalism and expansionism that attracted visits from Japanese intellectuals, entrepreneurs, and politicians when they visited the United States for the Louisiana Purchase Exhibition in 1904.[56] Students in Japanese agricultural colleges saw Saibara as an idol, as one of their popular songs described their ideal postgraduation career path based on his story:[57]

> Twenty years have passed since I graduated from college
> Now I am a big landlord in Texas
> In the place where fawns bleat in the fall
> There are golden waves of crops of 90 thousand chō.[58]

Aside from the success of his farm, other factors also contributed to the ascension of Saibara Seitō as the face of Japanese agricultural expansion. Aware of the rise of anti-Japanese sentiment on the West Coast, he understood that obtaining American citizenship and the associated political rights was crucial to the migration endeavor in the long run, thus he immediately applied for naturalization after the land purchase in Texas. However, as the Naturalization Act of 1870 permitted the naturalization of only Caucasian and African immigrants, the immigration authority in the state of Texas received Saibara's application without giving him a clear answer.[59] The ambivalent attitude of Texas authority led the Japanese expansionists to believe that there was a possible pathway to naturalization for them. In their imaginations, Saibara's success in developing rice farming in Texas and his resolution of permanent settlement would eventually earn him citizenship in the most civilized country of the world.

To the Japanese expansionists, the development of rice farming and the existing race relations in Texas made the state a perfect place for the Japanese to subvert white racism. After an investigation of Saibara's farm, politician Matsudaira Masanao observed that unlike the West Coast, Texas did not have a lot of Chinese or black people due to racial animosity; in contrast, the Japanese migrants were welcomed by the white settlers. Armed with their

---

[56] Ino Masayoshi, *Kyojin Saibara Seitō* (Tosa-shi: Saibara Seitō Sensei Shōtokuhi Kensetsu Kiseikai, 1964), 116.
[57] Ibid., 319.
[58] The area of 90,000 chō is equal to approximately 222,400 acres of land (900 square kilometers).
[59] Mamiya, *Saibara Seitō Kenkyū*, 330.

world-famous expertise in rice farming, the Japanese were treated even better than Caucasians from Italy and Spain.

While the lower-class Japanese laborers were targeted by white exclusionists on the West Coast, Matsudaira believed that capable and educated Japanese migrants like Saibara could easily gain American citizenship in Texas. As Japanese success in Texas would prove their assimilability into the white men's world, it would win for Japanese the right of naturalization in the entire country. Such a development would allow the Japanese settlers to participate in American politics in order to consolidate Japanese frontiers in the United States.[60]

Seeing rice farming in Texas as a promising model that could bring about a better future for Japanese migrants in the United States, Japan's Ministry of Foreign Affairs also provided political support to the movement. At the turn of the twentieth century, in order to avoid provoking further anti-Japanese sentiment on the American West Coast, the ministry had reduced Japanese labor migration to the United States. However, it gave a green light to those who intended to migrate to Texas as farmers, including both wealthy men like Saibara who would become big farm owners and small owner-farmers who would like to collectively manage a farm by pooling together their funds and labor. The Ministry of Foreign Affairs categorized the latter as collective farmers (*kumiai nōfu*) and managed to negotiate for their rights to migrate under the Gentlemen's Agreement.[61] As a result, the doors of Texas remained open to Japanese agricultural migration, at least in theory, until the passage of Immigration Act of 1924.

The End of the Texas Migration Campaign

To the severe disappointment of most Japanese expansionists of the day, the wave of Texas migration quickly ebbed and faded out from Japanese public discourse before the first decade of the twentieth century came to an end. While natural disasters and drops in rice prices due to overproduction had dealt substantial setbacks to Japanese farms in Texas,[62] it was the shortage of labor that fundamentally doomed these ventures. Matsuhara Ichio, the Japanese consul in Chicago, observed in a report to Tokyo in 1908 that after migrating to the United States, many Japanese farmhands quickly abandoned their posts.

[60] Matsudaira Masanao, "Hokubei Gasshūkoku Tekisasushu Beisaku Shisatsu Dan," *Chigaku Zasshi* 17, no. 8 (1905): 534.
[61] "Nōgyō Kumiai Beikoku Ijū Mōshikomi no Ken," in Gaimusho Gaikō Shiryōkan, *Hokubei Gasshūkoku Oyobi Kanada Nōgyō Kumiaiin Tokō Shutsugan Zakken* (1906), microfilm (Tokyo: Japan Microfilm Service Center, 1967).
[62] Thomas K. Walls, *The Japanese Texans* (San Antonio: University of Texas, Institute of Texan Cultures at San Antonio, 1987), 62–63.

Most of them left for California, where they picked up better-paying labor jobs.[63] The lack of leisure facilities in rural Texas was another reason why Japanese migrants were eager to quit the farm life and move elsewhere.[64]

These migrants had high mobility because of the particular way in which they were recruited. Since it was difficult to persuade those who had either fortune or land to abandon their properties in Japan, Japanese farm owners in Texas did not require their employees to make any financial commitment to the farm. As a result, contrary to the expectation of the Japanese agricultural expansionists, Japanese farms in Texas ended up recruiting laborers, not shareholding farmers, from Japan. In order to circumvent the government restrictions on labor migrants, these farm laborers applied for their passports as collective farmers and presented themselves as small shareholders of Japanese farms in Texas. However, with little actual commitment to the farms, it was easy for these farm laborers to quit and move on.[65]

Most Japanese farm owners preferred migrants from Japan to the local white, black, or Mexican farmers for two reasons. First, they trusted the farming skills of their compatriots because most of these migrants were previously farmers in Japan. Second, there was a language barrier between the Japanese farm owners and the locals.[66] The migrants from Japan thus constituted the primary labor source for Japanese farms in Texas, and their remigration to California and urban Texas left the farms mired in crisis.

Japanese farm owners responded to this crisis by working together to form the Texan Japanese Association (Tekisasu Nihonjin Kyōkai) in 1908. Immediately after its establishment, the association submitted an appeal to Japan's minister of foreign affairs, Komura Jutarō, urging the imperial government to stop the remigration of the Japanese farm laborers from Texas through diplomatic means. However, this effort was doomed from the start because there were no legal ways for Tokyo to control the mobility of its subjects outside of the imperial territory.

The failure of the Texan Japanese Association's appeal announced the end of Japanese agricultural migration in Texas. Faced with both a labor shortage and a drop in the price of rice, most Japanese farms went bankrupt before the end of the 1910s; their employees and owners either returned to Japan or remigrated to California.[67] Only a handful of them, including the farm owned by Saibara Seitō, were able to survive by reducing size and cultivating alternative crops.

[63] Mamiya, *Saibara Seitō Kenkyū*, 350.   [64] Ibid., 351.   [65] Ibid., 350–351.   [66] Ibid., 351.
[67] Ibid., 360.

A New Beginning: Farmer Migration and Brazil

Although the Texas campaign was short-lived, it marked a turning point in the evolution of Japanese Malthusian expansionism. It opened up a new chapter in the history of Japan's migration-driven expansion marked by farmer migration. In response to anti-Japanese campaigns in North America and the deterioration of Japan's rural economy during the first decades of the twentieth century, Japan's migration-driven expansion underwent a major paradigm shift from labor migration to agrarian settlement.

Due to their diverse social and political backgrounds, during the previous decades Malthusian expansionists had imagined very different futures for Japan's migrants—from businessmen to company employees, from plantation owners to farm laborers. The failure of the Texas campaign, however, convinced a growing number of Malthusian expansionists that becoming land-owning farmers was the only viable career path for Japanese migrants. This paradigm change was further cemented by the failed Japanese American enlightenment campaign in the 1910s and 1920s, a subject that will be examined in the next chapter.

The failure in Texas also forced Japanese expansionists to explore alternative destinations, leading them to cast their gaze on the "empty and rich lands" of Latin America. The initial architect of Texas campaign Uchida Sadatsuchi became the Japanese consul in the state of São Paulo, Brazil, in 1907. He immediately found Brazil to be a more suitable place for Japanese migration than the United States due to a perceived absence of racism. He did not hesitate to support migration leader Mizuno Ryū through diplomatic means, enabling him to bring the first official group of Japanese migrants to Brazil on the ship *Kasato-maru* in 1908.[68] The growing Japanese communities in Brazil also attracted the attention of Saibara Seitō. Disappointed by the rejection of his citizenship application in the United States, Saibara entrusted his Texan farm to his son and joined Japanese expansion in Brazil by starting a farm in the state of São Paulo in 1918. While his farming career in São Paulo was not as successful as expected, he moved north to the state of Pará in 1928 as an employee of Japan's South America Colonization Company (Nanbei Takushoku Kabushiki Gaisha) to experiment with Japanese farming at the mouth of the Amazon River.[69]

Conclusion

At the end of the 1906 novel *The Broken Commandment*, protagonist Segawa Ushimatsu decides to sail to Texas and start his new life there as a rice farmer.

---

[68] Tsuchida, "Japanese in Brazil," 61–62, 125–126.
[69] Mamiya, *Saibara Seitō Kenkyū*, 365–368.

Though a work of fiction, this book was an example of the Japanese general public's awareness of the opportunity of taking up rice farming in Texas. The rise of Japanese farmer migration to Texas, while similar to the wave of labor migration to the US West Coast in terms of its heimin-centered base, represented a turning point in the evolution of Japanese migration-based expansion. It marked the beginning of farmer-centered expansion with the goal of long-term agricultural settlement.

At the end of the nineteenth century, Japan lost its self-sufficiency in rice. As a result, it had to import its main staple food from Taiwan and the Korean Peninsula. The decline of the agricultural sector triggered a debate on agriculture's importance to the nation. Representing two opposing sides of the debate, Yokoi Toshiyoki and Nitobe Inazō held contrasting views on the nation's best course of development, but they both believed that agriculture had a fundamental role to play in Japan's overall economic growth, arguing for agriculture's centrality in both Japan's national identity and cultural tradition.

Malthusian expansionism provided a convenient solution for Japanese thinkers who sought to reverse the decline of agriculture while maintaining that the development of industry and commerce was vital to the empire's success. They attributed the fundamental cause of rural depression to overpopulation in the countryside, which in turn led to the overall decline of agricultural productivity. Based on this assumption, they argued that the revival of agriculture could be achieved by relocating the surplus population overseas without major changes in the existing economic structure in society. Moreover, these surplus farmers in Japanese countryside, through migration and farming, would become powerful vanguards of the empire's expansion project.

Aside from the calls for "rescuing" Japanese agriculture, the promotion of farmer migration to Texas was also a response to rising anti-Japanese sentiment on the American West Coast that primarily targeted Japanese labor migrants. In this context, rice farming in Texas was deemed as the best alternative because Japanese farmers, the expansionists believed, would find a warmer welcome in the United States than would laborers. Moreover, they were better equipped to put down permanent roots, thereby establishing the Japanese as an expansionist race in the American frontier. They expected that the success of Japanese rice farmers in Texas would reassert the racial superiority of the Japanese in the world through their achievements in agriculture.

However, a structural labor shortage quickly led to the decline of Japanese rice farming in Texas. The failure of this project and the enactment of the Gentlemen's Agreement forced the Japanese expansionists to revise their blueprint of agricultural migration. The Gentlemen's Agreement had shut America's doors to Japanese migrant laborers, but it was still possible for Japanese to migrate to America through familial relations. It thus ushered in the era of picture brides, when hundreds of thousands of Japanese women moved to the US West Coast. Japanese migration leaders strived to appease the anti-Japanese sentiment by encouraging Japanese Americans, through education and moral suasion, to assimilate into the mainstream – in other words, Caucasian – society. At the same time, thinkers and doers of Japanese expansion began to explore alternative migration destinations in Northeast Asia, Latin America, and the South Seas to carry out their versions of farmer-centered expansion.

In response to the ongoing Japanese exclusion campaigns in the United States represented by the promulgation of Alien Land Laws in a few states in the American West, Japanese policymakers, intellectuals, and migration movement leaders conducted heated debates that redefined the meaning, pattern, and direction of the empire's future expansion. Yoshimura Daijirō's failure to sustain his Texan farm and the enactment of the Gentlemen's Agreement did not hamper his zeal for embracing Western civilization. He participated in the activities of the Great Japan Civilization Association (Dai Nihon Bunmei Kyōkai), an organization founded by leading politician Ōkuma Shigenobu with the goal of winning Japan membership in the white men's world.[70] The mission of the Great Japan Civilization Association was similar to that of another organization formed in 1914, the Japanese Emigration Association (Nihon Imin Kyōkai), in which Ōkuma also played a central role. As the next chapter discusses at length, the Emigration Association became a headquarters for campaigns launched by Japanese expansionists to facilitate Japanese American assimilation into white American society. The next chapter also discusses how the model of farmer migration evolved in the years between the enactment of the Gentlemen's Agreement and the passage of the Immigration Act of 1924, when the American doors were completely shut to Japanese immigration. It explains in detail why, among the different campaigns in various areas around the Pacific Rim, it was in Brazil that the Japanese farmer migration turned out to be the most successful.

---

[70] Yoshimura helped to translate *Heredity in Relationship to Eugenics* by the American eugenics movement leader Charles B. Davenport into Japanese, published by the association in 1914 under the title *Jinshu Kairyō Gaku* (*The Study of Eugenics*). It advocated the improvement of the qualities of the American population by discouraging those who had genetic defects for reproduction and by banning those who had biologically undesirable traits from migrating to the United States.

5   "Carrying the White Man's Burden": The Rise
     of Farmer Migration to Brazil

The decline of Japanese labor migration to the United States ushered in
a new phase in Japan's migration-based expansion as Japanese intellectuals, policymakers, and migration promoters began to propose and carry
out farmer migration campaigns in regions both inside and outside of the
imperial territory. Following the failure of the rice cultivation campaign
in Texas, the period between the late 1900s and 1924 was marked by two
general courses of action taken jointly by Japan's government and social
groups. The first was to explore alternative routes and models of expansion, and the second was to facilitate Japanese immigrants' assimilation
into American society with the aim of placating anti-Japanese sentiment
in the United States and removing the restriction on Japanese immigration. Both of these courses of action were legitimized by the logic of
Malthusian expansionism.

The formation of the Japanese Emigration Association (Nihon Imin
Kyōkai) in 1914 was a milestone event in the Japanese state's involvement in migration management and promotion. As the embodiment of
synergy between the government and social groups, the association
worked to appease anti-Japanese sentiment in the United States.
Through both education and moral suasion, it carried out campaigns
that aimed at helping Japanese Americans assimilate into mainstream
American society. Members of the Emigration Association believed that
if all Japanese men and women in the United States could behave like
civilized white Americans, the Japanese race would eventually be able to
gain admission to the white men's world and anti-Japanese sentiment in
the United States would automatically disappear.

In response to the decline of Japanese migration to the United States,
the years following the Gentlemen's Agreement witnessed three general
campaigns of expansion launched under the collaboration of the Japanese
government and private groups. These campaigns included expansion to
Northeast Asia (the Korean Peninsula and Manchuria), the South Seas,
and South America. As Malthusian expansionism continued to legitimize
the migration-based model of expansion itself, the ongoing anti-Japanese
movement in the United States became the midwife of these campaigns.

All three campaigns were expected to change the image of the Japanese as an unwelcome intruder into the white men's domain. They were aimed at directing Japanese migration to alternative political spaces beyond North America so that Japanese expansion could be tolerated by Western colonial powers.

The proposal of redirecting migration into Japan's own spheres of influence in Northeast Asia was designed to avoid any direct confrontation with the West; the call for expansion to the South Seas, areas already under Western colonial influence, was presented as joining the West in the mission of spreading civilization to remote corners of the world; while the plan of directing migration to Latin America was based on the assumption that Latin America was still operating in a political vacuum – that is, yet unclaimed by any colonial power. The Japanese government had an unprecedented level of involvement in all of these campaigns. It sponsored semigovernmental and private associations to investigate the possibilities and means of migration and built up public appetite for expansion.[1] It also provided political and financial support for private migration companies that put these new migration plans into practice.

Japan's efforts to placate anti-Japanese sentiment in the United States and to explore alternative migration destinations were fundamentally intertwined: both were justified as solutions to the issue of overpopulation at home. Building upon the Texas farmer migration experience, both campaigns stemmed from the belief that the project of labor migration to the United States was irrevocably flawed and should be replaced by the model of farmer migration. Moreover, Japanese expansionists believed that Japanese immigrants' successful assimilation into American society would further facilitate Japanese expansion to other parts of the globe. Once these Japanese immigrants won the acceptance of the white Americans, it would not only justify Japanese colonial expansion as a mission of spreading civilization but also dispel the fear of the Japanese "yellow peril" among the Western powers. For this reason, in addition to leading the campaigns to facilitate Japanese American assimilation, the Emigration Association also played a central role in exploring migration destinations elsewhere.

This chapter examines the interactions and confluence of these two courses of action from the late 1900s to the mid-1920s. It shows how farmer migration, buttressed by the logic of Malthusian expansionism, became entrenched as the dominant mode of Japanese migration-driven expansion. The Japanese American assimilation campaign's hopes were dashed by the Immigration Act of 1924, which closed US doors to all Asian immigrants. The collaborative efforts made

---

[1] For *Hankan Hanmin* (semigovernmental) organizations of expansion, see Hyung Gu Lynn, "A Comparative Study of Tōyō Kyōkai and Nan'yō Kyōkai," in *The Japanese Empire in East Asia and Its Postwar Legacy*, ed. Harald Fuess (Munich: Iudicium, 1998), 65–95.

by the government and social groups in migrant expansion to Northeast Asia and the South Seas also resulted in disappointment. However, the initial success in farmer migration in Brazil invited an increasing number of Japanese expansionists to cast their gaze to the biggest country in South America.

The Beginning of Japanese Farmer Migration in Northeast Asia

After the Russo-Japanese War cemented Japan's political ascendancy in Northeast Asia, the Korean Peninsula and Manchuria became convenient alternatives to North America following the demise of the Texas campaign and the enactment of the Gentlemen's Agreement. The most famous proponent for Japan's expansion into Northeast Asia was Komura Jutarō, the minister of foreign affairs in the second Katsura Cabinet, who proposed the strategy of "concentrating on Manchuria and Korea" (Man Kan Shūchū) in a speech to the Imperial Diet in 1909. The formation of the Oriental Development Company (Tōyō Takushoku Kabushiki Gaisha) in 1908, under the political and financial support of the Prime Minister Katsura Tarō, brought the proposal of Northeast Asian expansion into action. The company acquired farmland on the Korean Peninsula, recruited Japanese farmers, and settled them there.[2]

Japan's migration-based expansion in Northeast Asia, both in ideology and in practice, was a replica of the failed Texas migration campaign, in terms of both the discourse of Malthusian expansionism and the idea of farm migration. Komura, for example, reasoned that the spacious land in the Korean Peninsula and Manchuria would be more than enough to accommodate Japan's surplus population. He further argued that migration would also help to stimulate Japanese population growth by an extra thirty million.[3]

The idea of farmer migration to the Korean Peninsula was further articulated by Kanbe Masao, a professor of law at Kyoto Imperial University. He published *On Agricultural Migration to Korea* (*Chōsen Nōgyō Imin Ron*) in 1910, on the eve of Japan's formal annexation of Korea. Like Komura, Kanbe believed that instead of Hawai'i, the US mainland, or Latin America, the Korean Peninsula should be the premier destination for Japanese migrants. For Kanbe, agricultural migration from Japan to Korea was not merely a solution to the issue of overpopulation but also a mission of spreading civilization because the unenlightened and incompetent Koreans had to be guided by the Japanese in order to cultivate their own land.[4]

[2] Hyung Gu Lynn, "Malthusian Dreams, Colonial Imaginary: The Oriental Development Company and Japanese Emigration to Korea," in Elkins and Pedersen, *Settler Colonialism in The Twentieth Century*, 30, 33.
[3] Iriye Toraji, *Hōjin Kaigai Hatten Shi* (Tokyo: Ida shoten, 1942), 2:510.
[4] Kanbe Masao, *Chōsen Nōgyō Imin Ron* (Tokyo: Yūhikaku Shobō, 1910), 44–45.

In addition, the proposal of expansion into Northeast Asia was also a strategic response to anti-Japanese sentiment in the United States. It was in line with Komura's acceptance of the Western imperialist world order and his efforts to gain Japan entry to the club of civilized powers. A longtime diplomat, Komura played a key role in forming the Anglo-Japanese Alliance in 1902 and in renewing it in 1911. In 1907, while serving as Japan's ambassador to the United Kingdom, he contributed to Japan's diplomatic efforts to placate the anti-Japanese sentiments in Canada.[5] Taking the cabinet post of minister of foreign affairs soon after the Gentlemen's Agreement was reached, Komura fulfilled the government's promise to ban Japanese labor migration to the United States. Adopting a pro-Anglo-American stance, he proved instrumental in negotiating the Root-Takahira Treaty with the United States in 1908. The treaty clarified the two countries' colonial privileges in the Asia-Pacific region in order to avoid possible conflicts between these two Pacific powers.[6] For its part, the policy of Man Kan Shūchū was in line with Katsura Cabinet's efforts to find a way for Japan to expand without rousing American suspicion and hostility.[7]

As will be discussed in the following paragraphs, Komura's notion of achieving conciliation with the United States in exchange for Japan's membership in the club of civilization was shared by contemporary advocates for Japan's southward expansion (*nanshin*) in the South Seas. These campaigns for exploring alternative routes of expansion were intertwined with Tokyo's efforts in facilitating Japanese American assimilation. During the interactions between the course of exploring alternative routes of expansion and that of fostering Japanese assimilation into the American society, farmer migration with the goal of permanent settlement was further solidified as the most desirable mode of Japanese expansion in the following decades.

White Racism and Malthusian Expansionism: The Formation of the Emigration Association

In the history of Japan's migration-driven expansion, if the campaign of Texas migration marked the beginning of the paradigm shift from labor to agriculture, the enactment of the Alien Land Law in California in 1913 was another critical event. Aimed at excluding Japanese farmers from the domestic agricultural sector and creating a social climate that was pointedly inhospitable for

---

[5] Tsuchida, "Japanese in Brazil," 74.

[6] Shinobu Jūnhei, *Komura Jutarō* (Tokyo: Shinchōsha, 1932), 267–275.

[7] For more details on Komura's stance, see Okamoto Shumpei, "Meiji Japanese Imperialism: Pacific Emigration or Continental Expansionism?," in *Japan Examined: Perspectives on Modern Japanese History*, ed. Harry Wray and Hilary Conroy (Honolulu: University of Hawai'i Press, 1983), 141–148.

immigrants, the California Alien Land Law of 1913 denied issei Japanese Americans the right to land ownership and restricted their legal tenancy to three years. It not only damaged the agricultural development of Japanese American communities but also gave a bitter lesson to the Japanese Malthusian expansionists about the importance of land ownership. It thus further cemented the centrality of land-acquisition-based farmer migration in the history of Japanese migration-driven expansion in the following decades.

In response to the Alien Land Law, Japanese politicians and social groups redoubled their efforts to placate anti-Japanese sentiment in the United States. Entrusted by business tycoon Shibusawa Ei'ichi, the first president of Industrial Bank of Japan (Nihon Kōgyō Ginkō), Soeda Jū'ichi and Kamiya Tadao, an employee of the Brazil Colonization Company, went to the United States to investigate the issue.[8] Soeda and Kamiya concluded that a moral reform was needed to "civilize" Japanese immigrants because their backward behaviors and lifestyle had been fueling anti-Japanese sentiment. Based on this conclusion, Shibusawa, Soeda, and Nakano Takenaka – the director of the Tokyo Chamber of Commerce – jointly submitted two proposals to the Ministry of Foreign Affairs. The first proposal contained their plans to smooth over anti-Japanese sentiment in the United States, including promoting mutual understanding between the two nations and turning Japanese Americans in the United States into better civilized subjects. The second proposal, however, called for looking to the South Seas and Latin America as alternative destinations for Japanese migration in the following decades.

These two proposals found supporters within the imperial government. In 1914, the government and social groups collaborated to form the Japanese Emigration Association to facilitate Japanese overseas migration and expansion by giving public lectures, conducting workshops, and publishing journals/ books on the subject. Its members included top government officials, Imperial Diet members, business elites, intellectuals, and migration agents.

The inaugural meeting of the Emigration Association was held in the hall of Tokyo Geographical Association,[9] the founding site of the Colonial Association (Shokumin Kyōkai), and there were indeed parallels between these two organizations. Like the Colonial Association, the Emigration Association was formed in response to Asian exclusion campaigns in the United States, and both membership rosters included Japanese politicians, social elites, and intellectuals. Members of the Emigration Association supported migration for different purposes: policymakers saw migration as essential for expansion, business tycoons expected it to boost international trade,

---

[8] Azuma, *Between Two Empires*, 53.
[9] Sakaguchi Mitsuhiko, "Kaisetsu," in *Nihon Imin Kyōkai Hōkoku*, vol. 1 (Tokyo: Fuji Shuppan, 2006), 6.

while intellectuals believed it would make Japan rise through the global racial hierarchy. Yet as a whole they were, like the Colonial Association members before them, adherents to Malthusian expansionism who lamented the issue of overpopulation in Japan but simultaneously avowed the necessity of further population growth.

As the manifesto of the Emigration Association claimed, among the nations of the world, the Japanese nation had an outstanding population growth rate as well as impressive population density. The goal of the association was to facilitate overseas migration so that the nation would not be mired in poverty and revolutions. Emigration, however, was not simply aimed at offloading of the surplus population. As the founders of the association also emphasized in the manifesto, "Western scholars often use the terms of colonial nation (*shokumin koku*) and non-colonial nation (*hi shokumin koku*) to differentiate successful nations from the unsuccessful ones." As a few European empires continued to strive as colonial nations, "Japan and the U.S. also began to take part in this imperial competition." The association's mission, then, was to serve Japan's national interests by facilitating migration-based expansion and cementing Japan's status as a member of the colonial nations' club.[10]

While the Colonial Association aimed to promote shizoku expansion in order to prepare for racial competition with the West, the Emigration Association was founded when anti-Japanese sentiment in the United States was at its peak. Yet instead of adopting a combative stance toward the West, the association hoped to keep the general avenues of Japanese overseas migration open by reconciling with Anglo-American colonial hegemony. Members of the association believed that widening the channel for Japanese immigration into the United States was not only crucial for Japan's future expansion but also feasible in practice. As Soeda Jū'ichi articulated, they were optimistic for two reasons. First, they denied the existence of racism against Japanese among white Americans and argued that Japanese immigrants themselves should be blamed for anti-Japanese sentiment because of their lack of social manners and backward lifestyle. As they saw it, at the heart of the problem was the insular national character of the Japanese, a product of the long-term isolationist (*sakoku*) policy of the backward Tokugawa regime. If this trait could be altered, then the anti-Japanese sentiment would disappear.[11] Second, they perceived World War I as a turning point that would lift the migration restriction in the United States: as the European battlefields demanded manpower, the flow of European migration to the United States would dry up after the war began, and Japanese immigrants would thus again be welcomed to fill the labor vacuum. In

[10] "Nihon Imin Kyōkai Setsuritsu Shushi," *Nihon Imin Kyōkai Hōkoku* 1, no. 1 (October 1914): 3 (repr., Tokyo: Fuji Shuppan, 2006).

[11] Soeda Jū'ichi, "Daisensō to Imin Mondai," *Nihon Imin Kyōkai Hōkoku* 1, no. 6 (February 1916): 6–7 (repr., Tokyo: Fuji Shuppan, 2006).

addition, Japanese Canadians who voluntarily joined the Canadian military to fight in the war would also improve Japan's international image.[12]

In the Emigration Association's blueprint for Japanese global expansion, the removal of migration restrictions in the United States was of paramount importance. This was not only because the United States still had spacious, fertile, and sparsely populated land, but also because the acceptance of Japanese immigrants by Americans would provide irrefutable evidence for Japan's status as a civilized nation equal to the Westerners. It would legitimize Japan's expansion in the future by opening the doors of other countries, both "civilized" and "uncivilized" alike, to Japanese migration. As the director of the Emigration Association Ōkuma Shigenobu envisioned, American acceptance of Japanese immigration would prove that Japan was capable of synthesizing the essences of the East and West. Standing on the top of the hierarchy of civilizations, Japan's expansion was destined to bring enlightenment to the entire world.[13]

The Enlightenment Campaign for Japanese American Assimilation and Women's Education

Members of the Emigration Association such as Shibusawa Eiichi and Soeda Jū'ichi played leading roles in the enlightenment campaign (keihatsu undō), a collaborative initiative launched by government officials and social leaders in Japan as well as Japanese Americans community leaders. It employed a two-pronged approach to achieve its goal of Japan-US conciliation that included both "external enlightenment" (*gai teki keihatsu*) and "internal enlightenment" (*nai teki keihatsu*). The former sought to improve the image of Japan and Japanese among the white Americans by increasing commercial, religious, and cultural exchanges between Japan and the United States. The latter, on the other hand, was targeted at the Japanese immigrants in the United States. If the Japanese immigrants' "problems" could be corrected, the campaign leaders believed, the anti-Japanese sentiment in the United States would naturally give way to acceptance. To this end, they identified a variety of problems common to Japanese Americans. These issues included ignorance of American customs, inadequate English proficiency, insufficient interaction with white Americans, engagement in gambling and prostitution, as well as reluctance to make social investment in the United States.[14]

In the campaign leaders' blueprint of civilizing the Japanese American communities, women played a critical role. Though Shimanuki Hyōdayū, the

---

[12] Ibid., 4.

[13] Ōkuma Shigenobu, "Sekai no Daikyoku to Imin," *Nihon Imin Kyōkai Hōkoku* 1, no. 2 (August 1915): 6–7 (repr., Tokyo: Fuji Shuppan, 2006).

[14] Suehiro Shigeo, *Hokubei no Nihonjin* (Tokyo: Nishōdō Shoten, 1915), 195–228.

first president of the Japanese Striving Society, died as early as 1913 and was not an official participant in the enlightenment campaign, his ideas on how women could contribute to the Japanese American assimilation actually set the agenda for the enlightenment campaign. Between the late 1900s and early 1920s, Japanese women began to migrate to the United States as marriage partners of the Japanese male immigrants in a growing number. This was because the Gentlemen's Agreement shut the American doors to Japanese migrant laborers but left them open to family members of the existing immigrants. Responding quickly to this situation, Shimanuki started raising fund for the establishment of women's school (*Rikkō Jogakkō*) inside the Striving Society in 1909, which became true at the end of that year.[15] Referring to their racial struggles in the United States, Shimanuki argued, the Japanese American immigrants were fighting a peaceful war, one as significant as the Russo-Japanese War. To support their battle to win the Japanese race deserved recognition from the white Americans, the society was dedicated to facilitating the migration of Japanese women to the United States so that they could become marriage partners and domestic assistants to male immigrants.[16]

The migration of Japanese women, Shimanuki reasoned, would placate anti-Japanese sentiment in the United States in two ways. First, the most important reason for the overall success in the worldwide colonial expansion of the European powers was that the male settlers migrated overseas with their wives. Just like the wives of the European colonial settlers, the Japanese women could give their husbands in the United States physical assistance and emotional comfort to overcome the material difficulties and loneliness in the foreign land. This family life would not only help the Japanese male immigrants to restrain themselves from indulgence in immorality and crimes but also solidify their resolution of permanent settlement in the United States. The improvement of Japanese immigrants' lifestyle would change the white Americans' attitude toward Japanese immigration. Second, women could also give birth to the next generation of the Japanese in the United States, who enjoyed the birthright citizenship and political rights attached to it. Because most of the first generation of Japanese immigrants had no access to US citizenship, the more children they had, the stronger the Japanese American communities would become politically. The growth of Japanese population with citizenship would prevent anti-Japanese campaigns from having political consequences.[17] However, for Shimanuki, not all Japanese women were qualified to take on this mission. Only those who were physically and mentally ready were qualified. The goal of the Women's School of the Japanese Striving

---

[15] The opening ceremony of the women's school was held on November 3, 1909. *Kyūsei* 5, no. 81 (November 1909): 4.
[16] "Rikkō Jogakkō Sanjoin Boshū," *Kyūsei* 5, no. 81 (November 1909): 1.
[17] Shimanuki, *Rikkō Kai to wa Nan Zo Ya*, 173–141.

Society was to prepare these women to become good wives and mothers in the frontiers of Japanese expansion before their migration.[18]

In the minds of the leaders of the enlightenment campaign, the female migrants were far from ready to take on this glorious mission. Most of the Japanese women who reached the American shore between late 1900s and early 1920s were picture brides (*shashin hanayome*) from poor families in rural Japan.[19] Japanese educators criticized them for bringing shame on the Japanese race and nation because of their "inappropriate" manners and "outdated" makeup and dress. Kawai Michi, national secretary of Japanese Young Women's Christian Association (JYWCA) and a central figure in the enlightenment campaign, attributed American anti-Japanese sentiment in part to the "uneducated" behavior of these women. Having studied in the United States under the support of the scholarship established by Tsuda Umeko, Kawai firmly believed that the image of a nation was judged by the education level of its women. Under her leadership, the JYWCA and its main branch in California initiated education campaigns to discipline picture brides so that they could represent Japan in more desirable ways.[20] With support from the local government and politicians, the JYWCA established an emigrant women's school in Yokohama, providing classes on housework, English, child rearing, American society, Western lifestyles, and travel tips for the picture brides before they left for the United States.[21] Besides training, the JYWCA disseminated pamphlets with similar guidance among emigrant women. The JYWCA's California branch also offered accommodation and similar training to picture brides after their arrival.[22] Through these efforts, the campaign leaders expected to showcase civilized Japanese womanhood to the white Americans.

In addition, the female migrants were also expected to solidify families and give birth to children for Japanese American communities. For this reason, the mission of disciplining rural women's wrongdoings did not stop at

---

[18] Ibid., 144–146.

[19] In order to get married, many Japanese immigrants asked their relatives in Japan to choose partners for them because they could not afford to travel back to Japan to find their own partners due to financial limitations and possible military service conscription. After the two sides exchanged photos by mail and agreed to get married, the husband in the United States would mail a steamship ticket to his bride-to-be so that she could come to the United States to meet him and live with him. This type of marriage, which became increasingly popular among Japanese immigrants in the United States at the beginning of the twentieth century, was called "picture marriage"; women who immigrated to the United States through this form of marriage were known as "picture brides." Although scholars now commonly use the term "picture bride," it was originally coined by Japanese educators to label poor Japanese women who were obsessed with the idea of a good life abroad and were willing to marry men whom they had never met to obtain a steamship ticket to the United States.

[20] Abiko, "Zaibei Nihonjin Kirisutokyō Joshi Seinen Kai Sōritsu no Shidai," 17–18.

[21] Yokohama YWCA 80-Nenshi Henshū Iinkai, *Kono Iwa no Ue ni: Yokohama YWCA 80-Nenshi* (Yokohama: Yokohama YWCA, 1993), 10.

[22] Abiko, "Zaibei Nihonjin Kirisutokyō Joshi Seinen Kai Sōritsu no Shidai," 16.

Figure 5.1 Members of an American congressional committee investigating the Japanese picture brides at the Angel Island immigration station. This photograph was taken on July 25, 1920. Courtesy of Getty Images, Bettmann Archive Pictures and Images.

correcting their manners in daily life but went as far as regulating their marriage and occupation. Owing to limitations of communication and understanding between the two sides before marriage, not all marriages of Japanese immigrants ended happily. In order to find a good partner, some Japanese male immigrants used fake pictures to appear younger and more handsome than they really were. Others lied about their financial situation, claiming that they were successful businessmen or rich landowners, while in reality they were merely agricultural laborers.[23] As a result, many picture brides felt either disappointed or cheated when they faced reality. Since there were far fewer women than men in Japanese communities in California, it was relatively easy for a single female to find a job and live by herself. Some

---

[23] Yuji Ichioka, "Amerika Nadeshiko: Japanese Immigrant Women in the United States, 1900–1924," *Pacific Historical Review* 9, no. 2 (1980): 347–348. See also Yanagisawa Ikumi, "'Shashin Hanayume' wa 'Otto no Dorei' Datta no Ka: 'Shashin Hanayume' Tachi no Katari wo Chūshin ni," in *Shashin Hanayome Sensō Hanayome no Tadotta Michi: Josei Iminshi no Hakkutsu*, ed. Shimada Noriko (Tokyo: Akashi Shoten, 2009), 64–65.

disappointed brides thus chose divorce.[24] Leaders of the enlightenment campaign attributed these wife-initiated divorces to "the weakness of Japanese females" and "degradation of female morality."[25] They warned that these "degraded women" were the cause of American anti-Japanese sentiment, and urged all Japanese immigrant women to remain loyal to their husbands and fulfill their duty to raise children.[26] Local Japanese Christian women's homes sometimes even intervened and managed to prevent such divorces.[27]

Responding to financial difficulties and the hardship of agricultural life, most Japanese immigrant women living in rural areas had no choice but to work in the fields with their husbands.[28] White exclusionists accused them of transgressing gender boundaries, in which a man should be the only breadwinner while a woman should stay at home taking care of the family. They described the Japanese women in the field as the slaves of their husbands and attributed such "transgression" to the racial inferiority and uncivilized tradition of Japanese immigrants.[29] Replicating claims of the exclusionists, Kawai argued that if women went out to work, their housework and child-rearing duties would be neglected. She maintained that Japanese female immigrants' farm work was driven by their greed for money and assumed that it was a cause of American anti-Japanese sentiment.[30]

Permanent Settlement and the Intellectual Shift from "Increasing People" to "Planting People"

This campaign of educating Japanese picture brides in the United States was also part of the ideological transition of Japanese expansionism in response to the rise of anti-Japanese sentiment in North America. The threat of racial exclusion in the United States reminded the expansionists in Tokyo the importance of permanent settlement of the Japanese migrants abroad. Unlike Ōkawadaira Takamitsu and Tōgō Minoru who called for Japanese expansion elsewhere in the late 1900s, the enlightenment campaign's goal was to remove the restrictions on Japanese migration to the United States. Yet the enlightenment campaign was also an offspring of the intellectual debates since the late

[24] Rumi Yasutake, *Transnational Women's Activism: The United States, Japan, and Japanese Immigrant Communities in California, 1859–1920* (New York: New York University Press, 2004), 125.
[25] Ibid.; Kusunoki Rokuichi, "Beikoku Kashū Engan no Dōhō," *Joshi Seinen Kai* 11, no. 7 (July 1914): 8.
[26] Yasutake, *Transnational Women's Activism*, 133.
[27] Kusunoki, "Beikoku Kashū Engan no Dōhō," 7–8.
[28] Yanagisawa, "'Shashin Hanayume' wa 'Otto no Dorei' Datta no Ka," 69–76.   [29] Ibid., 77.
[30] Tanaka Kei, "Japanese Picture Marriage in 1900–1924 California: Construction of Japanese Race and Gender" (PhD diss., Rutgers University, 2002), 211; and Kawai Michiko, "Tobei Fujin wa Seikō Shitsutsu Ari Ya?," *Joshi Seinen Kai* 13, no. 10 (October 1916): 11.

1900s that attempted to make sense of the rise of anti-Japanese sentiment in the United States. Replicating the ideas of Ōkawadaira and Tōgō, the campaign leaders identified the immigrants' sojourner mentality (*dekasegi konsei*) as the root of all evil, thus they believed that the ultimate solution was for the immigrants to commit to permanent settlement. As rural peasants came to constitute the majority of the migrant population and the domestic rice riots continued, agricultural settlement was naturally favored by the campaign leaders as the most desirable model of migration. In their minds, the enactment of the California Alien Land Law of 1913 reinforced the central importance of land ownership in order for Japanese immigrants to succeed in permanent settlement.[31]

To prepare migrants for the long-term commitment, the campaign leaders stressed the importance of training the migrants before they left Japan. To this end, the Emigration Association held regular lectures in Tokyo and Yokohama, published journals and books that disseminated migration-related information, and organized annual workshops from 1916 to 1919. These workshops were attended by teachers from high schools and professional schools throughout the archipelago.[32] The association also established an emigration training center in Yokohama in 1916, directly offering emigrants classes on social manners, hygiene, foreign languages, child rearing, and housework. Over four hundred migrants – two-fifths were women – attended the classes at the training center within two months after it opened. The center was jointly founded by funds from the Japanese Ministry of Foreign Affairs and donations from entrepreneurial tycoons. Nagata Shigeshi, the president of Japanese Striving Society, served as its first director.[33]

The Japanese expansionists' growing interest in permanent settlement was reflected by the ascendency of the term 植民 over 殖民 when referring to the concept of colonial migration. As written forms for the concept *shokumin*, the Japanese translation for the Western word "colonization,"[34] both terms first appeared during the early Meiji era. Even though their characters (*kanji*) differed, the Meiji intellectuals at times used the two terms interchangeably because they shared the same pronunciation, a common practice in the modern Japanese language.

The word 殖民, with the implication of reproducing, clearly dominated in governmental documents and intellectual works throughout most of the Meiji

[31] Yamawaki Haruki, "Beikoku Imin ni Kansuru Shokan," *Nihon Imin Kyōkai Hōkoku* 1, no. 7 (March 1916): 11–12 (repr., Tokyo: Fuji Shuppan, 2006).
[32] Sakaguchi, "Kaisetsu," 12.
[33] Soeda Jū'ichi, "Kojin no Kansei," *Nihon Imin Kyōkai Hōkoku* 1, no. 8 (April 1916): 4 (repr., Tokyo: Fuji Shuppan, 2006).
[34] Nagata Saburō, "Shokumin Oyobi Shokumichi no Jigi," *Kokumin Keizai Zasshi* 43, no. 2 (August 1927): 123.

period – as the first chapter of this book had illustrated, Meiji colonial expansion was developed hand in hand with the original accumulation of modern Japanese capitalism. However, 植民 gained increasing popularity among Japanese intellectuals in response to the rise of anti-Japanese sentiment in the United States in the beginning of the twentieth century.[35] The first Japanese book that adopted 植民 instead of 殖民 was *On Japanese Colonial Migration* (*Nihon Shokumin Ron*), authored by Tōgō Minoru in 1906. As the previous chapter showed, while Tōgō did not explain his choice of wording, this book marked only the beginning of the Japanese expansionists' intellectual exploration of the model of permanent migration. In 1916, Nitobe Inazō, Tōgō's coadvisor at Sapporo Agricultural College, penned an article that clarified the difference between these two written forms. As Nitobe pointed out, while 殖民 was a combination of the character 殖, literally meaning "reproducing," with the character 民, literally meaning "people," 植民 was a combination between 植, with the meaning of "planting," with "people," 民.[36] The fact that Nitobe used 植民 instead of 殖民 throughout the article demonstrated that the choice of this written form was deliberate. From the 1900s onward, 植民 gradually replaced 殖民 as the written form of *shokumin* in Japanese. Its increasing popularity among Japanese expansionists mirrored the affirmation of agriculture-centered permanent migration as the dominant model of Japanese expansion throughout the Taishō and early Shōwa years.

Japanese Expansion in Northeast Asia and the South Seas

The transformation in the discourse of Japanese expansion was further solidified by Japan's participation in World War I (1914–1918). As historian Frederick Dickinson forcefully argues, this first global war offered Japan a golden opportunity to join the club of modern empires as a valuable member.[37] Although its proposal to write the clause of racial equality into the charter of the League of Nations was rejected at the Paris Peace Conference, Japan, as a victor of the war, was able to secure a position of leadership in the postwar world as a charter member of the league.[38] It was also rewarded with Germany's colonies in Micronesia and colonial privileges in the Shandong Peninsula in China. At the turn of the 1920s, it seemed that Japan had much to gain and little to lose by embracing the new world order. Under Anglo-

---

[35] Ibid., 123–127.
[36] Nitobe, *Nitobe Hakushi Shokumin Seisaku Kōgi Oyobi Ronbunshū*, 41. As Yanaihara mentioned in the preface, this book is a collection of his note on Nitobe's seminars on colonial studies between 1916 and 1917. So we can assume that Nitobe made this statement.
[37] Frederick Dickinson, *World War I and the Triumph of a New Japan, 1919–1930* (Cambridge: Cambridge University Press, 2013), 12.
[38] Ibid., 69–70.

American hegemony, this new order professed to reject territorial expansion in favor of peace and cooperation. Japan had to halt its military expansion, but migration with the expectations of permanent settlement and local engagement seamlessly fitted into this new world order as a peaceful means of expansion.[39] Thus the years during and right after World War I witnessed increased Japanese efforts to expand via alternative routes by nonmilitary means.

The career trajectories of individual members of the Emigration Association around this time demonstrate how the Japanese American enlightenment campaign was intertwined with Japanese expansion campaigns in other part of the world that emerged at this time. Ōkuma Shigenobu, the president of the Emigration Association, was a long-standing advocate of Japanese conciliation with the West. Ōkuma was a passionate supporter of the enlightenment campaign, and his promotion of Japanese immigrants' assimilation into white society was tied to his agenda of integrating Japanese expansion in Northeast Asia into the existing imperial world order. It was also Ōkuma who, during his tenure as the prime minister of Japan, forced the Yuan Shikai regime to accept the Twenty-One Demands in order to deepen Japan's political and economic penetration in China while avoiding challenging the Western powers' existing colonial interest in China.[40] The aim of Japanese expansion in Northeast Asia, Ōkuma argued, should not only be solving the issue of domestic overpopulation and food shortage; Japan also needed to contribute to the economic prosperity and peace of local societies.[41]

The call for expansion to the South Seas emerged prior to the first two decades of the twentieth century – the Seikyō Sha leaders in the 1890s had advocated nanshin as a way to prepare Japan for the inevitable race war against the West. However, the later proposals of expansion to the South Seas were shaped by the experiences of Japanese American enlightenment campaign and World War I. As a result, this new discourse of southward expansion was centered on cooperation with the Western powers instead of challenging them. Takekoshi Yosaburō, a politician-cum-journalist and member of the Emigration Association, was a leading proponent of this trend of thought. In order for Japan to shed its image of the invader (as American exclusionists described Japan), Takekoshi argued, Japan's expansion must be carried out not

---

[39] Akira Iriye, "The Failure of Economic Expansionism: 1918–1931," in *Japan in Crisis: Essays on Taishō Democracy*, ed. Bernard Silberman and H. D. Harootunian (Princeton: Princeton University Press, 1974), 251.

[40] Frederick Dickinson insightfully points out that the Twenty-One Demands were proposed by a pro-West political faction in Japan in order to prevent the anti-West faction from taking on a more aggressive plan of expansion in Asia that would lead to an intense confrontation between Japan and the Western powers. See Frederick Dickinson, *War and National Reinvention: Japan in the Great War, 1914–1919* (Cambridge, MA: Harvard University Asia Center, 2001), 84–116.

[41] Ōkuma, "Sekai no Daikyoku to Imin," 7–8.

via military invasion but instead by focusing on bringing civilization to the world: while Japan was a latecomer to the civilized world, it was now already a full-fledged member, thus it was time for the Japanese to partake in carrying the "White Man's Burden" (*Hakujin no Omoni*).[42] The ideal direction for such a Japanese expansion was southward. Its targets included the South Pacific islands, originally proposed by the nanshin thinkers in the 1880s and 1890s, and Southeast Asia, which came under the Japanese colonial gaze after the annexation of Taiwan following the Sino-Japanese War.

Takekoshi acknowledged the fact that the majority of these areas were already under Western colonial rule. Yet Westerners, he contended, were too occupied with extracting profits from the colonies and ignored the task of civilizing these backward regions. Therefore, Japan should take this opportunity to bring civilization to Western colonies, guiding local peoples to make progress in developing commerce and acquiring education. If Japan took up the task to share the blessings of civilization with the native peoples, Takekoshi argued, its expansion would no longer be met with criticism.[43]

The calls for southward expansion also gained material support from the imperial government. In the 1910s, in addition to taking over Micronesia from Germany, the government also sponsored private Japanese enterprises to purchase lands for emigration in North Borneo. It also reached out to the French government in order to facilitate Japanese business expansion in Indochina.[44] Another member of the association, a politician and entrepreneurial tycoon named Inoue Masaji, played a leading role in Japanese mercantile and migrant expansion in the South Seas from the 1910s to the 1940s. He was the founder of the South Asia Company (Nan'a Kōshi), a Singapore-based Japanese trading company operating in Southeast Asia. He also cofounded the South Seas Association (Nan'yō Kyōkai), a semigovernmental association that promoted Japanese expansion in Southeast Asia and the South Pacific.[45] He later became the head of the government-sponsored Overseas Development Company (Kaigai Kōgyō Kabushiki Gaisha) and was in charge of the majority of the activities in Japanese Brazilian migration throughout the 1920s and 1930s.

The empire's expansion in Northeast Asia and the South Seas in the 1910s provided new colonial privileges for Japanese agricultural migrants. Japan's annexation of Korea not only safeguarded the land properties previously acquired by Japanese settlers but also gave them legal privileges for further land grabbing.[46] The Twenty-One Demands allowed Japanese subjects to lease land throughout Manchuria. The empire's annexation of German Micronesia in

[42] Takekoshi Yosaburō, "Nanpō no Keiei to Nihon no Shimei," *Taiyō* 16, no. 15 (1910): 20.
[43] Ibid., 20–21. [44] Lynn, "Comparative Study of Tōyō Kyōkai and Nan'yō Kyōkai," 83–84.
[45] Ibid., 72–73.
[46] Peter Duus, *The Abacus and the Sword: The Japanese Penetration of Korea, 1895–1910* (Berkeley: University of California Press, 1998), 376.

1915 as a mandate territory gave Japanese expansionists a free hand for land acquisition and migration there.

However, despite the imperial government's enthusiastic encouragement and political support by the end of the 1920s, the Malthusian expansionists were never fully satisfied with the state of Japanese agricultural migration to Northeast Asia and the South Seas. While the Korean Peninsula had one of the biggest Japanese overseas communities in the first half of the twentieth century, relatively few Japanese settlers there were farmers. Instead, they were either landlords or urbanites who worked for the colonial government and Japanese companies.[47] The Oriental Development Company had originally planned to move three hundred thousand Japanese farming households to the Korean Peninsula, but it managed to settle only fewer than four thousand households by 1924.[48] By 1931, only about eight hundred Japanese farmers were living inside Japan's sphere of influence in Manchuria, constituting a tiny portion of the primarily urban settler population.[49]

A direct reason for this failure was that Japanese agricultural settlers had serious difficulty competing with local Korean and Chinese farmers, whose cost of living and labor were substantially lower than theirs.[50] Japanese expansion to the South Seas in general primarily focused on commerce, accompanied by Japanese contract laborer migration to local sugar plantations. Specifically, Japanese farmer migration to the South Pacific began in the 1920s and the migrants mainly settled in the empire's mandate territory in Micronesia. While the number of settlers steadily increased under governmental support from the 1920s to the end of World War II, the total size of Japanese population in the South Pacific did not exceed twenty thousand by 1930.[51]

The Rise of Migration to Brazil, 1908–1924

While the migration experiments in Northeast Asia and the South Seas proved disappointing, Brazil, with its relatively friendly immigration policy toward the Japanese, turned out to be the most promising option for the Malthusian expansionists in Tokyo. Between 1908 and 1924, Japanese immigrants in

---

[47] As the data collected by Jun Uchida demonstrate, the vast majority of the Japanese settlers in the Korean Peninsula throughout the colonial period were urban residents who made a living as merchants, government employees, and workers and managers at manufacturing companies. Uchida, *Brokers of Empire*, 67–68.

[48] Iriye, "Failure of Economic Expansionism," 253.   [49] Wilson, "New Paradise," 252.

[50] Iriye, "Failure of Economic Expansionism," 254. As early as 1928, the president of the Southern Manchuria Railway Company, Yamamoto Jōtarō, made a similar argument. See Yamamoto Jōtarō, "Manmō no Hatten to Mantetsu no Jigyō," *Seiyū*, no. 330 (1928): 13–17, cited from Wilson, "New Paradise," 256.

[51] Peattie, "The Nan'yō: Japan in the South Pacific," 197. Peattie did not explain why the Japanese migration to the South Pacific was not fruitful, but a possible reason would be that the tropical climate was not attractive to farmers from the Japanese archipelago.

Brazil not only grew steadily in number but also succeeded in agricultural settlement. In 1920, before the arrival of the bigger waves of Japanese migrants to Brazil, there were over twenty-eight thousand Japanese settlers in Brazil, 94.8 percent of whom were engaging in rural agriculture. By the time the Immigration Act of 1924 passed, the number of Japanese migrants in Brazil had already climbed to thirty-five thousand.[52] In the same year, an unprecedented number of migrants from rural Japan, fully subsidized by Tokyo, also began to arrive on the shores of the state of São Paulo. From then until 1936, Brazil remained the single country that received the most Japanese migrants outside of Asia.[53] In that year, Japanese migrants to Manchuria eventually outnumbered those to Brazil. The following pages of this chapter discuss the reasons why Japanese agricultural migration eventually found success in Brazil.

Japanese expansionists had set their sights on Brazil decades before the Russo-Japanese War. As a result of the efforts of Enomoto Takeaki and his followers, Japan established diplomatic relationship with Brazil in 1895. This was soon followed by a Yoshisa Emigration Company project that recruited 1,592 laborers from Japan to work on coffee plantations in Brazil. However, this plan was suddenly canceled by Yoshisa Emigration Company's partner in Brazil, Prado Jordão & Company, due to the coffee market's collapse the same year. This aborted project revealed that the Brazilian government and

Table 5.1 *Annual numbers of Japanese migrants to Brazil and Manchuria in comparison (1932–1939)*

	1932	1933	1934	1935	1936	1937	1938	1939
Japanese migrants to Brazil	15,092	23,229	22,960	5,745	5,375	4,675	2,563	1,314
Japanese migrants to Manchuria	2,569	2,574	1,553	2,605	5,778	20,095	25,654	39,018

Data regarding Japanese migrants to Brazil are drawn from Gaimushō Ryōji Ijūbu, *Wa Ga Kokumin no Kaigai Hatten: Ijū Hyakunen no Ayumi –Shiryōhen* (Tokyo: Gaimushō Ryōji Ijūbu, 1972), 140. Data regarding Japanese migrants to Manchuria are drawn from Louise Young, *Japan's Total Empire: Manchuria and the Culture of Wartime Imperialism* (Berkeley: University of California Press, 1998), 395.

[52] Tsuchida, "Japanese in Brazil," 167, 197.
[53] This conclusion is based on data for Japanese migration to different parts of the world in Okabe Makio, *Umi wo Watatta Nihonjin* (Tokyo: Yamakawa Shuppansha, 2002), 14–15.

coffee plantation labor contractors did not take Japanese migrants seriously, as European immigrant laborers' numbers remained high while the global coffee market continued to lag. The failure of this migration project forced the policymakers in Tokyo to suspend all future plans of migration to Brazil in order to avoid economic loss and any further damage to Japan's international prestige.[54]

After the Russo-Japanese War, the resurgent interest in migration to Brazil was a direct result of anti-Japanese sentiment in the United States. In 1905, Japan's minister in Brazil, Sugimura Fukashi, sent a report to Tokyo that advocated Japanese migration to Brazil. Later published by *Osaka Asahi News* (*Osaka Asahi Shimbun*), this report pointed out that the Italian government's decision to suspend migration to Brazil had led to a labor shortage in the country. While white racism against Japanese in the United States, Canada, and Australia had worsened, Sugimura argued, Brazil would be an ideal alternative for Japanese migrants. He also encouraged migration agents in Japan to visit Brazil in order to explore the opportunities firsthand.[55]

The state of São Paulo in Brazil welcomed the Japanese immigrants for two reasons. The first was that it expected these migrants' arrival would foster the further growth of its coffee economy. The migrants would fill the labor vacuum created by the suspension of migration from Italy and open up Japanese market to Brazilian coffee – the ships that ferried the migrants to Brazil were expected to carry local coffee back to Japan. Paulista elites also believed that the Japanese migrants would turn the sparsely populated lowlands along the coast into productive farms.[56] With such expectations in mind, the state of São Paulo offered financial support for the endeavor.

Two migration projects, spearheaded by Mizuno Ryū and Aoyagi Ikutarō, respectively, were carried out with Brazilian support. Both Mizuno and Aoyagi believed that overseas migration was necessary not only to solve Japan's overpopulation issue but also to strengthen the Japanese empire,[57] and both men had previous migration experience elsewhere.[58] While their Brazilian migration projects represented two different models of migration – Mizuno's focused on contract labor while Aoyagi's focused on farmer migration with

---

[54] Tsuchida, "Japanese in Brazil," 31–37.
[55] Kōyama Rokurō, ed., *Imin Yonjūnen Shi* (São Paulo: Kōyama Rokurō, 1949), 14–17.
[56] Ibid., 128–129, 185–186.
[57] For Mizuno Ryō, see Mamiya Kunio, "Mizuno Ryō to Kōkoku Shokumin Gaisha ni Tsuite no Oboegaki," *Shakaigaku Tōkyū* 44, no. 2 (1999): 37. For Aoyagi Ikutarō, see Yabiku, *Burajiru Okinawa Iminshi*, 6.
[58] Mizuno served as president of the Imperial Colonial Migration Company (Kōkoku Shokumin Gaisha), which previously sent a small group of Japanese laborers to the Philippines. Aoyagi Ikutarō studied at the University of California in the 1880s and authored a book promoting migration to Peru in 1894. See Tsuchida, "Japanese in Brazil," 98, and Aoyagi Ikutarō, *Perū Jijō* (Tokyo: Aoyagi Ikutarō, 1894).

land acquisition—they were both ideological heirs to the earlier Texas migration project.

Uchida Sadatsuchi, the initial architect of Japanese agricultural migration to Texas, became the Japanese consul in the state of São Paulo in 1907. He served as an advocate for Mizuno's plan of Brazil-bound migration within the Japanese government. Japanese labor migration to Brazil, he reasoned, would eventually result in agricultural settlement like it had in Texas. He further argued that this time around, the settlement project was destined for success because, unlike the Americans, the Brazilians were not racist against the Japanese.[59] Uchida also played a central role during the initial negotiations between the state of São Paulo and the Japanese Ministry of Foreign Affairs that made it possible for Mizuno Ryū to transport 781 Japanese migrants to Brazil in June 1908 via the ship *Kasato-maru*.[60]

The state of São Paulo had partially subsidized the migrants' trip expenses with the expectation that they would work in the designated coffee plantations (*fazendas*) as laborers (*colonos*). The initial phase of the project, however, was not met with success, as Mizuno's poor planning led to company bankruptcy and caused misery for many of the first-wave migrants.[61] Nevertheless, Mizuno was able to continue his migration career via the newly established Takemura Colonial Migration Company (Takemura Shokumin Shōkai).[62] Between 1908 and 1914, Japanese labor migration to Brazil remained unsuccessful due to conflicting expectations of the Japanese migrants and the Brazilian plantation owners. The former, misled by migration companies to a degree, thought they could quickly make a fortune in Brazil. The latter, on the other hand, saw the migrants as exploitable cheap laborers who would accept a low standard of living and below-average wage. In 1914, unsatisfied with the Japanese immigrant laborers' performance, the state of São Paulo suspended its subsidy for Japanese migration. Worried that anti-Japanese sentiment would raise its head in South America like it had in the United States, Tokyo decided to halt further labor migration to Brazil.[63]

Aoyagi Ikutarō's migration project, on the other hand, closely resembled the earlier Japanese rice farming experience in Texas. Its participants arrived in Brazil as owner-farmers with long-term settlement plans. To take advantage of a law enacted by the state of São Paulo in 1907 that provided subsidies and land concessions to any migration companies that brought in agricultural settlers, a group of Japanese merchants and politicians formed the migration company Tokyo Syndicate. As the head of this company, Aoyagi planned to establish Japanese farming communities in Brazil by purchasing the lands at a low price in São Paulo and then selling portions to individual Japanese farmers. In 1912,

[59] Tsuchida, "Japanese in Brazil," 125.   [60] Ibid., 125–134.   [61] Ibid., 137–155.
[62] Ibid., 157.   [63] Ibid., 170–171.

the state of São Paulo granted fifty thousand hectares of uncultivated land in the Iguape region to Tokyo Syndicate under the condition that the company would relocate two thousand Japanese families there within four years.[64]

The year 1913 was crucial to Aoyagi's success. The California Alien Land Law of 1913 showed the Japanese leaders how important landownership was to successful migrant expansion. Aoyagi's efforts in Brazilian land acquisition thus caught the attention of Shibusawa Ei'ichi, a founding member of the Emigration Association and the central figure in the Japanese American enlightenment campaign. Shibusawa was well aware of how Japanese immigrants in California had suffered when they were deprived of their landownership; he became a passionate donor to and supporter for Aoyagi's campaign in Brazil. Under Shibusawa's leadership, a group of Japanese entrepreneurial elites formed the Brazil Colonization Company (Burajiru Takushoku Gaisha). With endorsements from the second Katsura Cabinet, the Brazil Colonization Company took over from Tokyo Syndicate to further expand land acquisition in the state of São Paulo while keeping Aoyagi Ikutarō at its helm.

This new company not only secured the ownership of the Iguape Colony but also purchased fourteen hundred hectares of land in the Gipuvura region from the state of São Paulo. In recognition of the support offered by the Japanese government, the company named their new property Katsura Colony after Katsura Tarō, the prime minister.[65] The imperial government was not the only party that was interested in experimenting with farmer migration in Brazil. Beginning with Shibusawa Ei'ichi, there was a number of Japanese entrepreneurial elites who also played a key role in Aoyagi's Brazilian land acquisition initiative. As most of their businesses depended heavily on Japan-US bilateral trade, they were interested in exploring alternative overseas markets to make up for the possible profit loss caused by the Americans' anti-Japanese stance. They believed that land acquisition in Brazil, coupled with Japanese farmer migration and permanent settlement, would open up more business opportunities for them.

Aside from government officials and business tycoons, Aoyagi Ikutarō's project also had supporters in the intellectual circles. In 1914, Kyoto Imperial University professor Kawada Shirō published his study of Brazil as a potential colony for Japan. Titled *Brazil as a Colony* (*Shokuminchi Toshite no Burajiru*), this book was the most representative product of the Japanese Malthusian expansionists' debate during the 1910s in response to the enactment of the Gentlemen's Agreement and the passage of the Alien Land Law in California.

---

[64] "Iguape Colony," in National Diet Library, Japan, *100 Years of Japanese Emigration to Brazil*, www.ndl.go.jp/brasil/e/s3/s3_2.html.
[65] Ibid.

It pointed to Brazil as the most pragmatic alternative to the United States for Japan's surplus people. Brazil was the ideal destination for Japan's surplus population because it had fertile and spacious land, a small population, and no race-based restrictions on citizenship or property rights.[66] At the same time, Kawada also pointed out, not all types of migration were desirable. Like Tōgō and Ōkawadaira, he stressed the difference between the less desirable emigration (*imin*) and the more desirable colonial migration (*shokumin*). Kawada paid special attention to the Brazilian Colonial Company as the first Japanese company to conduct "colonial migration" (shokumin), which was different from the previous migration endeavors that exported only the less desirable imin – that is, the contract laborers and temporary emigrants.[67] Kawada argued that Aoyagi's campaign, with its mission of acquiring farmland and helping Japanese peasants to permanently settle overseas, represented colonial migration rather than emigration. More importantly, it was the former that best served the interests of the Japanese empire.[68]

The Success of Farmer Migration in Brazil

Farmer migration with land acquisition in Brazil was the Japanese expansionists' answer to American racism against their compatriots. It was also ideologically complementary to the Japanese American enlightenment campaign that was under way at around the same time. However, the actual success of Aoyagi's project depended on a few contingent but indispensable global and local factors. The outbreak of World War I, the existing flow of Japanese laborers to Brazil, and the specific conditions of coffee and cotton plantations in the state of São Paulo all contributed to the campaign's success.

Although Aoyagi was successful in securing financial support, he had considerable difficulty recruiting migrants from Japan to Brazil. Japanese farmers were naturally reluctant to join this venture: not only did they have to permanently leave their homeland, they also had to fork over a significant amount of cash in order to purchase farmlands from the Brazil Colonization Company. Farmers who already owned land in Japan had few reasons to take the risk, while the landless farmers struggled to meet the financial requirement. For the latter group, migrating to Brazil as plantation laborers was only possible if their trips were subsidized. As a result, a majority of the initial setters in the company's colonies were Japanese contract laborers in coffee plantations who were already living in Brazil. For example, among the first thirty-three families who settled in the Katsura Colony in 1913, only three were recruited

---

[66] Kawada Shirō, *Shokuminchi Toshite no Burajiru* (Tokyo: Yūhikaku Shobō, 1914), 242.
[67] Ibid., 162.   [68] Ibid., 170.

from the archipelago; all the rest were Japanese laborers who had left their previous plantations in Brazil.[69]

Thus, in a stroke of irony, even though agricultural migration was slated to replace the "outdated and undesirable" model of laborer migration, it was the latter that provided the former with sufficient human capital for its initial success. The revival of Japanese labor migration was an immediate result of World War I, as the outbreak of the war led to a catastrophic decline in labor supply for the Brazilian coffee plantations. The annual number of new immigrants arriving in Brazil dropped from 119,758 in 1913 to a mere 20,937 in 1915. To make matters worse for the plantations, some European laborers already in their employment returned to their home countries, while still many others left for the cities to work in the more lucrative war-related industries.[70] Such an unexpected and urgent need for coffee plantation laborers eventually pushed the state government of São Paulo to resume its subsidy for labor migration from Japan in 1916.[71]

While the constant flow of laborers from rural Japan to coffee plantations in São Paulo provided a stable supply of potential farmer-settlers, the very structure of the Brazilian rural economy made it not only possible but also necessary for the Japanese laborers working on coffee plantations to gradually transform themselves into landowning farmers. The low wages these laborers received caused them much disappointment, but it also made it impossible for them to quickly return to Japan; thus they had to focus on improving their station in life while staying in Brazil. At the same time, the cultivation of alternative crops such as rice and cotton proved to be highly lucrative. While urbanization and industrialization increased the demand for rice as food and cotton as raw material, most of Brazil's rural landlords showed little interest in switching from coffee to these crops. The increasing demand for rice and cotton and the lack of local supply left a niche spot that the Japanese immigrants could ably fill. Having grown up in rural Japan, most of them had farming skills before coming to Brazil, and a lack of competition from the locals all but guaranteed their profits. In addition, unlike coffee, which required a multiple-year cycle to yield investment return, rice and cotton were annual crops that allowed farmers to quickly accumulate wealth with little initial investment. Therefore, even though their income levels were low, it was not difficult for Japanese migrants working on coffee plantations to purchase their own lands by cultivating rice and cotton in their spare time.

Under the management of Brazil Colonization Company, the region of Iguape became highly attractive to Japanese migrant laborers. In addition to dividing its land into small portions and allowing immigrants to purchase them by annual installments, the company's management of Iguape

---

[69] Tsuchida, "Japanese in Brazil," 188 and 190.   [70] Ibid., 172.   [71] Ibid., 173.

Figure 5.2 Japanese immigrants harvesting cotton in the field. This picture
was used by Japanese Striving Society's president Nagata Shigeshi for his
speeches around Nagano prefecture in the late 1910s to promote Japanese
migration to Brazil. Courtesy of the Japanese Striving Society.

provided the Japanese immigrants with a sense of community. For example, the residents of Katsura Colony, the first settler community in Iguape,
were able to communicate in Japanese in daily life, enjoy Japanese food
such as rice and miso, and purchase Japanese goods at reasonable prices in
local stores.[72] The Registro Colony, the second settler community in
Iguape, founded in 1916, featured a medical clinic and its own brick and
tile factories. Later on, both Katsura and Registro colonies also established
schools.[73] In 1917, the Brazil Colonization Company started offering loans
to every Japanese family – be they located in Japan or Brazil – that would
come live in Registro. As a result, the number of new families who moved
in grew from twenty in 1916 to one hundred fifty in 1918.[74]

[72] Ibid., 190.   [73] Ibid., 192. By 1924, four schools were established in Katsura and Registro.
[74] Ibid., 191.

Figure 5.3 Hundreds of bags of rice produced by Japanese immigrants piled up on a railway that connected the Japanese community in Registro with other parts of Brazil. This picture was also used by Japanese Striving Society's president Nagata Shigeshi for his speeches around Nagano prefecture in late 1910s to promote Japanese migration to Brazil. Courtesy of the Japanese Striving Society.

Iguape: A Turning Point

Between 1914 and 1917, while the total settler population in Iguape remained low, the number of recruits grew rapidly every year. The growth and stability of Japanese settler communities in Iguape during these years marked a turning point in the history of Japanese migration in Brazil for two reasons. For one thing, long-term opportunities in Iguape attracted more and more Japanese immigrants who came to Brazil as contract laborers to stay and give up their plan of returning. For another, the prosperity of Iguape also drew increasing support from the imperial government in Brazilian migration.

First, to those who initially migrated from Japan to Brazil as plantation laborers with the goal of returning home, the success of their peers in Iguape helped to motivate them to settle down and acquire lands for themselves. By 1920, Japanese immigrants in Brazil were more likely to own farmland than any other ethnic group. During that year, the Japanese immigrants held 5.3 percent of the alien-owned farmland in São Paulo, while they constituted only 4.3 percent of the state's foreign population.[75] In the same year, 94 percent of Japanese living in Brazil were engaged in agriculture in one way or another,[76] a figure that was in sharp contrast to the Japanese communities in Northeast Asia and the South Seas. By then, expansionists in Tokyo were convinced that agricultural migration was the most desirable migration model for the expanding empire. Yet only in Brazil, buoyed by specific local and global contextual factors, did agricultural settlement prove to be the most profitable choice for Japanese migrants.

Second, the prevailing trend of Japanese laborers in Brazil repositioning themselves as independent farmer also prompted the imperial government to take a fresh look at the value of labor migration. Indeed, the Ministry of Foreign Affairs endorsed Mizuno Ryū's initial campaign of labor migration to Brazil in 1908 because it expected that these labor migrants would eventually settle down in South America as independent farmers.[77] However, it was the growing size of laborer-turned-independent farmers in Japanese Brazilian communities that proved the model's merits to Tokyo. Thus convinced, the Japanese government became further involved in expanding and managing labor migration projects overseas in general and to Brazil in particular.

Between 1917 and 1918, four leading Japanese migration companies, including the South America Colonial Company (Nanbei Shokumin Kabushiki Gaisha), managed by Mizuno Ryū, merged into the Overseas Development Company (Kaigai Kōgyō Kabushiki Gaisha), commonly known as Kaikō for short.[78] After acquiring the Morioka Emigration Company (Morioka Imin Gaisha) in 1920, the Kaikō became the only government-authorized Japanese migration company operating in Brazil. At the time of its formation, the Kaikō primarily ran on private funds, but it maintained close ties with the government.[79] Not only was its first director Kamiyama Jūnji a former bureaucrat, its very inception was endorsed by Tokyo with the goal of consolidating the migration companies so that the government could monitor and manage overseas migration more effectively.[80]

---

[75] Ibid., 198.   [76] Ibid., 197.   [77] Ibid., 125.

[78] The other three migration companies that also merged into the Kaikō included Tōyō Imin Gōshi Gaisha, Nittō Shokumin Kabushiki Gōshi Gaisha, and Nihon Shokumin Gōshi Gaisha. See Kumamoto Yoshihiro, "Kaigai Kōgyō Kabushiki Gaisha no Setsuritsu Keii to Imin Kaisha no Tōgō Mondai," *Komazawa Daigaku Shigaku Ronshū*, no. 31 (April 2001): 60.

[79] The merger was initiated and supervised by the imperial government. Tsuchida, "Japanese in Brazil," 174.

[80] See the comments of the Japanese minister of finance on the Kaikō in 1918. Kaigai Kōgyō Kabushiki Gaisha, *Kaigai Hatten ni Kansuru Katsuta Ōkura Daijin Kōen* (Tokyo: Kaigai Kōgyō Kabushiki Gaisha, 1918), 28–32.

The Kaikō's initial task was recruiting farmers from rural Japan and relocating them overseas as contract laborers. Aside from coffee plantations in Brazil, it also sent migrants to work on sugar plantations and mines in other places around the Pacific Rim such as the Philippines, Australia, and Peru. Nevertheless, labor migration to Brazil claimed an increasing share of the Kaikō's business and became its dominant source of revenue from 1920 onward.[81]

In 1919, the Kaikō expanded into South America by merging with Aoyagi's Brazil Colonization Company, taking over the latter's land property and business in Brazil. Through this merger, the Kaikō combined the previously separate labor migration and farmer migration projects. More human and financial resources were then poured into the program of land acquisition in Iguape.[82] During the next year, the Kaikō established a third settler community named Sete Barras Colony in Iguape next to Registro. The company built roads to interconnect the three Japanese communities, linking them with river ports and adjacent Brazilian towns. With support from the imperial government, the Kaikō also began to integrate the domestic aspects of the migration campaign such as public promotion, candidate selection, and predeparture training. The migrants were expected to show their absolute dedication to the empire by permanently settling overseas as independent farmers, extending the Japanese empire's influence to the other side of the Pacific.

While the social mobility of the Japanese laborers-turned-owners in Brazil attracted increasing support from Tokyo, it also prompted the state of São Paulo to suspend its subsidy to Japanese immigrants. As more and more Japanese laborers left their original plantations to take up independent farming, São Paulo's policymakers became convinced that it was no longer cost-effective for their coffee plantations to seek out laborers from Japan.[83] This conclusion was also made at the moment when migrants from Europe once again began to pour into Brazilian plantations at the end of World War I. Despite the Japanese perception of racial equality in Brazil, the Brazilian government had always deemed European immigrants to be more desirable than those from Asia. In 1922, the state of São Paulo officially ended its subsidy for Japanese labor migration.

---

[81] See graph 3 in Sakaguchi, "Dare Ga Imin wo Okuridashita no Ka," 57.
[82] Tsuchida, "Japanese in Brazil," 192.   [83] Ibid., 176.

Toward a New Era of Japanese Settler Colonialism

The decline of São Paulo's interest in Japanese laborers, however, did not put an end to the flow of Japanese migration to Brazil. On the contrary, the number of Japanese immigrants in Brazil grew at a rapid pace after the turn of the 1920s. Growth of the Japanese migration flow to Brazil was accompanied by the overall changes in Japanese migration-based expansion in general, marked by the emphases on permanent settlement and the importance of women and the increasing involvement of the Japanese government in migration promotion and management. These changes were consolidated by a series of international and domestic events that took place in the first half of the 1920s.

In 1920, the California Alien Land Law was revised to close many significant loopholes that had existed in the original 1913 version. With Japanese American farmers as its primary target, the revised law banned aliens ineligible for citizenship from purchasing land in the names of their American-born children or in the names of corporations. Both practices were popular with Japanese immigrant farmers in California as ways to circumvent the original law. In addition to the right of purchasing and long-term leasing lands, the Japanese immigrants' right of short-term land leasing was also taken away from them. This revised law not only dealt a fatal blow to Japanese American farmers in California but also convinced Tokyo that the Japanese American enlightenment campaign had failed. In 1922, the Japanese government had to "voluntarily" stop issuing passports to picture brides to avoid fanning further anti-Japanese sentiment in the United States. In the meantime, while Asia and the South Pacific appeared to be unattractive destinations, white racism in North America spurred the Japanese expansionists to gaze into Brazil. The success of Japanese agricultural settlement in Iguape convinced Japanese policymakers that migration to Brazil was worth the financial investment.

Emerging amid the waves of anti-Japanese sentiment in the United States and the Japanese American enlightenment campaign, Japanese Brazilian migration immediately inherited the campaign leaders' emphasis on the principle of permanent settlement and the importance of women in Japanese community building. The Brazilian migration was carried out with efforts in fostering both land acquisition and family-centered settlement. For example, the Overseas Development Company that sent most of Japanese migrants to Brazil in the 1920s and 1930s, recruited migrants in family units instead of individually. To be qualified to sign the contract of migration with the Kaikō, each migrant family had to comprise at least three adults (above the age of twelve).[84]

---

[84] Sakaguchi, "Dare Ga Imin wo Okuridashita no Ka," 58.

Figure 5.4 Kaikō poster from around the mid-1920s to recruit Japanese for
Brazilian migration. It clearly illustrates two expectations on the migrants: (1)
they were supposed to migrate in the unit of family; (2) with the hoe in hand,
the central figure in the poster is a farmer. This indicates that migration should
be agriculture centered. Courtesy of Museu Histórico da Imigração Japonesa
no Brasil, São Paulo.

Figure 5.5 Magic lantern slide that the Japanese Striving Society's president Nagata Shigeshi used during his speeches around Nagano prefecture in late 1910s to promote Japanese migration in Brazil. It is a picture of the family of Nakamura Sadao, a schoolteacher from Kamiminochi County in Nagano prefecture, who migrated to Registro, Brazil, together in 1918. Family migration had begun to be the norm for Japanese migration to Brazil around that time. Courtesy of the Japanese Striving Society.

White racism in North America not only made Brazil increasingly attractive as a colonial target for Japanese Malthusian expansionists but also convinced them of the importance of permanent settlement and the role of women in Japanese overseas community building. On the other hand, the continuation of rural depression in Japan brought about a structural change in the imperial government's support for migration. Two years after the Rice Riots (Kome Sōdō) of 1918, the government created a Bureau of Social Affairs under the Ministry of Internal Affairs. Aside from tending to issues such as unemployment and poverty, the Bureau of Social Affairs was also tasked with promoting and managing overseas migration. This institutional change signaled that the Japanese government had come to recognize overseas migration as an important tool to combat domestic social issues; it was no longer a purely diplomatic matter under the sole management of the Ministry of Foreign Affairs.

The Great Kantō Earthquake (Kantō Dai Shinsai) of 1923 further stimulated the Bureau of Social Affairs' migration promotion. To forestall unrests following the disaster, the bureau began to provide full subsidies for migration to Brazil through the Kaikō. It offered thirty-five Japanese yen for each Brazil-bound migrant whom the company recruited, a sum that covered the costs of both enrollment and transportation, making migration to Brazil free of charge for the migrants themselves.[85] The number of Japanese migrants to Brazil jumped from 797 in 1923 to 3,689 in 1924.[86]

Meanwhile, the Immigration Act of 1924 put a complete stop to Japanese immigration to the United States. At the Imperial Economic Conference held in Tokyo in the same year, Japanese Diet members, government officials, and public intellectuals reached an agreement that the existing government policy on overseas migration needed an overhaul. The participants recognized the importance of overseas migration both as a way to alleviate overpopulation and rural poverty at home and as a means of peaceful expansion abroad. To avoid repeating the migration project's failure in North America, they demanded that the government increase its support for migration by playing a central role in protecting and training the emigrants.

The imperial government carried out this conference's agenda in the following years, and a new era of Japan's migration-based expansion thus began. From 1924 onward, the Japanese state – at both central and local levels – took on an unprecedented degree of responsibility in financing, promoting, and organizing emigration programs to Brazil and later Manchuria. This new era of migration also saw a radical departure from its past practices in terms of the migrants' social status. Given the continuing rural depression and full government subsidy for the migrants, the most destitute residents in the Japanese countryside became involved in the imperial mission of expansion.

Conclusion

This chapter has examined the two courses of action in Japanese overseas expansion between the enactment of the Gentlemen's Agreement in 1907 and the passage of the Immigration Act of 1924. Seeing overseas migration as an effective solution to the ever-growing surplus population in Japan, the Malthusian expansionists sought to placate the anti-Japanese sentiment in the United States while exploring alternative migration destinations. Both courses of action were marked by their efforts at embracing the logic of Western imperialism so that Japan's own expansion could fit into the existing world

---

[85] Tsuchida, "Japanese in Brazil," 177.   [86] Ibid., 178.

order as to share the "White Man's Burden" instead of challenging the hegemonic powers.

At the same time, most migration-related campaigns during these years were ultimately unfruitful. In the United States, the enlightenment campaign spearheaded by the Emigration Association ended with the passage of the Immigration Act of 1924. While the period between the late 1900s and the 1920s witnessed an expansion of Japanese colonial presence in Northeast Asia and the South Seas, Japanese farmer migration and settlement in these parts remained disappointing when measured against the expansionists' visions. An exception to this norm was Brazil, where Japanese migrants were able to build and expand their farming communities. Encouraged by what happened in Brazil, the Japanese government began to provide unprecedented support to expand Japanese migration to Brazil when the outlook for US-bound migration grew dim. The history of Japan's migration-based expansion entered a new era (from the mid-1920s to 1945) with a radical departure from the past in terms of the degree of the state's involvement, the social statuses of migrants, and the relationship of Japanese expansion with Western imperialism. The next two chapters will examine these radical changes and explain the new ways in which the discourse of overpopulation legitimized and shaped Japanese expansion in this new era.

Part III

Culmination, 1924–1945

6   Making the Migration State: Malthusian Expansionism and Agrarianism

In August 1919, a few months after the League of Nations Commission rejected Japan's proposal to write the clause of racial equality to the Covenant of the League, in Shanghai Kita Ikki drafted one of his most influential books, *An Outline for the Reorganization of Japan* (*Nihon Kaizō Hōan Taikō*). Kita pointed out in the book that Japan's rapidly growing population and the racism of the Western empires made Japan the only righteous empire in the world, who was destined to overthrow the tyranny of Western imperialism and liberate all peoples of color through its own colonial expansion. With its population doubled every fifty years, Kita argued, acquiring more territories overseas was the only way of the empire to avoid chaos in the archipelago caused by overpopulation.[1] Due to the low population densities, Kita saw Australia and Siberia in particular the rightful targets of Japanese expansion. As the new rulers of these lands, Kita envisioned, the Japanese would be different from the racist white occupiers who reserved these vast and empty territories only for themselves by excluding others. The Japanese, instead, would open the borders by welcoming the Chinese and Indians in Australia and the Chinese and Koreans in Siberia and turning these lands into cosmopolitan paradises.[2]

Kita was later known as a doyen of Japanese fascism in the 1930s whose ideas had a central responsibility for the terrifying coup d'état on February 26, 1936, and the rise of Japanese militarism in the 1930s in general. However, he was hardly an anomaly among the educated Japanese in the 1920s to promote expansion as a solution to the crisis of overpopulation in the archipelago. The 1920s was a special era in the evolution of Japanese Malthusian expansionism. On the one hand, the influence of the overpopulation discourse expanded beyond the circles of political and social elites and reached at the grassroots level throughout

---

[1] Kita Ikki, *Nihon Kaizō Hōan Taikō* (Tokyo: Nishida Mitsugi, 1928), 3–4.   [2] Ibid., 103.

the archipelago.[3] The anxiety over the "population problem" (*jinkō mondai*), as prominent scholar of colonial studies Yanaihara Tadao described in 1927, was spreading like a "wildfire" in the public discourse. Mass media engaged in nationwide debates on how to deal with overpopulation. On the other hand, the Japanese government was also undergoing a series of institutional changes in the decade to morph into what I call a migration state – a state that promoted and controlled overseas migration on an unprecedented scale backed by the logic of Malthusian expansionism.

After decades of preparation, Japan conducted its first national census in 1920. To encourage mass participation, the imperial government and public intellectuals alike went to great lengths to publicize the census's importance in articles, books, and even popular ballads.[4] Their efforts, together with data from the first census, further stirred the common people's national pride in the empire's burgeoning population; at the same time, however, they also fanned the flames of overpopulation anxiety in the archipelago.[5]

A series of international and domestic events between the late 1910s and early 1930s were also directly responsible for the escalation of overpopulation anxiety in Japan's public sphere. The most significant and large-scale rice riots broke out in 1918, bringing the issue of food shortage into the ongoing debate about Japan's overpopulation crisis. The global wave of post–World War I disarmament led to substantial layoffs in munitions and commercial shipbuilding industries in Japan, exacerbating the unemployment problem that had plagued Japan since 1920, adding fuel to the flame of Malthusian crisis.[6] The devastating Great Kantō Earthquake in 1923 further amplified national anxiety over the ever-growing surplus population within the archipelago, while the passage of the Immigration Act in the United States one year later led many to believe that previous outlets for these surplus people were no longer viable. The Japanese government also established the Commission for the Investigation of

---

[3] Yanaihara Tadao observed in 1927 that though overpopulation anxiety had existed in Japan for a long time, ordinary Japanese had only recently begun to realize that the archipelago might be plagued by overcrowding due to the rapid growth of the Japanese population. Yanaihara Tadao, "Jiron Toshite no Jinkō Mondai," *Chūō Kōron* 42, no. 7 (July 1927): 31–32.

[4] The Temporary Bureau of Census (Rinji Kokusei Chōsa Kyoku) that was in charge of conducting the census, for example, published a book of folk songs to advertise the census among the public in 1920. Rinji Kokusei Chōsa Kyoku, *Kokusei Chōsa Senden Kayōkyoku* (Tokyo: Tokyo Insatsu Kabushiki Gaisha, 1920).

[5] The book, Hayashi Shigeatsu, *Kokusei Chōsa ni Tsuite: Kokumin Hitsudoku* (Tokyo: Ginkōdō, 1920), aiming to encourage the mass participation in the first national census, both argued that the census would provide precise information on how fast the Japanese population grew and raised concern about the issue of overpopulation by restating the classic theory of Thomas Malthus.

[6] Nagai, *Nihon Jinkō Ron*, 170.

the Issues of Population and Food (Jinkō Shokuryō Mondai Chōsa Iinkai) directly under the cabinet.[7]

The escalation of nationwide anxiety regarding overpopulation was accompanied by an explosion of texts in the forms of books and articles in both public media and academic circles. Scholars, politicians, and social activists rushed to the fore, each of them offering different diagnoses and remedies. This chapter examines the changes in the discourse of Malthusian expansionism in the sociopolitical context of the 1920s and 1930s. It illustrates how the sudden outburst of nationwide overpopulation anxiety ushered in a new version of Japanese expansionism that radically differed from its predecessors. This new model of expansion not only disavowed white supremacy but also directly challenged the universal applicability of Western civilization. Thinkers and doers of migration began to seek homegrown justifications for Japan's expansion. To this end they looked to Japan's own culture, tradition, and history, though much of these were recent inventions just like their counterparts in the West.

While the enactment of the Immigration Act of 1924 in the United States had a huge impact on the transformation of Japan's Malthusian expansionism, rising sentiments of Japanese agrarianism also contributed to the development of Japan's own version of Manifest Destiny. The migration of Japanese farmers overseas was considered not only as a means to combat rural depression but also as a way for Japan to enlighten and guide other countries. The agrarian expansionists claimed that Japan was uniquely qualified as the harbinger of a new world order due to its distinct agrarian tradition, nonwhite cultural/racial identity, and marvelous success with modernization. These traits meant that Japan could lead the world to overthrow the triple tyranny of white racism, Western imperialism, and capitalism; and by doing so, it would bring true justice, peace, and freedom everywhere on earth.

The partnership of agrarianism and overseas expansion was reinforced by growing Japanese migration to Brazil since the beginning of the 1920s. The widening doors of Brazil to Japanese rural migrants and their success in becoming owner-farmers convinced the Japanese expansionists that farmer migration was indeed feasible. Driven by the promising future of Brazil-bound migration abroad and the intensified overpopulation anxiety at home, the Japanese government became increasingly involved in the migration scheme.

The formation of the migration state marked a turning point in the evolution of Japanese Malthusian expansionism. After the times of the shizoku and heimin, the imperial government devoted resources and power to catapult the most destitute and unprivileged class in the Japanese society, the rural masses,

---

[7] Yanaihara, "Jiron Toshite no Jinkō Mondai," 31–32.

onto the grand stage of overseas expansion. It was these landless farmers, the agrarian expansionists believed, who would spearhead the Japanese empire's ultimate mission by acquiring and farming land abroad. The centrality of the masses in Japanese overseas migration was well captured by contemporary writer Ishikawa Tatsuzō's 1932 novel *Sōbō*, which highlighted the misery of the rural Japanese during the entire process of migration to Brazil. The novel has been commonly known for its criticism of the imperial government for abandoning its own subjects through emigration;[8] its story, nevertheless, revealed that rural masses had become the backbone of Japan's overseas migration. The fact that the novel won Japan's first Akutagawa Prize in 1935 also confirmed the emergence of the rural masses as a dominating political force of the empire.

Overpopulation Anxiety and the Denunciation of White Racism

A direct trigger of the overpopulation anxiety was the passage of the Immigration Act of 1924 in the United States, the country that had received the largest number of Japanese migrants outside of Asia during the first two decades of the twentieth century. The shutting of the American doors to Japanese immigration immediately impacted the mind-sets of Japanese intellectuals and policymakers in diverse ways. Some took the Immigration Act as evidence of the overall failure of overseas migration as a way to relieve Japan's population pressure and urged the government to turn to more realistic solutions. They advocated measures such as increasing food production by introducing new crops with higher productivity, accelerating the process of industrialization, and expanding international trade.[9] Some previous migration promoters, like Abe Isoo, also joined the fledgling birth control and eugenics movement in order to solve the alleged population crisis.

While the birth control and eugenics movement gained momentum in Japan amid growing nationwide anxiety about overpopulation, nevertheless, apart from laborers' and women's rights activists the opinion leaders did not view population increase by itself in a negative light. Reducing the size of the population and reining in its growth rate through birth control remained unacceptable to the government of the day. Like most countries in the West, Japan did not legalize contraception until the latter half of the twentieth century. Instead of birth control, the main question that Japanese policymakers and intellectuals in the 1920s and 1930s wrestled with was how to maintain

---

[8] Thus those who left Japan as migrants were also described as *kimin* (people abandoned by the nation). Kimura Kazuaki, *Shōwa Sakka no "Nan'yō Kō"* (Tokyo: Sekai Shisō Sha, 2004), 59–60.
[9] Hasegawa, "1920 Nendai Nihon no Imin Ron (3)," 94–96.

migration-driven expansion so that the Japanese population could continue to grow.

Other thinkers and doers of migration-based expansion saw the passage of the Immigration Act as a remarkable opportunity to further advance their migration agenda by describing Japan as a victim of the Western empires. They denounced Japanese exclusion campaigns in the United States and the European colonies across the Pacific as fundamentally unjust. Nasu Shiroshi, a University of Tokyo professor, was a highly influential figure in Japan's agricultural policies circle from the 1920s to the end of World War II. He presented Japan as a victim of the population crisis at home and white racism abroad. Japan not only had a population that grew as fast as the Western nations, Nasu argued, but also a small territory. While Japan's territory was no more than one-twentieth that of the United States, it had to feed a population that was more than half the United States populace.[10] Furthermore, most of the land in the archipelago was covered by mountains and volcanoes; only 15.8 percent of it was arable – and this paltry figure was growing smaller each year because some of the land known as arable turned out to be arid.[11] Such an unbalanced ratio of population and arable land, Nasu claimed, was a breeding ground for social tensions. Japan's limited natural resources would soon fail to adequately provide for the archipelago's inhabitants, and it was only a matter of time before social unrest become a national plague. While the best way to solve Japan's current crisis was the migration of surplus population overseas, Nasu lamented, the Immigration Act had unfairly closed off this avenue for the Japanese.

Nasu spared no efforts to let his voice heard internationally. In 1927, the Institute of Pacific Relations held an international conference in Honolulu with the issue of population and food as one of its central themes. At that conference, Nasu pointed out that the Japanese people were confined to an isolated and overcrowded archipelago while the more fortunate nations not only occupied huge, unexplored lands but also had reserved them for their descendants by excluding other races. It was unfair, he contended, to confine the civilized Japanese race to the small archipelago and deprive them of expansion opportunities.[12]

According to Nasu, human history itself was a story of mass migrations of peoples. Contemporary national boundaries were only artificial constructs, and to stop peaceful transnational migrations was to go against the natural flow of people. In this sense, Nasu claimed, Japan's struggle for its right to survive and prosper through migration was also an effort to open up future possibilities for the entire world. Japan would demonstrate to the world how humankind could solve the inherent tension between population and food supply in a "reasonable

---

[10] Nasu, *Jinkō Shokuryō Mondai*, 105.   [11] Ibid., 108–111.   [12] Ibid., 86–87.

Table 6.1 *Comparison between the size of arable land and population among the countries of the world in 1924*

Country	Area in ten thousand hectares	Population in ten thousand persons	Population per 100 *chōbu**
United States	13,820	11,200	79.6
British India	12,210	31,880	260.9
Russia	9,900	9,590	96.9
Canada	2,750	920	33.4
France	2,290	3,918	171.1
Argentina	2,130	950	44.7
Germany	2,020	6,260	309.6
Spain	1,600	2,170	135.7
Italy	1,320	3,960	299.4
Australia	870	564	64.8
Brazil	760	3,060	398.5
Japan	620	5,900	950.4
Czechoslovakia	590	1,360	230.4
Great Britain	570	4,370	761.4
Hungary	540	820	149.8
Sweden	380	600	158.5
Egypt	340	1,552	408.4
Denmark	260	330	128.7
Belgium	120	770	629.1
Netherlands	90	720	629.1
New Zealand	74	130	170.7

This chart was made by Nasu Shiroshi based on data provided by Yokoi Toshiyoki. It shows that Japan had the highest population density vis-à-vis arable land among the listed countries. Nasu Shiroshi, *Jinkō Shokuryō Mondai* (Tokyo: Nihon Hyōronsha, 1927), 107.
* 1 *chōbu* is equal to approximately 0.99 hectares.

and constructive" way, thereby allowing mankind to overcome its eventual fate.[13]

While Nasu's criticism of Japanese exclusion was comparatively mild and his blueprint for Japanese expansion rested on achieving reconciliation with the West, other expansionists had more radical takes on the issue by directly attacking Western imperialism and white racism. Kyoto University professor Yano Jin'ichi warned his readers that Western nations were hypocrites who only paid lip service to the principles of justice and equality. The current global inequality in land and resource distribution, he argued, was not a mere coincidence; instead it rose out of centuries-long European invasions and appropriation of other peoples' ancestral lands. Even though the white settlers did not

[13] Ibid., 162–163.

have enough people to utilize the land resource they had deprived of others, they reserved the land for their posterity by refusing entry to migrants from overpopulated countries. This behavior itself, Yano argued, violated the principles of justice and equality and was a threat to the world peace.[14]

Another scholar, Tazaki Masayoshi, echoed Yano's criticism of Western imperialism and attributed global inequality in land distribution to white racism. He wrote in 1924, "When one looks at the world's map, there is an abundance of spacious and sparsely populated lands in the Americas, Australia, and Africa. Those lands have been unjustly colonized by a handful of white empires, and now the white settlers are prohibiting other people from immigrating to those places simply because of their skin color. How could this be acceptable according to the international standards of morality?"[15] In order to bring justice to the world and break the monopolization of land resource by white men, Tazaki argued, the world's lands should be redistributed based on the actual need of nations according to their population sizes.[16]

Nasu, Yano, and Tazaki held different opinions about how Japan should deal with its current tension with the Western empires. However, their problems with Western imperialism were quite similar. For all three of them, what was unjust was *not* that the Western empires deprived other peoples of their land and property per se, but that they wouldn't *share* the spoils with people from other civilized nations like Japan. Nasu, Yano, and Tazaki also all embraced the logic of Malthusian expansionism: the crisis of overpopulation not only deeply plagued the Japanese society, but also justified Japan's demands for its right to conduct overseas migration. They saw Japan as a victim of both overpopulation at home and racial exclusion abroad, and they believed that such injustices established Japan as the natural and rightful leader of all peoples of color, poised to challenge the global hegemony of Western imperialism and racism.

While the overpopulation was further agitated and diffused in the 1920s, the overall increase of Japanese population continued to be celebrated as evidence that the empire was growing ever stronger. For Japanese expansionists, Japan's population growth appeared even more important than before, as the empire began to depart from the Western model and take on the mission of challenging Anglo-American world order. The most representative articulation of this belief was voiced by economist Takata Yasuma. In a 1926 article titled "Be Fruitful, and Multiply!" ("Umeyō! Fueyō!"), Takata argued that birth control would hold back population growth and lead to a decline of national strength, equaling national suicide. He believed that population was not the cause of trouble but the source of national power. Not only was a large population

---

[14] Hasegawa, "1920 Nendai Nihon no Imin Ron (3)," 99–101.
[15] Tazaki, "Yukizumareru Wa Ga Kuni no Jinkō Mondai," 46, cited from Hasegawa, "1920 Nendai Nihon no Imin Ron (3)," 102.
[16] Ibid., 102.

needed for prosperity and expansion, Takata reminded his readers, it was also an essential weapon for the peoples of color in their fight against the white people.[17]

At the same time, some intellectuals in the West echoed the Japanese expansionists' calls for free international migration and land redistribution on a global level. As the need for extra land to accommodate surplus population had served as a central justification for Anglo-American expansion in the recent past, a number of influential Anglophone scholars, in particular, shared the logic of Japanese Malthusian expansionists. Raymond Pearl, director of the Institute of Biological Research at Johns Hopkins University, validated the anxiety of overpopulation through scientific calculations. In a speech at the World Population Conference in Geneva in 1927, Pearl argued that a society's population density had to be kept below a certain degree, otherwise it would lead to a decrease in birth rate and an increase in mortality rate.[18] Also at the conference was Warren Thompson, director of the Scripps Foundation and one of the most influential sociologists in the English-speaking world. In 1929, Thompson would publish a book calling for global land redistribution as a way to avoid another world war. In this book, *Danger Spots in World Population*, Thompson pointed to regional overpopulation as an important cause of international wars. He urged the United Kingdom, Australia, and the Netherlands to concede their territories in New Guinea to Japan in order to forestall a possible Japanese invasion due to Japan's population explosion. The Philippines, Thompson argued, was similarly expendable for the United States if it meant keeping a desperate Japan at bay.[19]

The Marriage of Population Crisis and Agrarianism

Japanese Malthusian expansionists' attack on white racism and Western imperialism was accompanied by a challenge against capitalist modernity. The criticism of Western capitalism reflected a surge of agrarianism in response to the continuous rural depression during the 1920s. The deterioration of the rural economy, growing rural-urban tensions, as well as mounting conflicts between different rural interest groups all added fuel to the spreading fire of population anxiety.

During the early twentieth century, except for a short period during World War I,[20] Japan's rural economy had suffered due to the accelerating processes

[17] Takata Yasuma, *Jinkō to Binbō* (Tokyo: Nihon Hyōronsha, 1927), 93–95. As stated in this book, the article "Umeyō! Fueyō!" was originally published in the journal *Keizai Ōrai* (August 1926).
[18] Pearl's presentation was a summary of his book *The Biology of Population Growth*, initially published in 1925. Bashford, "Nation, Empire, Globe," 180.
[19] Thompson, *Danger Spots in World Population*, 123–126.
[20] As Louise Young points out, the outbreak of World War I triggered a boom of urbanization throughout the archipelago. Louise Young, *Beyond the Metropolis: Second Cities and Modern Life in Interwar Japan* (Berkeley: University of California Press, 2013), 15–33. The rapid

of urbanization and industrialization. Higher wages and upward mobility in urban industries drained the most productive labor pool from agricultural production, while villages had to shoulder the burden of urban industries by absorbing the laid-off returnees whenever there was an economic downturn.[21] As historian Louise Young convincingly shows, the interwar period witnessed a flourishing of cities throughout the archipelago.[22] For the countryside, however, it was a particularly difficult time. The end of World War I was immediately followed by a steep drop in the prices of rice and silk, the two pillars of Japan's rural economy in both international and domestic markets. The situation grew catastrophic at the turn of the 1930s: a global depression sent the prices of Japan's agricultural products into free fall, while countless laid-off factory workers had to return to their home villages. On top of it all, famines caused by natural disasters claimed almost half a million victims in Hokkaido and the Northeast.[23]

As a result of the continuing devastation of the rural economy, the average profit from paddy field leasing in Japan fell from 7.92 percent in 1919 to 5.67 percent in 1925, then to 3.69 percent in 1931.[24] The prolonged depression pushed tenant farmers to demand further rent reductions.[25] Such tensions led to an exponential increase in tenant disputes throughout Japan. Nationwide, rent dispute incidents rose from 256 in 1918 to 1,532 in 1924, then to 2,478 in 1930.[26] In addition to rent disputes, the number of land-related disputes also grew steadily beginning in the mid-1920s. The drop in profit left many small and midsize landlords bankrupt, as they could no longer live on tenant rents. They began to demand their land back from tenants, in many cases even before the lease had expired, because they wanted to farm the land on their own in order to make ends meet. The number of land-related disputes reached its peak in 1936.[27]

Influenced by the global trend of democratization and socialism in the years immediately after World War I,[28] a group of new bureaucrats who sympathized with the rural poor rose to power in the agriculture section of the imperial government. These bureaucrats gathered around the figure of Ishiguro Tadaatsu, who began his political career in 1919 as the head of the Department of Agricultural Policy in the Bureau of Agricultural Affairs. To protect the interest of tenant farmers in rampart rent disputes, Ishiguro ushered in the Tenant Mediation Law (Kosaku Chōtei Hō). Under this law, the

expansion of urban population and industry increased the demand for agricultural products, leading to a temporary boom in the rural economy.

[21] Young, *Japan's Total Empire*, 324.   [22] Young, *Beyond the Metropolis*, 3.
[23] Young, *Japan's Total Empire*, 324.   [24] Ibid.   [25] Havens, *Farm and Nation*, 145.
[26] Young, *Japan's Total Empire*, 324.
[27] Shōji Shunsaku, *Kingendai Nihon no Nōson: Nōsei no Genten o Saguru* (Tokyo: Yoshikawa Kōbunkan, 2003), 130–136.
[28] Dickinson, *World War I and the Triumph of a New Japan*, 9–10.

government assigned a tenant mediator (*kosakukan*) to each prefecture, putting him in charge of mediating the disputes.[29] However, such efforts did not stem the tide of growing rural tensions.

The burgeoning crisis in the Japanese countryside became a breeding ground for agrarianist ideologies and movements. When compared with the dominant discourse in Japanese agrarianism at the turn of the twentieth century, this new wave of agrarianism was, as a whole, markedly more critical of capitalism and industrialization. In 1927, when disputes over land and tenant rent had reached a crescendo, the doyen of Japanese agrarianism, Yokoi Tokiyoshi, published his final book, *A Study on Small Farmers* (*Shōnō ni Kansuru Kenkyū*). The book, a closing statement from a lifelong critic of capitalism, attributed the root of the ongoing rural crisis to the profit-driven capitalist economy. Yokoi argued that Japan's traditional small-scale farming would free its people from the yokes of capitalism because owner-farmers did not trade their labor for profit; they provided labor out of moral obligation, took pleasure in their work, and found happiness in "nurturing the growth of plants and animals" with consideration for the environment.[30]

Yokoi's rejection of capitalist economy and his glorification of small-scale farming became increasingly attractive to the majority of the Japanese rural dwellers who had lost their hope in the status quo amidst the waves of depression. These included small owner-farmers who could lose their land at any time, tenant farmers who decried their exploitive landlords, and small landlords who, under economic pressure, had to take their land back from tenant farmers in order to farm it on their own. For all of them, living in a society where everyone farmed their own land with no debt or exploitation was the solution to all the countryside's economic problems. Although Yokoi died shortly after the book's publication, his teaching inspired a new generation of agrarianists in the 1920s and 1930s, represented by men such as Tachibana Kōzaburō and Katō Kanji. They not only brought small-scale farming to the core of Japanese national identity but also put Yokoi's ideas into practice.

The teachings and doings of Tachibana and Katō also demonstrated that compared to the previous decades, the agrarian movement in the 1920s and 1930s targeted people on a more grassroots level. In their imaginations, the ideal Japanese society would be composed of owner-farmers. Yet as the majority of rural residents were in reality landless, they embarked on a mission to help these farmers to acquire land. Tachibana, for example, saw owner-farmers as the backbone of the Japanese nation-empire. He believed that Japanese owner-farmers were the only people immune from the corrupted system of Western capitalism, thus they alone were qualified to save the society

---

[29] Shōji, *Kingendai Nihon no Nōson,* 111–113.
[30] Vlastos, "Agrarianism without Tradition," 86–87.

from the abyss of depression. Fostering prosperous self-sufficient villages and self-governed communities of owner-farmers was regarded as the ultimate solution to the current crisis. A passionate activist, Tachibana founded the Village Loving Society (Aikyō Kai) in 1929, and it became the engine of his farm cooperative campaign to create and cultivate owner-farmers. The cooperative movement aimed not only to provide poor farmers with financial aid but also to nurture the spirit of "true brotherhood" among them by promoting "diligent labor" with a "pure heart." They believed that by doing so, collective small-scale farming could achieve its goal of harmonizing the interest of self with that of others, thereby offering an effective remedy to a nation-empire that was suffering from both material and spiritual crises.[31]

While the call for supporting owner-farmers as the foundation of Japanese society continued to mount at the grassroots level, this agrarianist solution faced serious resistance from policymakers. As the government had no intention to alter the existing system of landownership, the competing interests of landlords and tenant farmers remained irreconcilable.[32] The most noteworthy action the imperial government took to cultivate owner-farmers in the 1920s was to provide long-term, low-interest loans to help them purchase the land they farmed. However, given that the land prices were far too high, few tenant farmers found these loans useful.[33]

Compared with calling for land redistribution in Japan, defining the entire archipelago as suffering from a shortage of land and demanding more land abroad were much more politically expedient, as they could avoid provoking the existing rural tensions and the unchallengeable power of the big landlords. The land shortage was ultimately attributed to the rapidly growing surplus population within the archipelago. In fact, overpopulation served as a tenable explanation for all the major problems that plagued Japanese society in the 1920s, such as farm land shortage, increased food costs, the growth of unemployment, economic stagnation, a shortage of natural resources, as well as deadlocked social progress.[34]

The thoughts and activities of Katō Kanji, another prominent leader of Japanese agrarianist movement, illustrated that agrarianism not only lent power to Malthusian expansionism but also became an ideological weapon for the empire to challenge Western imperialism and legitimize its own expansion. After investigation tours in Denmark, the United Kingdom, and the United States in 1922 and 1926, Katō concluded that the current distribution of land vis-à-vis population in the world was unfair, with a few Western powers

[31] Vlastos, "Agrarianism without Tradition," 88–90; and Havens, *Farm and Nation*, 163–273.
[32] Young, *Japan's Total Empire*, 334.   [33] Havens, *Farm and Nation*, 147.
[34] For a summary of the leading opinions on how the overpopulation issue affected Japanese society in the 1920s, see Jinkō Shokuryō Mondai Chōsakai, *Jinkō Mondai ni Kansuru Yoron* (Tokyo: Jinkō Shokuryō Mondai Chōsakai, 1928), 1–35.

monopolizing the vast majority of land on the one hand and the starvation of the colored people due to land shortage on the other. Just as the United States claimed its sphere of influence in the two Americas under the Monroe Doctrine, Katō believed, Japan had to monopolize the land of the Korean Peninsula, Manchuria, and Siberia.[35]

Katō further argued in a public speech in 1927 that among all the Asian nations, only the Japanese could save their brethren from the Western imperialism. The depression that plagued the Japanese countryside was not merely an issue for Japan but a crisis that had engulfed the entire Asia. Therefore, rescuing Japan from the rural crisis was to rescue Asia itself from the evil clutches of Western imperialism and white racism. Since the root of the problem was overpopulation in the countryside, merely reducing tenant rents would mean little. The real solution was to settle landless farmers overseas to acquire and work new land. The Korean Peninsula, in Katō's imagination, had abundant and fertile tracks of land waiting for Japanese farmers to work. Japanese farmer migration to the Korean Peninsula would not only save Japan from rural depression but also protect Korea from further American penetration.[36] To this end, Katō began to build schools that provided agricultural training to young Japanese students who would become empire builders in Northeast Asia.

While Katō later emerged as a political leader and ideological advocate of Japanese mass migration to Manchuria, he did not gain prominence until the latter half of the 1930s. Japanese colonial privilege in leasing land in Manchuria met strong resistance from local Chinese residents. Due to their higher costs of living, Japanese farmers could not compete with local Chinese and Korean farmers either. For these reasons, Japanese agrarian migration in Manchuria remained unsuccessful in the 1920s. By 1931, only 308 of the 64,662 farm families living inside Japan's sphere of influence in Manchuria were Japanese.[37] The plan of the Oriental Development Company (Tōyō Takushoku Kabushiki Gaisha) to expand Japanese farming communities in the Korean Peninsula also proved to be a disappointment.[38]

The Ascendancy of Brazilian Migration

Compared to Northeast Asia, from the 1920s to the mid-1930s, a locale that received a much more robust inflow of Japanese rural migrants was Brazil. Brazil

---

[35] Katō Kanji, "Nihon Nōson Kyōiku," in *Katō Kanji Zenshū*, vol. 1 (Uchihara-machi, Ibaraki-ken: Katō Kanji Zenshū Kankōkai, 1967), 84, cited from Hasegawa, "1920 Nendai Nihon no Imin Ron (3)," 102–103.

[36] Katō, "Nōson Mondai no Kanken," 229–232.   [37] Havens, *Farm and Nation*, 287.

[38] By 1926, around twenty thousand Japanese farmers, many of whom were landlords, resided on the Korean Peninsula. See Young, *Japan's Total Empire*, 316.

Table 6.2 *Comparison of Japanese migration to Brazil, the continental United States, and Hawai'i, 1906–1941*

Time period	Brazil	Continental US	Hawai'i
1906–1910	1, 714	7, 715	46, 650
1911–1915	13, 101	20, 773	17, 846
1916–1920	13, 576	30, 756	16, 655
1921–1925	11, 349	14, 849	10, 935
1926–1930	59, 564	1, 256	1, 546
1931–1935	72, 661	N/A	N/A
1936–1941	16, 750	N/A	N/A

This table compares the different dynamics of Japanese migration to Brazil, the continental United States, and Hawai'i – the three destinations with the highest average annual numbers of Japanese migrants between 1906 and 1941 outside of Asia. Based on data taken from Okabe Makio's *Umi wo Watatta Nihonjin* (Tokyo: Yamagawa Shuppansha, 2002), 14–15.

was an attractive destination for Japanese expansionists due to two reasons. First, Japanese exclusion in North America and an unfavorable outlook for agricultural migration in Northeast Asia left Japanese expansionists few alternatives to choose from. Second, not only did Brazil's door remain open to Japanese immigration, but Aoyagi Ikutarō's success in acquiring land and expanding Japanese farming communities in the state of São Paulo convinced the expansionists that Japanese agrarian settlement could in fact succeed there.

The steady growth of Japanese migration to Brazil throughout the 1920s constituted a crucial step in the fermentation of Japanese agrarian expansionism because it successfully put the combination of agrarianism and Malthusian expansionism into practice. The public media's growing enthusiasm for Brazil as a migration destination occurred at the same time when overpopulation anxiety intensified in the depressed Japanese countryside, and migration to Brazil seemed like a natural solution.

As one of the leading migration promotion journals in Japan in the 1920s and 1930s, *Shokumin* disseminated information about the prospects of migration to different areas of the world. It was founded by Kanda Hideo in 1921, after he returned from an investigative trip to Brazil. Kanda established the magazine as a response to the nationwide Rice Riots of 1918, providing a solution to the rural crisis by ways of overseas migration.[39] While *Shokumin* boasted a global scope, judging from the number of pages and articles devoted to Brazil, the journal's focus was undoubtedly this Amazonian country. Latin America in general also received more coverage than other parts of the world. The magazine's content

[39] "Zasshi Shokumin no Sōkan to Watashi," *Shokumin* 7, no. 11 (November 1928): 10.

mirrored the actual general public interests of the day. According to a survey conducted by *Shokumin* in 1925 about the most popular migration destination among its readers, Brazil was the overwhelming favorite, with 2,101 votes, far ahead of the South Seas (Nan'yō), which came in second with 409 votes; the rest were Manchuria (78 votes), Karafuto (9 votes), and Korea (3 votes). In fact, Brazil was so popular that in order to promote migration to the Korean Peninsula, a 1926 article in *Shokumin* had to showcase the similarities between Brazil and the northern Korean Peninsula: it labeled the latter as the "Brazil of the frigid zone" (*kantai Burajiru*) in the hopes of making the Korean Peninsula more attractive to the domestic readers.[40]

Figure 6.1 Set of cartoons published in *Shokumin* highlighting Brazil as the ideal place for surplus people in Japan by contrasting a spacious, wealthy, and prosperous South America with a crowded, impoverished, and troublesome Japan. *Shokumin* 9, no. 8 (August 1930): 112–113.

[40] Kawamura, "Naisen Yūwa no Zentei Toshite Hōyoku Naru Hokusen o Kaitaku Seyo," 45.

In the 1920s, even some of the most passionate supporters of Japanese expansion in Asia cast their gazes to Brazil. After spending five months in South America, Nanba Katsuji, who had been promoting Japanese migration to Manchuria for over ten years, gave up his earlier agenda and became a vocal supporter of migrant expansion to Brazil.[41] He authored the book *A Grand View of the Sources of Wealth in South America* (*Nanbei Fugen Taikan*) in 1923. Published in Dalian (*Dairen*), the political center of Japanese-occupied Southern Manchuria, this book aimed to encourage Japanese settlers in Northeast Asia to remigrate to Brazil.

A Grand View is representative of the enormous number of texts on Brazilian migration (in forms of books, articles, and pamphlets) that emerged in the 1920s, and it provides us with a valuable window into how Japanese Malthusian expansionists perceived Brazil during the age of agrarian expansion. Nanba began his book by lamenting Japan's social problems as a result of overpopulation, asserting the urgency of overseas migration as a solution. The bulk of the book was devoted to describing Brazil as an empty and rich land waiting for the Japanese to settle. In Nanba's imagination, unlike North America and Manchuria, which were either controlled by white racists or occupied by dangerous Chinese bandits, the natives of Brazil were not only few in number but also docile in nature. With a vast land that was four times Japan's size, Brazil was also blessed with countless natural resources like gold and diamonds. In addition, unlike Manchuria and Taiwan, Brazil possessed incredible agricultural potential because of its suitable climate.[42] No place on earth, concluded by Nanba, was better than Brazil for Japan's surplus population.[43]

The Making of the Migration State

The nationwide "Brazil fever" and the growing flow of migration to South America could not have taken place without the imperial government's endorsement. The period from the 1920s to the mid-1930s was marked by a gradual but steady expansion of the government's power in migration-related affairs. The imperial government intervened in both promotion and management of overseas migration on an unprecedented scale. A series of institutional changes in the 1920s led to the birth of what I call "the migration state," one that continued to function in Japan until the end of World War II. Its formation occurred at both central and local levels.

---

[41] Nanba, *Nanbei Fugen Taikan*, preface, 6.   [42] Ibid., 2–20.   [43] Ibid., 10.

State Expansion at the Central Level

The imperial government had been involved in migration management since the Meiji era, but the migration state that emerged in the 1920s marked a substantial departure from past practices. Overseas migration became an increasingly important method for the central government to deal with domestic social issues. While it was common practice for policymakers to use overseas migration to solve domestic problems, migration management had been historically separated from governmental institutions that handled domestic affairs. Colonial migration to Hokkaido was first monitored by the Hokkaido Development Agency and, after the said agency was abolished, managed by the authority of Hokkaido. Policies on colonial migration to Taiwan and the Korean Peninsula were decided through negotiations between the cabinet and local colonial authorities. Emigration to places beyond the imperial territories, such as the Americas, was primarily managed by the Ministry of Foreign Affairs (Gaimushō). As such, migration was not institutionally tied to social management until 1920, when the Bureau of Social Affairs was established under the Ministry of Home Affairs (Naimushō). The bureau was assigned to both combat domestic unemployment and manage migration outside of the imperial territories.[44] Its creation signaled the government's official recognition of overseas emigration as a critical solution to domestic social problems.

The Japanese government further integrated overseas migration into the sphere of domestic affairs in 1927, when it established the Commission for the Investigation of the Issues of Population and Food. Aiming to provide solutions to the alleged population crisis, the commission was headed by the prime minister and counted key policymakers and intellectuals among its members. Overseas migration was one of the key solutions proposed by the commission. In 1929, the government further involved itself in migration affairs by establishing the Ministry of Colonial Affairs (Takumushō), bringing the management of migration and other affairs inside the empire with that of migration beyond the imperial territories under one roof. The Ministry of Culture and Education (Monbushō) also created three migrant training centers (takushoku kunren sho) that prepared prospective migrants both mentally and physically for their upcoming undertakings.[45]

In addition to these institutional changes, the government gradually increased its financial support for overseas migration by working with migration and transportation companies, as was discussed in the previous chapter. In 1920, with governmental endorsement, the Overseas Development Company

---

[44] Sakaguchi, "Daire Ga Imin wo Okuridashita no Ka," 55.
[45] Burajiru Nihon Imin 100-Shūnen Kinen Kyōkai Hyakunenshi Hensan Iinkai, *Burajiru Nihon Imin Hyakunenshi*, vol. 1 (Tokyo: Fūkyōsha. 2008), 124.

(Kaikō) merged with the Morioka Migration Company to form Japan's sole migration company. In 1921, the government began to allocate funds to the Bureau of Social Affairs, which in turn provided funds for the Kaikō in order to subsidize emigration. From 1923 onward, the Kaikō received further financial assistance from the government and was able to waive the registration fees for all recruited migrants. Also starting in the same year, the government halved the railway fare for all migrants from their home villages to the ports of departure.[46]

The government spared no effort to promote Brazil-bound migration through media channels and public gatherings. Nearly every issue of *Shokumin* contained contributions from officials in the Ministries of Home Affairs and Foreign Affairs – articles that disseminated information about the government's overseas migration subsidies and the many opportunities abroad. The chorus of the government and public media for migration promotion in the 1920s reached a crescendo at the Conference for Overseas Colonial Migration (Kaigai Shokumin Taikai). This gathering was held in Tokyo in 1930, cohosted by the Colonial Migration Association (Shokumin Dōshi Kai) and the Tokyo Daily News Agency (Tokyo Nichi Nichi Shinbun Sha). Its aim was promoting Japanese migration to South America by presenting it as Japan's contribution to world peace and human progress.

The conference's three keynote speakers were the heads of the two hosting organizations and that of the Overseas Development Company. Their addresses were followed by speeches from the minister of colonial affairs, the emissary of the Vatican, the ambassador of Brazil, as well as the consulate generals of Argentina, Peru, and Mexico. The conference concluded with the screening of two films, one being an introduction to Brazil and the other a historical account of European colonial expedition in Africa.[47]

Above all else, the purpose of the migration state was to facilitate agrarian migration to Brazil. Growing amounts of government funds were being poured into the Kaikō and transportation companies in order to recruit the rural masses, especially tenant farmers, for migration. Even though they were identified as surplus population and ideal migration candidates, due to growing land disputes, most tenant farmers were unable to migrate due to sheer poverty. Whereas their predecessors – the shizoku migrants during the early Meiji period and the common youth at the turn of the twentieth century – possessed a certain capacity to finance their own attempts to move up in the world, these tenant farmers had neither the material means for social climbing nor the ambition for it. They were, as a whole, preoccupied by the fight for physical

---

[46] Ibid., 122.
[47] For the list of the programs at the conference, see "Shijō Mizōu no Kaigai Shokumin Daikai Tokushū no Ki," *Shokumin* 9, no. 3 (March 1930): 4.

survival and rent reduction. Therefore, convincing them to migrate overseas was a far more difficult task, demanding unprecedented undertakings. The growing government subsidies were intended to lift these most powerless people up and utilize them for overseas expansion by releasing them from financial burdens. If the overall poverty of the prospective migrants was an internal factor that contributed to the formation of the migration state, the state of São Paulo's suspension of its subsidy for Japanese migrants served as an external impetus for the Japanese government's increased financial aid to migrants.

Aside from the unfavorable outlook for Japanese migration to North America and agricultural expansion in Northeast Asia, the possibility for Japanese laborers in coffee plantations to become owner-farmers, as demonstrated by Aoyagi Ikutarō's Iguape communities, made Brazil especially attractive. The imperial government's subsidies through the Kaikō were decidedly generous for migrants to Brazil. In 1924, the Ministry of Home Affairs began to provide full coverage of steamship fare (two hundred yen per migrant) plus the handling fee (thirty-five yen); and beginning in 1932, it provided start-up funds for all Brazil-bound migrants.[48]

In addition to financial aid, the government also built facilities to provide temporary accommodations and training to migrants before their departure. Out of these centers, the establishment of Kobe Migrant Accommodation Center (Kobe Imin Shūyō Jo) in 1924 by the Ministry of Home Affairs was a milestone event.[49] Its functional priority was to serve Brazil-bound migrants, and it was open to migrants bound for other parts of the world only when it had extra space available. Migrants to Brazil could stay in the center gratis for up to eight days before their departure, during which time they would learn Portuguese, geography, custom, hygiene, religion, agriculture, and other information about Brazil.[50] The choice of location for the center also signified that Japan's primary departure port of overseas migrants had shifted from Yokohama to Kobe: the westbound sea route across the Indian and Atlantic oceans, one that eventually brought Japanese migrants to the Southeast coast of Brazil, had replaced the trans-Pacific route to the American West Coast as the primary route for Japanese emigration.

The expansion of Japanese government in migration promotion and management in the archipelago was further accompanied by the institutional growth of Japan's Ministry of Foreign Affairs in Brazil. A Japanese consulate was

---

[48] Tsuchida, "Japanese in Brazil," 177.
[49] After the Colonial Ministry was formed and took control of migration-related issues, the Kobe Migrant Accommodation Center also began to be managed by the Ministry of Colonial Affairs in 1932 and changed its title to the Kobe Migrant Education Center (Kobe Iminjū Kyōyō Jo).
[50] Burajiru Nihon Imin 100-shūnen Kinen Kyōkai Hyakunenshi Hensan Iinkai, *Burajiru Nihon Imin Hyakunenshi*, 124.

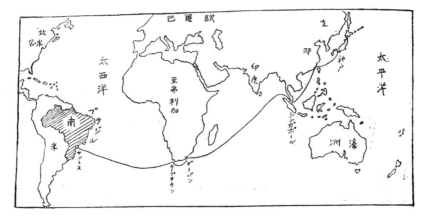

Figure 6.2 This map appeared in *Shokumin* and illustrated the standard sea route for Japanese migration to Brazil in the 1920s. *Shokumin* 3, no. 3 (March 1924): 45.

established in the state of São Paulo in 1915, and its branch was open in 1927 in Santos, the port where most of the Japanese migrants landed. The expansion of Japanese diplomatic branches in Brazil did not stop even after 1934, when the Getúlio Vargas regime restricted the number of annual Japanese immigrants to 2,849, 2 percent of the total Japanese immigrant population in Brazil that year. To support the growth of Japanese farming communities in northern and southern Brazil, two more Japanese consulates were established in the states of Amazonas in 1936 and Paraná in 1941.[51]

State Expansion at the Local Level

Another departure of the migration state from the previous model was the remarkable degree of initiative taken by local/prefectural governments and semigovernmental organizations in starting and managing migration campaigns. Prefectural governments had been involved in migration management as early as 1897. In that year, the central government transferred the responsibility of reviewing Japanese subjects' overseas travel applications (other than to Qing China and Joseon Korea) for labor migration and the power of granting passports to the government of each prefecture (*fu* and *ken*). During this early period, the prefectural governments' authority on migration-related matters was limited to deciding who could legally leave the archipelago and who could not. From the 1920s onward, however, the prefectural governments themselves

[51] Ibid., 120–124.

became engines of migration promotion and migrant training. As the next chapter discusses in detail, some, such as Nagano and Kumamoto, even managed to establish prefecture-centered Japanese settler communities in South America and later in Manchuria.

As it was at the national level, the rapid growth of local governmental involvement in migration management during the 1920s was triggered by the boom of migration to Brazil; like Tokyo, the local governments had the direct aim of promoting Japanese settlement in Brazil. The specific ways in which the prefectural governments involved themselves in Brazil-bound migration, however, were quite different from those of Tokyo. Under the sponsorship of the central government, the primary goal of the Kaikō's migration project was to export contract laborers to São Paulo coffee plantations, expecting that these laborers would later become owner-farmers. The migration campaigns spearheaded by the local authorities, however, were aimed at resettling poor farmers from Japan to Brazil directly as owner-farmers. Their settlement in Brazil was organized by the administrative divisions in the migrants' home prefectures.

Prefecture-centered Brazilian migration campaign first appeared in Nagano, and it grew into a nationwide movement after the Imperial Diet enacted the Overseas Migration Cooperative Societies Law (Kaigai Ijū Kumiai Hō) in March 1927. The law facilitated the formation of an Overseas Migration Cooperative Society (Kaigai Ijū Kumiai) in each prefecture. These societies were open to anyone in the prefecture who purchased a certain number of shares. In turn, the societies offered loans, migration-related facilities, and access to land in Brazil to their members who planned to resettle in South America. August of the same year saw the birth of the Federation of Overseas Migration Cooperative Societies (Kaigai Ijū Kumiai Rengōkai), which oversaw the existing societies and assisted with the establishment of new societies at the prefectural level. The imperial government immediately granted the federation a 1.7-million-yen land acquisition loan, enabling it to provide the existing societies with land and facilities in Brazil to be distributed to individual migrant households.[52]

By the mid-1930s, forty-four out of Japan's forty-seven prefectures had established their own Overseas Migration Cooperative Societies. Soon after its formation, the federation created the Brazilian Colonization Company Limited (Burajiru Takushoku Kumiai, Burataku for short) as its agent to carry out land acquisition and community building in Brazil.[53] By the end of the 1930s, when the Japanese migration to Brazil was suspended, Burataku was managing four major Japanese settler communities, including Bastos, Tietê,

---

[52] Tsuchida, "Japanese in Brazil," 250–251.
[53] "Emigration Incentives as a Means of Solving Population and Unemployment Problems," in National Diet Library, Japan, *100 Years of Japanese Emigration to Brazil.*

and Aliança in the state of São Paulo as well as Tres Barras in the state of Paraná. In total, these communities had 537,668 acres of land and 18,317 Japanese residents. Most settlers were farmers, with the majority of agricultural households owning land, while other settlers pursued commerce and manufacturing.[54]

Conclusion

In the history of Japanese colonial expansion, the 1920s was a crucial turning point despite the absence of military conflicts. On one hand, the empire substantially expanded its involvement in the establishment of the post–World War I war order and strengthened its ties with all of the major Western powers.[55] On the other hand, in sharp contrast with the turbulent 1910s, the metropolis maintained relatively peaceful relationships with its Asian colonies and semicolonies. However, two important changes signaled that the empire's expansion was undergoing a radical transformation. The first was the growing divergence between Japanese and Western ideologies of migration. The second was the expansion of state power in the promotion and management of overseas migration.

As overpopulation anxiety quickly spread throughout the archipelago in the 1920s, Malthusian expansionism's appeal continued to grow. However, instead of emulating the models of British settler colonialism and American westward expansion, as the empire had done during the Meiji and early Taishō periods, the thinkers and doers of colonialism collectively turned to the newly invented tradition of Japanese agriculture as their source of legitimacy.[56] This ideological split was directly triggered by both the passage of the Immigration Act of 1924 and the deterioration of Japanese rural economy since the early 1920s. The American ban on Japanese immigration created a strong backlash among Japanese intellectuals who became increasingly vociferous critics of white racism and Western imperialism. At the same time, the continuous depression in the countryside ushered in a surge of agrarianism that attributed the rural crisis to Japan's adoption of urban/industry-centered mode of development. The agrarianist thinkers contended that Japan needed to restore the centrality of owner-farmer-based agricultural production in the national economy and recapture the spirit of self-sufficiency in everyday life. Embracing Malthusian expansionism allowed this wave of agrarianism to gain increasing

---

[54] Tsuchida, "Japanese in Brazil," 269.
[55] Dickinson, *World War I and the Triumph of a New Japan,* 40–42, 67–83.
[56] Stephen Vlastos's salient research demonstrates how Japanese intellectuals challenged Western capitalist modernity by collectively inventing an ideal past of Japanese agriculture as an alternative future to Japanese economic development in the early twentieth century. Vlastos, "Agrarianism without Tradition," 79–94.

popularity without exacerbating the existing tensions in the countryside. As it was politically unfeasible to redistribute land in the archipelago to create the much-vaunted owner-farmers, the agrarian expansionists called for sending the landless, thus "surplus," farmers abroad to acquire more land. In addition to relieving population pressure and save the rural economy, agricultural migration would also create more owner-farmers on the frontiers of the empire.

While the paradigm shift of Japanese Malthusian expansionism toward farmer migration began with the campaign of rice farming in Texas around the time of the Russo-Japanese War, by the time the shift was complete in the 1920s, both the goal and practice of farmer migration had departed significantly from that of the Texas campaign. The Texas campaign had targeted Japanese rural elites who were financially prepared to migrate to the United States and become big farm owners. The promoters of farmer migration in the 1920s, however, appealed to more grassroots audiences in a much wider social stratum. Now the ideal recruits were either landless farmers or owner-farmers barely scraping by, and the ultimate goal of overseas migration was to turn these unfortunate rural subjects into owner-farmers by allowing them to acquire foreign land. Moreover, while the Texas migration campaign was ideologically patterned after the Anglo-American mode of expansion, the Japanese agrarian mode of expansion in the 1920s and 1930s was based on the time-honored Japanese agricultural tradition; and it was the vehicle through which Japan would fulfill its own manifest destiny as the liberator of the world's colored races.

What made this agrarian version of expansionism convincing was the steady development of Japanese migration to Brazil. For the expansionists in Tokyo, the recent failure of Japanese migration projects in North America, Hawai'i, and Australia proved the cruelty of white racism. At the same time, their attempts at creating Japanese owner-farmers in Northeast Asia and the South Seas were also unsuccessful. Brazil, however, was regarded as a shining beacon for the advocates of farmer migration and the Japanese public at large – its steady growth of migration inflow and the flourishing Japanese own-farmer communities seemed to prove that agrarian migration was more than just an enticing slogan.

The promising future in Brazil and the nationwide recognition of emigration as a solution to poverty drew an unprecedented level of involvement from the imperial government in the areas of migration promotion and management. The formation of the migration state and its financial and political aids, in turn, made the migration of the hundreds of thousands of rural poor possible. In collaboration with the Kaikō, the central government began providing full subsidies to any authorized Japanese subject who would like to pursue a future in Brazil. Some of the prefectural governments also came to the fore and launched their own campaigns of land acquisition and settler migration. The birth of the migration state thus perpetuated the marriage between the grassroots agrarianism and Brazilian migration. It allowed the landless farmers, deemed by the Malthusian expansionists as the most desirable subjects for migration, to participate in Japan's migration-driven expansion in South America.

The formation of the migration state paved the way for Japan's state-led mass migration to Manchuria during the late 1930s in order to facilitate its total war in Asia. One cannot fully grasp this historical transformation without understanding how the Japanese government inserted itself into the Brazilian migration project in the 1920s. Due to intensive involvement by the prefectural governments, the tale of Japanese migration and settlement in Brazil in the 1920s and 1930s was also a rich collection of local histories. The next chapter delves into the migration campaigns led by the government of Nagano prefecture, one that was the most active and successful in promoting and managing migration to Brazil, to illustrate how Malthusian expansionism functioned at the local level. Not coincidentally, Nagano was also the prefecture that exported the greatest number of migrants to Manchuria between the late 1930s and 1945. The study of migration promotion and management in Nagano pinpoints the nexus between Japanese migration to Brazil and Manchuria from the 1920s to the end of World War II.

7   The Illusion of Coexistence and Coprosperity: Settler Colonialism in Brazil and Manchuria

Among Japanese settler communities in Brazil, Aliança deserves special attention. It was the first community that attempted to put the new principles of Japanese expansionism that emerged in the 1920s into practice. As a model project of Japanese settler colonialism in Brazil, the establishment of Aliança laid the foundation for a new phase of Japanese expansion during the 1930s and 1940s in both ideology and practice.

Aliança was the first Japanese overseas community established under the principle of "coexistence and coprosperity" (*kyōzon kyōei or kyōzon dōei*). This principle of expansion challenged Western imperialism and capitalism by promoting Japan's own expansion as a mission to bring genuine peace, liberation, and happiness to the world. During the 1930s, the very same slogan was used in the puppet state of Manchukuo to justify escalated Japanese expansion. More broadly, it also served as the ideological framework of the Greater East Asia Co-Prosperity Sphere (Daitōa Kyōei Ken), the new world order envisioned by the Japanese empire during World War II.

In addition to radical ideological divergence, Aliança also saw the birth of a new model of recruiting and relocating migrants. While previous Japanese migrants undertook the journey either individually or under the auspice of migration companies, Aliança migrants collectively moved and resettled in groups that were based on their native prefectures and villages. Beginning in the late 1930s until the empire's demise in 1945, the Aliança model served as a central reference for the imperial government to relocate hundreds of thousands of rural Japanese to Manchuria and other parts of Asia.

What also distinguishes Aliança from the all previous migration projects is that it was the first prefecture-initiated project of migration. It was launched by the Shinano Overseas Association (Shinano Kaigai Kyōkai) in 1923 with support

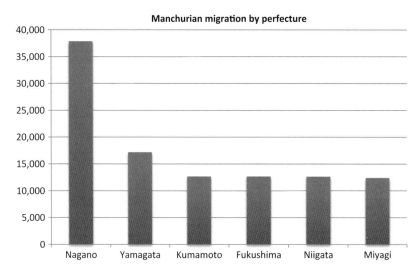

Figure 7.1 The six prefectures that exported the largest numbers of migrants among all Japanese prefectures to Manchuria from the beginning of the 1930s to the end of World War II were Nagano, Yamagata, Kumamoto, Fukushima, Niigata, and Miyagi. However, as the chart illustrates, among these six prefectures, the number of migrants from Nagano (37,859) was much larger than the number of migrants from any other prefectures and was even more than the numbers of migrants from Yamagata (17,177) and Kumamoto (12,680; the second and third in the rank) combined. See Louise Young, *Japan's Total Empire: Manchuria and the Culture of Wartime Imperialism* (Berkeley: University of California Press, 1998), 329–330.

from Nagano's prefectural government.[1] Nagano's success in Brazilian land acquisition and settler community management brought on a nationwide campaign of building prefectural Overseas Migration Cooperative Societies (Kaigai Ijū Kumiai) for Brazil-bound migration. As a pioneer of this campaign, Nagano prefecture became one of the most active participants in the mass migration movement during the late 1930s. Out of all the prefectures in the archipelago, it was Nagano that sent out the most men and women to Manchuria.[2]

The central role of Nagano prefecture in Manchurian migration in the 1930s and 1940s cannot be fully explained without an understanding of the

[1] The Shinano Overseas Association was named after Shinano no Kuni (State of Shinano), an ancient state of which the Nagano region was a part.
[2] In addition to the migration of men, Nagano prefecture was also one of the earliest and most activist prefectures to train and settle women to Manchuria in the 1930s. See Aiba Kazuhiko, Chen Jin, Miyata Sachie, and Nakashima Jun, eds., *Manshū "Tairiku no Hanayome" wa Dō Tsukurareta Ka?* (Tokyo: Akashi Shotten, 1996), 348–385.

prefecture's participation in Brazilian migration right before it. This chapter analyzes the process of Japanese community building in Aliança and Nagano prefecture's role in it. It also explains how the experience of Japanese migration in Brazil paved the way for Japan's later expansion into Manchuria. Through the story of Nagano prefecture, this chapter illustrates the ways in which the discourse of Malthusian expansionism drove migration-based expansion at the prefectural level. The chapter ends with a brief discussion of how the previous experiences of Japanese migration on both sides of the Pacific were reinterpreted to support the empire's expansion on the Asian continent during the total war.

Nagano Prefecture and Overseas Migration

Out of all the Japanese prefectures, Nagano had one of the longest histories of overseas migration. Historian Louise Young has traced the history of emigration promotion of the Prefectural Board of Education (Shinano Kyōiku Kai) back to 1888.[3] Stimulated by multiple wars and waves of migration, the board encouraged migration to Hokkaido, Taiwan, Manchuria, and the Korean Peninsula through publications and public lectures.[4] The prefecture's migration promotion substantially intensified in the 1910s, when Japanese expansionists began to explore alternative migration destinations due to anti-Japanese sentiment in North America. In this context, the expansionists believed that introducing migration preparation as a central element of Japan's national education agenda would enhance the quality of the migrants to forestall Japanese exclusion and to attract more Japanese subjects to the grand mission of overseas expansion.[5] Nagano's Board of Education responded quickly by adopting the promotion of overseas migration as one of the five principle goals of education in the prefecture. It published and assigned *Shinano Colonial Migration Reader* (*Shinano Shokumin Dokuhon*), a textbook promoting overseas migration, to be used in elementary schools. In order to further stimulate public interest and disseminate information about overseas migration, during the next few years the board organized hundreds of events for the schools of different levels throughout the prefecture, including public lectures, magic lantern shows, and photo exhibitions.[6]

Such efforts from Nagano's Prefectural Board of Education would not have been possible without cooperation from the Japanese Striving Society. The society was established by Christian Socialist Shimanuki Hyōdayū in Tokyo in

---

[3] Young, *Japan's Total Empire*, 331.
[4] Kobayashi Shinsuke, *Hitobito wa Naze Manshū e Watatta no Ka: Nagano Ken no Shakai Undō to Imin* (Kyōto: Sekai Shisōsha, 2015), 127–128.
[5] Nagata, *Kaigai Hatten*, 9–19.   [6] Nagata, *Shinano Kaigai Ijūshi*, 50–51.

1897. Under Shimanuki's leadership, the society promoted and facilitated the migration of young Japanese students to the United States as laborers. Following Shimanuki's death, Nagata Shigeshi became the president of the society in 1914. This leadership change ushered in a fundamental shift in the society's agenda as a migration organization. While it continued to smuggle laborers into the United States even after the Gentlemen's Agreement banned laborer migration from Japan, it became increasingly focused on exploring alternative migration destinations, particularly those in South America.

The change of leadership also reflected a discursive shift in Japan's migration-based expansion from laborers to agriculture workers. Nagata previously had edited the *North American Agricultural Journal* (*Hokubei Nōhō*), a Japanese American agricultural journal based in San Francisco, and now he quickly directed the society's migration promotion to target the rural population. A Nagano native, he also moved the geographical focus of the society's promotion from urban Tokyo to the countryside of Nagano. Working closely with the Nagano Prefectural Board of Education, the society provided speakers for most of the public lectures organized by the board during the 1910s. At the peak of the lecture campaign, between 1915 and 1916, Nagata alone delivered 250 lectures that were attended by a total of 120,000 prefecture residents.[7]

Nagata found a collaborator on the other side of the Pacific Ocean in Wako Shungorō, another Nagano native. Like Nagata, Wako migrated to the United States immediately after the Russo-Japanese War. Disappointed by institutionalized racism, Wako remigrated to Brazil after the passage of California Alien Land Law of 1913. In the state of São Paulo, he served as the editor of a Japanese immigrant newspaper *Noticias Do Brazil* (*Burajiru Jihō; Brazilian Times*) and became an active promoter of Nagano migration to Brazil.[8]

By the end of the 1910s, hundreds of Nagano residents had migrated to Iguape in the state of San Paulo as farming settlers, and they soon constituted a majority of the Japanese settlers in the Registro region.[9] By the late 1910s, Japanese communities in Iguape were, to various degrees, plagued by financial difficulties. Under pressure from Tokyo, the administrative authority of all these communities was transferred into the Kaikō's hands in 1919. Unsatisfied with this change, Nagata and Wako began to plan for an autonomous settler community in Brazil. They conceived that such a community,

[7] Ibid., 51.
[8] Kimura Kai, "Wako Shungorō no Kieta Ashiato o Tadoru," *Ariansa Tsūshin*, no. 13 (August 1, 2003), www.gendaiza.org/aliansa/lib/1301.html.
[9] Kimura Kai, "Ariansa to Shinano Kaigai Kyōkai," *Ariansa Tsūshin*, no. 8 (November 30, 2000), www.gendaiza.org/aliansa/lib/0803.html and Kimura Kai, "Ariansa e no michi," *Ariansa Tsūshin*, no. 23 (July 30, 2008), www.gendaiza.org/aliansa/lib/23-05.html.

primarily made up of Nagano natives, would be independent from both the imperial government and the Kaikō.[10]

In order to fund their land purchase and other expenses along the way, Nagata and Wako formed the Shinano Overseas Association (Shinano Kaigai Kyōkai) with cooperation from the prefecture government, the Board of Education, and the Japanese Striving Society. With the governor of Nagano and the head of the Prefectural Diet as its director and vice director, the association was a semigovernmental, nonprofit migration organization funded by both public grants and private donations. Established in 1922, the association gradually expanded beyond Nagano prefecture and Japan itself, establishing branches in Tokyo, San Francisco, Los Angeles, Mexico, Brazil, the Korean Peninsula, Manchuria, and China proper through a network of Nagano natives. It conducted a variety of activities such as hosting public lectures, publishing an official journal called *Beyond the Seas* (*Umi no Soto*), sponsoring investigative trips, as well as building Japanese communities in Asia and South America.[11]

Migration promotion in Nagano demonstrated how Malthusian expansionism worked at the prefectural level. As early as 1899, due to a shortage of farmland within the prefecture, Nagano's Board of Education had already begun to perceive a necessity of relocating farmers to Hokkaido and Taiwan.[12] The logic of Malthusian expansionism later gained more adherents amongst Nagano expansionists who were disappointed by Japanese exclusion in North America. The opening article in the inaugural issue of *Umi no Soto* in 1922 was the script of a speech of Nagano governor Okada Tadahiko, delivered at the founding ceremony of the journal and titled "The Overseas Development of Nagano People." Okada claimed that the Japanese people were troubled by poverty because the country had one of the highest population densities in the world, even while white people all over the world enjoyed a more prosperous life because of their low population densities. The population of the United States, for example, was smaller than that of Japan while its territory was much larger. The population densities of the United Kingdom, Belgium, and the Netherlands were originally as high as that of Japan, but their people were able to enjoy spacious land resources because these countries engaged in overseas expansion. The British had acquired Canada, Australia, India, and some territories in Southeast Asia and Africa, the Belgians took Congo, while the Dutch claimed the Dutch East Indies. These white settlers, Okada further pointed out, not only occupied foreign land throughout the world but also set aside these territories for their own descendants by excluding others.[13]

---

[10] Nagata Shigeshi, *Burajiru ni Okeru Nihonjin Hattenshi*, vol. 2 (Tokyo: Burajiru ni Okeru Nihonjin Hattenshi Kenkōkai, 1953), 32–34.

[11] Nagata, *Shinano Kaigai Ijūshi*, 57–66.

[12] Kobayashi, *Hitobito wa Naze Manshū e Watatta no Ka*, 127.

[13] Okada Tadahiko, "Nagano Kenjin no Kaigai Hatten," *Umi no Soto* 1, no. 1 (1922): 1–4.

After presenting the unequal state of land resource distribution around the world, Okada emphasized that the Malthusian crisis was particularly severe in Nagano. As the prefecture had relatively little arable land, its farmers had to plant crops on mountaintops and still could barely make ends meet. To make things worse, the speed of population growth in Nagano was faster than the national average, which was already among the highest of the world. To rescue the prefecture from Malthusian doom, it was imperative for Nagano residents, like the Westerners, to set out and explore land overseas. The prefecture's unfavorable natural environment, Okada predicted with confidence, had made Nagano people every bit capable as the Anglo-Saxons to overcome challenging environments around the world.[14]

As Okawa Heikichi, another speaker at the ceremony, would remind the same audience, however, population growth itself was not a bad thing at all. A Nagano native, Okawa served the imperial government as the head of the Bureau of Statistics. He argued that while international competitions of the day took a variety of forms, the winners were always nations with growing populations. The Jewish people, for example, were able to maintain their strength through population growth even though they did not have a home country. With their unparalleled solidarity and growth rate, the Japanese had a most promising future. Remarkably, Okawa used racial discrimination against Japanese immigrants in the United States to prove his point. He argued that the exclusion of the Japanese was rooted in the fear of white Americans because the Japanese people had the highest fertility rate among all the ethnic groups in the United States. While America was closing its doors, Okawa pointed out, Brazil was waiting for the Japanese with its spacious and empty land for the taking. By migrating to Brazil, the Japanese could not only explore and acquire local resources but also ensure that the Japanese population would continue its superior growth rate.[15]

Aliança, Malthusian Expansionism, and the Illusion of Coexistence and Coprosperity

The most significant campaign that the Nagano prefecture accomplished during the 1920s was the founding of Aliança in Brazil in 1923. Like Iguape, the farming community of Aliança was built by taking advantage of the 1907 law of the state of São Paulo that provided subsidies and land concessions to any migration company that would bring in agricultural settlers. The successful promotion campaign in Nagano, however, made Aliança the first Japanese community in Brazil that was primarily composed of farmers directly migrating from Japan, not those who arrived in Brazil initially as plantation laborers

[14] Ibid. [15] Ogawa Heikichi, "Kaigai Ijūsha no Shitō," *Umi no Soto* 1, no. 1 (1922): 9–11.

and then turned into farmers. With the continuous inflow of migration, the population of Aliança grew steadily from 54 settlers in 16 households to 1,335 settlers in 280 households from 1924 to 1934.[16]

Even more significantly, Aliança was the first Japanese overseas community that was established to consciously exemplify the new model of Japanese migration-driven expansion based on the principle that later came to be known as "coexistence and coprosperity." Along with Japan-centered Pan-Asianism, coexistence and coprosperity served as the overarching discourse legitimizing Japanese expansion in Asia beginning in the 1930s, eventually becoming the ideological basis of the Greater East Asia Co-Prosperity Sphere. Historians have long dismissed this slogan as a piece of empty propaganda that merely testified to the hypocrisy of Japanese imperialism and militarism, yet as the following paragraphs will illustrate, *kyōzon kyōei*, as the core principle of this new version of Japanese expansion, emerged as early as the 1920s during Japan's mass migration to Brazil. It was a product of specific international and domestic factors of the day and included multiple dimensions of meaning. Analyzing how the discourse of coexistence and coprosperity emerged will also help to elucidate the ideological and organizational connection between Japanese migration to Brazil in the 1920s and 1930s and later Japanese colonial expansion in Northeast Asia until the end of World War II.

First and foremost, as an expansionist discourse, coexistence and coprosperity was a direct response to the exclusion of Japanese from North America. It claimed that unlike racist Caucasians, the Japanese would treat people of color as equal partners. Both Nagata Shigeshi and Wako Shungorō, central figures in the establishment of Aliança, had experienced institutionalized white racism against Japanese immigrants firsthand in California. As early as 1917, Nagata published a book that defined white Americans as hypocrites who only paid lip service to justice and freedom. As he pointed out, "Their freedom was the freedom of the white Americans, not the freedom of the colored people. Their equality was the equality among the Euro-Americans, not the equality among different races of the entire world!" In the same book, Nagata also connected American anti-Japanese campaigns with white racism against black people in the United States and against the colonized people within the British Empire. He recalled his conversations with an African American and three Indians in California. The black person complained to Nagata that while African Americans were liberated from racial slavery, they were subject to racial segregation and discrimination in almost every aspect of US society. Similarly, the three Indians lamented that in all colonies of the British Empire around the world, Asians were excluded from benefits and opportunities enjoyed by the British. Both the African Americans and the Indians,

---

[16] Nagata, *Shinano Kaigai Ijūshi*, 92.

according to Nagata, saw Japan as the only possible liberator who would destroy the tyranny of white racism and imperialism. They pledged their allegiance to the Japanese empire if it would fight a war against the United States and the United Kingdom.[17]

As a faithful Malthusian expansionist, Nagata had no doubt that the destiny of the Japanese empire lay in overseas expansion. However, he further glorified Japanese expansion as a righteous mission to defeat global white hegemony by leading and uniting all peoples of color, thereby bringing genuine peace, freedom, and equality to the entire world. In his imagination, the people in Latin America, already suffering from the tyranny of white racism, were waiting for the Japanese empire to take on this global mission as their liberators – unlike the hypocritical white settlers, the Japanese would truly cohabit and cooperate with other racial groups.[18] As a reaction to the anti-Japanese campaigns in the United States, the racial denotation of coexistence and coprosperity made the project of Aliança particularly appealing to Japanese American immigrants. A substantial portion of its initial fund for land acquisition was contributed by Japanese Americans, and some issei also migrated to Aliança permanently.[19] The slogan of "coexistence and coprosperity" was quickly enshrined by other Japanese expansionists as a general guideline for Japanese migration to Brazil as well as other destinations.[20]

Its professed antiracist principle, however, only masked the Japanese empire builders' desire to overtake white men as the champion in the global racial hierarchy. In fact, the very name of Aliança spoke to this slogan's inherent hypocrisy. As was customary of naming organizations affiliated with Nagano prefecture, the new community was originally to be named Shinano colony (Shinano Shokuminchi). Yet this name was scrapped because the word Shinano sounded similar to Chino, the Portuguese word for Chinese. The Japanese founders wanted to avoid being confused with the Chinese, who were considered inferior in both Japan and Brazil. As a goodwill gesture, Wako Shungorō eventually named the community Aliança, meaning "alliance" in Portuguese.[21] From its very start, an understanding of racial hierarchy thus was ingrained in the slogan of "coexistence and coprosperity."

Nagata described the residents in Brazil as products of miscegenation between the Portuguese, the aborigines, and African immigrants. He argued that as a result of their mixed racial origin, the Brazilians not only harbored no racism against the Japanese migrants but also had little sense of nationhood. They had no plan to reserve the spacious land of their country exclusively for their own use, nor did they have the ambition to conduct colonial expansion

---

[17] Nagata, *Kaigai Hatten*, 19–21.   [18] Ibid., 21–22.
[19] Nagata, *Shinano Kaigai Ijūshi*, 83–84.
[20] See, for example, Arai, "Shokumin to Kyōiku," 84.
[21] Nagata, *Shinano Kaigai Ijūshi*, 79–80.

themselves, all of these making them extremely pliable to Japanese manipulation.[22] This racial hierarchy was later replicated in the relationship between the Japanese and the other peoples of Asia as coexistence and coprosperity became the guiding ideology of the empire's expansion in Asia during the 1930s and 1940s.

Second, aside from the professed antiracism element, coexistence and coprosperity was also a discourse of internationalism that emerged in Japan right after World War I in an era of Wilsonianism. Working in conjunction with Malthusian expansionism, it described the exportation of surplus Japanese population overseas as a mission to bring civilization and peace to the world. As a victor of the Great War, Japan responded quickly to the call for international cooperation in maintaining the security of the imperial world order in post–World War I era. Politicians, businessmen, and opinion leaders, old and new, urged their fellow countrymen to abandon traditional militarism in favor of the new and peaceful way of expansion through trade and migration. The purpose of expansion was no longer to conquer foreign land through warfare but to bring peace and progress to the entire humankind.[23]

As Diet member Tsuzaki Naotake pointed out in 1929, Aliança was a pioneer of Japan's new approach in global expansion.[24] By exporting surplus population to the less populated and less developed land abroad, the Japanese empire was helping local people to tap the sources of wealth and bringing enlightenment and prosperity to remote corners of the world. Migration of the rural poor from Nagano to Aliança as farmers instead of laborers fitted well with this magnanimous image of Japanese expansion. Unlike the labor migrants who had little investment in the long-term outlook of the host country, the agricultural migrants were joining the local society as permanent members. To highlight the difference between the model of Aliança and the previous model of migration that exported Japanese laborers to Brazilian coffee plantations, Nagata argued that the goal of Aliança was to "cultivate people rather than coffee" (*kōhī yori hito wo tsukure*).[25]

The success of the Aliança project spurred even more enthusiasm for Japanese land acquisition in Brazil in the name of peaceful expansion and shared development. Expansionists in Tokyo began to look beyond the state of São Paulo and sought to establish similar Japanese communities in other parts of Brazil. In 1928, Brazilian Colonization Company Limited purchased 74,750 acres of land in northern Paraná, where the Japanese farming community of Tres Barras was established in the early 1930s.[26] In the same year, answering the call of the Japanese prime minister and minister of foreign affairs, Tanaka

---

[22] Nagata, *Nōson Jinkō Mondai to Ishokumin*, 219.
[23] Iriye, "Failure of Economic Expansionism," 251–259.
[24] Tsuzaki Naotake, "Nihon no Genjō to Kaigai Hatten," *Rikkō Sekai*, no. 300 (December 1929): 9.
[25] Nagata, *Shinano Kaigai Ijūshi*, 134.   [26] Tsuchida, "Japanese in Brazil," 266–267.

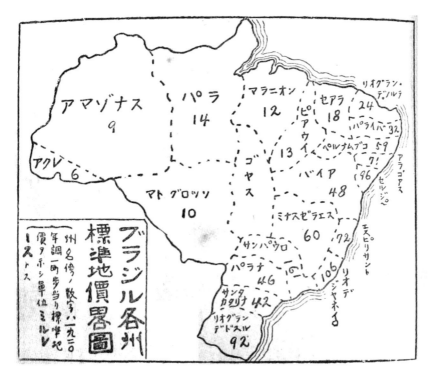

Figure 7.2 This map was made by the South America Colonial Company based on a 1920 survey that marked the land prices of different states in Brazil in thousands of Brazilian reals. *Shokumin* 7, no. 12 (December 1928): 71.

Gi'ichi, a group of Japanese entrepreneurs founded the South America Colonization Company (Nanbei Takushoku Kabushiki Gaisha, or Nantaku for short). Nantaku was created to take advantage of the state of Pará's policy of attracting foreign immigrants to develop the Amazon Basin. Dionysio Benetes, the governor of Pará, granted Nantaku one million hectares of land, including six hundred thousand hectares in the municipality of Acará and four hundred thousand in the municipality of Monte Alegre. In Acará, the company built its colony around Tomé-Acu.[27] Nantaku, however, did not limit its ambition to land acquisition in the Amazon Basin; it sought to raise more funds from the archipelago to acquire land in other parts of Brazil as well. The map in figure 7.2, marking out the land prices of all states in Brazil, was published by Nantaku in the journal *Shokumin* in 1928.

[27] Ibid., 271.

Coexistence and coprosperity's claim of internationalism, like its supposed pursuit of racial equality, did not come to pass in Aliança. After all, the ultimate goal of building Aliança was not to usher in global peace but to see if this new model of migration-driven expansion was indeed tenable.[28] The Aliança model rejected the traditional conquest of sword and fire in favor of spade and hoe. However, the shift occurred not because expansionists wished to share the benefits of migration with the Brazilians but because they perceived this model as a better one to put down the roots of the Japanese empire in South America. Even during the height of Japanese immigration, Aliança failed to live up to its cosmopolitan promise. Until 1936, when the annual number of Japanese migrants to Brazil began to drop sharply, the inhabitants of Aliança were almost entirely Japanese.[29]

Third, coexistence and coprosperity was also an agrarian discourse that had its root in the growing agrarianist movement in Japan during the 1920s and 1930s. Japanese expansionists promoted it as the embodiment of a community-building spirit from ancient Japan that was centered on self-sufficiency and mutual aid. Many of the leading agrarianists of the day, including Tachibana Kōzaburō, Gondō Seikyō, and Katō Kanji, attributed Japan's rural depression to the capitalist economic system and individualism – evils that were imported from the West. For them, the remedy for the ills plaguing the Japanese countryside was to return to Japan's traditional rural-centered life and mode of production. Shaped by the agrarianist movement of the day, the principle of coexistence and coprosperity called for owner-farmer-based collective farming in which all members of a village would preserve their economic autonomy while maintaining mutual support. In the minds of the agrarianists, subsistence farming was the ideal way of living because villagers would not rely on others or exploit them. Through mutual aid, each village would achieve self-sufficiency at the community level.[30] Such self-sufficiency and autonomy, the agrarianists believed, would rescue the Japanese countryside from capitalist exploitation and individualist self-interest.

This agrarianist approach was put into practice through the rapid expansion of the Producers' Cooperative Association (Sangyō Kumiai) among Japanese farmers during the 1920s. This association was founded in 1900 in Japan with the aim to protect the economic interests of low-income farmers and workers through mutual aid. In 1921, the imperial government endorsed the formation

---

[28] Historian Akira Iriye argues that the Japanese empire did not seek to challenge the post–World War I global imperial order, but sought to conduct its own expansion by following its principles. See Iriye, "Failure of Economic Expansionism," 239–240.

[29] Beginning in 1936, the Japanese immigration slowed down and stopped due to immigration restrictions in Brazil. Accordingly, the Japanese population in Aliança began to decrease and more and more Brazilian settlers began to move in. Nagano Ken Kaitaku Jikōkai Manshū Kaitakushi Kankōkai, *Nagano Ken Manshū Kaitaku Shi: Sōhen* (Nagano-shi: Nagano Ken Kaitaku Jikōkai Manshū Kaitakushi Kankōkai, 1984), 113.

[30] Hon'iden Yoshio, "Nōson to Kyōdō," *Ie no Hikari* 3, no. 1 (January 1927): 10–13.

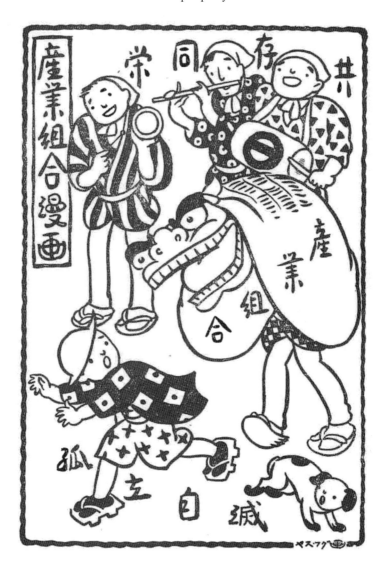

Figure 7.3 Cartoon from the first page of the January 1927 issue of *Ie no Hikari*. It promoted the slogan of coexistence and coprosperity (*Kyōzon Dōei*) as a spirit of the Producers' Cooperative Association. Isolation and selfishness, as this picture indicated, would lead only to extinction.

of a national headquarters of the Association (Zenkoku Rengōkai) under the newly revised Producers' Cooperative Law (Sangyō Kumiai Hō). The number of association members reached 3.64 million in 1925, almost half of them being farmers. To monitor and manage the association's activities, the government established the Department of the Producers' Cooperation under the Ministry of Agriculture and Forestry (Nōrinshō) in the same year.[31] At the same time, the association began to publish its official magazine, the *Light of Family* (*Ie no Hikari*). Promoting owner-farmer-based collective farming under the principle of coexistence and coprosperity, the magazine grew into one of the most popular periodicals in rural Japan during the 1930s, reaching one million in monthly circulation by 1935.[32]

    The founders of Aliança did not believe that the domestic agrarianist movement alone would be sufficient to save the Japanese countryside. For them, overseas migration was the ultimate solution. However, they did loyally follow the agrarianist principles of community building in their migration campaigns. Aliança was first conceived when Nagata Shigeshi and Wako Shungorō were disappointed by the Kaikō taking over the management of Japanese communities in Iguape. Certain that a settler community's autonomy was of the utmost importance, they began to undertake the first prefecture-centered migration project. While Aliança received financial aid from the imperial government, it was established as a farming community independent from managerial intervention of both the Kaikō and the imperial government.[33]

    In addition to its prized autonomy, Aliança also followed the principle of collective farming. Unlike Western colonial expansions that allowed the elites to monopolize wealth and power, Nagata argued, Japanese overseas expansion should benefit the common people.[34] To this end, the Aliança project was derived from the growth of Producers' Cooperative Association in Japan. Different from previous campaigns that recruited migrants from all over the country, Aliança's fund-raising and recruitment campaigns were conducted with in Nagano prefecture. Aliança's settlers were primarily Nagano farmers who were expected to possess a strong sense of community and willingness for mutual aid because of their homegrown ties. To ensure its socioeconomic autonomy, Aliança had facilities such as construction companies, a rice mill, and a coffee refinery in addition to its administrative office, clinic, elementary school, hotel, dormitories, church, and newspaper agency.[35]

    The establishment of Aliança by the Shinano Overseas Association paved the way for a wave of prefecture-based Japanese expansion projects in Brazil. The overseas associations of Tottori, Toyama, and Kumamoto, with support

[31] Tagawa Mariko, "'Imin' Shichō no Kiseki" (PhD diss., Yūshōdō Shuppan, 2005), 105.
[32] Ibid., 109.   [33] Kimura, "Ariansa to Shinano Kaigai Kyōkai."
[34] Nagata Shigeshi, "Sangyō Kumiai no Kaigai Enchō," *Rikkō Sekai,* no. 232 (April 1924): 3.
[35] Nagata, *Shinano Kaigai Ijūshi,* 91–92.

Figure 7.4 Copy of the front cover of the inaugural issue of *Ie no Hikari*, published in May 1925, with the words "coexistence" and "coprosperity" (*kyōzon dōei*) on top. These words, like the motto of the Producers' Cooperative Association, appeared on the cover of almost every issue of the journal.

from their own prefectural governments, acquired lands adjacent to Aliança and established migrant communities. Replicating Aliança's prefecture-centered model, Tottori's community was formed in 1926 as Aliança II. Toyama and Shinano Overseas Associations collaborated to build Aliança III in 1927, while Kumamoto Overseas Association established Vila Nova during the same year.[36]

To further encourage prefecture-centered collective migration to Brazil, the Imperial Diet in 1927 enacted the Overseas Migration Cooperative Societies Law (Kaigai Ijū Kumiai Hō). This legislation facilitated the formation of an Overseas Migration Cooperative Society (Kaigai Ijū Kumiai) in each prefecture that raised funds and recruited migrants based on the model of the Producers' Cooperative Association. In order to synchronize the campaigns in each prefecture, the government also established the Federation of Overseas Migration Cooperative Societies. The fact that Umetani Mitsusada, the former governor of Nagano who played a key role in the establishment of Aliança, served as the first director of the federation testified to the impact of Aliança on this movement.[37]

The agrarianist spirit of self-sufficiency and mutual aid also became a requirement for Japanese overseas migrants in general. In a 1928 issue of *Shokumin* (*Colonial Review*), its editor Naitō Hideo reminded his readers that the issue of overpopulation had caused numerous social problems in Japan, including economic depression, greater social inequality, and the monopolization of wealth and power by a small group of elites. Naitō urged his countrymen to explore new land abroad where they could establish progressive societies with equality for all through the spirit of coexistence and coprosperity. "I believe," he contended, "the success of colonial migration is not valued by the amount of money or wealth you make. Instead, it is . . . judged by whether you can achieve true freedom and live together with each other in happiness and equality."[38]

However, like the internationalist and racial equality aspects of coexistence and coprosperity, its self-proclaimed agrarianist dimension also turned out to be a mere illusion. None of the three settler communities (Bastos, Tietê, and Tres Barras) established by Burataku, the agent of the Federation of Overseas Migration Cooperative Societies in Brazil, copied the prefecture-centered model of Aliança. Due to financial and organizational barriers, they all became mixed communities that had settlers from all over the archipelago.[39] Moreover,

[36] Ibid., 95–96; Tsuchida, "Japanese in Brazil," 267.
[37] Nagata Shigeshi, "Sangyō Kumiai no Kaigai Enchō," *Rikkō Sekai,* no. 232 (April 1924): 3.
[38] Nagata, *Shinano Kaigai Ijūshi*, 91–92. *Shokumin* 7, no. 6 (June 1928): 1.
[39] Kimura Kai, "Ikken Isson Kara Ikkatsu Daijūchi e," in "Ariansa Undō no Rekishi (3): Burajiru Ijūshi no Nazo–Kaigai Ijū Kumiai Hō," *Ariansa Tsūshin*, no. 26 (August 1, 2009), www.gendaiza.org/aliansa/lib/26–05.html.

Figure 7.5 Cover of a brochure for the migration of Japanese owner-farmers to Brazil published by the Federation of Overseas Migration Cooperative Societies in March 1932. This brochure was distributed by the Overseas Migration Cooperative Society in Kagawa prefecture. National Diet Library, Japan, *100 Years of Japanese Emigration to Brazil*, www.ndl.go.jp/brasil/e/data/R/042/042-001r.html.

Aliança II, Aliança III, and Vila Nova quickly lost their autonomy. Due to financial and political pressure from the federation, the leadership of these three communities was handed over from the Overseas Migration Associations of Tottori, Toyama, and Kumamoto to the Burataku soon after their establishment. Collective farming also turned out to be detrimental to Aliança's well-being as individual farmers' economic condition successively deteriorated. Though it managed to maintain the autonomy of Aliança for more than a decade, the Shinano Overseas Association eventually handed the community over to Burataku in 1938 due to financial problems.[40]

From Aliança to Manchuria: The Heyday of Malthusian Expansionism

Japan's military expansion in Manchuria in 1931 and the formation of Manchukuo as the empire's puppet state inspired Japanese expansionists to reconsider Northeast Asia as an optimal migration destination. By the mid-1930s, migration promoters, old and new, had not only debated about strategies and plans but also conducted a number of experimental migration campaigns under sponsorship from the military. None of these campaigns prevailed, however, due to violent Chinese resistance as well as the lower living cost of local farmers that the Japanese farmers failed to compete with in Manchuria.[41] Though anxiously seeking ways to lift the countryside out of depression, Tokyo did not offer substantial policy support for migration to Manchuria.

The malaise of migration to Manchuria was in stark contrast with – as well as partially a result of – the further development of Japanese expansion in Brazil during the first half of the 1930s. Though Brazil's coffee economy took a serious hit from a sudden price drop during global depression, the country in general continued to welcome migrants from Japan as plantation laborers and farmers due to shrinking immigration numbers from Italy and Portugal. The number of annual Japanese migrants to Brazil kept growing from the 1920s. In 1932, Japanese accounted for 37 percent of the immigrants who entered Brazil, becoming the largest group of immigrants in terms of annual number. The inflow of Japanese migrants reached its peak in 1933 and 1934, with about twenty-three thousand migrants each year that accounted for an absolute majority of the overall number of immigrants to Brazil.[42]

The early 1930s was also marked by further growth of Japanese communities in Brazil. In response to the commonwealth nations' boycott against Japanese textile in 1932, Tokyo turned from India to Brazil as Japan's cotton supplier.[43] Technical assistance from Tokyo and financial subsidies from major Japanese textile companies began to pour into Japanese Brazilian communities to stimulate cotton cultivation. It contributed to the prosperity of Japanese agriculture in Brazil in general and the success of cotton production in particular throughout the 1930s. By 1939, the Japanese communities in São Paulo single-

---

[40] Nagano Ken Kaitaku Jikōkai Manshū Kaitakushi Kankōkai, *Nagano Ken Manshū Kaitaku Shi*, 113–114.

[41] Wilson, "New Paradise," 261–273.   [42] Tsuchida, "Japanese in Brazil," 235, 241.

[43] Ibid., 310.

handedly contributed 20.4 percent of the state's annual agricultural output. In terms of cotton, Japanese communities accounted for as much as 43.3 percent.[44] Until the outbreak of the Pacific War in 1941, Japanese communities in Brazil continued to serve as one of the major cotton suppliers for the textile industry of the Japanese empire.[45]

Compared with the success of Japanese expansion in Brazil, Manchuria appeared much less attractive to common farmers and migration promoters even after the empire secured military and political control of Manchuria between 1931 and 1932. By 1936, despite enthusiastic support from the Kwantung Army, none of the Japanese migration endeavors in Manchuria prevailed.[46] During the early 1930s, even some Japanese government officials maintained that Brazil was a better place for Japanese migration than Manchuria would be.[47]

Two political changes in the mid-1930s, however, altered this situation. Japanese military expansion in Manchuria led to a resurgence of " yellow peril" rhetoric in Brazil. The idea of protecting the nation from Japanese imperialism joined forces with the old race-based anti-Japanese sentiment that first emerged in Brazil during the first two decades of the twentieth century.[48] The constitution of 1934 following the Vargas Revolution eventually included an amendment modeled after the Immigration Act of 1924 in the United States. It imposed a 2 percent annual quota of the numbers of immigrants from each nation based on the numbers of the existing immigrants who had arrived in the past half a century. Based on this quota, only 2,775 (later revised to 2,849) Japanese subjects were allowed for immigration.[49] Though the amendment did not immediately come into effect, Japanese immigration still plummeted in response – from more than 23,000 in 1933 to fewer than 2,000 in 1941.[50]

Japan's migration-driven expansion eventually took another major direction change in 1936, shifting its destination from South America to Manchuria. As the Japanese military dramatically increased its political influence following the February 26 Incident, the Hiroda Kōki cabinet successfully turned the Kwangtung Army's agenda of mass migration to Manchuria into a national policy. The imperial government began to organize a project that would relocate five million farmers in one million households from Japan to

[44] Ibid., 307.
[45] "Establishment of the Quota System and Movements for Japanese Immigrants Exclusion," in *100 Years of Japanese Emigration to Brazil.*
[46] See Wilson, "New Paradise," 264–277.   [47] See ibid., 258.
[48] Tsuchida, "Japanese in Brazil," 289–290.
[49] Jeffery Lesser, *Negotiating National Identity: Immigrants, Minorities, and the Struggle for Ethnicity in Brazil* (Durham, NC: Duke University Press, 1999), 120.
[50] Tsuchida, "Japanese in Brazil," 239.

Manchuria within the next two decades.[51] The heyday of migration to Manchuria had begun.

After the Manchurian Incident, and with the same passion that they previously had demonstrated for Brazil-bound migration, the elites of Nagano prefecture quickly responded to the political changes in Northeast Asia. Aliança pioneers such as the Shinano Overseas Association, the Prefectural Board of Education, the Japanese Striving Society, and the prefectural government enthusiastically committed themselves to the promotion of migration to Manchuria long before the imperial government had launched its mass migration project in 1936.[52] By the end of World War II, Nagano had sent out the largest number of migrants to Manchuria among all the prefectures. The number of migrants from Nagano was more than twice the number from Yamagata, which came in second, and was just slightly less than the combined figure of migrants from Yamagata, Kumamoto, and Fukushima (ranked second, third, and fourth).[53] The readiness of Nagano prefecture in migration to Manchuria could not be fully explained without understanding the important role the prefecture had played in migration to Brazil a decade earlier.

The story of Nagano prefecture during the 1920s and 1930s reveals the intrinsic connections between Japanese migration to Brazil and Manchuria. Malthusian expansionism, which had justified Japanese migration to Brazil, continued to serve as the central principle for Japan's expansion in Manchuria. This new migration campaign saw the coinage of the term "lifeline" (*seimeisen*), indicating that the rich and conveniently empty land in Northeast Asia, similar to the empire's source of wealth (*fugen*) in South America of yesteryear, would provide a panacea to Japan's social problems brought on by overpopulation. In the logic of Malthusian expansionism, Manchuria was now vital to Japan's continued existence as an empire – for the sake of self-defense, the Japanese needed to occupy and colonize it.[54]

The outwardly benevolent discourse of coexistence and coprosperity that guided Japanese expansion in Brazil remained in effect for its Manchurian expansion. In fact, it became enshrined as the guideline of racial relations in Manchukuo: different from the Anglo-Saxons who not only invaded the domain of peoples of color but also excluded Asian immigrants from their territories, the Japanese would treat all people around the world equally and lead them to establish a new world of genuine peace.[55] The Japanese pointed to the supposed racial harmony with local residents achieved by Japanese communities in Brazil as evidence that they would be able to accomplish the same

[51] Tagawa, "'Imin' Shichō no Kiseki," 129–130.
[52] Nagano Ken Kaitaku Jikōkai Manshū Kaitakushi Kankōkai, *Nagano Ken Manshū Kaitaku Shi*, 89, 150–166.
[53] Young, *Japan's Total Empire*, 329–330.   [54] Ibid., 89.
[55] Nagata, *Nōson Jinkō Mondai to Ishokumin*, 212.

task in Manchuria.[56] As it was in Brazil, far from simply dumping the surplus people onto the Asian continent, the empire expected the migrants to be the vanguard in the fight for a new Japan-centered world order.

The expected roles of the migrants were clarified in a 1938 anthology titled *Agriculture and the Building of East Asia* (*Tōa Kensetsu to Nōgyō*). The book outlined the government's plan of accelerating farmer migration to Manchuria in order to support the total war. Aside from an essay by Katō Kanji, it also featured the writings of Ishiguro Tadaatsu and Kodaira Gon'ichi, central figures in the government's agricultural section, as well as Nasu Shiroshi, the leading agrarianist scholar. The book's contributors believed that not everyone in Japan was qualified to shoulder the task of agricultural expansion. Only the owner-farmers, they argued, were competent empire builders under the principle of coexistence and coprosperity.

Katō Kanji's essay pointed out that the owner-farmers' spirit of self-sufficiency was essential for the Japanese to cohabit and coprosper with others in Manchuria. Businessmen and landlords, he argued, made profits by exploiting others, thus their settlement in Manchuria could only create conflicts between the colonists and the local people. In contrast, owner-farmers were the sons of toil who earned their own bread and clothes by their bare hands. Since their livelihood did not depend on exploiting others, they could live peacefully with their neighbors and exchange knowledge, technology, and goods with them on an equal footing.[57]

Nasu Shiroshi's piece reaffirmed Katō's arguments from another angle by integrating the principle of coexistence and coprosperity into the school of Pan-Asianism. The production mode of owner-farmers, Nasu believed, represented the success and superiority of Japanese agriculture. According to Nasu, despite some difficulties, the Japanese empire was able to accommodate a huge number of farmers within an extremely small size of land, all the while maintaining a high standard of civilization. No other nation on earth could boast the same achievement, and the Japanese were able to achieve such an extraordinary success only after a long period of hard work, beginning in the Meiji era, in combining universal scientific principles with East Asian characteristics. This experience made Japanese owner-farmers natural tutors to their Chinese brethren: with a high density of farming population, the state of Chinese agriculture mirrored that in Tokugawa Japan and was in sharp contrast with the big-farm mode of Euro-American agriculture. Similarities between the states of Chinese

[56] Nagata Shigeshi, "Ajia Tairiku e no Shinshutsu," *Rikkō Sekai*, no. 286 (October 1928): 4.
[57] Katō Kanji, "Manshū Imin wa Naze Daimondai Ka," in *Tōa Kensetsu to Nōgyō*, ed. Asahi Shinbunsha (Tokyo: Tokyo Asahi Shinbunsha, 1939), 49–50.

and Japanese agriculture meant that the Japanese owner-farmers were more qualified than Westerners to bring progress to the Asian continent.[58] Institutional and human connections between Japanese expansion to Brazil and that to Manchuria were also evident. For example, Umetani Mitsusada, the first director of the Federation of Overseas Migration Cooperative Societies that carried out most of the Japanese land acquisition projects in Brazil after 1927, became the head of the migration department of the Kwantung Army in 1932 to orchestrate Japanese migration campaigns and land acquisition in Manchuria.[59] A former governor of Nagano, Umetani was also the one who provided the crucial financial support for the Aliança project. Nagata Shigeshi, a founder of Aliança, began to participate in the Manchuria-bound migration movement in 1932; he would also serve on the planning committee established by the imperial government that drafted the blueprint for the five-million-people migration project.[60] Under his leadership, the Japanese Striving Society launched campaigns to send men and women to Java and the Philippines as the empire expanded into Southeast Asia during World War II.[61] The Overseas Women's Association (Kaigai Fujin Kyōkai) that focused on facilitating the migration of Japanese women to Brazil since the mid-1920s also gradually shifted its focus from South America to Asia. It began to relocate Japanese women to Manchuria and China proper in 1935, through either marriage with local Japanese male setters or employment opportunities.[62] The association also responded to the mass migration policy during the late 1930s by vowing to contribute to the construction of a Japan-centric new order in East Asia.[63]

While there were important connections between Japanese migration campaigns to Brazil and Manchuria, the latter began in the late 1930s as a nationwide sociopolitical movement orchestrated by the "total empire," to borrow a phrase from Louise Young. As such, the Manchurian campaign differed substantially from its forerunners; indeed, it marked the culmination of Japan's migration-driven expansion, during which the state and civil society were integrated in an unprecedented scope and depth for the purpose of achieving the same goal. The Aliança model of collective migration, for example, remained an outlier in Japanese migration to Brazil. It was the

[58] Ishigurō Tadaatsu, "Shintōa Kensetsu to Wa Ga Nōgyō," in *Tōa Kensetsu to Nōgyō*, ed. Asahi Shinbunsha (Tokyo: Tokyo Asahi Shinbunsha, 1939), 72–74.

[59] Nagata Shigeshi, "Manshū no Shinano Mura (1)," *Rikkō Sekai*, no. 347 (November 1933): 21.

[60] Nippon Rikkō Kai, *Nippon Rikkō Kai*, 213.   [61] Ibid., 260–273.

[62] See "Kaigai Fujin Kyōkai Kankei," no. 9, *Honpō Shakai Jigyō Kankei Zakken*, Archive of Japanese Foreign Ministry, retrieved from Japan Center Asian Historical Records, National Archives of Japan (Reference code: B04013226500).

[63] Ibid. Also see Sidney X. Lu, "Japanese American Migration and the Making of Model Women for Japanese Expansion in Brazil and Manchuria, 1871–1945," *Journal of World History* 28, nos. 3–4 (December 2017): 461–465.

rehabilitation movement launched throughout the Japanese countryside in the 1930s that turned the model of Aliança to the principal method of the state's choosing. Migrants were collectively recruited and settled in Manchuria according to their common home villages and prefectures.[64]

The global depression at the turn of the 1930s triggered a dramatic increase of land disputes in the Japanese countryside. An increasing number of land-lords could no longer survive on collecting rent from tenants, thus they began to take the land back from their tenants in order to farm on their own.[65] The exacerbated tension led the government to accelerate its cultivation of the class of owner-farmers. The driving force behind Tokyo's new policies in this era was agrarianist bureaucrat Ishiguro Tadaatsu, the vice-minister of agriculture and forestry. Under his leadership, the government ran its rural rehabilitation program between 1932 and 1935, providing financial and technical aid to farmers in a thousand villages each year in order to help the owner-farmers. In 1934, the Ministry of Agriculture and Forestry established the Association for Rural Rehabilitation (Nōson Kōsei Kyōkai), which carried out these poli-cies at local levels through campaigns of education and suasion. These cam-paigns were aimed at helping the rural poor to achieve economic independence and self-sufficiency.[66]

The owner-farmer-centered nature of the rural rehabilitation program was evident in the writings of Sugino Tadao, a director of the Association for Rural Rehabilitation. The rehabilitation program, Sugino argued, was targeted only at helping the owner-farmers. Through their own labor, the owner-farmers were able to produce sufficient agricultural products; as such, they could lead a life of economic independence without being exploited by – or exploiting – others. These farmers, claimed Sugino, were the true foundation of nation and empire.[67]

However, since the landlords maintained a firm grip on political power, the rural rehabilitation program, like other government programs aimed at redu-cing rural tensions, accomplished little. Given that land redistribution within the archipelago was impossible, the *overall* shortage of land was readily offered as an explanation for the lack of owner-farmers. The solution, therefore, lay in land acquisition beyond the archipelago. Malthusian expansionism allowed the agrarian expansionists to connect the domestic efforts of cultivat-ing owner-farmers with the campaign of agricultural migration to Manchuria.

---

[64] Young, *Japan's Total Empire*, 328, 336.   [65] Shōji, *Kingendai Nihon no Nōson*, 130–136.
[66] Hiraga Akihiko, *Senzen Nihon Nōgyō Seisakushi no Kenkyū: 1920–1945* (Tokyo: Nihon Keizai Hyōronsha, 2003), 214–226.
[67] Ibid., 224. Sugino defined these ideal farmers as "chūnō," literally meaning "middle-class farmers." But based on his description, it is better to understand this group as owner-farmers. For an in-depth analysis of the idea of chūnō during the rural rehabilitation movement, see Young, *Japan's Total Empire*, 338–339.

Joining hands with longtime agrarian expansionist Katō Kanji, Ishiguro welcomed agrarian migration to Manchuria as an essential cure for land shortage in the overpopulated Japanese countryside.[68] Japan itself, argued Ishiguro in 1936, was like a tenant farmer on the world stage, rejected for landownership everywhere due to the stranglehold of white hegemony.[69] Accordingly, in Ishiguro's imagination, Japan's expansion into Manchuria was a landless farmer's just demand for land to survive.

More specifically, the impact of the rehabilitation movement differentiated the Manchuria-bound migration campaign from the empire's previous waves of migration-based expansion. Aiming to create owner-farmers through land rationing, the rehabilitation movement brought about a rash of local initiatives to define the minimal size of land needed for a farming household to achieve self-sufficiency. Based on their own calculations, different local authorities created various standards. Through a nationwide survey, the Ministry of Agriculture and Forestry concluded in 1937 that a farming household needed an average of 1.6 chō (4 acres) of land.[70] The Japanese colonial authority in Manchuria devised its own standard for Japanese farming settlers in 1935, which was as big as 20 chō.[71]

These surveys and standards, though invariably arriving at different numbers, together vested the logic of Malthusian expansionism with a veneer of scientific respectability. It presented Japanese land acquisition in Manchuria as a reasonable action based on objective calculations. Japan's migration-based expansion was no longer legitimized only by the growing number of the empire's surplus population; it was now also justified by the concrete calculability of the amount of land these surplus people would actually need. The scope of Japanese expansion, as this logic went, was entirely driven by the objective need of the surplus population, as if the expansion would indeed come to an end if the imagined standard of land per household of all Japanese farmers was eventually met.

On the other hand, the imperial government showed little interest in setting a cap on Japanese population growth. Instead, it continued to demand the birth of more people instead of less. Such a demand was further advanced by the outbreak of the total war and the mass migration to Manchuria. Worried by shortages of manpower after millions were drafted into military service,[72] the cabinet issued a guide for making new population policies in 1941, titled *The Principle to Establishing Population Policies* (*Jinkō Seisaku Kakuritsu Yōkō*). The principle set the goal to increase the Japanese population to one million by

---

[68] Namimatsu, "Nōson Keizaikosei to Ishigurō Tadatsu Hōtoku Shisō to no Kanren o Megutte," 119–120.
[69] Ōtake Keisuke, *Ishiguro Tadaatsu no Nōsei Shisō* (Tokyo: Nōsan gyoson Bunka Kyōkai, 1984), 194.
[70] Young, *Japan's Total Empire*, 340–341.   [71] Ibid., 343.   [72] Ibid., 392–393.

1960 by lowering the age for legal marriage by three years and having each couple give birth to five children on average. To this end, it planned policies like encouraging marriage via governmental financial subsidies, restricting employment opportunities for women over twenty years old, taxing single people heavily while reducing the taxes of those with large families, and banning birth control.[73]

Past in Present: From "Emigrants" to "Overseas Compatriots"

In addition to Brazil, the empire's other experiences of migration-driven expansion, real or imagined, were also called into service to promote and legitimize Japanese migration to Asia from the 1930s to 1945. Empire builders now portrayed the migration of farmer-soldiers to Hokkaido in early Meiji as a resounding success in order to justify similar programs in Manchuria.[74] They also offered the supposed benevolence of Japanese colonizers toward the Ainu as evidence that the Japanese expansion in Asia was truly for the purpose of coexistence and coprosperity.[75] In 1936, the imperial government hired historian Iriye Toraji to author a massive two-volume epic of Japanese overseas migration that chronicled various Japanese migration activities in different parts of the world (Hawai'i, Southeast Asia, North and South America, etc.) from the dawn of Meiji to the present. The central message contained in these over a thousand pages was straightforward: with the glorious past achievement of overseas expansion and the unprecedented support from the imperial government at present, the empire's mass migration to Manchuria was destined for unparalleled future success.[76]

The efforts in weaving the past and present experiences of Japanese migration-based expansion culminated in November 1940, when the imperial government held the Tokyo Conference of the Overseas Compatriots (Kaigai Dōhō Tokyo Daikai) to celebrate the 2,600th anniversary of the Japanese empire. The conference was attended by Japanese representatives from all over the world. To downplay the political boundaries between the Japanese inside and outside the empire's sphere of influence, the representatives were divided into several sections solely by geography, including sections for Hawai'i, North America, Latin America, the South Seas, and East Asia. Prime Minister Konoe Fumimaro chaired

---

[73] Yoshida Tadao, *Myōnichi no Jinkō Mondai: "Man'in Nihon" wa Kaishōsareru Ka* (Tokyo: Shakai Shisōsha, 1962), 120–121. Also see Takeda, *Political Economy of Reproduction in Japan*, 79–80.

[74] Taga Muneyuki, *Hokkaido Tondenhei to Manshū* (Tokyo: Teikoku Zaikō Gunjinkai Honbu, 1932), 1–2, and 63–65.

[75] Takakura Shin'ichirō, *Ainu Seisaku Shi* (Tokyo: Nihon Hyōronsha, 1942), 1–6.

[76] Iriye, *Hōjin Kaigai Hatten Shi*, cited from Azuma, "'Pioneers of Overseas Japanese Development,'" 1198–1199.

the conference and delivered the opening address. Several ministers also contributed remarks. In addition to holding exhibitions and speeches to glorify the
sacrifices and achievements the overseas Japanese had made, the conference
honored many figures from the overseas communities for their contributions to
the empire. Such recognition and appreciation naturally came with a price: overseas Japanese across the globe were all called on to serve the grand mission of the
empire – "eight corners under one roof" (*hakkō ichiu*). As the speech of Konoe
made it clear, "Our glorious history of overseas expansion has been written by the
blood and sweat of your forefathers ... and the world has now come to a turning
point. ... Our empire, under the reign of our emperor, is on a mission to bring true
justice and true happiness to all mankind, as well as uniting the entire world. ...
Unite, and be ready to make sacrifices!"

The commemoration of the glorious and patriotic history of Japanese
trans-Pacific migration at the 1940 conference was accompanied by an
identity transformation of the overseas Japanese during the total war.
Under the reign of the migration state, Japanese emigrants came to be
hailed as "overseas compatriots" (*kaigai dōhō*). The identity of "overseas
compatriots" downplayed the difference between the Japanese abroad and
those living in the home archipelago. It transcended time, geography,
generation, social class, and gender by tying every individual of Japanese
ancestry to one sacred mission: the destined expansion of the empire.

This identity transformation was well illustrated by a radio drama that
the Japanese Broadcasting Cooperation (NHK) aired nationwide on
November 9, 1940, a day after the closure of the Tokyo Conference of
the Overseas Compatriots. Titled "Thousands of Miles of Waves" ("Hatō
Banri"), the drama depicted an exchange between several Japanese emigrants
in a third-class cabin of a ship bound overseas, and the conversation took
place when the ship encountered a storm on the sea. Among these passengers,
only one character – a second-generation Japanese American – was specifically identified. He was depicted as a young man of promise who had just
completed a three-year study period in Japan during the Sino-Japanese War;
proud of being a Japanese American, he decided to return to the United States
in order to carry on the great cause of his forefathers. After showing his
approbation for this nisei, another passenger said, "We used to be called
'emigrants' (*imin*), but now it's time to completely change this perception
(of the Japanese back home). We went overseas not for material gains, but to
expand the frontier of Japanese people." In this way, the overseas Japanese
sought to shake off the negative label of "emigrants" and become the
respected "overseas compatriots," the pioneers of the empire's global expansion. This sublimation was realized in the drama through a Japanese
American's affirmation of his loyalty to the empire by coming back to Japan

for study, then returning to his host country and vowing to contribute to Japan from abroad.[77]

This sought-after recognition by the empire and its people, however, had a price tag. As the passenger continued, "Yet the true overseas development of our nation will start from now!" After recounting the past pains and sacrifices of the overseas Japanese, he reminded his audience that Japan had secured the leadership of East Asia; now the overseas Japanese needed to shoulder more responsibilities than ever in order to support the empire's mission. Since none of the passengers' destinations were indicated except for the young Japanese American, the audience could assume that the ship was bound for the United States. Yet at the end of the drama, when a female passenger turned on a radio in the cabinet, everyone on board heard "The Song of Patriotic March" ("Aikoku Kōshin Kyoku"), popularized by a program that was broadcasted from Tokyo to China and Southeast Asia. The direction of the radio broadcast followed the route of the empire's current expansion. The seemingly strange fact that the song that was broadcast toward China and Southeast Asia was received on the emigrant ship bound for the United States highlighted the ties between Japanese migrations to both sides of the Pacific Ocean.[78]

The drama also carefully demonstrated to its audience that Japanese expansion was a story of women as much as of men. Of the nine characters in the drama, four were female. Unlike the male characters, who were uniformly depicted as decisive, courageous, and patriotic, the female characters were portrayed with a touch of delicacy: they were physically and mentally weaker, but had the potential to become as strong as their male counterparts. When the ship encountered a storm and shook severely, three women began to complain and a young wife even burst into tears and began to regret her decision of giving up a peaceful life in Japan's countryside. Disappointed by her weakness, her husband reminded her that they could achieve success abroad only by overcoming such hardships. In contrast to those who complained, the fourth woman, who did not have a single line of dialogue, was in the throes of labor. She was praised by the men on board as living proof that the strong spirit existed in the blood of Japanese women. The nisei also brought up the name of Okei, a fictional female figure in Japanese American history, praising her as a pioneer of Japanese overseas expansion.[79] The drama used the stories of a pioneering Japanese American woman and a mother silently giving birth on the ship together to urge Japanese women to leave the overpopulated archipelago and become mothers and wives on the empire's overseas frontiers.[80]

---

[77] Yamashita Sōen, ed., *Hōshuku Kigen Nisenroppyakunen to Kaigai Dōhō* (Tokyo: Hōshuku Kigen Nisenroppyakunen to Kaigai Dōhō Kankō Kai, 1941), 219–221.
[78] Ibid., 221–223.   [79] Ibid., 220.   [80] Ibid., 221–222.

Conclusion

The history of Japanese community building in Aliança by the Nagano prefecture offers a valuable lens through which one may examine the characteristics of Japan's migration-driven expansion during the 1920s and 1930s. First of all, the establishment of Aliança in the state of São Paulo, Brazil, a brainchild of expansionists based in Nagano, was the first prefecture-led migration project in imperial Japan. The success of Aliança ushered in a wave of prefecture-centered Brazilian migration throughout the archipelago in the latter half of the 1920s. Many prefectural governments, following Nagano's example, established their own Overseas Migration Cooperative Society to promote overseas expansion. Some also managed to establish exclusive settler communities in Brazil.

Second, Aliança was also a direct response to the institutionalized racism against Japanese immigrants in the United States. The architects of Aliança carefully designed it to exemplify the new model of Japanese settler colonialism. It marked Japanese expansion's ideological departure from Western imperialism by advocating the principle of coexistence and coprosperity. The project of Aliança, followed by other Japanese settler communities established in Brazil, was to demonstrate the benevolence of the Japanese: the Japanese expansionists believed that unlike the racist and hypocritical Westerners, the Japanese would treat the unenlightened people as equals and bring them genuine peace and progress. Influenced by Japanese agrarianism in the 1920s and 1930s, the principle of coexistence and coprosperity also grounded itself in self-sufficiency and mutual aid-centered agricultural production, which was claimed to be a uniquely Japanese tradition.

Nagano prefecture's history of migration also offers an example of the intrinsic connections between Japanese migration to Brazil and later to Manchuria. State institutions involved in the promotion and management of migration, at both central and prefectural levels, were first established for Japanese Brazilian migration but later became engines of mass migration to Manchuria. Core leaders of Brazilian migration, such as Nagata Shigeshi and Umetani Tadaatsu, also enthusiastically participated in the government-led Manchurian migration campaign. The principle of coexistence and coprosperity, first exemplified in Japanese Brazilian communities, was later applied to Japanese expansion in Manchuria and eventually became the ideological core of the Greater East Asia Co-Prosperity Sphere.

Ironically, even as the total war drained manpower from the archipelago, the anxiety of overpopulation continued to legitimize Japan's migration-driven expansion. In addition to Brazil, the experiences of migration in Hokkaido and North America of yesteryear were also reinvoked as justification for the empire to send more subjects, not fewer, to the Asian continent. When the empire collapsed in August 1945, approximately 6.9 million Japanese subjects, around 9 percent of the entire Japanese population, were living overseas, mostly in Asia.[81] The return of these former settlers and soldiers eventually paved the way for the restart of a new wave of Japanese overseas migration in the 1950s. Like the migration waves before 1945, this new wave of migration to South America was also legitimized by Malthusian expansionism. How did this new wave of migration start? To what extent was it a continuation of Japan's pre-1945 migration-driven expansion? These questions are answered in the next chapter.

---

[81] Lori Watt, *When Empire Comes Home: Repatriation and Reintegration in Postwar Japan* (Cambridge, MA: Harvard University Asia Center, 2009), 2.

Part IV

Resurgence, 1945–1961

8   The Birth of a "Small" Japan: Postwar Migration to South America

Japan's defeat in World War II marked a sharp turning point in the history of Japanese overseas migration. As Japan lost most of its colonies and imperial territories beyond the archipelago, colonial migration came to an abrupt end. The GHQ (General Headquarters of the Allied occupation of Japan) not only cut off most of the contact between ordinary Japanese and people living in other parts of the world,[1] but also dismantled the set of mechanisms that was responsible for relocating Japanese overseas during the past decades. It abrogated the Overseas Migration Cooperative Societies Law that had turned prefectural governments into engines of emigration; it also disbanded the migration companies, including the Kaikō, which had relocated most of the migrants from the archipelago to South America and the South Seas since the - mid-1920s.[2]

However, Japanese overseas migration quickly began anew following the end of the occupation, with Malthusian expansionism continuing to serve as its central justification. During the 1950s, a prime decade for overseas migration, over ten thousand Japanese annually settled overseas. In 1957, when overseas migration was at its postwar zenith, the Federation of Japanese Overseas Associations (Nihon Kaigai Kyōkai Rengōkai), a government proxy organization in migration management, issued a pamphlet vowing to further expand emigration in the years to come. Titled *Japan and Emigration* (*Nihon to Ijū*), the pamphlet outlined the government's view on migration. It began with familiar rhetoric, presenting a sharp contrast between the spacious and empty Americas and the small and overpopulated Japan. While Japan's territory was halved after the empire's collapse, the pamphlet continued, its population continued on a path of rapid growth. In 1956, Japan's population exceeded ninety million, making the country one of the five most

---

[1] Yukiko Koshiro, *Trans-Pacific Racism and the U.S. Occupation of Japan* (New York: Columbia University Press, 1999), 125.
[2] Nagata Shigeshi, *Kankō Imin to Min'ei Ijū: Keikaku Imin to Yobiyose Ijū* (Tokyo: Nippon Rikkō Kai, 1954), 8.

populated nations in the world. In terms of population density, Japan climbed up to claim the third place, behind only the Netherlands and Belgium.[3] In the cities, with an estimated 670,000 people entering the job market annually, Japan had to keep its economic growth at a rate of 6 to 7 percent in order to accommodate new job seekers every year. This goal appeared impossible to achieve. Meanwhile, in the countryside, more than a decade of land exploration had failed to provide sufficient new land to accommodate all the surplus people. The reason for this failure, argued the pamphlet, was not that Japanese people did not work hard enough but that the archipelago no longer had extra farmland available.[4]

Overpopulation, the pamphlet lamented, had devastated Japan: people from all walks of life had to struggle to survive the unhealthy competition, students had to quit school in order to get into the queue for jobs early, while millions of the second and third sons of farming families were bereft of land – and along with it, a future.[5] The only remedy, the pamphlet concluded, was overseas migration. It would not only reduce the population pressure within the archipelago but also bring benefit to Japan via remittance and international trade, thereby creating more job opportunities at home.

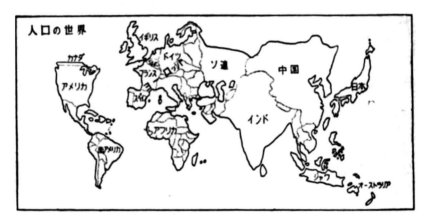

Figure 8.1 This world map, titled "Sekai no Jinkō" (The Population of the World), appeared on the first page of the book *Japan and Emigration*. It recalculated the land sizes of the major countries and continents based on the sizes of their populations. It thus emphasized the unbalance of population distribution vis-à-vis land in the contemporary world.

---

[3] Nihon Kaigai Kyōkai Rengōkai, *Nihon to Ijū: Naze Ijū wa Sokushinsareneba Naranaika* (Tokyo: Nihon Kaigai Kyōkai Rengōkai, 1957), 2–3.
[4] Ibid., 4–6.   [5] Ibid., 1–2.

Overseas migration, the pamphlet further claimed, was crucial to the construction of Japan's new national identity. Standing at the crossroads of history and living in a time of the two Cold War superpowers, Japan would follow the path of pacifism and democracy; it was destined to share these blessings with the rest of the world. Exporting migrants would help Japan to achieve this mission by eliminating poverty and food shortage at home while exploring untapped wealth in other parts of the world.[6]

The Federation of Japanese Overseas Associations was directly funded by the Japanese government, and it took primary responsibility in migration promotion and management during the postwar era. As the pamphlet demonstrated, just like in the decades before 1945, overpopulation served as an easy explanation for deeply rooted social tensions. It highlighted overseas migration as a panacea to the existing social issues that appeared otherwise unsolvable. Once again, the promoters of migration did not cast it in a light of casting off dead weight – instead, they urged prospective migrants to embrace the noble goal to glorify their nation from afar.

This chapter examines the history of Japanese overseas migration from the end of World War II to the beginning of the 1960s, when it began to decline following Japan's economic boom. It highlights the similarities between postwar Japan's overseas migration and the migration-based expansion that came before it. These similarities, the chapter argues, were rooted in institutional and discursive continuities that survived Japan's defeat. After the occupation ended, institutions and personalities formerly in charge of the empire's migration matters found themselves once again playing vital roles to steer the ship of postwar migration, and they continued to embrace Malthusian expansionism to legitimize their agendas. This continuity in the history of Japanese overseas migration, maintained through both defeat and the occupation, is crucial for our understanding of the trans-Pacific legacies of Japanese settler colonialism in the postwar era.

From War to Peace: The Birth of a "Small" Japan and the Resurgence of the Discourse of Overpopulation

The end of the war led to a sudden increase in the archipelago's population. The empire's collapse brought 5 million civilian and military repatriates back to Japanese shores by the end of 1946.[7] Long-absent peace also stimulated a baby boom that peaked between 1947 and 1949, producing 7.5 million new citizens within three years. The mortality rate, on the other hand, dropped to the lowest point in Japanese history.[8]

---

[6] Ibid., 18–20.   [7] Watt, *When Empire Comes Home*, 2.
[8] Yukiko, *Trans-Pacific Racism*, 126.

These demographic changes were also accompanied by the immediate territorial change of Japan. The defeat and decolonization of the empire ushered in the rise of the discourse of "small" Japan among the Japanese intellectuals and policy makers in the postwar era. Only a few days after Japan's official surrender, wartime bureaucrat Ōta Masataka published an article in *Asahi Shinbun*, titled "Seven Million People in a Small Territory." Ōta claimed that the defeat had imposed a formidable challenge that Japan had never faced before: the nation had to accommodate an unprecedented size of population in a substantially reduced territory.[9] Also reminiscing about the empire, Sugino Tadao, a member of the think tank behind the wartime Manchurian migration, lamented that before the defeat Japan's territory was much larger than its current size, with a smaller population in it. But now, it not only lost much of its previous territory but also gained more population. As such, Sugino argued, it was impossible for the nation to sustain the livelihood of its population with the limited resources in this small archipelago.[10]

It is in this context that the anxiety of overpopulation quickly reemerged in Japanese public discourse right after the war. But more significantly, behind the anxiety of overpopulation lay the government's inability to provide livelihoods for people whose lives were completely upended by the war. The total war had led to the creation of a welfare state in Japan that introduced both national health insurance and labor pensions, thereby assuming unprecedented responsibilities for the well-being of its people. Reforms during the occupation years further cemented the scope of this welfare state,[11] even as it found itself increasingly unable to adequately address the human costs of the war.

Soldiers needed pensions, the injured needed care, the homeless needed shelters, and everyone needed food. The return of the repatriates was joined by an even larger flow of people within the archipelago due to wartime evacuations. From December 1943 to June 1945, following government mandates, approximately 7.7 million residents in thirteen major Japanese cities such as Tokyo, Yokohama, Osaka, Kobe, and Nagoya left their homes to flee from American air attacks.[12] They relocated to either the countryside or other

---

[9] Ōta Masataka, "Semai Kokudo ni Nana Sen Man Nin," *Asahi Shinbun*, August 21, 1945, 2.

[10] Sugino, *Kaigai Takushoku Hishi*, 36.

[11] For example, Article 24 of the New Constitution requires the Japanese government to provide social welfare, freedom, and democracy to its people by protecting children, promoting public health and social security, standardizing working conditions, and fixing wages and working hours. Laws established following the constitution include the welfare law for children, promulgated in December 1947, followed by the welfare law for the physically handicapped, in effect in 1949, as well as the law on social welfare work of 1951 and the law on the promotion of social welfare work of 1953. See Mutsuko Takahashi, *The Emergence of Welfare Society in Japan* (Aldershot: Avebury, 1997), 64–65.

[12] Yasuoka Ken'ichi, *Tashatachi no Nōgyōshi: Zainichi Chōsenjin Sokaisha Kaitaku Nōmin Kaigai Imin* (Kyoto: Kyoto Daigaku Gakujutsu Shuppankai, 2014), 111–112.

small cities, and a majority of them remained jobless until the end of the war.[13] Japan's defeat also crushed the empire's military industry, creating a large number of laid-off workers.[14]

Terming the archipelago as "overpopulated" was an easy way to reconcile the growing responsibility of the Japanese government for social welfare and its inability to effectively help the people in its charge. The claim of over-population also provided justification for the government to limit the scope of its welfare policy, by excluding the unwanted and the disqualified. The empire's Korean and Taiwanese soldiers, for example, were stripped of their Japanese citizenship immediately after the war, which allowed the Japanese government to deny these colonial soldiers their veteran pensions.[15] When the comprehensive national welfare system was implemented in 1959, the government further excluded former colonial subjects (Koreans and Taiwanese) residing in Japan by defining them as foreigners. In the same year, the Japanese government and civic groups began to repatriate the Koreans residents of Japan on a mass scale, sending them to North Korea in order to reduce the population of Koreans in Japan.[16]

The claim of overpopulation was also used by Japanese eugenicists to advance their agendas on the issues of abortion and birth control. Japan, they argued, had turned into a militant empire primarily because of its uncontrollable population pressure at home. To avoid the same mistake, the new nation should lessen the population pressure by introducing birth control regulations and legalizing abortion.[17] These views were well received by a government that desperately sought to bridge the gap between its welfare obligations and its constrained financial capacity. The enactment of the Eugenic Protection Law in 1948 made Japan one of the first countries in the world to legalize abortion, while the law's 1952 revision further loosened the requirement for abortion, allowing women to conduct legal abortion because of "economic hardship and difficulty,"[18] which became the number one reason for abortion conducted in the decades to come. From the beginning of the 1950s, birth control also became a part of Japanese public health administration.[19]

Though many promoters of unlimited population growth during wartime Japan quickly turned into postwar advocates of birth control,[20] there remained opponents to birth control in both government and civic society. Seeing population as the crucial source for national strength, opponents of contraception

---

[13] Ibid., 138.   [14] Ibid., 148.   [15] Fujitani, *Race for Empire*, 379–380.

[16] Tessa Morris-Suzuki, "Exodus to North Korea Revisited: Japan, North Korea, and the ICRC in the 'Repatriation' of Ethnic Koreans from Japan," *Asia-Pacific Journal* 9, Issue 22, no. 2 (May 30, 2011): 7–8.

[17] Fujime, *Sei no Rekishigaku*, 371–372; Takeda, *Political Economy of Reproduction in Japan*, 109.

[18] Takeda, *Political Economy of Reproduction in Japan*, 103.   [19] Ibid., 106–107.

[20] Fujime, *Sei no Rekishigaku*, 361.

worried about the long-term damage of slowing population growth. The minister of health and welfare, Ashida Hitoshi, argued that it was difficult for any nation to reverse the trend in birth rate once it began to drop.[21] Nagata Shigeshi, the president of the Japanese Striving Society, had an even stronger opinion. India and China, he contended, survived the tyranny of Western colonialism because of their huge populations. Similarly, Great Britain's rise as the most powerful colonial empire should also be attributed to its strength in numbers. France, on the contrary, was plagued by a succession of problems both at home and abroad ever since its government adopted the policy of birth control. For Nagata, population was not only crucial for a nation's survival but also its most important source of strength. The white hegemony in the United States, Nagata warned, was in danger due to the insidious influence of Margaret Sanger. The birth rate of white people in America dropped quickly while that of black people continued to climb. Based on this observation, Nagata made a splendid prediction that within a hundred years the United States would be led by a black president. Japan was indeed an overpopulated country, but such a big population was precisely the foundation of Japan's national wealth. The practice of birth control, he warned, was like another nuclear bomb that would ultimately destroy Japan's national strength.[22]

For Malthusian expansionists who, like Nagata Shigeshi, continued to strive in the postwar era, overseas migration undoubtedly remained the best course of action for the overpopulated archipelago. In 1947, only two years after the end of the war, the leaders of the Japanese Striving Society and other pre-1945 migration organizations formed the Overseas Migration Association (Kaigai Ijū Kyōkai), vowing to start sending Japanese migrants abroad again. To this end, the association began to hold public gatherings and publish journals to promote overseas migration among the general public and frequently appealed to the government calling for its action.[23]

However, the Japanese government was initially hesitant to endorse overseas migration. Such a response was natural, as the policymakers in Kasumigaseki were fully aware that due to the close tie between migration and colonial expansion in the preceding years, getting the green light from the United States would be no easy matter. Their concerns were well founded: under pressure from the SCAP (Supreme Commander for the Allied Powers), Kagawa Toyohiko, a symbolic figure of Japanese pacifism, withdrew his commitment to serve as the first director of the Overseas Migration

[21] Tama Yasuko, "Shōsanka to Kazoku Seisaku," in *Gendai Shakaigaku: 19: Kazoku no Shakaigaku*, ed. Inoue Shun, Ueno Chizuko, Ōsawa Masachi, Mita Munesyke, and Yoshimi Shun'ya (Tokyo: Iwanami Shoten, 1996), 159–187.

[22] "Imin Chūshin no Jinkō Mondai," *Rikkō Sekai*, no. 628 (July 1957): 5.

[23] Wakatsuki Yasuo and Jōji Suzuki, eds., *Kaigai Ijū Seisaku Shiron* (Tokyo: Fukumura Shuppan, 1975), 97; Koshiro, *Trans-Pacific Racism*, 129–131.

Association.[24] Moreover, even after the United States changed its stance, Australia proved to be an intransigent opponent on the issue.[25] It was the project of domestic land exploration that eventually brought overseas migration once again to the forefront of policy debates in Japan.

Domestic Land Exploration, Land Reform, and the Discourse of Overpopulation Transformed

The domestic land exploration project was the linchpin of the Japanese government's efforts to assist people who had lost their homes and livelihoods due to the war. Land exploration was not a new policy: during the war, the government had already adopted it to utilize those who were evacuated from the major cities. Under the slogan of "returning to farming" (kinō), the government encouraged these evacuees to take up farming to increase the food supply for the empire.[26] In this way, the evacuation-driven migration in the wartime archipelago was closely tied to farming, with the Ministry of Agriculture and Forestry (MAF) playing a leading role in the process.[27]

Even after the war ended, the archipelago remained in dire need of food. The countryside continued to see inflows of displaced people, though this time mainly those returning from the empire's colonies and overseas territories.[28] The new government responded to this situation in an extension of wartime policy, with the intention of turning the homeless returnees into productive subjects. In November 1945, the cabinet passed the Guidelines of Conducting Emergent Land Exploration (Kinkyū Kaitaku Jigyō Jisshitsu Yōryō) to provide more food and build new villages following the return of the military and civilians from overseas. These guidelines stipulated that the government would mobilize the repatriates to conduct a massive campaign of land exploration (kaitaku) and improvement (kairyō) throughout the archipelago. The goal was to create 1.55 million hectares of new land (either unclaimed or previously in use by the military) and settle one million new farming households within five years,[29] an ambitious agenda that dwarfed even the state-led wartime migration to Manchuria in its size. Notably, this new campaign was mainly staffed with the same bureaucrats who orchestrated the Manchuria migration project and the "returning to farming" campaign during the war, and the MAF continued to play a crucial role in the postwar land exploration program. In October 1945,

[24] Koshiro, *Trans-Pacific Racism*, 129.   [25] Ibid., 139.
[26] Yasuoka, *Tashatachi no Nōgyōshi*, 130, 136–137.   [27] Ibid., 137.
[28] Many evacuees in the countryside eventually returned to their original homes after the government removed the ban that prevented them from returning to their cities in March 1947. The majority of the people to be resettled in the countryside after the war were repatriates who came back to archipelago from overseas. Ibid., 164–165.
[29] Ibid., 147.

the Bureau of Land Exploration (Kaitaku Kyoku), the organ directly in charge of the land exploration program, was established as a part of the ministry.[30] From the end of 1946 onward, the MAF also took over the responsibility of settling the repatriates from the Ministry of Foreign Affairs.[31]

The campaign of emergent land exploration took place around the same time as postwar land reform, another nationwide policy initiative. Beginning at the end of 1946, under the supervision of the GHQ, the Japanese government began to nationalize land throughout the archipelago by purchasing private land from landlords and confiscating lands used by the imperial military before 1945. It then redistributed land by selling it at low prices to the landless people in the countryside.[32] As was the case for land exploration, MAF bureaucrats, many of them carry-overs from wartime, played a central role in implementing the reform. Adherents to agrarianism and faithful disciples of Ishiguro Tadaatsu, the actual executors of the reform Wada Hiroo and Tōbata Shirō saw this campaign as a golden opportunity to realize their pre-1945 dream of creating an owner-farmer society.[33] Land reform dramatically transformed the landscape of land property distribution within Japan: tenant farming rate plummeted from 46 percent in 1941 to 14 percent in 1949,[34] and the class of big landlords quickly faded out from view.[35]

The campaign of land reform was also closely intertwined with that of emergent land exploration. The agrarianist bureaucrats of the MAF, figures who had orchestrated the wartime migration to Manchuria, were now central architects of both campaigns. They carried out both to turn Japan into a nation of owner-farmers by redistributing land to the formerly landless. The repatriates were among the intended beneficiaries of both campaigns, which expected to resettle them in the archipelago by land grant. However, even as the reform did quickly create a society of owner-farmers and the land exploration campaign quickly increased the size of arable land in the archipelago, neither of these campaigns was successful in settling the repatriates. As the following paragraphs illustrate, the Japanese government's failure to resettle the repatriates in these two campaigns moved the issue of overpopulation from cities to the countryside, turning the primary source of overpopulation anxiety from the shortage of food and jobs into the shortage of land.

The primary beneficiaries of the emergent land exploration and land reform campaigns, in reality, turned out to be local farmers, not the repatriates. While

---

[30] Ibid., 147.   [31] Ibid., 185.   [32] Ibid., 245.

[33] Shōji Shunsaku's study shows that the Japanese bureaucrats were more radical than the GHQ in terms of the goal of the reform. The GHQ saw the land reform as a means to achieve the goal of Japan's democratization and had sympathy toward the property loss of the landlords. In contrast, the Japanese bureaucrats targeted an overhaul of the system of land ownership itself. Shōji, *Kingendai Nihon no Nōson*, 194.

[34] Shōji, *Kingendai Nihon no Nōson*, 185.   [35] Yasuoka, *Tashatachi no Nōgyōshi*, 246.

the Bureau of Land Exploration initially sought to settle the repatriates back in their home prefectures, this plan did not work as expected. The case of Shimoina County in Nagano prefecture shows that the local farmers had formed ties with each other through the Village Renewal Cooperative (Nōson Kōsei Kumiai), a nationwide network composed of village-level branches established throughout the archipelago in the 1930s, while most returnees did not have such connections. During both land exploration and land reform campaigns, properties were distributed to farmers through this network. Returnees without the cooperative's membership, accordingly, were excluded from obtaining a share in the redistribution of local land.[36] As a result, after temporarily returning to their home prefectures, many repatriates had to remigrate elsewhere with assistance from their home prefectures. Ibaraki and Hokkaido became the two prefectures that received the biggest numbers of the repatriates from other prefectures.[37] However, many repatriates had difficulties in settling in their nonnative prefectures as well. With strong resentment, local farmers treated them as outsiders who would steal their ancestral land, and local governments also had imposed policies aimed at reducing the number nonnative repatriates that they had to accommodate. Even Hokkaido, the prefecture that had been a destination for Japanese migrants ever since early Meiji, imposed requirements on the amount of start-up fund and farming equipment each farmer should possess before they could settle in, the responsibility of providing which then fell onto the shoulders of the repatriates' home prefectures.[38] With their own budget limitations, however, many prefectures quickly ceased their support for the remigration of repatriates. It was reported that in 1948 alone, with no hope of acquiring land, thirty thousand households quit the land exploration campaign.[39]

Sensing insurmountable difficulties to reach the goal set up by the Guidelines of Conducting Emergent Land Exploration on time, the government reduced the expected number of household resettlement from 1 million to 0.34 million in 1947. It abandoned the emergent land exploration project entirely in the next year, and then disbanded the Bureau of Land Exploration in the year after that. By 1950, the efforts to relocate repatriates within the archipelago had ended in failure.[40] The campaign moved on to a new stage, focusing on assisting existing landowners to expand and develop their existing land. During this stage, the campaign sought to provide land to a small and selective

---

[36] Aoki Takeshi, "Gaichi Hikiagesha Shuyō to Sengo Kaitaku Nōmin no Sōshutsu: Nagano Ken Shimoinagun Igaryōmura no Jirei," *Shakai Keizai Shigaku* 77, no. 2 (August 2011): 99–100.
[37] Nagano Ken Kaitaku Jikōkai Manshū Kaitakushi Kankōkai, *Nagano Ken Manshū Kaitaku Shi*, 741.
[38] Ibid., 742.   [39] Yasuoka, *Tashatachi no Nōgyōshi*, 167.
[40] Nagano Ken Kaitaku Jikōkai Manshū Kaitakushi Kankōkai, *Nagano Ken Manshū Kaitaku Shi*, 743.

group of people, primarily the second and third sons of owner-farmers who did not have the right to inherit land. The repatriates ceased to be beneficiaries – even if in name only – of the land exploration campaign.[41]

The emergent land exploration and land reform campaigns brought dramatic changes to the Japanese countryside. They turned the majority of the rural population into owner-farmers and eliminated the landlord class from Japanese society. However, local farmers who were not displaced during the war refused to share their newly gained land with the repatriates. Local protectionism also limited the capacity of prefectures to accommodate repatriates who remigrated from their native prefectures. As a result, the short-lived emergent land exploration campaign failed to provide farmland to a majority of the repatriates, leaving a significant number of landless people in the countryside even after land reform. In addition to fueling further Malthusian anxiety, this development would transplant the primary focus of such anxiety from the cities to the countryside, from the supply of food and jobs to the supply of arable land.

The discourse of overpopulation was a boon for the Japanese government in general and the agrarianist MAF bureaucrats in particular: it allowed them to celebrate the achievements of land reform while excusing themselves for the failure to provide land to most of the repatriates. Ishiguro Tadaatsu, the doyen of state agrarianism, claimed that the fundamental problem of the Japanese rural economy was overpopulation that led to a shortage of farmland.[42] The current land holdings by owner-farmer households were already modest enough; any further division would lead to overintensive farming and production inefficiency. The question, therefore, had morphed into how to provide sufficient land to each household in order to maintain a healthy agricultural economy.

The discourse of land shortage emerged from the failure of the emergent land exploration program. Not only did it change the nature of overpopulation anxiety in postwar Japan, it also legitimized the Japanese government's official resumption of its promotion and management of overseas migration. In 1949, the Ministry of Foreign Affairs issued a report, claiming that there was little hope for Japanese economic development to reach a level that could provide livelihood for all people in the archipelago in the foreseeable future.[43] In the same year, the House of Representatives issued a plan that was endorsed by all parties, vowing to take action against Japan's current population pressure, and overseas migration was listed as one of the three proposed measures.[44]

---

[41] Yasuoka, *Tashatachi no Nōgyōshi*; Zenkoku Kaitaku Nōgyō Kyōdō Kumiai Rengōkai, *Sengo Kaitakushi*, vol. 2 (Tokyo: Zenkoku Kaitaku Nōgyō Kyōdō Kumiai Rengōkai, 1967), 8.

[42] Ōtake Keisuke, ed., *Ishiguro Tadaatsu no Nōsei Shisō* (Tokyo: Nōsan Gyoson Bunka Kyōkai, 1984), 340.

[43] Wakatsuki and Jōji, *Kaigai Ijū Seisaku Shiron*, 84.

[44] The other two plans were the continuation of land exploration and the promotion of birth control. See Yasuoka, *Tashatachi no Nōgyōshi*, 285.

Together, these two events signaled the Japanese government's readiness to embrace Malthusian expansionism once again, a decisive step leading to the resumption of state-sponsored overseas migration right after the end of the occupation.

The Remarriage of Agrarianism and Malthusian Expansionism and the Rebirth of the Migration State

Like overseas migration campaigns conducted by the Japanese empire between the late 1920s and 1945, Japanese migration during the 1950s and 1960s was primarily funded and managed by the state. In 1952, the first group of postwar Japanese overseas migrants left the archipelago for the Amazon Basin in northern Brazil. A few government-led migration projects that resettled Japanese to different parts of Brazil soon followed. Japanese migrants had set their feet again in the Americas and Southeast Asia. Between 1952 and 1962, when the number of overseas migration began to drop sharply, over twelve thousand Japanese migrated overseas every year. Among them, approximately 40 percent settled in Brazil.[45] In many ways, the 1950s and 1960s saw the reemergence of the same migration state from the prewar era, and at the center of this organizational continuity was the MAF's leadership in migration management. When mass migration to Manchuria in the late 1930s was presented as the cure for Japanese rural depression, it was the MAF, led by agrarianist bureaucrats that recruited, trained, and resettled the migrants.[46] Though mass migration came to an end after the collapse of the empire, the MAF had survived in the postwar government, and the agrarianist bureaucrats managed to weather the political purges during the occupation years with their control of the ministry intact.

The drive of MAF bureaucrats and nonstate actors during these campaigns – land exploration and land reform at first, then the promotion of overseas migration – was closely tied to their design for postwar Japan. Remaining loyal to their pre-1945 dream, they believed that the new Japan should become a model nation of owner-farmers. However, whereas Japanese agrarianism between the 1920s and 1945 presented a fundamental challenge to modern capitalism, Western imperialism, and white racism, most of the postwar agrarianists had revised their ideas in response to Japan's defeat and the US occupation. This revised postwar version of agrarianism imagined the

---

[45] The annual number of overseas migrants between 1952 and 1962 was around 12,013, while the annual number of those who settled in Brazil around the same time period was 4,816. These numbers are calculated based on data provided by Itō Atsushi. See Itō, *Nihon Nōmin Seisaku Shiron*, 216.

[46] Itō, *Nihon Nōmin Seisaku Shiron*, 127. The Ministry of Colonization (Takumushō), which also played an important role in migration to Manchuria, was disbanded in 1942.

construction of an owner-farmer society in Japan as an ideal way for the nation to embrace American global hegemony as a surrogate of the West during the Cold War. Ishiguro Tadaatsu, that spiritual leader of the state-led anticapitalist agrarianism before 1945, was quick to refer to the United States as an ideal example for Japan to emulate. The splendid capitalist civilization and democracy of the United States, Ishiguro argued, was solidly rooted in an own-farmer economy originally established by Thomas Jefferson. As the Japanese nation was striving to catch up with the progress of Western democracy, the American example demonstrated that owner-farmers were the indispensable foundation of postwar Japanese society.[47]

Though overseas migration was suspended during the occupation years, the sections of the MAF that concerned themselves with migration matters continued to function by facilitating the repatriation and resettlement of Japanese settlers living in the former colonies. The Bureau of Land Exploration that took the primary role in attempting to turn the repatriates into land-owning farmers was staffed with many of the same people who had orchestrated the mass migration to Manchuria.[48] To the agrarianists, both domestic land exploration and land reform campaigns were important steps in creating their ideal farming society. Katō Kanji, one of the central architects of mass migration to Manchuria, wholeheartedly dedicated himself to mobilizing the repatriates *from* Manchuria to explore new lands in the archipelago. Back in 1927, Katō had founded an educational institution known as the Japanese National High School (Nihon Kokumin Kōtō Gakkō) to cultivate colonial farmers who later migrated to the Asian continent. During the postwar era, Katō repurposed the same institution to prepare the repatriates for domestic land exploration.[49] By "maximizing the labor of the people who came back to the countryside and returned to farming (*kinō*)," Katō claimed, Japan could create the most ideal agricultural society in the world.[50] The land reform represented another major endeavor of the Japanese agrarianists, and it indeed eliminated the landlord class, a chief barrier in Japan's path to an owner-farmer society before 1945. However, as explained previously in this chapter, the campaigns of land exploration and land reform failed to provide land and livelihood to the majority of the repatriates.

Overpopulation was a handy explanation for such a failure. As Ishiguro reasoned in 1950, as it was during the prewar era, it was impossible for Japan to become a true owner-farmer society as long as surplus population existed in the countryside. As a result, these surplus people had to find alternative livelihoods.[51] As it was in the pre-1945 era, Ishiguro and his loyal followers

---

[47] Ōtake, *Ishiguro Tadaatsu no Nōsei Shisō*, 335.   [48] Yasuoka, *Tashatachi no Nōgyōshi*, 183.
[49] Kitasaki Kōnosuke, *Sengo Kaitakuchi to Katō Kanji: Jizoku Kanō na Nōgyō no Genryū* (Tokyo: Nōrin Tōkei Shuppan, 2009), 37.
[50] Itō, *Nihon Nōmin Seisaku Shiron*, 75.   [51] Ibid., 267–268.

within and outside of the MAF saw overseas migration as the best solution. They expected that migration would ease the domestic population pressure, enabling Japan to finally transform itself into an ideal owner-farmer society with a perfectly balanced population/land ratio.

The marriage between the anxiety of overpopulation and the discourse of land shortage brought the MAF again to the forefront of migration promotion and management. In December 1952, the ministry took primary responsibility in sending a group of government-sponsored migrants abroad, for the first time in the postwar era, to northern Brazil's Amazon Basin. While the Ministry of Foreign Affairs provided lodging and training for the migrants when they stayed at the Kobe Migration Center (Kobe Ijū Assen Sho) before departure, the MAF was in charge of the promotion and recruitment of these migrants by working closely with prefectural governments.[52] During the next year, the MAF established its own facility to train migrants in a farm in Fukushima as its answer to the Kobe center managed by the Ministry of Foreign Affairs. The farm was previously used to train farmers for domestic land exploration.[53]

As the postwar migration tide began to rise, the Ministry of Foreign Affairs tried to further its influence by extending control over the project. In 1953, it established the Department of Migration (Imin Ka) under the Bureau of Euro-American Affairs (Ōbei Kyoku). The department assumed the responsibility for conducting investigations into overseas migration in South America and mediating the relationship between social groups and the government in migration-related matters.[54] In the same year, the Ministry of Foreign Affairs began to revive the prefecture-based overseas associations – the same institution that had played a vital role in migration promotion and recruitment at the local level in previous campaigns of migration to Brazil and Manchuria. In 1954, the ministry sponsored the formation of the Federation of Overseas Associations (Kaigai Kyōkai Rengōkai, or Kaikyōren for short) to coordinate the activities of all local overseas associations and place them under its own direction. Through this move, the ministry aimed to expand its power in migration management by monopolizing the process of migrant recruitment.

Naturally, the MAF strongly opposed the attempted power grab of the Ministry of Foreign Affairs. Pointing out the fact that the majority of the migrants were farmers, the leaders of MAF argued that it was crucial for the selection and recruitment of migrants to be performed by the MAF, a matter in which they had both expertise and experience.[55] A 1954 cabinet decision put the contention to rest; it decided that while the Ministry of Foreign Affairs would take charge of overseas migration-related affairs, the domestic selection and recruitment of migrants would be conducted under the

---

[52] Nōgyō Takushoku Kyōkai, *Sengo Kaigai Nōgyō Ijū no Shokan to Kikō*, 10–11.   [53] Ibid., 18.
[54] Ibid., 19–20.   [55] Yasuoka, *Tashatachi no Nōgyōshi*, 295.

cooperation of both ministries.[56] Even after the Ministry of Foreign Affairs became the central state organ in charge of migration management, the MAF continued to play an important role in promoting and managing the migration of Japanese farmers to the Americas. The MAF's involvement in overseas migration was mainly through two proxy organizations, the Association for International Collaboration of Farmers (AICF; Kokusai Nōyū Kai) and the National Federation of Agricultural Migration Cooperative Associations (JATAKA; Zenkoku Takushoku Nōgyō Kyōdō Kumiai Rengōkai), respectively in charge of farmer migration to North America and South America.

In sum, the Japanese overseas migration trend that resumed in the 1950s was managed by a migration state that mirrored its pre-1945 incarnation. Like its imperial counterpart, the postwar government tasked itself with managing the selection, recruitment, and training of migrants; it also provided subsidies for their transportation and settlement. This similarity sprang from a striking institutional and personnel continuity between the two governments despite a crushing defeat in World War II. The MAF, the state organ that played a central role in the mass migration to Manchuria during the war, had led the resettlement of the repatriates and the domestic land exploration project immediately after the war, and now it was initiating overseas migration for the new Japanese nation.

Farmer Migration for a New Nation: Representing Past for Future

The central role of the MAF revealed the farmer-centered nature of the Japanese overseas migration in the postwar era. During the 1950s and 1960s, as from the 1920s to 1945, tensions rising from land shortage continued to be the main fuel that powered the migration machine. Though usually self-proclaimed as the migration of technicians and developers (*gijutsu imin* and *kaihatsu imin*), postwar Japanese overseas migration remained, like it was for Brazil and Manchuria, predominantly an agricultural one that focused on land acquisition. Most migrants were those who were denied access to land, such as repatriates, urban war evacuees, and sons without inheritance rights from farming households.

Once again, the migration state did not plan to simply transplant these people and leave them to their own fates abroad. The postwar agrarianists, still adherents of Malthusian expansionism, believed that migration would fashion these surplus persons, potential sources of unrest at home, into model subjects of the new nation – only now instead of the Empire of Japan, the object of their allegiance was a democratic state. By taming lands of wildness in underdeveloped countries, these

---

[56] Nōgyō Takushoku Kyōkai, *Sengo Kaigai Nōgyō Ijū no Shokan to Kikō*, 81.

consummate farmers were expected to bring the blessings of modernization to backward people around the globe and present Japan on the international stage as a splendid proxy nation of the free world. This postwar reinvention of Japanese national identity as well as its representation through farmer migration were made possible by the legacy of Japan's migration-driven expansion in the previous decades. The following paragraphs take a closer look at how leaders of the postwar Japan legitimized overseas migration by reinterpreting the history of Japanese expansion before 1945.

Eulogizing Colonialism as Modernization

Immediately following Japan's surrender, the Allies' International Military Tribunal for the Far East, the purge of hundreds of thousands of politicians and public figures, as well as the censorship policy imposed by the occupation authority together set the tone on how World War II should be understood and remembered in Japan. However, how the history of Japanese colonialism should be remembered remained a contested topic. While the United States and its allies termed the pre-1945 Japan as an evil empire of invaders, the Americans nevertheless understood that an all-out attack on Japanese colonial expansion would leave the United States itself vulnerable to similar criticism.[57] Moreover, with the consent of the occupation authorities, many wartime politicians, intellectuals, and bureaucrats quickly returned to government service after the temporary purge, giving rise to a rose-tinted perspective of Japan's colonial history in the public sphere. As a result, the denunciation of wartime fascism and militarism right after the war emerged hand in hand with the acknowledgment and even celebration of the colonial expansion of the empire in Japanese public discourse.

In September 1946, one year after the collapse of the Japanese empire, the Ministry of Finance began a comprehensive investigation of Japanese activities beyond the archipelago from the beginning of the Meiji era to the end of World War II. The result of this investigation was a thirty-volume collection that documented the details of Japanese overseas communities around the Pacific. With the majority of the volumes dedicated to the experience of the settler communities inside the empire, the immediate goal of this investigation was to allow the Japanese government to claim ownership of Japanese colonial assets in lost imperial territories.[58] In keeping with this purpose, the Japanese

---

[57] Marlene J. Mayo, "Literary Reorientation in Occupied Japan: Incidents of Civil Censorship," in *Legacies and Ambiguities: Postwar Fiction and Culture in West Germany and Japan*, ed. Ernestine Schlant and J. Thomas Rimer (Washington, DC: Woodrow Wilson Center Press, Johns Hopkins University Press, 1991), 147.
[58] Paku Kyonmin, "Kaigai Jigyōsha no Zaigai Zaisan no Hōshō Yōkyu to Shokuminchi Ninshiki, 1945–1948 Nen: Chōsen Jigyōshakai o Chūshin ni," *Hōgaku Seijigaku Tōkyū: Hōritsu, Seiji, Shakai*, no. 108 (Spring 2016): 24.

government argued that the Japanese assets in the colonies were obtained not through military invasion but accumulated, over a long period of time, by the efforts of hardworking Japanese people. In order to persuade the GHQ and the allied powers, the collection was not only rich in details but also written by specialists of different fields citing meticulous studies.[59] It could be considered the first comprehensive history of the Japanese empire compiled in the post-war era.

A careful look at the narrative of the collection reveals how the new government chose to represent Japan's colonial history immediately after the war. The Japanese empire, the collection emphasized, was extraordinarily successful in transplanting Western civilization onto the archipelago, and Japan's population explosion was a result of such success. As the population continued to grow, the existing territory's resources proved to be too limited, which left the empire no choice but to conduct territorial expansion. The expansion of the empire, in other words, was primarily driven by the desire to gain additional land and other resources to accommodate the ever-growing Japanese population.[60] On the other hand, the collection described Japanese expansion as a successful process of transplanting progress and modernization from the archipelago to the colonies, something mutually beneficial to both the Japanese and the local populations.[61] The Pacific War, the collection argued, had unfortunately terminated this process and destroyed much of the achievement accomplished by the Japanese empire.[62]

The Japanese Overseas Migration as a Story of Cosmopolitanism

Postwar Japanese elites also linked the presentation of Japanese colonial expansion as a project of modernization and the colonial settlers as modernizers with the virtues of altruism and cosmopolitanism, two traits that Japanese overseas migrants were believed to possess in abundance. Sugino Tadao, the brain behind both Japanese wartime migration to Manchuria and the postwar South American migration campaign, argued that Japanese migration to Manchuria was driven by neither imperialism nor colonialism. Instead, it was a part of Japan's effort to establish a new world order under which all people could coexist and coprosper. Such a spirit of altruism, Sugino intoned, should continue to buttress Japan's overseas migration in the postwar era.[63]

---

[59] Ibid., 18.
[60] Ōkurashō Kanrikyoku, *Nihonjin no Kaigai Katsudō ni Kansuru Rekishi Teki Chōsa*, vol. 1, *Sōron*, edited by Kobayashi Hideo (Tokyo: Yumani Shobō, 2002), 151–152.
[61] Ibid., 269–270.   [62] Ibid., 184–185.
[63] Yamamoto Yūzō, *Manshū Kioku to Rekishi* (Kyoto: Kyoto Daigaku Gakujutsu Shuppankai, 2007), 312.

They also reinterpreted the history of Japanese migration to the United States as an example of cosmopolitanism. In 1950, Japanese singer Yamaguchi Yoshiko came to the United States as a member of a Japanese cultural delegation. This delegation was a part of the effort made by the postwar Japanese government to rehabilitate Japan's international image, presenting Japan as a close American ally rather than the evil enemy from an all too recent past.[64] During the visit, she performed for Japanese American communities in Sacramento, California.[65] More famously known by her Chinese name, Li Xianglan, Yamaguchi was one of the most popular singers in Manchukuo and Japanese-occupied China during the war, singing songs in Chinese to propagate Pan-Asianism as well as Sino-Japanese coexistence and coprosperity. For her Sacramento audience, Yamaguchi performed two of the most popular songs from her wartime repertoire, "Ye Lai Xiang" ("The Night Willow") and "Suzhou Yequ" ("Nocturne of Suzhou"), in both Japanese and Chinese. Through these performances, the delegation expressed gratitude on Japan's behalf to the Japanese Americans for their sufferings and hardships during the war.[66]

Tokyo interpreted the Japanese American experience as a resounding success of Japanese overseas migration. Japanese Americans endured unbearable but necessary difficulties rising from decades of institutionalized racism that culminated in wartime internment. They also successfully proved their loyalty to their host country through the heroism of nisei soldiers in the European theater of World War II, which eventually won them true membership of the white men's society when the McCarran-Walter Act in 1952 granted Japanese immigrants the right of naturalization. The cultural delegation's expression of gratitude connected the experience of the Japanese Americans with the fate of Japan, as if the Japanese Americans, by bearing the unbearable in the past, earned not only their citizenship in the United States but also the eventual acceptance of Japan into the Western world after the war. Yamaguchi Yoshiko's performances to the Japanese Americans also brought the experiences of Japanese migration to Asia and to the United States before 1945 together to construct a coherent story of Japanese migration on both sides of the Pacific, marked by altruism and cosmopolitanism. The overseas Japanese in any part of

---

[64] Michael Bourdaghs, *Sayonara Amerika, Sayonara Nippon: A Geopolitical Prehistory of J-Pop* (New York: Columbia University Press, 2012), 58–59.

[65] Ibid., 58.

[66] "Moto Joyū no Yamaguchi Yoshiko San 1950 Sengo Bei Kōen no Ōngen wo Kakunin," *Hokukoku Shinbun*, Yūkan (August 18, 2012): 1; "Yamaguchi Yoshiko San Bei Kōen no Ongen," *Shinano Mainichi Shinbun*, Yūkan (August 18, 2012). I would like to thank Professor Michael Bourdaghs at the University of Chicago for generously sharing with me the information regarding Yamaguchi Yoshiko's tour in Sacramento and related newspaper clips.

the world, as this logic implied, were neither invaders nor spies, but hearty contributors to the progress and prosperity of the host societies.

This perceived happy ending for the Japanese American story was celebrated by migration promoters as a testament to the cosmopolitan nature of Japanese migrants, who would give their wholehearted loyalty to whichever country they migrated to.[67] Nagata Shigeshi, the president of the Japanese Striving Society, looked at the history of Japanese Brazilian migration through the same lens. Recycling the discourse of coexistence and coprosperity that guided Japanese settlement in Aliança, Nagata argued that Japanese Brazilian migration in the postwar era would continue to prioritize the cultivation of people instead of the cultivation of crops, encouraging Japanese immigrants to assimilate into their host societies.[68] Sugino Tadao also concluded that the experience of Japanese migration on both sides of the Pacific before 1945 proved the Japanese to be cosmopolitans; he called the Japanese postwar migrants "international farmers" because they were willing to plant down their roots wherever they migrated to in order to bring peace and mutual understanding to the entire world.[69]

Reembracing White Racism and Cold War Colonialism and the Making of New Japanese Frontiers

In addition to modernizers and cosmopolitans, the postwar migration promoters also strived to portray the Japanese as frontier explorers, thereby reinserting Japan into the global racial hierarchy as a colored proxy of white supremacy. The claim of Japanese as frontier explorers emerged during the period of US occupation as migration promoters in Japan attempted to persuade the United States to rescind the ban on overseas migration and to open the doors of the countries under American political influence in South America and Southeast Asia to Japanese migrants. Being a master race like the Anglo-Saxons, the migration promoters argued, the Japanese deserved the privilege to explore the underdeveloped world for the good of all human beings.

In the postwar era, as Japanese Malthusian expansionists strived to restart Japanese overseas migration by embracing a US-centered world order, they saw the American West as a particularly important frontier of the new Japan. In their minds, it was a perfect place for the Japanese to be reimbued with "the vigorous pioneer spirit" of the Americans.[70] They saw Japanese migration to the United States as a shortcut to relocate the Japanese to the top of the global racial hierarchy under the umbrella of white supremacy.

---

[67] Nagata, *Shinano Kaigai Ijūshi*, 244.
[68] Nagata Shigeshi, "Zahaku Dōhō no Shinro," *Rikkō Sekai*, no. 563 (February 1952): 1.
[69] Sugino, *Kaigai Takushoku Hishi*, 100–101.
[70] Nōgyō Takushoku Kyōkai, *Sengo Kaigai Nōgyō Ijū no Shokan to Kikō*, 156.

A telling example was the decade-long Japanese Agricultural Workers Program (Nōgyō Rōmusha Habei Jigyō, or Tannō). Launched by the Association for International Collaboration of Farmers (AICF), the Tannō program brought forty-one hundred Japanese to rural California as fixed-term farm workers. AICF was led by Ishiguro Tadaatsu and Nasu Shiroshi,[71] and a substantial part of its founding members were brains and arms of Japanese wartime migration campaigns. Many AICF members, in their official positions, also worked on postwar repatriation of overseas Japanese.[72] Established only a few months before state-sponsored migration officially began, the AICF quickly become a proxy for the MAF to carry out its programs of overseas migration and training. Aside from running the Fukushima migration training center and exchange programs between Japanese and American farmers,[73] the main undertaking of the AICF during the 1950s and 1960s was the Tannō program. It shows the unexpected ways in which Japanese postwar agrarianists reimagined the American West as a new frontier of postwar Japanese migration. In the mind of these expansionists, Japanese farmer migration to the United States would regain Japan a desired location in the global racial hierarchy, which would in turn legitimize Japan's own agricultural expansion in backward countries in South America and Southeast Asia.

While the McCarran-Walter Act of 1952 reopened American doors to Japanese immigration, the annual quota assigned for Japan was only 185.[74] Though the fixed-term agricultural workers program was not subject to the quota limit, it was not intended for immigration. Nevertheless, in the mind of the AICF leaders, the program could temporarily relieve rural population pressure and provide landless farmers with opportunities to gain a livelihood. They further claimed that Japanese farmers' participation in postwar agricultural development in the American West would allow them to once again bask

---

[71] Eiichiro Azuma, "Japanese Agricultural Labor Program: Temporary Worker Immigration, U.S.-Japan Cultural Diplomacy, and Ethnic Community Making among Japanese Americans," in *A Nation of Immigrants Reconsidered: US Society in an Age of Restriction, 1924–1965*, ed. Maddalena Marinari, Madeline Y. Hsu, and María Cristina García (Urbana: University of Illinois Press, 2019), 162; Itō, *Nihon Nōmin Seisaku Shiron*, 113–114.

[72] Nasu Shiroshi, the first president of the association, Ishiguro Tadaatsu, a key member in the advisory board, and Sugino Tadao and Kodaira Gon'ichi, on the council of directors, were central architects of migration to Manchuria. In addition, many other founding members of the association were previous members of the Association of Exploration and Self-Striving (Kaitaku Jikō Kai), an association established right after the war to facilitate the repatriation of Japanese settlers in Manchuria and to resettle them in Japan through domestic land exploration. See Itō, *Nihon Nōmin Seisaku Shiron*, 113–114; Nōgyō Takushoku Kyōkai, *Sengo Kaigai Nōgyō Ijū no Shokan to Kikō*, 4–5.

[73] The farm training program in Fukushima offered by the MAF to the selected farmer migrants was managed by AICF. Nōgyō Takushoku Kyōkai, *Sengo Kaigai Nōgyō Ijū no Shokan to Kikō*, 18.

[74] Azuma, "Japanese Agricultural Labor Program," 162.

in the light of democracy after postwar land reform.[75] The AICF members expected that with their natural industriousness, honesty, and talent, Japanese farmers would be welcomed by white American farm owners as superior to Mexican bracero workers.[76] The perception of Japanese farmers as model minority workers in California, they envisioned, would help Japan to join the US-centered world order as a model-minority nation.[77] Ultimately, this would help Japan to secure US permission to export migrants inside the American sphere of influence to South America and Southeast Asia.[78]

The AICF's programs of Japanese farmer migration and exchanges in the United States were thus intertwined with the ideas and activities to reopen the doors of South America and Southeast Asia for Japanese expansion in the postwar era. In 1958, Ishiguro visited Brazil as the head of the Japanese farmers' delegation to celebrate the fiftieth anniversary of Japanese migration to Brazil. Believing that Japanese farmers' achievements in the United States had won them respect from white Americans and Brazilians alike, he happily noted that the Japanese were now welcomed in Brazil as highly civilized people who were also humble, hardworking, and willing to bring progress to the most primitive land of the country.[79]

The postwar reintegration of South America and Southeast Asia as frontiers on the map of Japanese expansion was best represented by the ideas and activities of Sugino Tadao and Nagata Shigeshi. Sugino, an AICF leader who brought a Japanese farmer delegation to California in 1953,[80] became the founding professor of the degree program of colonial agriculture (*nōgyō takushoku gakka*) at Tokyo Agricultural University (Tokyo Nōgyō Daigaku) in 1956.[81] Under his guidance, the school trained the leaders of Japanese farmer migration to both South America and Southeast Asia.

Like Ishiguro and Nasu, Sugino was a passionate supporter of the Japanese agrarianist movement in the 1930s and 1940s who embraced migration to Manchuria as a way to create an owner-farmer society. After the war, Sugino also quickly reemerged as an advocate of farmer migration overseas, for he still regarded it as the ultimate remedy for the ills that haunted an overpopulated Japan. As demonstrated by the modern history of

---

[75] For the statement of Ishiguro Tadaatsu, see Nōgyō Takushoku Kyōkai, *Sengo Kaigai Nōgyō Ijū no Shokan to Kikō*, 155–156. For the statement of Nasu Shiroshi, see Azuma, "Japanese Agricultural Labor Program," 171.

[76] Azuma, "Japanese Agricultural Labor Program," 163. Growers in California, too, embraced these Japanese agricultural workers as the foil for the "inconvenient" braceros. Mireya Loza, "The Japanese Agricultural Workers' Program Race, Labor, and Cold War Diplomacy in the Fields, 1956–1965," *Pacific Historical Review* 86, no. 4 (2017): 671–675.

[77] To borrow a word from Takashi Fujitani, *Race for Empire*, 211.

[78] For the statement of Ishiguro, see Nōgyō Takushoku Kyōkai, *Sengo Kaigai Nōgyō Ijū no Shokan to Kikō*, 157. For the statement of Nasu, see Azuma, "Japanese Agricultural Labor Program," 163.

[79] Sugino, *Kaigai Takushoku Hishi*, 4.   [80] Ibid., 18.   [81] Ibid., 5.

European expansion, Sugino argued, frontiers were pivotal for a nation's fate, for nations that had conducted frontier expansion emerged stronger than others. When the metropolis began to decline, the frontier would fill up the void and become a new – and better – home for the people in the former metropolis. He saw the relationship between the United States, a shared frontier of the Europeans, and the European metropolis as a living example.[82] As the Northern Hemisphere now was caught in the confrontation between two nuclear superpowers, Sugino predicted, it was doomed to decline. With spacious, unexplored land and abundant natural resources, the peaceful Southern Hemisphere would become the new frontier of the entire human race. As a master race in agricultural production, the Japanese were eminently suited to become the leaders of the mission to conquer the virgin forests and tap the natural wealth in this new frontier.[83]

Nagata Shigeshi supported Sugino's view by arguing that Japanese farmers, superior to the white people in agricultural undertakings, could offer a unique remedy for the crisis of Brazilian agriculture. The traditional mode of agriculture, introduced to Brazil by the European settlers who exploited the farmland without a long-term vision, he argued, had been turning Brazilian farmland into deserts.[84] In contrast, the Japanese mode of intensive farming, which featured frequently fertilizing the land, improving crops, and preventing and controlling pests, could revitalize Brazilian agriculture.

Restarting Japanese migration to Brazil in the postwar era, Nagata further argued, was also crucial to sustain the prosperity of the existing Japanese communities in Brazil. As an adherent of agrarianism, Nagata was worried that as more Japanese immigrants left their rural homes for urban areas amid the process of rapid urbanization in postwar Brazil, Japanese Brazilians were losing their farmland, the foundation upon which their lives were built. He expected that postwar Japanese migration would reverse the decline of the farming population in Japanese Brazilian communities.[85] In this endeavor, the migration of well-trained women was especially important. These female migrants would balance the gender ratio in Japanese Brazilian communities and give birth to more members of the next generation. As mothers, they would also pass down their

[82] Ibid., 223–226.   [83] Ibid., 220.
[84] Nagata argued that previously agriculture in Brazil was primarily managed by European immigrants, who knew only large-scale farming. They first burned the forests and planted coffee trees in the ashes. After planting coffee without fertilizing the land for twenty-five years, they chopped down the coffee trees and planted cotton instead. After four or five years, when the land could no longer sustain cotton, they would use the weeds to feed cattle. After the land was completely exhausted and could not even support animals, they would sell it. See Nagata Shigeshi, "Hakkoku Nōgyō no Shūyakuka," *Rikkō Sekai*, no. 665 (August 1960): 1.
[85] "Burajiru ni Okeru Hōjin Nisei no Rison Mondai," *Umi no Soto,* postwar, no. 17 (October 1952): 1.

passion for farming to their children,[86] ensuring that agriculture would continue to be the foundation of Japanese Brazilian communities. Under his leadership, the Japanese Striving Society established the Association of the Southern Cross (Minami Jūji Kai), a reincarnation of the Striving Society's Women School and Women Home before 1945. The association facilitated the migration of Japanese women to South America as brides of male migrants and provided these women with migration-related training before they left Japan.[87]

In a similar way, Japanese expansionists applied the trope of frontier to other countries in South America and Southeast Asia. In 1956, the MAF and the Ministry of Foreign Affairs jointly initiated a failed attempt that aimed to relocate ten thousand Japanese men and women to Cambodia each year for five years. The plan was a close copy of the land-acquisition-centered Japanese migration programs in Brazil. Calling Cambodia Amazon of the East (*Tōyō no Amazon*), it once claimed to turn the surplus people in the "fully packed Japan" (*man'in Nihon*) into trailblazers of the nation's new frontier, this time in Asia.[88]

The Decline of Japanese Overseas Migration and the Demise of Malthusian Expansionism

Throughout the 1950s, though Japanese overseas migration was not impressive in terms of its absolute size, its annual numbers did steadily grow as more countries opened up their doors to Japanese migrants. At the end of the 1950s, Malthusian expansionism continued to serve as a guiding principle for the policymakers in Tokyo, who relied on overseas migration to both relieve population pressure and explore new frontiers of the new nation.[89] In 1958, the Ministry of Foreign Affairs made a plan to relocate 101,000 Japanese overseas in the next four years.[90] However, to the surprise of many, the annual numbers of Japanese overseas migration did not grow but plummeted at the beginning of the 1960s.

A few events in 1961 jointly marked the turning point of postwar Japanese migration. In that year, migrants who participated in the failed 1956 to 1959 migration campaign to the Dominican Republic began to return to the archipelago.[91] Around the same time, the migration project in Guatapara, Brazil, managed by JATAKA, also ran into trouble.[92] These failures, caused

[86] Ibid., 1; "Ijū Undō kara Tori Nokosaru Musume Tachi Yō, Ijū Seyō," *Rikkō Sekai*, no. 662 (May, 1960): 4; Nagata Shigeshi, "'Hito o Tsukure' kara 'Haha o Tsukure e,'" *Rikkō Sekai*, no. 677 (August, 1961): 1.
[87] Nippon Rikkō Kai, *Nippon Rikkō Kai*, 373.
[88] "Kanbojia Imin: Raishun Sōsōni Chōsadan Mazu Hitsuyōna Shikin no Enjo," *Asahi Shinbun*, December 19, 1955, 7.
[89] Nihon Kaigai Kyōkai Rengōka, *Nihon to Ijū*, 18–20.
[90] Wakatsuki and Jōji, *Kaigai Ijū Seisaku Shiron*, 106.   [91] Ibid., 779.
[92] Nagata Shigeshi, "Imin Saiaku no Sai," *Rikkō Sekai*, no. 684 (March, 1962): 1; "Postwar Emigration Agencies," in *100 Years of Japanese Emigration to Brazil*.

by poor planning and management on the Japanese government's part, triggered a substantial change in the image of overseas migration in public
discourse. Japan's mass media not only were increasingly critical of the
government's migration management ability but also became pessimistic
about the outlook of Japanese overseas migration itself.[93] However, while
a future in foreign lands looked increasingly uncertain, things were looking
up at home: Ikeda Hayato's cabinet set a plan to double Japanese national
income within the next ten years; implemented in 1961, this goal was reached
in as few as six years, marking the beginning of the period of Japan's rapid
economic growth (*kōdo keizai seichōki*) that lasted for more than two decades.
As the fast industrial development began to demand an increasingly large labor
force from the Japanese countryside, the anxiety of overpopulation quickly
dissipated; starting in 1961, annual overseas migration numbers continuously
declined.

The Japanese government tried to reverse this trend by unifying its proxy
organizations in migration management, combining the Federation of Overseas
Migration Associations (Kaigai Kyōkai Rengōkai) and the Japan Emigration
Promotion Company (Nihon Kaigai Iju Shinkō Kabushiki Gaisha) into the
Japan Emigration Service (Kaigai Ijū Jigyōdan) in 1963.[94] True believers of
migration also pressed on with their campaigns. Nagata Shigeshi, for example,
argued that further population increases should be implemented in tandem with
the Ikeda cabinet's plan to double the national income: Japan, he believed,
needed to double the size of its population within ten years in order to export
more migrants to occupy and utilize the wealth of undeveloped lands around
the world.[95] However, none of these efforts were able to reverse the rapid
decline of migration numbers.

In addition to the drop in numbers, as more and more rural people turned to
cities for job opportunities and personal advancement, Japanese overseas
migration in the 1960s also became less farmer centered. Urban-based skilled
workers and specialists in science and technology began to constitute a greater
portion of the migrants.[96] This change mirrored the overall decline of the
previously farmer-centered Japanese communities in North and South
America. As more second- and third-generation Japanese immigrants left the
countryside for education and job opportunities in the cities, the Japanese

---

[93] See "Kyō no Mondai," *Asahi Shinbun*, August 2, 1961; "Dominika Ijū no Kyōkun, " *Mainichi Shinbun*, April 12, 1962, cited from Wakatsuki and Jōji, *Kaigai Ijū Seisaku Shiron*, 779.

[94] Itō, *Nihon Nōmin Seisaku Shiron,* 228.

[95] "Nihon Minzoku Nioku Gosenman ni," *Rikkō Sekai*, no. 694 (January 1963): 6.

[96] As early as 1958, noticing the increase of urban skilled workers and technicians in the migration to Brazil, the Ministry of Foreign Affairs envisioned the establishment of several Tokyo villages (*Tokyo Mura*), new urban-based Japanese communities in Brazil. "Takamaru Imin Netsu: Burajiru e Tokyo Mura mo," *Asahi Shinbun*, June 4, 1958, 10.

Table 8.1 *Government-subsidized Japanese migration to Brazil, 1955–1965*

Year	1955	1956	1957	1958	1959	1960	1961	1962	1963	1964	1965
Agriculture	2,620	4,335	5,132	6,251	6,939	6,691	5,010	1,745	1,127	445	201
Technology	37	35	17	50	92	123	122	71	89	108	169
Other			23	11	10	18	14	14	14	198	161
Total no.	2,657	4,370	5,172	6,312	7,041	6,832	5,146	1,830	1,230	751	531

This table shows Japanese-Brazilian migrants between 1955 and 1965 who received subsidies from the Japanese government. Based on data provided in Itō Atsushi, *Nihon Nōmin Seisaku Shiron: Kaitaku Imin Kyōiku Kunren* (Kyoto: Kyoto Daigaku Gakujutsu Shuppankai, 2013), 223–224. It illustrates the sharp drop of migration numbers from 1962 onward and also the increase of urban, technology-related migrants since the turn of the 1960s.

communities in North and South America also became increasingly urbanized as a whole.

Japanese overseas migration experienced a further downturn in the 1970s. The Satō Eisaku cabinet extended the meaning of "overseas migration" (*kaigai ijū*) to Japanese citizens who stayed aboard only temporarily, such as short-term workers and students. This substantially broadened definition reflected changes to the mode of Japanese expansion itself – that is, from land-acquisition-centered farmer migration to investment- and trade-centered business expansion. The idea of relocating people overseas as a way of relieving domestic population pressure completely disappeared from the mission of this newly defined overseas migration.[97] The primary goal of the government's new migration policy, as announced by the Satō cabinet, was to facilitate the expansion of Japanese companies overseas by providing them with a sufficient labor supply. In 1974 the government-affiliated organizations for overseas migration further merged with the government proxies in charge of international affairs, such as foreign investment and trade, cultural and educational exchange, and technological cooperation. The result was the formation of the Japan International Cooperation Agency (JICA; Kokusai Kyōryoku Jigyōdan). The establishment of JICA demonstrated that overseas migration was no longer an independent field in the government's policymaking process. Instead, it became submerged into the field of international cooperation (*kokusai kyōryoku*). While the term "international cooperation" gained increasing popularity, "overseas migration" (kaigai ijū) had faded out of public discourse by the 1970s.

The decline of Japanese overseas migration in the 1960s was also accompanied by the demise of Malthusian expansionism as an expansionist discourse around the world. World War II and the Cold War confrontation right afterward escalated the processes of technological development and the discovery of new energy sources. As material production was gradually separated from the soil, the association between land and limits to food production and life capability was no longer convincing. In 1969, British historical demographer E. A. Wrigley reasoned in his book *Population and History* that industrial development would eventually bypass "the bottleneck caused by the problems of expanding organic raw material supply." As inorganic materials continued to replace organic materials, material production was increasingly less dependent on the fertility of soil.[98] Malthusian expansionism, which justified overseas migration as a solution to the overpopulation issue at home, had lost its logical foundation. In the 1960s and 1970s, the distribution of land versus population continued to be sharply unbalanced in the postwar era, and many societies

---

[97] Wakatsuki and Jōji, *Kaigai Ijū Seisaku Shiron,* 856–857.
[98] E. A. Wrigley, *Population and History* (New York: McGraw-Hill, 1969), 57, cited from Bashford, *Global Population*, 14.

continued to struggle against food shortages. However, overpopulation could no longer stand as a cogent explanation for social poverty. The pre–World War II call for redistribution of land around the world had been replaced by the two Cold War superpowers' competition in exporting technology and ideology to the Third World.

Conclusion

In many aspects, overseas migration in postwar Japan was a continuation of Japan's migration-driven expansion before 1945. The anxiety of overpopulation right after the war emerged in a context very different from the pre-1945 era, but the government's failure to provide farmland to the millions of repatriates directly resulted in the remarriage of overpopulation anxiety and the discourse of land shortage. As a result, Malthusian expansionism continued to serve as the primary justification for postwar overseas migration that began in 1952 until Japan's economy took off in the 1960s.

As it did during the migration campaigns to Brazil and Manchuria between the 1920s and 1945, the Japanese government took a central role in postwar migration management. The similar functions that it performed grew out from an institutional and personnel continuity that survived Japan's defeat in World War II. The MAF, the headquarters of pre-1945 agrarian expansionists that led the project of mass migration to Manchuria, continued to play a central role in orchestrating the campaigns of land exploration and land reform. Its leadership in these two domestic postwar campaigns also turned the ministry into one of the central sections of the government that oversaw overseas migration management during the 1950s and 1960s. Pre-1945 agrarian bureaucrats retained their influence in the ministry during the postwar era, and they once again became the engines of farmer migration projects.

Although the Japanese empire had given way to an avowed democratic state, an ideological continuity could also be traced in this new state's approach to migration: Japanese policymakers and advocates did not consider overseas migration simply as a solution to overpopulation; they saw it as a critical opportunity for postwar Japan to reembrace the world with a new identity: a pacifist, altruistic, and loyal member of the Western bloc. They expected the migrants, the model subjects of this new nation, to bring the blessings of Western modernization and progress to the backward countries around the globe during the Cold War.

Conclusion
Rethinking Migration and Settler Colonialism in the Modern World

The Nexus between Emigration and Colonial Expansion

In February 1977, Umesao Tadao, then the director-general of Japan's National Museum of Ethnology and one of the most highly regarded anthropologists in Japan, arrived in São Paulo. Umesao had come to assist the local Japanese communities in their efforts to establish a museum of Japanese immigration. Inspired by the Historical Museum of Hokkaido (Hokkaido Kaitaku Kinenkan) in Sapporo,[1] the Historical Museum of Japanese Immigration in Brazil (Museu Histórico da Imigração Japonesa no Brasil) was unveiled in 1978 in São Paulo as an important part of the celebration of the seventieth anniversary of the beginning of Japanese immigration to Brazil.

Under Umesao's guidance, the museum presented the history of Japanese Brazilian migration as a story of dazzling success. It recorded the achievements of Japanese immigrants in frontier exploration, agricultural innovation, and ethnic integration in Brazil. It also detailed Japanese contributions to Brazil's economic, social, and cultural development during different periods in general.[2] As Umesao put it, the triumph of Japanese Brazilians was a chapter of the glorious history of Japanese global migration. He acknowledged that the Japanese government, in the past, had to send its subjects overseas due to population pressures at home. However, as Japanese emigrants had made great contributions to their host societies, this development was undoubtedly a mutually beneficial one.[3] According to him, by settling in North and South

---

[1] The Historical Museum of Hokkaido (Hokkaido Kaitaku Kinenkan) was opened in 1971 to celebrate the hundred-year anniversary of the Japanese colonization of Hokkaido. It was renamed Hokkaido Museum (Hokkaido Hakubutsukan) in 2015. Historical Museum of Hokkaido, *Museum Survey and Guide* (Sapporo: Historical Museum of Hokkaido, 2014), 1.

Umesao was invited by Japanese Brazilian scholar Saitō Hiroshi to assist the establishment of a museum for Japanese immigration in Brazil. Saitō was impressed by the exhibitions at the Historical Museum of Hokkaido during a visit and wanted to create a similar one to record the history of Japanese migration to Brazil. Saitō Hiroshi, *Burajiru to Nihonjin* (Tokyo: Simul Press, 1984), 115–119.

[2] Saitō, *Burajiru to Nihonjin*, 121.

[3] Umesao Tadao, "Nihonjin to Shinsekai," *JICA Yokohama Kaigai Ijū Shiryōkan Kenkyū Kiyō*, no. 1 (2006): 4.

America the Japanese migrants "have joined the New World" (*Shinsekai ni sankasu*). On the other hand, Umesao dismissed Japan's colonial migration within Asia as a miserable but abrupt episode and excluded it from his splendid narrative of integration and development.[4]

In reality, however, the experiences of Japanese migration in Asia and in Hawai'i and North and South America were inseparable. This book has demonstrated the nexus between Japanese migration – both inside and outside of the empire's sphere of influence in Asia – and the multidimensional continuities in Japanese migration before and after 1945. I have examined these connections and continuities at four different but interlocked analytical loci. The first locus of analysis is the history of Malthusian expansionism in Japan throughout the modern era. I have focused on the central role that the Malthusian discourse played during Japan's migration-driven expansion in Asia, Hawai'i, and the Americas from the beginning of the Meiji era to two decades after World War II. The evolution of Malthusian expansionism in Japan can be divided into four stages: emergence, transformation, culmination, and resurgence. During each and all of these four stages, I hold Japanese expansionists of different generations accountable for inventing, disseminating, and manipulating the anxiety of overpopulation to advance expansionist agendas and legitimize emigration campaigns. These individuals presented overpopulation as the fundamental cause of whatever social tension was plaguing the Japanese archipelago at the time; they further propagated the belief that to relocate the "surplus" people overseas would not only rescue the archipelago from a Malthusian catastrophe but also turn these elements of discord into valuable subjects who would expand the nation and empire. As their blueprints of expansion transcended the territorial boundaries of the Japanese empire, Malthusian expansionism left deep imprints in almost every major locale of Japanese emigration around the Pacific Rim – from Hokkaido to California, from Hawai'i to Micronesia, from Texas to São Paulo, and from Manchuria to the Amazon River Basin.

The second locus of analysis is the human connections and institutional continuities between Japanese emigration campaigns in different time periods. The life trajectories of individual Malthusian expansionists such as Tsuda Sen, Fukuzawa Yukichi, Enomoto Takeaki, Katayama Sen, Saibara Seitō, Nagata Shigeshi, Ishiguro Tadaatsu, Sugino Tadao, and their associates all challenge the seemingly natural impermeability of temporal and territorial boundaries of the Japanese empire. Moreover, I have discussed a number of organizations that played leading roles in promoting migration-drive expansion in different

---

[4] Nihon Gaimushō Kokusai Kyōryoku Jigyōdan, *Kaigai Ijū no Igi o Motomete: Burajiru Ijū 70-Shūnen Kinen: Nihonjin no Kaigai Ijū ni Kansuru Shinpojumu* (Tokyo: Nihon Gaimushō, 1979), 20.

spaces and time periods, such as the Colonial Association, the Emigration Association, and the Japanese Striving Society. My analysis of the campaigns planned and carried out by these organizations uncovers the consistent trans-Pacific flows and connections of Japanese migration around the Pacific Rim from early Meiji to the postwar era. The role that the imperial government played in its control and management of migration-related affairs also demonstrated continuities between different waves of emigration. The state's institutional expansion culminated in the formation of "the migration state" in the late 1920s. First aimed at encouraging the rural poor to migrate to Brazil, the same set of state machinery later took the lead in orchestrating the empire's mass migration to the Asian continent from late 1930s to 1945. Though briefly suppressed during the period of the US occupation, the same institutions – indeed, often the same people – would once again steer Japanese migration to South America in the postwar years.

This book's third locus of analysis is the ideological interaction between Japanese migration campaigns on both sides of the Pacific. I have explained how Japanese exclusion in the Americas had formed and transformed Japanese colonial expansion in Asia. Japanese exclusion in the United States not only precipitated Japanese expansion in Asia and other areas across the Pacific but also spurred the Japanese expansionists to invent the idea of coexistence and coprosperity. As a new principle of Japanese settler colonialism, this idea attacked the hypocrisy of white racism and Anglo-American imperialism while highlighting the supposed benevolence of Japan's own expansion. What's more, the closing off of the white men's world reconfigured the pattern of Japanese migration itself. Amid their bitter struggles against anti-Japanese sentiments in North America, Japanese Malthusian expansionists gradually reached an agreement that placed the acquisition of land and permanent settlement at the top and center of their migration agendas. Drawing from the lesson of Japanese exclusion in the United States, they concluded that *dekasegi*, the migration of temporary laborers who stayed overseas for only a short period, was an ill-conceived venture. Instead, they came to see those who would acquire and farm foreign land as ideal migration candidates: agricultural settlement would secure long-term land ownership, and it could also effectively extract wealth from the land for the empire.[5] The ideas of farmer-centered Japanese settler colonialism were first experimented with in Texas in the first few years of the twentieth century and were soon applied in a few state-led colonial migration projects in Taiwan and the Korean Peninsula. Japanese agricultural settler colonialism reached its maturity in Brazil and Manchuria between the 1920s and 1945. During this period, to foster agricultural

---

[5] For a general analysis of the role of agriculture in settler colonialism, see Wolfe, "Settler Colonialism and the Elimination of the Native," 395.

settlement overseas family migration became a norm, of which the migration of women was an essential component. Japanese expansionists expected female migrants were expected to assist their male counterparts by performing household duties and rearing the next generation of empire builders; moreover, they were tasked with representing a civilized empire and showcasing their feminine morality to the unenlightened others.

This paradigm change of migration was captured by the gradual shift of the written form of the Japanese word for colonial migration from 殖民 to 植民. Both were invented by Japanese intellectuals in the mid-nineteenth century as the character forms of *shokumin*, the Japanese translation of the imported term "colonial migration." The fact that 殖民 was much more commonly used in print throughout the Meiji era was a clear indicator of how colonial migration was understood at the time: an action to increase manpower for the empire. However, 植民, a combination of 植 (meaning "to plant") and 民 (meaning "people"), gained increasing popularity during the 1900s and had become the dominant written form of *shokumin* by the 1910s.[6] The shift from 殖民 to 植民 in the writings of Japanese intellectuals took place at the exact same time when Japanese laborer migration in the United States was met with increasing hostility. As Sakiyama Hisae, the president of the School of Overseas Colonial Migration (Kaigai Shokumin Gakkō), explained in 1928, 植民 was the more appropriate term because much like how the planting of trees and grass called for careful location selection and cultivation, emigration, too, should be a long-term project, in which the emigrants should put down their roots overseas, build robust families and communities, and plan for further development.[7]

The fourth locus of my analysis is the intellectual conflation between migration and expansion in modern Japanese history. Japan's rise as a modern nation and empire took place in the dual context of territorial expansion and demographic expansion of the European powers in the modern era. Emigration was both a means and a result of Japan's participation in the global expansion of modern imperialism and capitalism. In the imaginations of Japan's leaders, the Japanese were a superior and civilized people, on par with the British and Americans who owned the most powerful empires, because the Japanese enjoyed a rate of population growth similar to the latter. For the same reason, they believed that Japan deserved the same right to export its surplus people out

[6] As early as 1906, Tōgō Minoru's book *Nihon Shokumin Ron* had already used the form 植民 in its title. See Tōgō, *Nihon Shokumin Ron*; Nagata, "Shokumin Oyobi Shokumichi no Jigi," 123–127. Nitobe Inazō made it clear in 1916 that while 殖民 meant reproducing or increasing people, 植民 indicated planting people. See Nitobe, *Nitobe Hakushi Shokumin Seisaku Kōgi Oyobi Ronbunshū*, 41. As Yanaihara mentioned in the preface, this book is a collection of his note on Nitobe's seminars on colonial studies between 1916 and 1917. So we can assume that Nitobe made this statement then.

[7] Sakiyama Hisae, "Shoku to Iu Ji o Kokoro Toshite," *Shokumin* 7, no. 2 (February 1928): 69–70.

of the overcrowded archipelago and claim rich and empty land overseas like its Western counterparts had done. Emigration, one of the central means of the United Kingdom and the United States to build their global empires, was thus never far away from expansion in the lexicon of the educated Japanese. Therefore, not only did the recent migration-driven expansion of the Western empires serve as a compelling example for Japan's project of empire building, the Western settler nations and colonies also became destinations of Japan's own expansionist migration. Subscribing to the Lockean definition of land ownership, Japanese Malthusian expansionists believed that the Japanese settlers deserved the right to the lands of the Americas, Hawai'i, and the South Pacific due to the low population density of the white population there. The Japanese could cooperate or compete with Western settlers to enlighten and replenish these lands while the Japanese empire was carving out its territorial Lebensraum by wrestling with Western colonialism in Asia.

Remembering Japanese Emigration in World History: Divergence and Convergence

This intellectual conflation between migration and settler colonialism provided the logical foundation for Umesao Tadao's historical narrative of Japanese overseas migration. Aside from those involved in the unfortunate episode on the Asian continent, Umesao argued, all Japanese migrants were bound for the "New World," like the Americas and Australia. In these global frontiers, Japanese migrants achieved glorious success by joining hands with European settlers to create a new and multicultural civilization for the entire mankind.[8] Under this mind-set, Umesao supervised the construction of Japan Overseas Migration Museum (Kaigai Ijū Shiryōkan) in Yokohama and designed its permanent exhibition.[9] With the theme of "We Have Joined the New World" (Warera Shinsekai ni Sankasu), this exhibition narrates a glorious saga of Japanese emigrants' struggles against racism and xenophobia and enumerates their contributions to the frontier explorations of various host countries across the Pacific. Though titled "The History of Overseas Migration" (Kaigai Ijū no Rekishi), the exhibition includes only the experiences of Japanese migration in Hawai'i and the Americas. The entire history of Japanese colonial migration in Asia, where most of the Japanese overseas had settled, is missing.[10]

Umesao's ideas and museum designs demonstrate the paradoxical logic upon which the history and memory of Japanese overseas migration had been

[8] Nihon Gaimushō Kokusai Kyōryoku Jigyōdan, *Kaigai Ijū no Igi o Motomete*, 22.
[9] Umesao, "Nihonjin to Shinsekai," 1.
[10] Detailed information about the exhibition can be found in Kaigai Ijū Shiryōkan, *Kaigai Ijū Shiryōkan Tenji Annai: Warera Shinsekai ni Sankasu* (Yokohama: Dokuritsu Gyōsei Hōjin Kokusai Kyōryoku Kikō Yokohama Sentā, 2004).

Figure C.1 Display board at the entrance to the exhibition "We Have Joined the New World" at the Overseas Migration Museum in Yokohama. The board states in Japanese, English, Portuguese, and Spanish that the exhibition is "dedicated to those Japanese who have taken part in molding new civilizations in the Americas." This photograph was taken by Tian Huang at the Overseas Migration Museum in Yokohama, Japan, November 1, 2018.

constructed during the Cold War era. After the nation quickly reemerged as a Western Bloc power, the history and memory of overseas emigration in postwar Japan have been generally marked by two seemingly contradictory paradigms of narrative, namely the separation between Japanese settler colonialism in Asia and Japanese emigration beyond the empire on the one hand and the integration of Japanese emigration to the Americas and Hawai'i into the triumph of Western settler colonialism on the other.

First, the experience of Japan's colonial migration in Asia (*shokumin shi*), as a part of the disgraceful but also disposable past of the Japanese empire, has been clinically removed from the epic of Japanese overseas migration (*imin shi*) – a battle hymn of industrious Japanese migrants who successfully overcame racial and cultural biases in their host societies. Second, the history of Japanese migration to the Western settler nations and colonies has been incorporated into the colonial narrative of European expansion around the world. The Japanese migrants, as the narrative goes, came to join the European settlers in their mission of spreading civilization to the unenlightened lands.

As one of the most highly cited anthropologists and most influential thinkers in postwar Japan, Umesao Tadao also integrated his account of Japanese migration history into his ecological theory of world history that placed Japan and Western Europe at the top of a global hierarchy of civilizations. Umesao famously argued that due to similarities in their ecological environments, Western European and Japanese civilizations had developed in a similar manner and at a comparable pace. Their shared ecological features also made these two civilizations the most superior and progressive in world history. In contrast, common ecological features shared by societies in Asian continent, including those of India, China, the Islamic world, and Russia, meant that their civilizations were doomed to decline.[11]

Fukuzawa Yukichi's thesis of de-Asianization (*datsuaron*) which urged Japan to embrace the West and leave Asia behind, Umesao argued, was only partially correct. Because, for Umesao, Japan had never been associated with Asia in the first place.[12] Just as Fukuzawa's thesis of de-Asianization mirrored Japan's acceptance of New Imperialism during the late nineteenth century, Umesao's ecological theory of civilizations was clearly influenced by the Cold War. It offered historical and even scientific legitimacy for postwar Japan's embrace of the Western Bloc and the colonial narrative of world history associated with it.

As Umesao saw it, the very nature of migration was for the migrants to partake in molding new civilizations: Japanese migrants in the "New World," like the European colonial settlers who came before them, were neither guests (*okyaku san*) nor invaders (*shinnyūsha*). Instead, they were participants

---

[11] Umesao, "Nihonjin to Shinsekai," 10.   [12] Ibid., 12.

Figure C.2 A section of the exhibition "We Have Joined the New World" is titled "Toil in the Soil." Demonstrating the farming tools the Japanese migrant farmers used in the Americas, it praises the contributions that Japanese migrants made to the land exploration and agricultural development of the host societies through diligence and integrity. This photograph was taken by Tian Huang at the Overseas Migration Museum in Yokohama, Japan, November 1, 2018.

(*sankasha*) who contributed to the making of new civilizations.[13] The equalization between the Japanese and European races in the "New World" was further strengthened by Umesao's differentiation between the Japanese and other East Asian ethnic groups. The Koreans and Chinese, he argued, were not qualified to be migrants (*imin*); due to their lack of interest in farming, they were merely "floaters" (*ryūmin*) with no commitment to their host societies. The Japanese, instead, were willing to put down their roots in the new lands by taking up farming.[14]

The "New World," Umesao further argued, was the future of mankind. The "Old World," one composed of nation-states, was destined to decline and be replaced by the multicultural "New World," established on the principle of

[13] Nihon Gaimushō Kokusai Kyōryoku Jigyōdan, *Kaigai Ijū no Igi o Motomete*, 22.
[14] Umesao Tadao, "Shin Sekai e no Sanka: Nikei Imin Shūdan no Sekaishi Teki Imi," *Kasumigaseki Fōramu*, no. 1 (June 1977), republished in Umesao Tadao, *Umesao Tadao Chosakushū*, vol. 2 (Tokyo: Chūō Kōronsha, 1993), 260.

coexistence and coprosperity that transcended racial and national boundaries.[15] As such, he interpreted the long history of European settler colonialism in the Americas as a cosmopolitan saga about the creation of a bright future for all human beings and highlighted Japanese migration as one of its critical components. In this splendid narrative, Umesao conveniently edited out the presence of the indigenous peoples in the Americas, people who had lived in this "New World" long before the "Old World" came into being. Needless to say, their tragic experiences of being deprived of livelihood, properties, and ancestral lands were also absent from Umesao's narrative.

Migration as Settler Colonialism: Thinking with the Indigenous Perspective

Umesao Tadao's description of Japanese overseas migration as contributing to the creation of a cosmopolitan "New World" may find its unexpected counterpart in the field of Asian American studies in the United States. Scholarship in Asian American studies has made great achievements in highlighting the contributions Asian immigrants have made to US society and explaining how Asian immigration has turned the United States into a more culturally and ethnically diverse nation. Together these studies have directly challenged the anti-Asian racism that has undergirded institutionalized discrimination, exclusion, and violence toward Asian immigrant communities throughout American history. However, as Candace Fujikane observes from the perspective of Hawai'ian history, this Asian-immigrant-centered narrative runs the risk of sabotaging the continued struggles of the indigenous peoples of Hawai'i to reclaim their ancestral lands. Inadvertently or not, writing the history of Hawai'i as one that begins with its colonization and ends with the creation of a multicultural society serves to cover up settler colonial violence with a veil of democracy. It masks "the realities of a settler colony that continues to deny indigenous peoples their rights to their lands and resources."[16] As such, Patrick Wolfe cautions, contemporary "antiracist" scholarship in Asian American history may inadvertently further empower the structure of settler colonialism disguised by multiculturalism and democracy.[17]

The critique of the "antiracist" narrative in Asian American history from the perspective of indigenous peoples also reveals the blurriness in the conceptual boundaries between migration and settler colonialism. To be sure, the history of migration is a complicated one. Not all experiences of migration in the modern

[15] Umesao, "Nihonjin to Shinsekai," 13.
[16] Candace Fujikane, "Introduction: Asian Settler Colonialism in the U.S. Colony of Hawai'i," in Fujikane and Okamura, *Asian Settler Colonialism*, 3.
[17] Patrick Wolfe, ed., *The Settler Complex: Recuperating Binarism in Colonial Studies* (Los Angeles: UCLA American Indian Studies Center, 2016), 15.

time should be understood through the lens of colonialism. Migration itself by no means equates to colonialism either. Yet, writing in the context of the Hawai'ian history, Dean Itsuji Saranillio argues that by moving into a territory governed by a settler colonial state, the immigrants may bolster the existing power system. It is particularly so when immigrants seek empowerment by participating in the existing sociopolitical structure.[18] From a similar perspective, Shu-mei Shih has questioned the value of "diaspora" as an analytical framework to understand the history of Chinese migration to Southeast Asia. The term "diaspora," Shih argues, masks the colonial nature of Chinese settlements there in the past, as some Han Chinese migrants had established independent regimes in indigenous lands even before European colonizers arrived. Later on, many Han Chinese were also hired by European settlers to collect taxes and manage plantations. They played the role of what Shih describes as "middlemen settler colonialism."[19]

As this book has explained, Japanese Malthusian expansionists saw Japanese migrants in the United States, both laborers on the West Coast and rice farmers in Texas, as Japan's equivalents to the Anglo-American colonial settlers. From their perspective, Japanese immigrants' struggle for inclusion in the US citizenry was a crucial step for the Japanese to secure membership in the white men's club. Though this was eventually denied to them by the Immigration Act of 1924, between the late nineteenth century and early twentieth, thinkers and doers of Japanese migration to the United States had no intention of challenging the US settler colonial structure itself. Instead, they saw Japanese American immigration was an intrinsic part of the Japanese empire's participation in the colonial order in the Americas and other parts of the world.

Recent research on the history of Latin America poses another challenge to the discrepancy between the definitions of migration and settler colonialism. In the history of Anglophone settler nations, the taking of indigenous land typically began in the formative period of the settler states – that is, immediately after the landing of the colonial settlers. However, Spanish and Portuguese colonialism in the Americas first began by exploiting the native peoples' labor and wealth rather than dispossessing them of their lands. In southern Brazil, Argentina, and Uruguay, large-scale immigration and appropriation of indigenous land did not take place until the late nineteenth century and early twentieth, long after the independence of the settler states themselves. The conventional periodization in the history of Anglophone settler nations, that of a period of colonial settlers followed by a period of immigrants, is thus incompatible in the case of Latin America.[20]

---

[18] Saranillio, "Why Asian Settler Colonialism Matters," 287.
[19] Shih, "Theory, Asia and the Sinophone," 478.
[20] Michael Goebel, "Settler Colonialism in Postcolonial Latin America," in *The Routledge Handbook of the History of Settler Colonialism*, ed. Edward Cavanagh and Lorenzo Veracini (London: Routledge, 2017), 139–140, 147.

The growth of Japanese migration to Brazil in the early twentieth century, discussed in this book, was part of a large-scale immigration wave in the Southern Cone. Japanese agricultural settlement in Brazil, which grew substantially during the 1920s and 1930s, was both a part and a result of the Brazilian government's appropriation of indigenous land. Moreover, this book has further demonstrated the nexus between Japanese migration in Brazil and Japanese settler colonialism in Asia. The Japanese expansionists' promotion of farmer migration to the state of São Paulo was intellectually tied with various colonial migration initiatives to the Korean Peninsula, Southeast Asia, and the South Pacific. The community of Aliança, established by the Shinano Overseas Association in the 1920s, became a prototype for the imperial government's mass migration and settlement campaigns in colonial Manchuria during the 1930s.

Settler Colonialism as Migration: Malthusianism and Expansion

This study has presented an account of Japanese expansion that transcends the territorial and temporal boundaries of the Japanese empire, arguing that we cannot fully grasp the history of Japanese expansion in Asia without an understanding of Japanese migration outside of the empire and vice versa. More importantly, it has taken a migration-centered approach in the study of settler colonialism. Instead of exploring the power structure inside the settler colonial space, it has focused on the process of settler migration itself, with both the sending and receiving ends of the migration in consideration. In particular, this book has demonstrated the close link between Malthusianism and settler colonial expansion. It has located Malthusian expansionism at the intellectual core of Japan's migration-driven expansion across the Pacific. This discourse endorsed colonial demands for additional land by both encouraging overpopulation anxiety and stressing the need for population growth. It rationalized emigration both as a panacea for social ills supposedly resulting from overpopulation and as a way of pursuing wealth and power abroad.

The ideas and practices of Japan's ideologues, social reformers, and settler community leaders, the protagonists of this book, should never be conflated with the voices and experiences of the individual Japanese emigrants themselves. Most of the men and women who left the archipelago had lived on the margins of society; emigration was usually their last option to escape destitution. Though Tokyo often hailed them as vanguards of the expanding empire, the emigrants did not automatically share these visions. Those who settled beyond the empire's sphere of influence often fell prey to institutionalized racism, violence, and exclusion. The history of Japanese migration to the United States, for example, contains ample evidence of such tragedies, including the wartime internment of over 110,000 innocent people of Japanese ancestry.

The empire builders of modern Japan did not invent Malthusian expansionism. Instead, this set of ideas was created by British expansionists during the seventeenth and eighteenth centuries to justify the colonial settlers' appropriation of aboriginal lands in North America. In fact, the emergence of Malthusian expansionism, a powerful discourse that legitimized the acquisition of foreign lands in the language of reason and progress, marked the birth of modern settler colonialism itself. While it was first exemplified by British settler colonialism in North America and then by US westward expansion, Malthusian expansionism was later also adopted by other modern empires to justify their own expansion in the nineteenth and twentieth centuries. The chorus of Axis powers' demands for "living space" in the early twentieth century was by no means an anomaly in the civilized world. Their intellectual roots can be traced back to the genesis of the modern world itself, when imperial nations in Europe redrew the world map through the lens of Enlightenment.

Bibliography

Abbreviations

AIFC	Association for International Collaboration of Farmers
FYZ	*Fukuzawa Yukichi Zenshū*
GHQ	General Headquarters of the Allied Occupation of Japan
HKZ	*Hokkaido Kaitaku Zasshi*
JATAKA	National Federation of Agricultural Migration Cooperative Associations
JICA	Japan International Cooperation Agency
Kaikō	Kaigai Kōgyō Kabushiki Gaisha
MAF	Ministry of Agriculture and Forestry
SCAP	Supreme Commander for the Allied Powers
Tannō	Nōgyō Rōmusha Habei Jigyō

Archives and Collections

Center for Modern Japanese Legal and Political Documents, University of Tokyo (Japan)

Collection of Overseas Migration, Wakayama Civic Library (Japan)

Collection for Social Issues Related to Christianity, Institute for Study of Humanities and Social Sciences, Doshisha University (Japan)

Diplomatic Archives of the Ministry of Foreign Affairs of Japan

Hoji Shinbun Digital Collection, Hoover Institution Library and Archives, Stanford University (United States)

Ichioka (Yuji) Papers, Library Special Collections, University of California, Los Angeles (United States)

Japan Center for Asian Historical Record, National Archives of Japan

Japanese Overseas Migration Museum (Japan)

Kajiyama Collection, University of Hawai'i at Mānoa Libraries (United States)

Museu Histórico da Imigração Japonesa no Brasil, São Paulo (Brazil)

Nagano Prefecture Museum of History (Japan)

Nagano Prefectural Library, Collection of Native Materials (Japan)

Nippon Rikkō Kai (Japan)

Published Government Documents

Gaimu Daijin Kanbō Iminka, *Mekishikokoku Taiheiyo Engan Shoshūn Jūnkai Hōkoku.* Tokyo: Gaimu Daijin Kanbō Imin Ka, 1891.

Gaimusho Gaikō Shiryōkan. *Hokubei Gasshūkoku Oyobi Kanada Nōgyō Kumiaiin Tokō Shutsugan Zakken* (1906). Microfilm. Tokyo: Japan Microfilm Service Center, 1967.

Gaimushō Ryōji Ijūbu. *Wa Ga Kokumin no Kaigai Hatten: Ijū Hyakunen no Ayumi – Shiryōhen.* Tokyo: Gaimushō Ryōji Ijūbu, 1972.

Kōseishō, Jinkō Minzokubu. *Yamato Minzoku o Chūkaku to Suru Sekai Seisaku no Kentō.* No. 1. In *Minzoku Jinkō Seisaku Kenkyū Shiryō: Senjika ni Okeru Kōseishō Kenkyūbu Jinkō Minzokubu Shiryō,* vol. 3. Reprint, Tokyo: Bunsei Shoin, 1982.

Yamato Minzoku o Chūkaku to Suru Sekai Seisaku no Kentō. No. 3 In *Minzoku Jinkō Seisaku Kenkyū Shiryō: Senjika ni Okeru Kōseishō Kenkyūbu Jinkō Minzokubu Shiryō,* vol. 5. Reprint, Tokyo: Bunsei Shoin, 1982.

Yamato Minzoku o Chūkaku to Suru Sekai Seisaku no Kentō. No. 6. In *Minzoku Jinkō Seisaku Kenkyū Shiryō: Senjika ni Okeru Kōseishō Kenkyūbu Jinkō Minzokubu Shiryō,* vol. 8. Reprint, Tokyo: Bunsei Shoin, 1982.

Jinkō Shokuryō Mondai Chōsakai. *Jinkō Mondai ni Kansuru Yoron.* Tokyo: Jinkō Shokuryō Mondai Chōsa Kai, 1928.

"Kaigai Fujin Kyōkai Kankei." No. 9. *Honpō Shakai Jigyō Kankei Zakken.* Archive of Japanese Foreign Ministry. Retrieved from Japan Center Asian Historical Records, National Archives of Japan (Reference code: B04013226500).

Kaigai Ijū Shiryōkan, *Kaigai Ijū Shiryōkan Tenji Annai: Warera Shinsekai ni Sankasu.* Yokohama: Dokuritsu Gyōsei Hōjin Kokusai Kyōryoku Kikō Yokohama Sentā, 2004.

Nagano Ken Kaitaku Jikōkai Manshū Kaitakushi Kankōkai. *Nagano Ken Manshū Kaitaku Shi: Sōhen.* Nagano-shi: Nagano Ken Kaitaku Jikōkai Manshū Kaitakushi Kankō Kai, 1984.

"Nōgyō Kumiai Beikoku Ijū Mōshikomi no Ken." In Gaimusho Gaikō Shiryōkan. *Hokubei Gasshūkoku Oyobi Kanada Nōgyō Kumiaiin Toko Shutsugun Zakken* (1906). Microfilm. Tokyo: Japan Microfilm Service Center, 1967.

Ōkurashō Kanrikyoku. *Nihonjin no Kaigai Katsudō ni Kansuru Rekishi Teki Chōsa.* Vol. 1, *Sōron,* edited by Kobayashi Hideo. Tokyo: Yumani Shobō, 2002.

Rinji Kokusei Chōsa Kyoku. *Kokusei Chōsa Senden Kayōkyoku.* Tokyo: Tokyo Insatsu Kabushiki Gaisha, 1920.

Historical Periodicals and Newspapers

Ajia　亜細亜
Amerika　亜米利加
Asahi Shinbun　朝日新聞
Burajiru: Ishokumin to Bōeki　ブラジル　移植民と貿易
Chigaku Zasshi　地学雑誌
Chūō Kōron　中央公論
Eigyō Hōkokusho　営業報告書 (東洋拓殖株式会社)
Ensei　遠征

Gaikō Jihō (Revue Diplomatique) 外交雑誌
Hokkaido Kaitaku Zasshi 北海道開拓雑誌
Ie no Hikari 家の光
Jiji Shinpō 時事新報
Jiyūtō Hō 自由党報
Joshi Seinen Kai 女子青年会
Kōchi Shokumin Kyōkai Hōkoku 高知殖民協会報告
Kokumin Keizai Zasshi 国民経済雑誌
Kokumin no Tomo 国民の友
Kyūsei (The Salvation) 救世
Mainichi Shinbun 毎日新聞
New York Times
Nihon Imin Kyōkai Hōkoku 日本移民協会報告
Nihonjin 日本人
Rikkō 力行
Rikkō Sekai 力行世界
Rōdō Sekai (Labor World) 労働世界
Sekai no Nihon 世界の日本
Shakai Shugi (Socialist) 社会主義
Shokumin (Colonial Review) 植民
Shokumin Kyōkai Hōkokusho 殖民協会報告書
Shōnen Sekai 少年世界
Taiyō 太陽
Tobei Shinpō 渡米新報
Tobei Zasshi 渡米雑誌
Tokyo Keizai Zasshi 東京経済雑誌
Tōyō 東洋
Tōyō Keizai Shinpō 東洋経済新報
Umi no Soto 海の外
Yūben 雄弁

Primary Sources

Abe Isoo. "Byō Teki Shakai." *Shakai Shugi* 7, no. 8 (March 18, 1903): 4.
  Hokubei no Shin Nihon. Tokyo: Hakubunkan, 1905.
  "Imin to Kyōiku." *Yūben* 3, no. 8 (1912): 37–47.
  Sanji Seigen Ron. Tokyo: Jitsugyō no Nihon Sha, 1922.
  "Seinen no Tameni Kaigai Tokō no To o Hiraku Beshi." *Shakai Shugi* 8, no. 4 (February 18, 1904): 4–7.
Abiko Yonako. "Zaibei Nihonjin Kirisutokyō Joshi Seinen Kai Sōritsu no Shidai." *Joshi Seinen Kai* 9, no. 9 (October 1912): 17–18.
Akamine Se'ichirō. *Beikoku Ima Fushigi*. Tokyo: Jitsugakkai Eigakkō, 1886.
  Ajia, no. 36 (February 28, 1894): 679–680.
Aoyagi Ikutarō. *Perū Jijō*. Tokyo: Aoyagi Ikutarō, 1894.
Arai Nobuo. "Shokumin to Kyōiku." *Shokumin* 3, no. 3 (March 1924): 84.
  "Asano." *HKZ*, no. 2 (February 14, 1880): 9.

"Budō Saibai no Rieki." *HKZ*, no. 5 (March 27, 1880): 97.

"Burajiru ni Okeru Hōjin Nisei no Rison Mondai." *Umi no Soto*, postwar, no. 17 (October 1952): 1.

Capron, Horace M. *Memoirs of Horace Capron*—Vols. 1 and 2: *Autobiography*. Special Collections, National Agricultural Library, 1884.

Condliffe, J. B. "The Pressure of Population in the Far East." *Economic Journal* 42, no. 166 (1932): 196–210.

Crocker, W. R. *The Japanese Population Problem: The Coming Crisis*. London: George Allen & Unwin, 1931.

Davenport, Charles B. *Jinshu Kairyō Gaku*. Translated by Yoshimura Daijirō. Tokyo: Dainihon Bunmei Kyōkai, 1914.

"Dominika Ijū no Kyōkun." *Mainichi Shinbun*, April 12, 1962.

Franklin, Benjamin. *Observations concerning the Increase of Mankind and the Peopling of Countries*. Boston: S. Kneeland, 1755.

Fukui Jūnko. "Kaidai." *Sekai no Nihon* 1. Reprint, Tokyo: Kashiwa Shobō, 1992.

Fukuoka Teru. *Kigyō Risshi no Kinmon: Ichimei Beikōsha Hikkei*. Tokyo: Nisshindō, 1887.

Fukuzawa Yukichi. "Beikoku wa Shishi no Seisho Nari." In *Fukuzawa Yukichi Zenshū*, vol. 9, 442–444. Tokyo: Iwanami Shoten, 1960.

"Danji Kokorozashi o Tatete, Kyōkan o Izu Beshi." In *Fukuzawa Yukichi Zenshū*, vol. 9, 457. Tokyo: Iwanami Shoten, 1960.

"Datsua Ron." In *Fukuzawa Yukichi Chosakushū*, vol. 8. Tokyo: Keio Gijuku Daigaku Shuppankai, 2003.

"Fuki Kōmyo wa Oya Yuzuri no Kuni ni Kagirazu." In *Fukuzawa Yukichi Zenshū*, vol. 9, 546. Tokyo: Iwanami Shoten, 1960.

"Hinkō Ron." In *Fukuzawa Yukichi Zenshū*, vol. 5, 545–578. Tokyo: Iwanami Shoten, 1970.

"Ijū Ron no Ben." In *Fukuzawa Yukichi Zenshū*, vol. 9, 458–460. Tokyo: Iwanami Shoten, 1960.

"Jinkō no Hanshoku." In *Fukuzawa Yukichi Zenshū*, vol. 15, 347–350. Tokyo: Iwanami Shoten, 1961.

"Jinmin no Ishoku." In *Fukuzawa Yukichi Zenshū*, vol. 15, 350–352. Tokyo: Iwanami Shoten, 1961.

"Jinmin no Ishoku to Shōfu no Dekasegi." In *Fukuzawa Yukichi Zenshū*, vol. 15, 362–363. Tokyo: Iwanami Shoten, 1961.

"Nihon Fujin Ron." In *Fukuzawa Yukichi Zenshū*, vol. 15, 448–466. Tokyo: Iwanami Shoten, 1961.

"Taiwan Eien no Hōshin." In *Fukuzawa Yukichi Zenshū*, vol. 15, 265–266. Tokyo: Iwanami Shoten, 1961.

"Hainichi Dai Nana Shūnen o Mukau." *Gaikō Jihō* 55, no. 614 (1930): 11–44.

"Hainichi Imin Hō Dai Hachi Shūnen o Mukau." *Gaikō jihō* 59, no. 638 (1931): 24–45.

"Hainichi Imin Hō Dai Jūgo Shūnen o Tomurau." *Gaikō Jihō* 87 (1938): 75–83.

"Hainichi Imin Hō Dai Jūni Shūnen." *Gaikō Jihō* 75 (1935): 44–56.

"Hainichi Imin Hō Dai Jūroku Shūnen o Tomurau." *Gaikō Jihō* 91 (1939): 80–89.

"Hainichi Imin Hō Dai Jūsan Shūnen o Tomurau." *Gaikō Jihō* 79 (1936): 79–90.

Hamata Kenjirō. "Shokumin Ron." *Tokyo Keizai Zasshi*, no. 600 (1891): 793–794.

"Harukani Gaimudaijin Enomoto Takeaki ni Agaru no Sho." *Ensei*, no. 13 (July 1892): 14.

Hasegawa Yūichi. "1920 Nendai Nihon no Imin Ron (3)." *Gaikō Jihō*, no. 1297 (June 1991): 94–102.

Hattori Tōru. *Nan'yō Saku*. Tokyo: Sanshōdō Shoten, 1891.

Hayashi Shigeatsu. *Kokusei Chōsa ni Tsuite: Kokumin Hitsudoku*. Tokyo: Ginkōdō, 1920.

Hiraoka Hikotarō. *Nihon Nōhon Ron*. Tokyo: Yasui Ukichi, 1902.

Hirayama Katsukuma, ed. *Kaigai Fugen Sōsho*. Tokyo: Ryūbunkan, 1905.

Historical Museum of Hokkaido. *Museum Survey and Guide*. Sapporo: Historical Museum of Hokkaido, 2014.

"Hokkaido wa Kosan no Chi Naru Setsu." *Hokkaido Kaitaku Zasshi*, no. 17 (September 11, 1880): 387.

Hon'iden Yoshio. "Nōson to Kyōdō." *Ie no Hikari* 3, no. 1 (January 1927): 10–13.

"Ijū Undō kara Tori Nokosaru Musume Tachi Yō, Ijū Seyō." *Rikkō Sekai*, no. 662 (May 1960): 4.

"Imin Chūshin no Jinkō Mondai." *Rikkō Sekai*, no. 628 (July 1957): 5.

"Imin no Kyūmu Tankenka no Ketsubō." *Ensei*, no. 32 (October 1893): 2–6.

Inahara Katsuji. "Hainichi Dai Yon Shūnen o Mukau." *Gaikō Jihō* 46, no. 542 (1927): 1–18.

Ino Masayoshi. *Kyojin Saibara Seitō*. Tosa-shi: Saibara Seitō Sensei Shōtokuhi Kensetsu Kiseikai, 1964.

Inoue Hikosaburō. *Suzuki Keikun and Taguchi Ukichi, Nantō Junkōki*. Tokyo: Keizai Zasshisha, 1893.

Inoue Kakugorō Sensei Denki Hensankai. *Inoue Kakugorō Sensei Den*. Tokyo: Inoue Kakugorō Sensei Denki Hensankai, 1943.

Iriye Toraji. *Hōjin Kaigai Hatten Shi*. Vols. 1 and 2. Tokyo: Ida shoten, 1942.

Ishida Kumataro and Shūyū Sanjin. *Kitare Nihonjin: Ichimei Sōkō Tabi Annai*. Tokyo: Kaishindō, 1886.

Ishiguro Tadaatsu. "Shintōa Kensetsu to Wa Ga Nōgyō." In *Tōa Kensetsu to Nōgyō*, edited by Asahi Shinbunsha, 72–74. Tokyo: Tokyo Asahi Shinbunsha, 1939.

Itagaki Morimasa, ed. *Itagaki Taisuke Zenshū*. Tokyo: Hara Shobō, 1980.

Itagaki Taisuke. "Shokumin Ron." *Jiyūdō Hō*, no. 10 (April 28, 1892).

Izumi Sei'ichi and Saitō Hiroshi. *Amazon: So no Fūdo to Nihonjin*. Tokyo: Kokin Shoin, 1954.

"Japan's Invasion of the White Man's World." *New York Times*, September 22, 1907, 4.

"Josei Mo Nisennin Hoshii: Kanbojia e no Imin." *Asahi Shinbun*, March 5, 1956, 7.

"Jyagatara Imo no Rieki." *Hokkaido Kaitaku Zasshi*, no. 3 (February 28, 1880): 56.

Kaigai Kōgyō Kabushiki Gaisha. *Kaigai Hatten ni Kansuru Katsuta Ōkura Daijin Kōen*. Tokyo: Kaigai Kōgyō Kabushiki Gaisha, 1918.

"Kaigai no Shin Kokyō." *Jiji Shinpō*, February 3, 1896.

"Kaitaku no Shisatsu." *Hokkaido Kaitaku Zasshi*, no. 2 (February 14, 1880): 1–4.

"Kaitaku Zasshi Hakkō no Shushi." *Hokkaido Kaitaku Zasshi*, no. 1 (January 31, 1880): 2–3.

Kanbe Masao. *Chōsen Nōgyō Imin Ron*. Tokyo: Yūhikaku Shobō, 1910.

"Kanbojia Imin: Raishun Sōsōni Chōsadan Mazu Hitsuyōna Shikin no Enjo." *Asahi Shinbun*, December 19, 1955, 7.

Katayama Sen. "Seinen Joshi no Tobei." *Shakai Shugi* 8, no. 1 (January 3, 1904): 17–19.

"Tekisasu Beisaku to Nihonjin (1)." *Tōyō Keizai Shinpō*, no. 305 (May 1904): 25.

Tobei Annai. Tokyo: Rōdō Shinbunsha, 1902. Reprinted in *Shoki Zai Hokubei Nihonjin no Kiroku, Hokubeihen,* vol. 44, 2–6, edited by Okuizumi Eizaburō. Tokyo: Bunsei Shoin, 2006.

Tsuzuki Tobei Annai. Tokyo: Tobei Kyōkai, 1902. Reprinted in *Shoki Zai Hokubei Nihonjin no Kiroku, Hokubeihen,* vol. 44, 1–4, edited by Okuizumi Eizaburō. Tokyo: Bunsei Shoin, 2006.

Katō Kanji. "Manshū Imin wa Naze Daimondai Ka." In *Tōa Kensetsu to Nōgyō*, edited by Asahi Shinbunsha, 49–50. Tokyo: Tokyo Asahi Shinbunsha, 1939.

"Nihon Nōson Kyōiku." In *Katō Kanji Zenshū*, vol. 1. Uchihara-machi, Ibaraki-ken: Katō Kanji Zenshū Kankōkai, 1967.

"Nōson Mondai no Kanken." In *Chihō Kairyō Kōenshū*, vol. 8, edited by Tokyo Chihō Kairyō Kyōkai, 229–232. Tokyo: Tokyo Chihō Kairyō Kyōkai, 1927.

Katō Tokijirō. "Kokumin no Hatten." *Shakai Shugi* 8, no. 9 (July 3, 1904): 248–249.

Katsuyama Kōzō. *Nihon Kaifu: Hokkaido Shokumin Saku*. Tokyo: Dainihon Shokuminkai, 1891.

Kawada Shirō. *Shokuminchi Toshite no Burajiru*. Tokyo: Yūhikaku Shobō, 1914.

Kawai Michiko. "Tobei Fujin wa Seikō Shitsutsu Ari Ya?" *Joshi Seinen Kai* 13, no. 10 (October 1916): 11.

Kawamura Toyomi. "Naisen Yūwa no Zentei Toshite Hōyoku Naru Hokusen o Kaitaku Seyo." *Shokumin* 5, no. 2 (February 1926): 45.

"Kazoku Shokun Shikiri ni Hokkaido no Chi o Aganau." *Hokkaido Kaitaku Zasshi*, no. 8 (May 8, 1880): 170–171.

Kikkawa Hidezō. *Shizoku Jusan no Kenkyū*. Tokyo: Yūhikaku, 1935.

Kita Ikki. *Nihon Kaizō Hōan Taikō*. Tokyo: Nishida Mitsugi, 1928.

"Kokumin no Katsuro." *Rōdō Sekai* 6, no. 16 (September 23, 1902): 16.

Konishi Naojirō, ed. *Hawai Koku Fūdo Ryakuki: Fu Ijūmin no Kokoroe*. Tokyo: Eishōdō, 1884.

Kotoku Shūsui. *Teikoku Shugi*. Tokyo: Iwanami Bunko, 1901.

Kōyama Rokurō, ed. Imin Yonjūnen Shi. São Paulo: Kōyama Rokurō, 1949.

Kudō Heisuke. *Akaezo Fūsetsukō: Hokkaido Kaitaku Hishi*. Translated by Inoue Takaaki. Tokyo: Kyōikusha, 1979.

Kuroda Ken'ichi. *Nihon Shokumin Shisōshi*. Tokyo: Kōbundō Shobō, 1942.

Kurose Hiroshi. "Kyōzon Kyōei ni Susume." *Burajiru: Ishokumin to Bōeki* 6, no. 5 (May 1932): 2.

Kusunoki Rokuichi. "Beikoku Kashū Engan no Dōhō." *Joshi Seinen Kai* 11, no. 7 (July 1914): 8.

"Kyō no Mondai." *Asahi Shinbun*, August 2, 1961.

"Kyūseigun o Ronzu." *Kyūsei* 1, no. 5 (July 1895): 1–11.

Lenin, V. I. *Imperialism, the Highest Stage of Capitalism*. Chippendale: Resistance Books, 1999.

Malthus, Thomas. *An Essay on the Principle of Population*. London: J. Johnson, 1789.

Matsudaira Masanao. "Hokubei Gasshūkoku Tekisasushu Beisaku Shisatsu Dan." *Chigaku Zasshi* 17, no. 8 (1905): 534.

Mori Kiyondo. *Matsuoka Yōsuke o Kataru*. Tokyo: Tōhō Bunka Gakkai, 1936.

"Moto Joyū no Yamaguchi Yoshiko San 1950 Sengo Bei Kōen no Ōngen wo Kakunin." *Hokugoku Shinbun*, August 18, 2012, 1.

Mutō Sanji. *Beikoku Ijū Ron*. Tokyo: Maruzen, 1887.

Nagai Tōru. *Nihon Jinkō Ron*. Tokyo: Ganshōdō, 1929.

Nagasawa Setsu (Betten). "Hawai'i Iyoiyo Isogi Nari." *Ajia* 2, no. 11 (1893): 291–295.

"Raisei no Nihon to Sanbei Kantsū Daitetsudō." *Nihonjin*, no. 2 (October 20, 1893): 113–114.

Yankii. Tokyo: Keigyōsha, 1893.

Nagata Saburō. "Shokumin Oyobi Shokumichi no Jigi." *Kokumin Keizai Zasshi* 43, no. 2 (August 1927): 123–127.

Nagata Shigeshi. "Ajia Tairiku e no Shinshutsu." *Rikkō Sekai*, no. 286 (October 1928): 4.

Burajiru ni Okeru Nihonjin Hattenshi. Vol. 2. Tokyo: Burajiru ni Okeru Nihonjin Hattenshi Kenkōkai, 1953.

"Hakkoku Nōgyō no Shūyakuka." *Rikkō Sekai*, no. 665 (August 1960): 1.

"'Hito o Tsukure' kara 'Haha o Tsukure e.'" *Rikkō Sekai*, no. 677 (August 1961): 1.

"Imin Saiaku no Sai." *Rikkō Sekai*, no. 684 (March 1962): 1.

Kaigai Hatten to Wa Ga Kuni no Kyōiku. Tokyo: Dōbunkan, 1917.

Kankō Imin to Min'ei Ijū: Keikaku Imin to Yobiyose Ijū. Tokyo: Nippon Rikkō Kai, 1954.

"Manshū no Shinano Mura (1)." *Rikkō Sekai*, no. 347 (November 1933): 21.

Nōson Jinkō Mondai to Ishokumin. Tokyo: Nihon Hyōronsha, 1933.

"Sangyō Kumiai no Kaigai Enchō." *Rikkō Sekai*, no. 232 (April 1924): 3.

Shinano Kaigai Ijūshi. Nagano: Shinano Kaigai Kyōryokukai, 1952.

"Zahaku Dōhō no Shinro." *Rikkō Sekai*, no. 563 (February 1952): 1.

Naitō Hideo. "Kaigai no Seikō to Wa?!" *Shokumin* 7, no. 6 (June 1928): 1.

Nanba Katsuji. *Nanbei Fugen Taikan*. Dairen: Ōsakaya-gō Shoten, 1923.

"Nanshin ya? Hokushin ya?" *Taiyō* 19, no. 15 (November 1913).

Nasu Shiroshi. *Jinkō Shokuryō Mondai*. Tokyo: Nihon Hyōronsha, 1927.

Nihon Gaimushō Kokusai Kyōryoku Jigyōdan. *Kaigai Ijū no Igi o Motomete: Burajiru Ijū 70-Shūnen Kinen: Nihonjin no Kaigai Ijū ni Kansuru Shinpojumu*. Tokyo: Nihon Gaimushō, 1979.

"Nihon Imin Kyōkai Setsuritsu Shushi." *Imin Kyōkai Hōkokusho* 1, no. 1 (October 1914): 3. Reprint, Tokyo: Fuji shuppan, 2006.

Nihon Kaigai Kyōkai Rengōkai. *Nihon to Ijū: Naze Ijū wa Sokushinsareneba Naranaika*. Tokyo: Nihon Kaigai Kyōkai Rengōkai, 1957.

"Nihon Kokumin no Shinshūkyō." *Kokumin no Tomo*, no. 201 (September 13, 1893): 1.

"Nihon Minzoku Nioku Gosenman ni." *Rikkō Sekai*, no. 694 (January 1963): 6.

"Nihon Minzoku no Bōchō." *Taiyō* 16, no. 15 (November 1910).

Nishiuchi Yōsan. "Shokumin Jigyō to Kokka Keizai no Kankei." *Kōchi Shokumin Kyōkai Hōkoku*, no. 1 (October 1893): 3–4.

Nitobe Inazō. *The Imperial Agricultural College of Sapporo*. Sapporo: Imperial Agricultural College, 1893.

Nitobe Hakushi Shokumin Seisaku Kōgi Oyobi Ronbunshū. Edited by Yanaihara Tadao. Tokyo: Iwanami Shoten, 1943.

Nōgyō Honron. 6th ed. Tokyo: Shōkabō, 1905.

Noboru Momotari. *Waga Chishima*. Tokyo: Gojōrō, 1892.

"Nōgu Kairyō Ron." *Hokkaido Kaitaku Zasshi*, no. 3 (February 28, 1880): 59.

Nōgyō Takushoku Kyōkai. *Sengo Kaigai Nōgyō Ijū no Shokan to Kikō*. Vol. 1. Tokyo: Nōgyō Takushoku Kyōkai, 1966.

Ogawa Heikichi. "Kaigai Ijūsha no Shitō." *Umi no Soto* 1, no. 1 (1922): 9–11.

Okada Tadahiko. "Nagano Kenjin no Kaigai Hatten." *Umi no Soto* 1, no. 1 (1922): 1–4.

Ōkawadaira Takamitsu. *Nihon Imin Ron*. Tokyo: Jōbudō, 1905.

Ōkuma Shigenobu. "Sekai no Daikyoku to Imin." *Imin Kyōkai Hōkokusho* 1, no. 2 (August 1915): 6–8. Reprint, Tokyo: Fuji Shuppan, 2006.

Ōkurashō Kanrikyoku. *Nihonjin no Kaigai Katsudō ni Kansuru Rekishi Teki Chōsa*. Vol. 1, *Sōron*. Edited by Kobayashi Hideo. Tokyo: Yumani Shobō, 2002.

Ōta Masataka. "Semai Kokudo ni Nana Sen Man Nin." *Asahi Shinbun*, August 21, 1945, 2.

Ōyama Ujirō. "Hainichi Imin Hō Dai Kyū Shūnen." *Gaikō Jihō* 63 (1932): 1–13.

Ozaki Yukio. "Beikoku Zakkan." In *Ozaki Gakudō Zenshū*, vol. 3, 343–354. Tokyo: Kōronsha 1955–1956.

Pearl, Raymond. *The Biology of Population Growth*. New York: Knopf, 1925.

"Raisei no shinajin narabini sono riyō (1)." *Ensei*, no. 14 (July 1892): 1–4.

"Raisei no shinajin narabini sono riyō (2)." *Ensei*, no. 16 (August 1892): 192–193.

"Rikkō Hyōron." *Kyūsei* 6, no. 87 (January 1, 1907): 1.

"Rikkō Jogakkō Sanjoin Boshū." *Kyūsei* 5, no. 81 (November 1909): 1.

"Rōdōsha no Koe." *Kokumin no Tomo*, no. 95 (September 23, 1890): 9.

"Sake no Setsu." *Hokkaido Kaitaku Zasshi*, no. 10 (June 5, 1880): 241.

Sakiyama Hisae. "Shoku to Iu Ji o Kokoro Toshite." *Shokumin* 7, no. 2 (February 1928): 69–70.

"Seinen Gakumon no Keikō." *Kokumin no Tomo*, no. 304 (August 21, 1896): 1–2.

"Sekai no Nihon Ya, Ajia no Nihon Ya." *Kokumin no Tomo*, no. 250 (April 13, 1895): 1–4.

"Sekishin Shain no Funhatsu (1)." *HKZ*, no. 6 (April 10, 1880): 122–123.

"Sekishin Shain no Funhatsu (2)." *HKZ*, no. 7 (April 24, 1880): 147.

Seya Shōji. *Hawai*. Tokyo: Chūaisha Shoten, 1892.

Shibue Tamotsu. *Beikokushi*. Vol. 1. Tokyo: Manganro, 1872.

Shiga Shigetaka. *Nan'yō Jiji*. Tokyo: Maruzen Shōsha Shoten, 1891.

"Shijō Mizōu no Kaigai Shokumin Daikai Tokushū no Ki." *Shokumin* 9, no. 3 (March 1930): 4.

Shimanuki Hyōdayū. *Rikkō Kai to wa Nan Zo Ya*. Tokyo: Keiseisha, 1911.

"Shokan Nisoku." *Kyūsei* 6, no. 92 (1910): 6.

Shimizu Ichitarō. *Nihon Shin Fugen: Ichibei Hokkaido Jimu*. Tokyo: Kinkōdō, 1890.

"Shin Kichōsha no Danwa." *Rikkō* 2, no. 6 (May 25, 1904): 2.

Shinobu Jūnhei. *Komura Jutarō*. Tokyo: Shinchōsha, 1932.

"Shokumin Kyōkai Setsuritsu Shoisho." *Shokumin Kyōkai Hōkokusho*, no. 1 (April 1893): 105–107.

"Shokuminchi ni Taisuru Honkai no Iken." *Ensei*, no. 5 (September 1891): 1–3.

Soeda Jū'ichi. "Daisensō to Imin Mondai." *Nihon Imin Kyōkai Hōkoku* 1, no. 6 (February 1916): 6–7. Reprint, Tokyo: Fuji Shuppan, 2006.

"Kojin no Kansei." *Nihon Imin Kyōkai Hōkoku* 1, no. 8 (April 1916): 4. Reprint, Tokyo: Fuji Shuppan, 2006.

Suehiro Shigeo. *Hokubei no Nihonjin*. Tokyo: Nishōdō Shoten, 1915.

Sugi Kōji. *Sugi Sensei Kōen Shū.* Tokyo: Chūaisha, 1902.

Sugino Tadao. *Kaigai Takushoku Hishi: Aru Kaitaku Undōsha no Shuki.* Tokyo: Bunkyō Shoin, 1959.

Sugiura Jūkō. *Hankai Yume Monogatari: Ichimei Shinheimin Kaitendan.* Tokyo: Sawaya, 1886.

Taga Muneyuki. *Hokkaido Tondenhei to Manshū.* Tokyo: Teikoku Zaikō Gunjinkai Honbu, 1932.

Taguchi Ukichi. "Hokkaido Kaitaku Ron." *Tokyo Keizai Zasshi*, no. 77 (1881): 669.

"Nan'yō Keiryaku Ron." *Tokyo Keizai Zasshi*, no. 513 (1890): 352–353.

Nihon Keizai Ron. Tokyo: Keizai Zasshisha, 1878.

"Wakare ni Nozomi Ichū o Arawasu." *Tokyo Keizai Zasshi*, no. 521 (1890): 631–632.

Takakura Shin'ichirō. *Ainu Seisaku Shi.* Tokyo: Nihon Hyōronsha, 1942.

"Takamaru Imin Netsu: Burajiru e Tokyo Mura mo." *Asahi Shinbun*, June 4, 1958, 10.

Takata Yasuma. *Jinkō to Binbō.* Tokyo: Nihon Hyōronsha, 1927.

Takekoshi Yosaburō. "Nanpō no Keiei to Nihon no Shimei." *Taiyō* 16, no. 15 (1910): 20.

Takezawa Taichi, Fukuda Kenshirō, and Nakamura Masamichi. *Mekishiko Tanken Jikki.* Tokyo: Hakubunkan, 1893.

Tazaki Masayoshi. "Yukizumareru Wa Ga Kuni no Jinkō Mondai." *Tōyō*, February 1924, 46.

Thompson, Warren S. *Danger Spots in World Population.* New York: Knopf, 1929.

"Tobe no Kōjiki." *Shakai Shugi* 7, no. 12 (May 18, 1903): 23–24.

Tōgō Minoru. *Nihon Shokumin Ron.* Tokyo: Bunbudō, 1906.

Tōkai Etsurō. *Mekishikokoku Kinkyō Ippan: Fu Nihon Fukoku Saku.* 1889.

Tokutomi Iichirō (Sōhō). *Dai Nihon Bōchō Ron.* Tokyo: Min'yūsha, 1894.

"Nihon Jinshu no Shin Kokyō." *Kokumin no Tomo* 6, no. 85 (June 13, 1890): 829–838.

"Shin Nihon no Seinen." In *Tokutomo Sōhō Shū*, edited by Uete Michiari, 118–119. Tokyo: Chikuma Shobō, 1974.

Shōrai no Nihon. Tokyo: Keizai Zasshisha, 1886.

Torii Akita. "Ijū Ron." *Tokyo Keizai Zasshi*, no. 514 (1890): 397–400.

Toyama Yoshifumi. *Nihon to Hawai: Kakumei Zengo no Hawai.* Tokyo: Hakubunkan, 1893.

"Tōyō Dendō Kaishi no Issaku." *Kyūsei*, no. 1 (March 1895): 2.

Tōyō Takushoku Kabushiki Gaisha. *Eigyō Hōkokusho*, no. 15 (1923).

Tsuda Sen. "Nihon Teikoku no Uchi ni Amerika Gasshūkoku wo Genshutsu Suru wa Atarasa ni Tōki ni Arazaru Beshi." *Hokkaido Kaitaku Zasshi*, no. 3 (February 28, 1880): 50–51.

Tsuneya Seifuku. *Kaigai Shokumin Ron.* Tokyo: Hakubunsha, 1891.

Tsuzaki Naotake. "Nihon no Genjō to Kaigai Hatten." *Rikkō Sekai*, no. 300 (December 1929): 9.

Turner, Frederick Jackson. *The Frontier in American History.* New York: Henry Holt, 1920.

Umesao Tadao. "Nihonjin to Shinsekai." *JICA Yokohama Kaigai Ijū Shiryōkan Kenkyū Kiyō*, no. 1 (2006): 1–4.

"Shin Sekai e no Sanka: Nikei Imin Shūdan no Sekaishi Teki Imi." *Kasumigaseki Fōramu*, no. 1 (June 1977). Reprinted in Umesao Tadao, *Umesao Tadao Chosakushū*, vol. 20, 253–264. Tokyo: Chūō Kōronsha, 1993.

Umetani Mitsusada. "Burajiru Ijūchi Jijō." *Rikkō Sekai*, no. 288 (December 1928): 11.
Wakayama Norikazu. *Wakayama Norikazu Zenshū*. Vol. 1. Tokyo: Tōyō Keizai Shinpōsha, 1940.
"Yamaguchi Yoshiko San Bei Kōen no Ongen." *Shinano Mainichi Shinbun*, August 18, 2012.
Yamamoto Jōtarō. "Manmō no Hatten to Mantetsu no Jigyō." *Seiyū*, no. 330 (1928): 13–17.
Yamashita Keitarō. *Kanata Fugen*. Tokyo: Maruzen Shōsha, 1893.
Yamashita Sōen, ed. *Hōshuku Kigen Nisenroppyakunen to Kaigai Dōhō*. Tokyo: Hōshuku Kigen Nisenroppyakunen to Kaigai Dōhō Kankō Kai, 1941.
Yamawaki Haruki. "Beikoku Imin ni Kansuru Shokan." *Nihon Imin Kyōkai Hōkoku* 1, no. 7 (March 1916): 11–12. Reprint, Tokyo: Fuji Shuppan, 2006.
Yanaihara Tadao. "Jiron Toshite no Jinkō Mondai." *Chūō Kōron* 42, no. 7 (July 1927): 31–32.
"Nanpō Rōdō Seisaku no Kichō." *Shakai Seisaku Jihō*, no. 260 (1942): 156–157.
Yokohama YWCA 80-Nenshi Henshū Iinkai. *Kono Iwa no Ue ni: Yokohama YWCA 80-Nenshi*, Yokohama: Yokohama YWCA, 1993.
Yoshida Hideo. *Nihon Jinkō Ron no Shiteki Kenkyū*. Tokyo: Kawade Shobō, 1944.
Yoshida Kensuke and Sudō Tokiichirō. *Kinsei Shidan*. Vol. 1. Tokyo: Kyōritsusha, 1872.
Yoshimura Daijirō. *Hokubei Tekisasushū no Beisaku: Nihonjin no Shin Fugen*. Osaka: Kaigai Kigyō Dōshikai, 1903.
Hokubei Yūgaku Annai. Tokyo: Okashima Shoten, 1903.
Seinen no Tobei. Tokyo: Chūyōdō, 1902.
Tekisasushū Beisaku no Jikken. Tokyo: Kaigai Kigyō Dōshi Kai, 1905.
Tobei Seigyō no Tebiki. Tokyo: Okashima Shoten, 1903.
Yoshimura Shigeyoshi. *Sakiyama Hisae Den: Ishokumin Kyōiku to Amazon Kaitaku no Senkakusha*. Tokyo: Kaigai Shokumin Gakkō Kōyūkai Shuppanbu, 1955.
"Yūshisha no Jimu." *Hokkaido Kaitaku Zasshi*, no. 27 (February 5, 1881): 50–51.
"Zasshi Shokumin no Sōkan to Watashi." *Shokumin* 7, no. 11 (November 1928): 10.
Zenkoku Takushoku Nōgyō Kyōdō Kumiai Rengōkai. *Kaigai Nōgyō Ijū*. Tokyo: Zenkoku Takushoku Nōgyō Kyōdō Kumiai Rengōkai, 1959.

Secondary Sources

Aiba Kazuhiko, Chen Jin, Miyata Sachie, and Nakashima Jun, eds. *Manshū "Tairiku no Hanayome" wa Dō Tsukurareta Ka?* Tokyo: Akashi Shotten, 1996.
Aoki Takeshi. "Gaichi Hikiagesha Shuyō to Sengo Kaitaku Nōmin no Sōshutsu: Nagano Ken Shimoinagun Igaryōmura no Jirei." *Shakai Keizai Shigaku* 77, no. 2 (August 2011): 79–100.
Armitage, David. "John Locke, Carolina, and the *Two Treatises of Government*." *Political Theory* 32, no. 5 (October 2004): 602–627.
"John Locke: Theorist of Empire?" In *Empire and Modern Political Thought*, edited by Sankar Muthu, 100–101. Cambridge: Cambridge University Press, 2012.
Arneil, Barbara. *John Locke and America: The Defense of English Colonialism*. Oxford: Oxford University Press, 1996.

Azuma, Eiichiro. *Between Two Empires: Race, History, and Transnationalism in Japanese America*. London: Oxford University Press, 2005.

In Search of Our Frontier: Japanese America and Settler Colonialism in the Construction of Japan's Borderless Empire. Berkeley: University of California Press, 2019.

"Japanese Agricultural Labor Program: Temporary Worker Immigration, U.S.-Japan Cultural Diplomacy, and Ethnic Community Making among Japanese Americans." In *A Nation of Immigrants Reconsidered: US Society in an Age of Restriction, 1924–1965*, edited by Maddalena Marinari, Madeline Y. Hsu, and María Cristina García, 161–190. Urbana: University of Illinois Press, 2019.

"Japanese Immigrant Settler Colonialism in the U.S.-Mexican Borderlands and the U.S. Racial-Imperialist Politics of the Hemispheric 'Yellow Peril.'" *Pacific Historical Review* 83, no. 2 (May 2014): 255–276.

"'Pioneers of Overseas Japanese Development': Japanese American History and the Making of Expansionist Orthodoxy in Imperial Japan." *Journal of Asian Studies* 64, no. 4 (November 2008): 1187–1226.

"A Transpacific Origin of Japanese Settler Colonialism: US Migrant Expansionists and Their Roles in Japan's Imperial Formation, 1892–1908." Paper presented at the Global Japan Forum, University of California, Los Angeles, May 9, 2014.

Banner, Stuart. *Possessing the Pacific: Land, Settlers and Indigenous People from Australia to Alaska*. Cambridge, MA: Harvard University Press, 2007.

Bashford, Alison. *Global Population: History, Geopolitics, and Life on Earth*. New York: Columbia University Press, 2016.

"Malthus and Colonial History." *Journal of Australian Studies* 36, no. 1 (March 2012): 99–110.

"Nation, Empire, Globe: The Spaces of Population Debate in the Interwar Years." *Comparative Studies in Society and History* 49, no. 1 (2007): 170–201.

"Population Politics since 1750." In *The Cambridge World History, Volume VII: Production, Destruction and Connection, 1750–Present*, Part I: *Structures, Spaces and Boundary Making*, edited by J. R. McNeill and Kenneth Pomeranz, 212–236. Cambridge: Cambridge University Press, 2015.

Bashford, Alison, and Joyce E. Chaplin, eds. *The New Worlds of Thomas Robert Malthus: Rereading the Principle of Population*. Princeton: Princeton University Press, 2017.

Belich, James. *Replenishing the Earth: The Settler Revolution and the Rise of the Anglo-World, 1783–1939*. Oxford: Oxford University Press, 2009.

Bourdaghs, Michael. *Sayonara Amerika, Sayonara Nippon: A Geopolitical Prehistory of J-Pop*. New York: Columbia University Press, 2012.

Burajiru Nihon Imin 100-Shūnen Kinen Kyōkai Hyakunenshi Hensan Iinkai. *Burajiru Nihon Imin Hyakunenshi*. Vol. 1. Tokyo: Fūkyōsha, 2008.

Burkholder, Mark. "Spain's America: From Kingdoms to Colonies." *Colonial Latin American Review* 25, no. 2 (2016): 125–126.

Burns, Susan L. "Gender in the Arena of the Courts: The Prosecution of Abortion and Infanticide in Early Meiji Japan." In *Gender and Law in the Japanese Imperium*, edited by Susan L. Burns and Barbara J. Brooks, 81–108. Honolulu: University of Hawai'i Press, 2014.

Choate, Mark I. *Emigrant Nation: The Making of Italy Abroad.* Cambridge, MA: Harvard University Press, 2008.

Cole, Joshua. *The Power of Large Numbers: Population, Politics, and Gender in Nineteenth Century France.* Ithaca, NY: Cornell University Press, 2000.

Crump, John. *The Origins of Socialist Thought in Japan.* London: St. Martin's Press, 1983.

Dickinson, Frederick. *Taishō Tennō: Ichiyaku Godaishū o Yuhisu.* Tokyo: Minerva Shobo, 2009.

  War and National Reinvention: Japan in the Great War, 1914–1919. Cambridge, MA: Harvard University Asia Center, 2001.

  World War I and the Triumph of a New Japan, 1919–1930. Cambridge: Cambridge University Press, 2013.

Drixler, Fabian. *Mabiki: Infanticide and Population Growth in Eastern Japan, 1660–1950.* Berkeley: University of California Press, 2013.

Dusinberre, Martin. *Hard Times in the Hometown: A History of Community Survival in Modern Japan.* Honolulu: University of Hawai'i Press, 2012.

  "Writing the On-Board: Meiji Japan in Transit and Transition." *Journal of Global History* 11, no. 2 (2016): 271–294.

Duus, Peter. *The Abacus and the Sword: The Japanese Penetration of Korea, 1895–1910.* Berkeley: University of California Press, 1998.

Ebihara Hachirō. *Kaigai Hōji Shinbun Zasshishi: Tsuketari Kaigai Hōjin Gaiji Shinbun Zasshishi.* Tokyo: Meicho Fukyūkai, 1980.

Elkins, Caroline, and Susan Pedersen, eds. *Settler Colonialism in the Twentieth Century: Projects, Practices, and Legacies.* London: Routledge, 2005.

Emori Susumu. *Ainu Minzoku no Rekishl.* Urayasu: Sōfūkan, 2007.

Ericson, Steve. "'Matsukata Deflation' Reconsidered: Financial Stabilization and Japanese Exports in a Global Depression, 1881–85." *Journal of Japanese Studies* 40, no. 1 (2014): 1–28.

Fitzpatrick, Matthew P. *Liberal Imperialism in Germany: Expansionism and Nationalism, 1848–1884.* New York: Berghahn Books, 2008.

Frühstück, Sabine. *Colonizing Sex: Sexology and Social Control in Modern Japan.* Berkeley: University of California Press, 2003.

Fujikane, Candace, and Jonathan Y. Okamura, eds. *Asian Settler Colonialism: From Local Governance to the Habits of Everyday Life in Hawai'i.* Honolulu: University of Hawai'i Press, 2008.

Fujime Yuki. *Sei no Rekishigaku: Kōshō Seido, Dataizai Taisei kara Baishun Bōshihō, Yūsei Hogohō Taisei e.* Tokyo: Fuji Shuppan, 1997.

Fujita, Fumiko. *American Pioneers and the Japanese Frontier: American Experts in Nineteenth-Century Japan.* Westport, CT: Greenwood, 1994.

Fujitani, Takashi. "Kindai Nihon ni Okeru Kenryoku no Tekunorojii: Guntai, Chihō, Shintai." Translated by Umemori Naoyuki. *Shisō*, no. 845 (November 1994): 164–166.

  Race for Empire: Koreans as Japanese and Japanese as Americans. Berkeley: University of California Press, 2011.

Fujitani, Takashi, Geoffrey M. White, and Lisa Yoneyama, eds. *Perilous Memories: The Asia-Pacific War(s).* Durham, NC: Duke University Press, 2001.

Garon, Sheldon. *Molding the Japanese Minds: The State in Everyday Life.* Princeton: Princeton University Press, 1998.

Geiger, Andrea. *Subverting Exclusion: Transpacific Encounters with Race, Caste, and Borders, 1885–1928*. New Haven, CT: Yale University Press, 2011.

Goebel, Michael. "Settler Colonialism in Postcolonial Latin America." In *The Routledge Handbook of the History of Settler Colonialism*, edited by Edward Cavanagh and Lorenzo Veracini, 139–152. London: Routledge, 2017.

Gordon, Andrew. *Labor and Imperial Democracy in Prewar Japan*. Berkeley: University of California Press, 1991.

Grafe, Regina, and Alejandra Irigoin. "A Stakeholder Empire: The Political Economy of Spanish Imperial Rule in America." *Economic History Review* 65, no. 2 (2012): 609–651.

Hankins, Joseph D. *Working Skin: Making Leather, Making a Multicultural Japan*. Berkeley: University of California Press, 2014.

Hasegawa Yūichi. "1920 Nendai Nihon no Imin Ron (3)." *Gaikō Jihō*, no. 1279 (June 1991): 94–105.

Havens, Thomas R. H. *Farm and Nation in Modern Japan: Agrarian Nationalism, 1870–1940*. Princeton: Princeton University Press, 1974.

Hayami Akira. "Jinkō Tōkei no Kindaika Katei." In *Kokusei Chōsa Izen, Nihon Jinkō Tōkei Shūsei*, reprint ed., vol. 1, edited by Naimushō Naikaku Tōkeikyoku, 3–11. Tokyo: Tōyō Shorin, 1992.

Rekishi Jinkōgaku de Mita Nihon. Tokyo: Bungei Shunjū, 2001.

Hiraga Akihiko. *Senzen Nihon Nōgyō Seisakushi no Kenkyū: 1920–1945*. Tokyo: Nihon Keizai Hyōronsha, 2003.

Hirano, Katsuya. "The Politics of Colonial Translation: On the Narrative of the Ainu as a 'Vanishing Ethnicity.'" *Asia-Pacific Journal* 4, no. 3 (January 12, 2009). https://apjjf.org/-Katsuya-Hirano/3013/article.html.

"Thanatopolitics in the Making of Japan's Hokkaido: Settler Colonialism and Primitive Accumulation." *Critical Historical Studies* 2, no. 2 (Fall 2015): 191–218.

Hirano, Katsuya, Lorenzo Veracini, and Toulouse-Antonin Roy, eds. "Vanishing Natives and Taiwan's Settler-Colonial Unconsciousness." *Critical Asian Studies* 50, no. 2 (2018): 196–218.

Hirobe, Izumi. *Japanese Pride and American Prejudice: Modifying the Exclusion Clause of the 1924 Immigration Act*. Stanford: Stanford University Press, 2002.

Hiroshima Kiyoshi. "Gendai Nihon Jinkō Seisaku Shi Shōron: Jinkō Shishitsu Gainen o Megutte, 1916–1930." *Jinkō Mondai Kenkyū*, no. 154 (April 1980): 51–54.

Hoff, Derek S. *The State and the Stork: The Population Debate and Policy Making in US History*. Chicago: University of Chicago Press, 2012.

"Hokkaido Nōgyō no Keisei." In *Nihon Nōgyō Hattatsushi: Meiji Ikō ni Okeru, vol. 4: Nihon Shihon Shugi Kakuritsuki no Nōgyō*, edited by Tōhata Sei'ichi and Norinaga Toshitarō, 559–560. Tokyo: Chūō Kōronsha, 1978.

Howell, David. "Early Shizoku Colonization of Hokkaido." *Journal of Asian History* 17 (1983): 40–67.

Ichioka, Yuji. "Amerika Nadeshiko: Japanese Immigrant Women in the United States, 1900–1924." *Pacific Historical Review* 9, no. 2 (1980): 339–357.

The Issei: The World of the First Generation Japanese Immigrants, 1885–1924. New York: Free Press, 1990.

Iino Masako, Kameda Kinuko, and Takahashi Yūko, eds. *Tsuda Umeko o Sasaeta Hitobito*. Tokyo: Yūhikaku, 2000.

Inoue Katsuo. "Sapporo Nōgakkō to Shokumingaku no Tanjō." In *Teikoku Nihon no Gakuchi*, vol. 1, edited by Yamamoto Taketoshi et al., 11–42. Tokyo: Iwanami Shoten, 2006.

Irish, Ann B. *Hokkaido: A History of Ethnic Transition and Development on Japan's Northern Island*. Jefferson, NC: McFarland, 2009.

Iriye, Akira. "The Failure of Economic Expansionism: 1918–1931." In *Japan in Crisis: Essays on Taishō Democracy*, edited by Bernard Silberman and H. D. Harootunian, 237–269. Princeton: Princeton University Press, 1974.

——. *Pacific Estrangement: Japanese and American Expansion, 1897–1911*. Cambridge, MA: Harvard University Press, 1972.

Itō Atsushi. *Nihon Nōmin Seisaku Shiron: Kaitaku Imin Kyōiku Kunren*. Kyoto: Kyoto Daigaku Gakujutsu Shuppankai, 2013.

Itō Hiroshi. *Tondenhei no Kenkyū*. Tokyo: Dōseisha, 1992.

Ittmann, Karl, Dennis D. Cordell, and Gregory H. Maddox, eds. *The Demographics of Empire: The Colonial Order and the Creation of Knowledge*. Athens: Ohio University Press, 2010.

Kaiho Mineo. *Kinsei no Hokkaido*. Tokyo: Kyōikusha, 1979.

Katayama Sei'ichi. *Kindai Nihon no Joshi Kyōiku*. Tokyo: Kenpakusha, 1984.

Kikugawa Sadami. "Tekisasu Beisaku no Senkusha: Saibara Seito to Ōnishi Rihei." *Keizai Keiei Ronsō* 32, no. 4 (March 1998): 39–58.

Kimura Kai. "Ariansa e no michi," *Ariansa Tsūshin*, no. 23 (July 30, 2008). 2018, www.gendaiza.org/aliansa/lib/23–05.html.

——. "Ariansa to Shinano Kaigai Kyōkai." *Ariansa Tsūshin*, no. 8 (November 30, 2000). www.gendaiza.org/aliansa/lib/0803.html.

——. "Ikken Isson Kara Ikkatsu Daiijūchi e." In "Ariansa Undō no Rekishi (3): Burajiru Ijūshi no Nazo—Kaigai Ijū Kumiai Hō." *Ariansa Tsūshin*, no. 26 (August 1, 2009). www.gendaiza.org/aliansa/lib/26–05.html.

——. "Wako Shungorō no Kieta Ashiato o Tadoru." *Ariansa Tsūshin*, no. 13 (August 1, 2003). www.gendaiza.org/aliansa/lib/1301.html.

Kimura Kazuaki. *Shōwa Sakka no "Nan'yō Kō."* Tokyo: Sekai Shisō Sha, 2004.

Kimura Kenji. "Nichiro Sengo Kaigai Nōgyō Imin no Rekishiteki Chii." In *Nihon Jinushi Sei to Kindai Sonraku*, edited by Abiko Rin, 149–168. Tokyo: Sōfūsha, 1994.

Kinmonth, Earl H. *The Self-Made Man in Meiji Japanese Thought: From Samurai to Salary Man*. Berkeley: University of California Press, 1981.

Kitasaki Kōnosuke. *Sengo Kaitakuchi to Katō Kanji: Jizoku Kanō na Nōgyō no Genryū*. Tokyo: Nōrin Tōkei Shuppan, 2009.

Kobayashi Shinsuke. *Hitobito wa Naze Manshū e Watatta no Ka: Nagano Ken no Shakai Undō to Imin*. Kyoto: Sekai Shisōsha, 2015.

Kodama Masaaki. "Kaisetsu." In *Shokumin Kyōkai Hōkoku Kaisetsu, Sōmokuji, Sakuin*. Tokyo: Fuji Shuppan, 1987.

——. *Nihon Iminshi Kenkyū Josetsu*. Tokyo: Keisuisha, 1992.

Kojima Reiitsu. *Nihon Teikoku Shugi to Higashi Ajia*. Tokyo: Ajia Keizai Kenkyūjo, Hatsubaijo Ajia Keizai Shuppankai, 1979.

Koshiro, Yukiko. *Trans-Pacific Racism and the U.S. Occupation of Japan*. New York: Columbia University Press, 1999.

Koyama Shizuko. *Ryōsai Kenbō Toiu Kihan*. Tokyo: Keisō shobō, 1991.

Kumamoto Yoshihiro. "Kaigai Kōgyō Kabushiki Gaisha no Setsuritsu Keii to Imin Kaisha no Tōgō Mondai." *Komazawa Daigaku Shigaku Ronshū*, no. 31 (April 2001): 57–69.

Kumei Teruko. *Gaikokujin o Meguru Shakaishi: Kindai Amerika to Nihonjin Imin*. Tokyo: Yūsankaku, 1995.

Lesser, Jeffery. *Negotiating National Identity: Immigrants, Minorities, and the Struggle for Ethnicity in Brazil*. Durham, NC: Duke University Press, 1999.

Levitan, Kathrin. "'Sprung from Ourselves': British Interpretations of Mid-Nineteenth-Century Racial Demographics." In *Empire, Migration and Identity in the British World*, edited by Kent Fedorowich and Andrew S. Thompson, 60–81. Manchester: Manchester University Press, 2013.

Loza, Mireya. "The Japanese Agricultural Workers' Program Race, Labor, and Cold War Diplomacy in the Fields, 1956–1965." *Pacific Historical Review* 86, no. 4 (2017): 661–690.

Lu, Sidney X. "Colonizing Hokkaido and the Origin of Japanese Trans-Pacific Expansion, 1869–1894." *Japanese Studies* 36, no. 2 (2016): 251–274.

"Japanese American Migration and the Making of Model Women for Japanese Expansion in Brazil and Manchuria, 1871–1945." *Journal of World History* 28, nos. 3–4 (December 2017): 437–467.

"The Shame of Empire: Japanese Overseas Prostitutes and Prostitution Abolition in Modern Japan, 1880s–1927." *Positions: Asia Critique* 24, no. 4 (November 2016): 839–873.

Lynn, Hyung Gu. "A Comparative Study of Tōyō Kyōkai and Nan'yō Kyōkai." In *The Japanese Empire in East Asia and Its Postwar Legacy*, edited by Harald Fuess, 65–95.Munich: Iudicium, 1998.

"Malthusian Dreams, Colonial Imaginary: The Oriental Development Company and Japanese Emigration to Korea." In *Settler Colonialism in the Twentieth Century: Projects, Practices, and Legacies*, edited by Caroline Elkins and Susan Pedersen, 25–40. London: Routledge, 2005.

Mamiya Kunio. "Mizuno Ryō to Kōkoku Shokumin Gaisha ni Tsuite no Oboegaki." *Shakaigaku Tōkyū* 44, no. 2 (1999): 27–49.

Saibara Seitō Kenkyū. Kōchi-shi: Kōchi Shimin Toshokan, 1994.

Manz, Stefan. *Constructing a German Diaspora: The "Greater German Empire," 1871–1914*. New York: Routledge, 2014.

Matthew, Laura, and Michel Oudijk. *Indian Conquistadors: Indigenous Allies in the Conquest of Mesoamerica*. Norman: University of Oklahoma Press, 2007.

Mayo, Marlene J. "Literary Reorientation in Occupied Japan: Incidents of Civil Censorship." In *Legacies and Ambiguities: Postwar Fiction and Culture in West Germany and Japan*, edited by Ernestine Schlant and J. Thomas Rimer, 135–161. Washington, DC: Woodrow Wilson Center Press, 1991.

McCormack, Noah. "Buraku Emigration in the Meiji Era—Other Ways to Become 'Japanese.'" *East Asian History*, no. 23 (June 2002): 87–108.

Milner, Clyde A., II, Carol A. O'Connor, and Martha A. Sandweiss, eds. *The Oxford History of the American West*. New York: Oxford University Press, 1994.

Minohara Toshihiro. *Amerika no Hainichi Undō to Nichi-Bei Kankei: "Hainichi Iminhō" wa Naze Seiritsushita Ka.* Tokyo: Asahi Shinbun Shoppan, 2016.

Hainichi Iminhō to Nichibei Kankei: Hanihara Shokan no Shinsō to Sono Jūdainaru Kekka. Tokyo: Iwanami Shoten, 2002.

Miwa Kimitada, ed. *Nichi-Bei Kiki no Kigen to Hainichi Iminhō.* Tokyo: Ronsōsha, 1997.

"Shiga Shigetaka (1863–1927): A Meiji Japanist's View of and Actions in International Relations." Research Papers, Series A-3, Institute of International Relations, Sophia University, 1970.

Mizuno Mamoru. "Ekkyō to Meiji Nashonarizumu 1889 Nen Jōyaku Kaisei Mondai ni Okeru Seikyō Sha no Shisō." *Nihon Gakuhō,* no. 22 (March 2003): 39–54.

Moriyama, Alan Takeo. *Imingaisha: Japanese Emigration Companies and Hawai'i, 1894–1908.* Honolulu: University of Hawai'i Press, 1985.

Morris-Suzuki, Tessa. "Exodus to North Korea Revisited: Japan, North Korea, and the ICRC in the 'Repatriation' of Ethnic Koreans from Japan." *Asia-Pacific Journal* 9, Issue 22, no. 2 (May 30, 2011). https://apjjf.org/2011/9/22/Tessa-Morris-Suzuki/3541/article.html.

Nagai Hideo. *Nihon no Kindaika to Hokkaido.* Sapporo: Hokkaido Daigaku Shuppankai, 2007.

Nakanome Tōru. *Seikyōsha no Kenkyū.* Kyoto: Shibunkaku Shuppan, 1993.

Namimatsu Nobuhisa. "Nōson Keizaikosei to Ishiguro Tadatsu Hōtoku Shisō to no Kanren o Megutte." *Kyōto Sangyō Daigaku Ronshū, Shakai Kagaku Keiretsu,* no. 22 (March 2005): 119–120.

National Diet Library, Japan. *100 Years of Japanese Emigration to Brazil.* www.ndl.go.jp/brasil/e/index.html.

Nelson, Robert L. "Colonialism in Europe? A Case against Salt Water." In *Germans, Poland, and Colonial Expansion to the East: 1850 through the Present,* edited by Robert Nelson, 1–10. New York: Palgrave Macmillan, 2009.

Nippon Rikkō Kai Sōritsu Hyaku Shūnen Kinen Jigyō Jikkō Iinkai Kinenshi Hensan Senmon Iinkai. *Nippon Rikkō Kai Hyakunen no Kōseki: Reiniku Kyūsai, Kaigai Hatten Undō, Kokusai Kōken.* Tokyo: Nippon Rikkō Kai, 1997.

Nippon Rikkō Kai Sōritsu Hyaku Shūnen Kinen Jigyō Jikkō Iinkai Kinenshi Hensan Senmon Iinkai. *Nippon Rikkō Kai Hyakunen no Kōseki: Reiniku Kyūsai, Kaigai Hatten Undō, Kokusai Kōken.* Tokyo: Nippon Rikkō Kai, 1997.

Oguma Eiji. *Nihonjin no Kyōkai: Okinawa Ainu Taiwan Chōsen Shokuminchi Shihai kara Fukki Undō made.* Tokyo: Shinyōsha, 1999.

Okabayashi Nobuo. "Jinkō Mondai to Imin Ron: Meiji Nihon no Fuan to Yokubō." *Doshisha Hōgaku* 64, no. 8 (March 2013): 75–167.

Okabe Makio. *Umi wo Watatta Nihonjin.* Tokyo: Yamakawa Shuppansha, 2002.

Okamoto, Shumpei. "Meiji Japanese Imperialism: Pacific Emigration or Continental Expansionism?" In *Japan Examined: Perspectives on Modern Japanese History,* edited by Harry Wray and Hilary Conroy, 141–148. Honolulu: University of Hawai'i Press, 1983.

Orii, Kazuhiko, and Hilary Conroy. "Japanese Socialists in Texas: Sen Katayama." *Amerasia Journal* 8, no. 2 (1981): 163–170.

Ōtake Keisuke. *Ishiguro Tadaatsu no Nōsei Shisō.* Tokyo: Nōsan gyoson Bunka Kyōkai, 1984.

Oxford, Wayne. *The Speeches of Fukuzawa: A Translation and Critical Study.* Tokyo: Hokuseido, 1973.

Paku Kyonmin. "Kaigai Jigyōsha no Zaigai Zaisan no Hōshō Yōkyu to Shokuminchi Ninshiki, 1945–1948 Nen: Chōsen Jigyōshakai o Chūshin ni." *Hōgaku Seijigaku Tōkyū: Hōritsu, Seiji, Shakai,* no. 108 (Spring 2016): 1–33.

Peattie, Mark. "The Nan'yō: Japan in the South Pacific, 1885–1945." In *The Japanese Colonial Empire, 1895–1945,* edited by Ramon Myers and Mark Peattie, 172–210. Princeton: Princeton University Press, 1987.

——— *Nan'yō: The Rise and Fall of the Japanese in Micronesia, 1885–1945.* Honolulu: University of Hawai'i Press, 1988.

Rao, Mohan. "An Imagined Reality: Malthusianism, Neo-Malthusianism and Population Myth." *Economic and Political Weekly* 29, no. 5 (January 29, 1994): 40–42.

Saitō Hiroshi. *Burajiru to Nihonjin.* Tokyo: Simul Press, 1984.

Sakada Yasuo. "The Enactment of the 1891 Immigration Law of the United States and Conflicting American and Japanese Perceptions: 'The Undesirable' and the 'Undesired.'" *Kokusaigaku Ronshū* 9, no. 1 (June 1998): 21–69.

Sakaguchi Mitsuhiko. "Dare Ga Imin wo Okuridashita no Ka: Kan Taiheyō ni Okeru Nihonjin no Kokusai Idō Gaikan." *Ritsumeikan Gengo Bunka Kenkyū* 21, no. 4 (March 2010): 53–66.

——— "Kaisetsu." In *Nihon Imin Kyōkai Hōkoku,* vol. 1, 3–13. Tokyo: Fuji Shuppan, 2006.

Sand, Jordan. "Gentlemen's Agreement, 1908: Fragments for a Pacific History." *Representations* 107, no. 1 (Summer 2009): 91–127.

——— "Reconfiguring Pacific History: Reflections from the Pacific Empires Working Group." *Amerasia Journal* 42, no. 3 (2016): 1–5.

Saranillio, Dean Itsuji. "Why Asian Settler Colonialism Matters: A Thought Piece on Critiques, Debates, and Indigenous Difference." *Settler Colonial Studies* 3, nos. 3–4 (2013): 280–294.

Sasaki Toshiji. "Enomoto Takeaki no Imin Shoreisaku to Sore o Sasaeta Jinmi." *Kirisutokyō Shakai Mondai Kenkyū,* no. 37 (March 1989): 535–549.

Sawada, Mitziko. *Tokyo Life, New York Dreams: Urban Japanese Visions of America, 1890–1924.* Berkeley: University of California Press, 1996.

Scheiner, Irwin. *Christian Converts and Social Protest in Meiji Japan.* Berkeley: University of California Press, 1970.

Shih, Shu-mei. "Theory, Asia and the Sinophone." *Postcolonial Studies* 13, no. 4 (2010): 465–484.

Shimazu, Naoko. *Japan, Race and Equality: The Racial Equality of 1919.* London: Routledge, 1998.

Shimizu Seisaburō. "Hokubei Tekisasushu Iminchi Torishirabe Hōkoku." In *Gaimushō Tsūshōkyoku, Imin Chōsa Hōkoku,* vol. 1, 1–28. 1908. Reprint, Tokyo: Yūshōdō Shuppan, 1986.

Shōji Shunsaku. *Kingendai Nihon no Nōson: Nōsei no Genten o Saguru.* Tokyo: Yoshikawa Kōbunkan, 2003.

Soloway, Richard A. *Demography and Degeneration: Eugenics and the Declining Birthrate in Twentieth-Century Britain.* Chapel Hill: University of North Carolina Press, 1995.

Stalker, Nancy. "Suicide, Boycotts and Embracing Tagore: The Japanese Popular Response to the 1924 US Immigration Exclusion Law." *Japanese Studies* 26, no. 2 (2006): 153–170.

Sumiya Kimio. *Katayama Sen, Kindai Nihon no Shisōka.* Vol. 3. Tokyo: Tokyo Daigaku Shuppankai, 1967.

Suzue Ei'ichi. "Yanagita Tokichi to Kariforunia Imin." *Fukuzawa Techō* 40 (March 1980): 1–5.

Tachikawa Kenji. "Meiji Kōhanki no Tobei Netsu: Amerika no Ryūkō." *Shirin* 69, no. 3 (May 1, 1986): 71–105.

"Meiji Zenhanki no Tobeinetsu (1)." *Tomiyama Daigaku Kyōyōbu Kiyō* 23, no. 2 (1990): 1–30.

Tadakaze Suganuma. *Shin Nihon Tonan no Yume.* Tokyo: Iwanami Shoten, 1888.

Tagawa Mariko. "'Imin' Shichō no Kiseki." PhD diss., Yūshōdō Shuppan, 2005.

Takahashi, Mutsuko. *The Emergence of Welfare Society in Japan.* Aldershot: Avebury, 1997.

Takahashi Yūko. *Tsuda Umeko no Shakaishi.* Tokyo: Tamakawa Daigaku Shuppanbu, 2002.

Takaki, Ronald. *Strangers from a Different Shore: A History of Asian Americans.* Berkeley: University of California Press, 1998.

Takasaki Sōji. *Tsuda Sen Hyōden: Mō Hitotsu no Kindaika o Mezashita Hito.* Urayasu: Sōfūkan, 2008.

Takeda Hiroko. *The Political Economy of Reproduction in Japan: Between Nation-State and Everyday Life.* London: Routledge, 2005.

Tama Yasuko. "Shōsanka to Kazoku Seisaku." In *Gendai Shakaigaku: 19: Kazoku no Shakaigaku,* edited by Inoue Shun, Ueno Chizuko, Ōsawa Masachi, Mita Munesyke, and Yoshimi Shun'ya, 159–187. Tokyo: Iwanami Shoten, 1996.

Tamanoi, Mariko. *Memory Maps: The State and Manchuria in Postwar Japan.* Honolulu: University of Hawai'i Press, 2008.

Tamura Norio, and Shiramizu Shigehiko, eds. *Beikoku Shoki no Nihongo Shinbu.* Tokyo: Keisō Shobō, 1986.

Tanaka, Kei. "Japanese Picture Marriage in 1900–1924 California: Construction of Japanese Race and Gender." PhD diss., Rutgers University, 2002.

Tomiyama Ichirō. "Colonialism and the Sciences of the Tropical Zone: The Academic Analysis of Difference in 'the Island Peoples.'" *Positions: Asia Critique* 3, no. 2 (1995): 385–386.

Tsuchida, Nobuya. "The Japanese in Brazil, 1908–1941." PhD diss., University of California, Los Angeles, 1978.

Tsunoyama Yukihiro, *Enomoto Takeaki to Mekishiko Ijū.* Tokyo: Dōbunkan Shuppan, 1986.

Uchida, Jun. *Brokers of Empire: Japanese Settler Colonialism in Korea, 1876–1945.* Cambridge, MA: Harvard University Press, 2011.

"From Island Nation to Oceanic Empire: A Vision of Japanese Expansion from the Periphery." *Journal of Japanese Studies* 42, no. 1 (2016): 57–90.

Usui Ryūichirō. *Enomoto Takeaki kara Sekaishi Ga Mieru.* Tokyo: PHP Kenkyūjo, 2005.

Veracini, Lorenzo. "'Settler Colonialism': Career of a Concept." *Journal of Imperial and Commonwealth History* 41, no. 2 (2013): 313–333.

Settler Colonialism: A Theoretical Overview. Houndmills: Palgrave Macmillan, 2010.

The Settler Colonial Present. Houndmills: Palgrave Macmillan, 2015.

Villella, Peter. *Indigenous Elites and Creole Identity in Colonial Mexico, 1500–1800.* Cambridge: Cambridge University Press, 2016.

Vlastos, Stephen. "Agrarianism without Tradition: The Radical Critique of Prewar Japanese Modernity." In *Mirror of Modernity: Invented Traditions of Modern Japan*, edited by Stephen Vlastos, 79–94. Berkeley: University of California Press, 1998.

"Opposition Movements in Early Meiji, 1868–1885." In *The Cambridge History of Japan, vol. 5: The Nineteenth Century*, edited by Marius Jansen, 367–431. Cambridge: Cambridge University Press, 1989.

Wakatsuki, Yasuo. "Japanese Emigration to the United States, 1866–1924: A Monograph." *Perspectives in American History* 12 (1979): 389–516.

Wakatsuki Yasuo, and Jōji Suzuki, eds. *Kaigai Ijū Seisaku Shiron.* Tokyo: Fukumura Shuppan, 1975.

Walls, Thomas K. *The Japanese Texans.* San Antonio: University of Texas, Institute of Texan Cultures at San Antonio, 1987.

Watt, Lori. *When Empire Comes Home: Repatriation and Reintegration in Postwar Japan.* Cambridge, MA: Harvard University Asia Center, 2009.

Webb, Walter Prescott. *The Great Frontier.* Boston: Houghton Mifflin, 1952.

Wheat, David. *Atlantic Africa & the Spanish Caribbean, 1570–1640.* Chapel Hill, NC: Omohundro Institute and University of North Carolina Press, 2016.

Wilson, Sandra. "The New Paradise: Japanese Emigration to Manchuria in the 1930s and 1940s." *International History Review* 17, no. 2 (May 1995): 249–286.

Wolfe, Patrick. "Settler Colonialism and the Elimination of the Native." *Journal of Genocide Research* 8, no. 4 (December 2006): 387–409.

Settler Colonialism and the Transformation of Anthropology: The Politics and Poetics of an Ethnographic Event. London: Cassell, 1999.

ed. *The Settler Complex: Recuperating Binarism in Colonial Studies.* Los Angeles: UCLA American Indian Studies Center, 2016.

Wrigley, E. A. *Population and History.* New York: McGraw-Hill, 1969.

Wrobel, David M. *Global West, American Frontier: Travel, Empire and Exceptionalism from Manifest Destiny to the Great Depression.* Albuquerque: University of New Mexico Press, 2013.

Yabiku Mōsei. *Burajiru Okinawa Iminshi.* São Paulo: Zaibu Okinawa Kenjinkai, 1987.

Yaguchi Yūjin. *Hawai'i no Rekishi to Bunka.* Tokyo: Chūō Kōron Shinsha, 2002.

Yamamoto Yūzō. *Manshū Kioku to Rekishi.* Kyoto: Kyoto Daigaku Gakujutsu Shuppankai, 2007.

Yanagisawa Ikumi. "'Shashin Hanayume' wa 'Otto no Dorei' Datta no Ka: 'Shashin Hanayume' Tachi no Katari wo Chūshin ni." In *Shashin Hanayome Sensō Hanayome no Tadotta Michi: Josei Iminshi no Hakkutsu*, edited by Shimada Noriko, 47–85. Tokyo: Akashi Shoten, 2009.

Yano Tōru. *"Nanshin" no Keifu.* Tokyo: Chūō Kōronsha, 1975.

Yasuoka Ken'ichi. *Tashatachi no Nōgyōshi: Zainichi Chōsenjin Sokaisha Kaitaku Nōmin Kaigai Imin.* Kyoto: Kyoto Daigaku Gakujutsu Shuppankai, 2014.

Yasutake, Rumi. *Transnational Women's Activism: The United States, Japan, and Japanese Immigrant Communities in California, 1859–1920.* New York: New York University Press, 2004.

Yoshida Tadao. *Myōnichi no Jinkō Mondai: "Man'in Nihon" wa Kaishōsareru Ka.* Tokyo: Shakai Shisōsha, 1962.

Young, Louise. *Beyond the Metropolis: Second Cities and Modern Life in Interwar Japan.* Berkeley: University of California Press, 2013.

Japan's Total Empire: Manchuria and the Culture of Wartime Imperialism. Berkeley: University of California Press, 1998.

Zenkoku Kaitaku Nōgyō Kyōdō Kumiai Rengōkai. *Sengo Kaitakushi.* Vol. 2. Tokyo: Zenkoku Kaitaku Nōgyō Kyōdō Kumiai Rengōkai, 1967.

Index

Note: Page numbers in italics indicate illustrative material.

Studies of the Weatherhead East Asian Institute, Columbia University

Selected Titles

(Complete list at: http://weai.columbia.edu/publications/studies-weai/)

Residual Futures: The Urban Ecologies of Literary and Visual Media of 1960s and 1970s Japan, by Franz Prichard. Columbia University Press, 2019.

Down and Out in Saigon: Stories of the Poor in a Colonial City, by Haydon Cherry. Yale University Press, 2019.

The Power of Print in Modern China: Intellectuals and Industrial Publishing from the end of Empire to Maoist State Socialism, by Robert Culp. Columbia University Press, 2019.

Beyond the Asylum: Mental Illness in French Colonial Vietnam, by Claire E. Edington. Cornell University Press, 2019.

Borderland Memories: Searching for Historical Identity in Post-Mao China, by Martin Thomas Fromm. Cambridge University Press, 2019.

Sovereignty Experiments: Korean Migrants and the Building of Borders in Northeast Asia, 1860–1949, by Alyssa M. Park. Cornell University Press, 2019.

The Greater East Asia Co-Prosperity Sphere: When Total Empire Met Total War, by Jeremy A. Yellen. Cornell University Press, 2019.

Thought Crime: Ideology and State Power in Interwar Japan, by Max Ward. Duke University Press, 2019.

Statebuilding by Imposition: Resistance and Control in Colonial Taiwan and the Philippines, by Reo Matsuzaki. Cornell University Press, 2019.

Nation-Empire: Ideology and Rural Youth Mobilization in Japan and Its Colonies, by Sayaka Chatani. Cornell University Press, 2019.

Fixing Landscape: A Techno-Poetic History of China's Three Gorges, by Corey Byrnes. Columbia University Press, 2019.

The Invention of Madness: State, Society, and the Insane in Modern China, by Emily Baum. University of Chicago Press, 2018.

Japan's Imperial Underworlds: Intimate Encounters at the Borders of Empire, by David Ambaras. Cambridge University Press, 2018.

Heroes and Toilers: Work as Life in Postwar North Korea, 1953–1961, by Cheehyung Harrison Kim. Columbia University Press, 2018.

Electrified Voices: How the Telephone, Phonograph, and Radio Shaped Modern Japan, 1868–1945, by Kerim Yasar. Columbia University Press, 2018.

Making Two Vietnams: War and Youth Identities, 1965–1975, by Olga Dror. Cambridge University Press, 2018.

A Misunderstood Friendship: Mao Zedong, Kim Il-sung, and Sino–North Korean Relations, 1949–1976, by Zhihua Shen and Yafeng Xia. Columbia University Press, 2018.

Playing by the Informal Rules: Why the Chinese Regime Remains Stable Despite Rising Protests, by Yao Li. Cambridge University Press, 2018.

Raising China's Revolutionaries: Modernizing Childhood for Cosmopolitan Nationalists and Liberated Comrades, by Margaret Mih Tillman. Columbia University Press, 2018.

Buddhas and Ancestors: Religion and Wealth in Fourteenth-Century Korea, by Juhn Y. Ahn. University of Washington Press, 2018.

Idly Scribbling Rhymers: Poetry, Print, and Community in Nineteenth Century Japan, by Robert Tuck. Columbia University Press, 2018.

China's War on Smuggling: Law, Economic Life, and the Making of the Modern State, 1842–1965, by Philip Thai. Columbia University Press, 2018.

Forging the Golden Urn: The Qing Empire and the Politics of Reincarnation in Tibet, by Max Oidtmann. Columbia University Press, 2018.

The Battle for Fortune: State-Led Development, Personhood, and Power among Tibetans in China, by Charlene Makley. Cornell University Press, 2018.

Aesthetic Life: Beauty and Art in Modern Japan, by Miya Elise Mizuta Lippit. Harvard University Asia Center, 2018.

Where the Party Rules: The Rank and File of China's Communist State, by Daniel Koss. Cambridge University Press, 2018.

Resurrecting Nagasaki: Reconstruction and the Formation of Atomic Narratives, by Chad R. Diehl. Cornell University Press, 2018.

China's Philological Turn: Scholars, Textualism, and the Dao in the Eighteenth Century, by Ori Sela. Columbia University Press, 2018.

Making Time: Astronomical Time Measurement in Tokugawa Japan, by Yulia Frumer. University of Chicago Press, 2018.

Mobilizing Without the Masses: Control and Contention in China, by Diana Fu. Cambridge University Press, 2018.

Post-Fascist Japan: Political Culture in Kamakura after the Second World War, by Laura Hein. Bloomsbury, 2018.

China's Conservative Revolution: The Quest for a New Order, 1927–1949, by Brian Tsui. Cambridge University Press, 2018.

Promiscuous Media: Film and Visual Culture in Imperial Japan, 1926–1945, by Hikari Hori. Cornell University Press, 2018.

The End of Japanese Cinema: Industrial Genres, National Times, and Media Ecologies, by Alexander Zahlten. Duke University Press, 2017.

The Chinese Typewriter: A History, by Thomas S. Mullaney. The MIT Press, 2017.

Forgotten Disease: Illnesses Transformed in Chinese Medicine, by Hilary A. Smith. Stanford University Press, 2017.

Borrowing Together: Microfinance and Cultivating Social Ties, by Becky Yang Hsu. Cambridge University Press, 2017.

Food of Sinful Demons: Meat, Vegetarianism, and the Limits of Buddhism in Tibet, by Geoffrey Barstow. Columbia University Press, 2017.

Youth For Nation: Culture and Protest in Cold War South Korea, by Charles R. Kim. University of Hawai'i Press, 2017.

Socialist Cosmopolitanism: The Chinese Literary Universe, 1945–1965, by Nicolai Volland. Columbia University Press, 2017.

The Social Life of Inkstones: Artisans and Scholars in Early Qing China, by Dorothy Ko. University of Washington Press, 2017.

Darwin, Dharma, and the Divine: Evolutionary Theory and Religion in Modern Japan, by G. Clinton Godart. University of Hawai'i Press, 2017.

Dictators and Their Secret Police: Coercive Institutions and State Violence, by Sheena Chestnut Greitens. Cambridge University Press, 2016.

The Cultural Revolution on Trial: Mao and the Gang of Four, by Alexander C. Cook. Cambridge University Press, 2016.

Inheritance of Loss: China, Japan, and the Political Economy of Redemption After Empire, by Yukiko Koga. University of Chicago Press, 2016.

Homecomings: The Belated Return of Japan's Lost Soldiers, by Yoshikuni Igarashi. Columbia University Press, 2016.

Samurai to Soldier: Remaking Military Service in Nineteenth-Century Japan, by D. Colin Jaundrill. Cornell University Press, 2016.